Memorable meals start with *Taste of Home!*

These are the heartwarming dishes home cooks love to serve their own families.

Since our founding over 25 years ago, *Taste of Home* has helped millions of family cooks set memorable meals on the table. What's our secret? Ask the thousands of home cooks who share their most-requested dishes with us. They'll tell you it's all about delicious family-favorite recipes made from easy-to-find ingredients.

Peek inside *Taste of Home Annual Recipes* and you'll find 468 delectable dishes as well as the heartwarming stories behind each one. Try any of these mouthwatering specialties, and you'll soon make them part of your own family story.

This exciting new edition offers an entire year's worth of recipes from the magazine, plus dozens of tasty bonus recipes never before seen in the publication. Just consider these handy chapters:

- **Main Dishes**
  Savor 50 beloved classics, including Sunday dinners, slow-cooked entrees and savory meat pies.
- **Potluck Pleasers**
  Bring-a-dish events are a snap when you cook from the crowd-pleasing recipes in this chapter.
- **Cookies, Bars & Candies**
  Whether you're planning a cookie exchange or need a pan of picnic-ready bars, there's fun by the dozen here.

Five icons help you make the most of kitchen time:

FAST FIX = Finished in 30 minutes or less
EAT SMART = Lower in calories, fat and sodium
SLOW COOKER = Made in a slow cooker
(5) INGREDIENTS = Made with 5 or fewer ingredients (excluding water, salt, pepper and canola/olive oil)
FREEZE IT = Includes freezing/reheating instructions

It all adds up to memorable meals just waiting to be shared. And with *Taste of Home Annual Recipes,* it's never been more heartwarming to do so. Happy cooking!

DELICIOUS DISHES

Quick dinners, exciting new favorites and frosty creations are just a few of the surprises you'll find in *Taste of Home Annual Recipes.* For a five-ingredient entree that's big on summer flavor, you'll love Cheesy Summer Squash Flatbreads (top). Mix up exciting meals with Korean Sausage Bowl (center), an authentically ethnic-tasting dish that uses common ingredients. And for a pair of merry treats, blend up cheery Chilly Snow-Day Floats (bottom).

Taste of Home

1610 N. 2nd St., Suite 102, Milwaukee WI
53212-3906

**BEEF & BEAN
TACO CHILI
PAGE 57**

Deputy Editor: Mark Hagen
Senior Art Director: Raeann Thompson
Editor: Christine Rukavena
Art Director: Maggie Conners
Senior Graphic Designer: Courtney Lovetere
Graphic Designer: Jazmin Delgado
Copy Editor: Dulcie Shoener
Cover Photographer: Mark Derse
Set Stylist: Stephanie Marchese
Food Stylist: Josh Rink

Pictured on front cover:
Beef Stew Skillet Pie, p. 89
Pictured on back cover:
Frosted Chocolate Delights, p. 237

International Standard Book Number:
D 978-1-61765-822-8
U 978-1-61765-823-5

International Standard Serial Number:
1094-3463

Component Number:
D 117400066H
U 117400068H

Printed in U.S.A.
1 3 5 7 9 10 8 6 4 2

Contents

Get Social with Us!

Like Us: facebook.com/tasteofhome

Pin Us: pinterest.com/taste_of_home

Follow Us: @tasteofhome

Tweet Us: twitter.com/tasteofhome

To find a recipe: tasteofhome.com

To submit a recipe: tasteofhome.com/submit

To find out about other *Taste of Home* products: shoptasteofhome.com

ROASTED RED PEPPER TRIANGLES, PAGE 15

APPETIZERS & BEVERAGES

Good times call for the perfect refreshments. Whether you're hosting a get-together or bringing a dish to share, here are dozens of delicious ways to get the party started.

FAB CRAB CAKES

Ann Girucky of Virginia makes a family classic that's crunchy on the outside and creamy on the inside. Just add a squeeze of lemon.

TANGIER ISLAND VIRGINIA CRAB CAKES

These crisp-on-the-outside, tender-on-the-inside crab cakes are what I grew up eating. They're absolutely delicious each and every time I make them.
—Ann Girucky, Norfolk, VA

PREP: 20 MIN. • **COOK:** 5 MIN./BATCH
MAKES: 12 CRAB CAKES

- **1 large egg, beaten**
- **1 Tbsp. mayonnaise**
- **1 tsp. ground mustard**
- **1 tsp. seafood seasoning**
- **1 tsp. prepared mustard**
- **1 tsp. minced fresh parsley**
- **½ tsp. salt**
- **¼ tsp. pepper**
- **1 lb. lump crabmeat, drained**
- **2 slices white bread, finely crumbled (about 1½ cups)**
- **3 Tbsp. canola oil**

1. In a large bowl, mix the first eight ingredients until blended. Fold in crab until well coated. Gently stir in breadcrumbs until well blended. Shape into twelve ½-in.-thick patties.

2. In a large skillet, heat oil over medium-high heat. Add crab cakes in batches; cook 2-3 minutes on each side or until dark golden brown.

1 CRAB CAKE: 90 cal., 5g fat (1g sat. fat), 52mg chol., 407mg sod., 3g carb. (0 sugars, 0 fiber), 8g pro.

FAST FIX

BEST EVER REMOULADE

This creamy remoulade recipe is the perfect way to add some Louisiana spice to your next sandwich, crab cake or burger.
—Lauren Knoelke, Milwaukee, WI

TAKES: 10 MIN. • **MAKES:** 12 SERVINGS

- **¾ cup mayonnaise**
- **¼ cup chopped dill pickle**
- **1 green onion, finely chopped**
- **2 garlic cloves, minced**
- **2 Tbsp. Creole mustard**
- **1 Tbsp. stone-ground mustard**
- **1 Tbsp. Louisiana-style hot sauce**
- **1 tsp. lemon juice**
- **½ tsp. paprika**
- **⅛ tsp. pepper**

In a bowl, stir together all ingredients until blended. Refrigerate until ready to use.

2 TBSP.: 97 cal., 10g fat (2g sat. fat), 1mg chol., 213mg sod., 1g carb. (0 sugars, 0 fiber), 0 pro.

SUCCESS TIPS

- **There are four grades of crabmeat:** claw, special, lump and jumbo lump. Using blue lump crabmeat for this recipe will result in the best texture and flavor.
- **Add the crabmeat after mixing the initial ingredients** to avoid breaking up the chunks of crab too much. Then, mix in the bread crumbs gently.
- **When adding the bread crumbs,** use only as much as you need to be able to form a patty that holds together.

ZUCCHINI PICO DE GALLO

5 INGREDIENTS

SPIKED LEMONADE

A touch of rum gives a tropical twist to this fabulous homemade lemonade. If you have vodka on hand, try that instead of the rum.
—Taste of Home *Test Kitchen*

PREP: 15 MIN. + CHILLING • **MAKES:** 8 SERVINGS (ABOUT 2 QT.)

- **2¼ cups sugar**
- **5 cups water, divided**
- **1 Tbsp. grated lemon zest**
- **1¾ cups lemon juice**
- **1 cup light rum or vodka**
- **6 to 8 cups ice cubes**

GARNISH

- **Lemon slices**

1. In a large saucepan, combine the sugar, 1 cup water and lemon zest. Cook and stir over medium heat until sugar is dissolved, about 4 minutes. Remove from the heat. Stir in lemon juice and remaining water. Pour into a 2-qt. pitcher; refrigerate until chilled.
2. Stir in rum. For each serving, place ¾-1 cup ice in a Collins or highball glass. Pour lemonade mixture into glass. Garnish with lemon slices as desired.
1 CUP: 296 cal., 0 fat (0 sat. fat), 0 chol., 1mg sod., 61g carb. (56g sugars, 0 fiber), 0 pro.

EAT SMART

ZUCCHINI PICO DE GALLO

I love the fresh veggies of summer. I make big bowls of this salsa, which we eat with pretty much everything when tomatoes are bountiful. My kids love it, though I leave out the jalapeno when making it for them.
—Amy Gattuso, Madison Heights, MI

PREP: 20 MIN. + CHILLING • **MAKES:** 4½ CUPS

- **2 large tomatoes, chopped**
- **1 medium zucchini, finely chopped**
- **1 poblano pepper, seeded and chopped**
- **½ cup chopped onion**
- **1 seeded and diced jalapeno pepper, optional**
- **2 Tbsp. minced fresh cilantro**
- **2 garlic cloves, minced**
- **½ tsp. salt**
- **¼ tsp. pepper**
- **3 Tbsp. lime juice**

Combine the first nine ingredients. Add lime juice; toss to coat. Cover and refrigerate at least 1 hour.
¼ CUP: 10 cal., 0 fat (0 sat. fat), 0 chol., 68mg sod., 2g carb. (1g sugars, 1g fiber), 0 pro.

SPIKED LEMONADE

CAULIFLOWER CEVICHE

EAT SMART

CAULIFLOWER CEVICHE

My 87-year-old mom showed me how to make this fantastic vegetarian recipe that tastes so much like seafood ceviche. I often serve it with crackers on the side.
—Beatriz Barranco, El Paso, TX

PREP: 20 MIN. + CHILLING • **MAKES:** 10 SERVINGS

- **1 medium head cauliflower, finely chopped**
- **1 cup ketchup**
- **1 cup orange juice**
- **3 medium tomatoes, chopped**
- **1 medium onion, finely chopped**
- **½ cup minced fresh cilantro**
- **¼ tsp. salt**
- **¼ tsp. pepper**
- **3 medium ripe avocados, peeled and cubed**
- **Lemon wedges, tortilla chip scoops and hot pepper sauce, optional**

1. In a large skillet, bring 1 cup water to a boil. Add cauliflower; cook, uncovered, just until crisp-tender, 5-8 minutes. Remove with a slotted spoon; drain and pat dry. Meanwhile, stir together ketchup and orange juice.
2. In a large bowl, combine cauliflower with tomatoes and onion. Add ketchup mixture, cilantro, salt and pepper; toss to coat. Refrigerate, covered, at least 1 hour.
3. Stir in avocado cubes. If desired, serve with lemon wedges, tortilla chip scoops and hot pepper sauce.
1 SERVING: 129 cal., 7g fat (1g sat. fat), 0 chol., 387mg sod., 18g carb. (11g sugars, 5g fiber), 3g pro.

FAST FIX

MEDITERRANEAN NACHOS

My husband once piled all the Middle Eastern dishes I had made on top of pita chips and ate it that way. It was delicious and fun, and we've kept doing it! I am half Lebanese, so we usually call these Lebanese nachos. Whatever you call them, they are delicious.
—Gina Fensler, Cincinnati, OH

TAKES: 30 MIN. • **MAKES:** 6 SERVINGS

- **½ lb. ground lamb or lean ground beef (90% lean)**
- **1 Tbsp. pine nuts**
- **¼ tsp. salt**
- **⅛ tsp. pepper**
- **6 Tbsp. plain yogurt, divided**
- **1 pkg. (7.33 oz.) baked pita chips**
- **1 cup prepared tabbouleh**
- **½ cup hummus**
- **1 large tomato, chopped**
- **¼ cup sliced ripe olives**
- **1 Tbsp. minced fresh parsley**
- **1 Tbsp. minced fresh mint**
- **Chopped red onion, optional**

1. In a small skillet, cook lamb over medium heat 4-6 minutes or until no longer pink, breaking into crumbles; drain. Stir in pine nuts, salt and pepper; cool slightly. Stir in 2 Tbsp. yogurt.
2. Arrange pita chips on a serving platter. Layer with lamb mixture, tabbouleh, hummus, tomato, olives, parsley, mint, remaining yogurt and, if desired, onion. Serve immediately.
1 SERVING: 299 cal., 14g fat (4g sat. fat), 27mg chol., 624mg sod., 29g carb. (2g sugars, 4g fiber), 13g pro.

MEDITERRANEAN NACHOS

EAT SMART

PEACH BRUSCHETTA

As a starter or light snack, this bruschetta is a wonderful way to savor the taste of summer, with just a bite of fresh peach amid a medley of lively flavors.
—Nikiko Masumoto, Del Ray, CA

PREP: 35 MIN. • **COOK:** 15 MIN.
MAKES: 2 DOZEN

¼ cup chopped walnuts
1 garlic clove
1½ cups fresh arugula
¼ cup extra virgin olive oil
Salt and pepper to taste

BRUSCHETTA

1 Tbsp. olive oil plus additional for brushing bread, divided
1 large red onion, thinly sliced (1½ cups)
1 tsp. minced fresh rosemary
24 slices French bread baguette (⅜ in. thick)
1 to 2 garlic cloves, halved
2 small ripe peaches, peeled and cut into ¼-in. slices
Shaved Parmesan cheese
Coarse salt

1. For pesto, place walnuts and garlic in a small food processor; pulse until finely chopped. Add arugula; process until blended. Continue processing while gradually adding oil in a steady stream. Season with salt and pepper to taste.
2. For bruschetta, in a large skillet, heat 1 Tbsp. oil over medium heat. Add onion and rosemary; cook 15-20 minutes or until onion is softened, stirring occasionally.
3. Brush both sides of bread slices with additional oil. Grill, covered, over medium heat or broil 4 in. from heat 1-2 minutes on each side or until golden brown.
4. Rub garlic halves on both sides of toasts; discard garlic. Spread toasts with pesto. Top with onion mixture, peaches and cheese. If desired, sprinkle with coarse salt. Serve immediately.
1 APPETIZER: 69 cal., 5g fat (1g sat. fat), 0 chol., 37mg sod., 5g carb. (1g sugars, 0 fiber), 0 pro.

PEACH BRUSCHETTA

MINIATURE CORN DOGS

Fun-sized corn dogs add a little wow to snack time or any time. Kids and adults love them equally, so expect them to disappear fast.
—Deb Perry, Bluffton, IN

PREP: 25 MIN. • **COOK:** 5 MIN./BATCH
MAKES: ABOUT 3½ DOZEN

1 cup all-purpose flour
2 Tbsp. cornmeal
1½ tsp. baking powder
¼ tsp. salt
Dash onion powder
3 Tbsp. shortening
¾ cup 2% milk
1 large egg
1 pkg. (16 oz.) miniature smoked sausages
Oil for deep-fat frying
Spicy ketchup

1. In a small bowl combine the flour, cornmeal, baking powder, salt and onion powder; cut in shortening until crumbly. Whisk milk and egg; stir into flour mixture just until moistened. Dip mini sausages into the batter.
2. In an electric skillet or deep fryer, heat oil to 375°. Fry sausages, a few at a time, until golden brown, 2-3 minutes. Drain on paper towels. Serve with ketchup.
1 MINI CORN DOG: 68 cal., 6g fat (1g sat. fat), 11mg chol., 136mg sod., 2g carb. (0 sugars, 0 fiber), 2g pro.

ROASTED BEETROOT & GARLIC HUMMUS

ROASTED BEETROOT & GARLIC HUMMUS

This beetroot hummus is so tasty and healthy, and it's the prettiest pink snack I've ever seen. This is also an ideal recipe to make in large batches and keep in the fridge for lunches and snacks throughout the week.
—Elizabeth Worndl, Toronto, ON

PREP: 25 MIN. • **BAKE:** 45 MIN.
MAKES: 16 SERVINGS

- **3 fresh medium beets (about 1 lb.)**
- **1 whole garlic bulb**
- **½ tsp. salt, divided**
- **½ tsp. coarsely ground pepper, divided**
- **1 tsp. extra virgin olive oil plus ¼ cup olive oil, divided**
- **1 can (15 oz.) garbanzo beans or chickpeas, rinsed and drained**
- **3 to 4 Tbsp. lemon juice**
- **2 Tbsp. tahini**
- **½ tsp. ground cumin**
- **½ tsp. cayenne pepper**
- **¼ cup plain Greek yogurt, optional**
- **Minced fresh dill weed or parsley**
- **Assorted fresh vegetables**
- **Sliced or torn pita bread**

1. Preheat oven to 375°. Pierce beets with a fork; place in a microwave-safe bowl and cover loosely. Microwave beets on high for 4 minutes, stirring halfway. Cool slightly. Wrap beets in individual foil packets.

2. Remove papery outer skin from garlic bulb, but do not peel or separate cloves. Cut in half crosswise. Sprinkle halves with ¼ tsp. salt and ¼ tsp. pepper; drizzle with 1 tsp. oil. Wrap in individual foil packets. Roast beets and garlic until cloves are soft, about 45 minutes.

3. Remove from oven; unwrap. Rinse beets with cold water; peel when cool enough to handle. Squeeze garlic from skins. Place beets and garlic in food processor. Add garbanzo beans, lemon juice, tahini, cumin, cayenne pepper and remaining olive oil, salt and pepper. Process until smooth.

4. If desired, pulse 2 Tbsp. Greek yogurt with beet mixture, dolloping remaining yogurt over finished hummus. Sprinkle with dill or parsley. Serve with assorted vegetables and pita bread.

¼ CUP: 87 cal., 5g fat (1g sat. fat), 0 chol., 131mg sod., 8g carb. (3g sugars, 2g fiber), 2g pro. **Diabetic exchanges:** 1 fat, ½ starch.

(5) INGREDIENTS FAST FIX

BRIE WITH ALMONDS

This nut-topped cheese is elegant and impressive for holiday occasions. No one will guess that the recipe is actually a snap to prepare.
—Mildred Aydt, Chanhassen, MN

TAKES: 15 MIN. • **MAKES:** 8 SERVINGS

- **1 round Brie cheese (8 oz.)**
- **2 Tbsp. butter, melted**
- **¼ cup sliced almonds**
- **1 Tbsp. brandy, optional**
- **Assorted crackers**

1. Place Brie in an ungreased ovenproof serving dish. Combine the butter, almonds and, if desired, brandy; pour over Brie.

2. Bake, uncovered, at 400° until the cheese is softened, 10-12 minutes. Serve with crackers.

2 TBSP.: 141 cal., 12g fat (7g sat. fat), 36mg chol., 199mg sod., 1g carb. (0 sugars, 0 fiber), 7g pro.

FRIED GREEN TOMATO NAPOLEONS WITH MANDARIN COLESLAW

Fried green tomatoes get stacked and smothered with pimiento cheese in this seriously comforting dish that doubles up on two of my favorite Southern classics. The mandarin coleslaw makes it bright and fresh.
—Amy Freeze, Avon Park, FL

PREP: 30 MIN. • **COOK:** 5 MIN. • **MAKES:** 4 SERVINGS

- **⅓ cup mayonnaise**
- **¼ cup white vinegar**
- **2 Tbsp. sugar**
- **1 tsp. salt**
- **1 tsp. garlic powder**
- **½ tsp. pepper**
- **1 pkg. (14 oz.) three-color coleslaw mix**
- **¼ cup finely chopped onion**
- **1 can (11 oz.) mandarin oranges, drained**

FRIED TOMATOES

- **1 large egg, lightly beaten**
- **Dash hot pepper sauce, or to taste**
- **¼ cup all-purpose flour**
- **1 cup dry bread crumbs**
- **2 medium green tomatoes, cut into four slices each**
- **Oil for frying**
- **½ tsp. salt**
- **¼ tsp. pepper**

TOPPINGS

- **½ cup pimiento cheese spread**
- **4 tsp. pepper jelly**

1. Combine first six ingredients. Add coleslaw mix and onion. Add mandarin oranges; stir carefully.
2. In a shallow bowl, whisk egg and hot sauce. Place flour and bread crumbs in separate shallow bowls. Dip tomato slices in flour to coat both sides; shake off excess. Dip in egg mixture, then in bread crumbs, patting to help coating adhere.
3. In an electric skillet or deep fryer, heat oil to 350°. Fry tomato slices, a few at a time, until browned, 1-2 minutes on each side. Drain on paper towels. Sprinkle with salt and pepper.
4. To assemble napoleons, layer one tomato slice with 1 Tbsp. pimiento cheese. Repeat layers. Top with 1 tsp. pepper jelly. Repeat with remaining tomato slices. Serve over coleslaw.
1 SERVING: 487 cal., 31g fat (7g sat. fat), 22mg chol., 1281mg sod., 45g carb. (26g sugars, 5g fiber), 7g pro.

TEST KITCHEN TIP

Mandarin oranges make a standout addition to this slaw, giving it a nice pop of freshness without making the taste overtly citrusy. To make the recipe gluten-free, dredge the tomatoes in cornmeal instead of flour and panko.

5 INGREDIENTS

RHUBARB PUNCH

I love the tart taste of rhubarb, and this lively, beautiful punch makes a refreshing treat at any get-together.
—Eleanor Martens, Rosenort, MB

PREP: 30 MIN. + COOLING • **MAKES:** 24 SERVINGS (16 OZ. EACH)

- **3 qt. diced fresh or frozen rhubarb**
- **4½ cups sugar**
- **3 qt. water**
- **1 can (6 oz.) frozen orange juice concentrate, thawed**
- **3 Tbsp. lemon juice**
- **Lemon-lime soda**

In a heavy saucepan, bring rhubarb, sugar and water to a boil. Boil 15 minutes; cool and strain. Stir in orange and lemon juices. Chill. For each serving, combine ½ cup rhubarb syrup and 12 oz. soda; serve in a chilled glass.
NOTE: If using frozen rhubarb, measure rhubarb while still frozen, then thaw completely. Drain in a colander, but do not press the liquid out.
1 SERVING: 329 cal., 0 fat (0 sat. fat), 0 chol., 39mg sod., 83g carb. (76g sugars, 1g fiber), 1g pro.

FRIED GREEN TOMATO NAPOLEONS WITH MANDARIN COLESLAW

HONEY & ALE
PULLED CHICKEN SLIDERS

SLOW COOKER

HONEY & ALE PULLED CHICKEN SLIDERS

Score big with your guests with a little bit of sweet heat! This recipe works well for a football party—the extra liquid in the slow cooker keeps the chicken nice and juicy all day long.
—Julie Peterson, Crofton, MD

PREP: 20 MIN. • **COOK:** 6 HOURS • **MAKES:** 12 SERVINGS

- ¼ **cup honey**
- 2 **Tbsp. cider vinegar**
- 2 **Tbsp. Sriracha Asian hot chili sauce**
- 1 **Tbsp. chili powder**
- 1 **tsp. smoked paprika**
- 1 **tsp. garlic powder**
- 1 **tsp. onion powder**
- ½ **tsp. salt**
- 2 **lbs. boneless skinless chicken thighs (about 8 thighs)**
- ¾ **cup brown ale**
- 3 **Tbsp. cornstarch**
- 3 **Tbsp. water**
- 12 **slider buns**
- **Sweet pickles and additional Sriracha sauce, optional**

1. In a 3- or 4-qt. slow cooker, combine the first eight ingredients. Add chicken and ale; toss to coat. Cook, covered, on low until chicken is tender, 6-8 hours. Remove meat; when cool enough to handle, shred with two forks.

2. Strain cooking juices; skim fat. Transfer juices to a small saucepan; bring to a boil. In a small bowl, mix cornstarch and water until smooth; stir into saucepan. Return to a boil, stirring constantly; cook and stir until thickened, about 5 minutes. Add chicken to the sauce; toss to coat. Serve on buns, with pickles and additional Sriracha sauce if desired.

1 SLIDER: 224 cal., 7g fat (2g sat. fat), 51mg chol., 357mg sod., 22g carb. (8g sugars, 1g fiber), 17g pro.

5 INGREDIENTS

STRAWBERRY-LAVENDER INFUSED WATER

A little bit of lavender goes a long way, so be sure not to overdo it! This pretty combo screams summer, but you can also dry out the lavender and enjoy this anytime.
—Taste of Home *Test Kitchen*

PREP: 5 MIN. + CHILLING • **MAKES:** 8 CUPS

- 1 **cup sliced fresh strawberries**
- 3 **fresh lavender sprigs or 1 tsp. dried culinary lavender**
- 2 **qt. water**

Combine all ingredients in a large glass carafe or pitcher. Cover and refrigerate 12-24 hours.

STRAWBERRY-LAVENDER INFUSED WATER

EAT SMART 5 INGREDIENTS

ORANGE SHRIMP MOJO

With jalapeno, orange and avocado, every bite of this enticing entree is spicy, tangy and fresh. The sauce beautifully glazes the tender shrimp.
—Don Thompson, Houston, OH

PREP: 25 MIN. • **COOK:** 45 MIN.
MAKES: 8 SERVINGS

- **1 Tbsp. cumin seeds**
- **1 Tbsp. whole peppercorns**
- **1 Tbsp. grated orange or tangerine zest**
- **½ tsp. dried oregano**
- **½ tsp. salt**
- **1 lb. uncooked jumbo shrimp, peeled and deveined**
- **4 tsp. olive oil**
- **3 cups orange juice**
- **3 Tbsp. rum or chicken broth**
- **1 garlic clove, minced**
- **1 large navel orange, peeled, sectioned and chopped**
- **½ cup chopped sweet onion**
- **1 cup cubed avocado**
- **½ cup minced fresh cilantro, divided**
- **1 tsp. chopped seeded jalapeno pepper**

1. In a small dry skillet over medium heat, toast cumin seeds and peppercorns until aromatic, 1-2 minutes. Remove from skillet. Crush seeds using a spice grinder or mortar and pestle.
2. In a small bowl, combine the orange zest, oregano, salt and crushed spices. Sprinkle 1 Tbsp. spice mixture over shrimp.
3. In a large skillet, cook shrimp in oil over medium-high heat 1 minute; turn shrimp. Add orange juice, rum, garlic and 1 Tbsp. spice mixture. Cook and stir until shrimp turn pink, 1-2 minutes longer; remove and keep warm.
4. Bring liquid in skillet to a boil. Cook until reduced to ⅔ cup, about 35 minutes. Meanwhile, for salsa, combine orange, onion, avocado, ¼ cup cilantro, jalapeno and remaining spice mixture in a small bowl.
5. Stir shrimp and remaining cilantro into sauce; heat through. Serve with salsa.
NOTE: Wear disposable gloves when cutting hot peppers; the oils can burn skin. Avoid touching your face.
1 SERVING: 172 cal., 6g fat (1g sat. fat), 69mg chol., 218mg sod., 16g carb. (11g sugars, 2g fiber), 11g pro. **Diabetic exchanges:** 1 starch, 1 lean meat, 1 fat.

ORANGE SHRIMP MOJO

EAT SMART FAST FIX

HOMEMADE GUACAMOLE

Nothing is better than fresh guacamole when you're eating something spicy. It's easy to whip together in a matter of minutes, and it quickly tames anything that's too hot.
—Joan Hallford, North Richland Hills, TX

TAKES: 10 MIN. • **MAKES:** 2 CUPS

- **3 medium ripe avocados, peeled and cubed**
- **1 garlic clove, minced**
- **¼ to ½ tsp. salt**
- **2 medium tomatoes, seeded and chopped, optional**
- **1 small onion, finely chopped**
- **¼ cup mayonnaise, optional**
- **1 to 2 Tbsp. lime juice**
- **1 Tbsp. minced fresh cilantro**

Mash avocados with garlic and salt. Stir in remaining ingredients.
¼ CUP: 90 cal., 8g fat (1g sat. fat), 0 chol., 78mg sod., 6g carb. (1g sugars, 4g fiber), 1g pro. **Diabetic exchanges:** 1½ fat.

MEATBALLS IN CHILI & JELLY SAUCE

Meatballs 8 Ways

Cook frozen meatballs according to package directions and toss with any of these sauces.

Bourbon Sauce
Cook and stir ¾ cup brown sugar, ¾ cup white vinegar, ¾ cup bourbon and 1 tsp. spicy brown mustard until mixture begins to simmer.

Chili & Jelly Sauce
Cook and stir 1 (12-oz.) bottle chili sauce and 1 (10-oz.) jar grape jelly until jelly is melted and mixture begins to simmer.

Cranberry
Cook and stir 1 (14-oz.) can jellied cranberry sauce, 1 cup ketchup, 3 Tbsp. brown sugar and 1 Tbsp. lemon juice until blended and hot.

Chimichurri Sauce
Chop 3 peeled garlic cloves in a small food processor. Add 1 cup fresh parsley, ¼ cup cilantro, 1 tsp. salt and ¼ tsp. pepper; pulse until finely chopped. Add 2 Tbsp. red wine vinegar. While processing, gradually add ½ cup olive oil.

Hoisin Sauce
Combine ¼ cup each rice vinegar and hoisin sauce, 2 Tbsp. each water, sesame oil and soy sauce, 1 Tbsp. honey, and 1 tsp. each minced garlic and ginger. Bring to a simmer.

Orange Glaze
Heat 1 (12-oz.) jar orange marmalade, ¼ cup orange juice, 2 chopped green onions and 1 chopped jalapeno.

Marinara Sauce
Heat 1½ cups marinara, ⅓ cup chopped ripe olives and ½ cup minced basil.

Swedish
In a large saucepan, melt 2 Tbsp. butter. Stir in 2 Tbsp. flour until smooth; gradually add 1 cup beef broth. Bring to a boil; cook and stir for 2 minutes. Stir in ½ cup heavy cream and ¼ tsp. dried dill; simmer 1 minute.

MEATBALLS WITH ORANGE GLAZE

SLOW COOKER

GREEN CHILI ADOBADO POUTINE

A Canadian comfort-food classic is even better when served southwestern-style, as either an appetizer or an entree. Although the ribs are done here without fuss in a slow cooker, you can also bake them at 325°, covered with foil, about 45 minutes. Then uncover and bake for another 20 minutes.
—Johnna Johnson, Scottsdale, AZ

PREP: 50 MIN. • **COOK:** 3 HOURS • **MAKES:** 8 SERVINGS

- **3 garlic cloves, unpeeled**
- **4 dried guajillo or ancho chilies, stemmed and seeded**
- **1 can (10 oz.) enchilada sauce, divided**
- **3 cans (4 oz. each) chopped green chilies, divided**
- **1 Tbsp. cider vinegar**
- **2 tsp. dried oregano**
- **½ tsp. ground cumin**
- **½ tsp. salt**
- **½ tsp. pepper**
- **⅛ tsp. ground cinnamon**
- **2 lbs. boneless country-style pork ribs, cut into 2-in. pieces**
- **1 pkg. (32 oz.) frozen french-fried potatoes**
- **1 cup queso fresco**
- **Pico de gallo, optional**

1. Lightly smash garlic cloves with the bottom of a heavy skillet to flatten. Cook garlic cloves in a large skillet over medium-low heat until softened and browned, about 10 minutes. Cool and peel.
2. In same skillet at the same time, cook dried chilies, pressing them against the bottom with a spatula or tongs until lightly toasted and fragrant, 1-2 minutes. Transfer to a bowl. Pour boiling water over chilies to cover; let stand 15 minutes. Drain.
3. Place softened chilies and garlic in a food processor. Add ½ cup enchilada sauce, two cans green chilies, vinegar, oregano, cumin, salt, pepper and cinnamon; process until blended. Stir in remaining enchilada sauce and green chilies. Transfer to a 5- or 6-qt. slow cooker. Add ribs; turn to coat. Cover and cook on high until the meat is tender, 3-4 hours. During the final 30 minutes, cook fries according to package directions.
4. Remove pork; shred with two forks. Top fries with shredded pork, cheese, enchilada gravy and, if desired, pico de gallo.
1 SERVING: 434 cal., 19g fat (7g sat. fat), 75mg chol., 1065mg sod., 31g carb. (2g sugars, 5g fiber), 28g pro.

ROASTED RED PEPPER TRIANGLES

I sandwich full-flavored meats, cheeses and roasted red peppers between layers of flaky crescent dough for this sensational treat. We like to have marinara sauce on hand for dipping.
—Amy Bell, Arlington, TN

PREP: 35 MIN. • **BAKE:** 50 MIN. • **MAKES:** 2 DOZEN

- **2 tubes (8 oz. each) refrigerated crescent rolls**
- **1½ cups finely diced fully cooked ham**
- **1 cup shredded Swiss cheese**
- **1 pkg. (3 oz.) sliced pepperoni, chopped**
- **8 slices provolone cheese**
- **1 jar (12 oz.) roasted sweet red peppers, drained and cut into strips**
- **4 large eggs**
- **¼ cup grated Parmesan cheese**
- **1 Tbsp. Italian salad dressing mix**

1. Preheat oven to 350°. Unroll one tube of crescent dough into one long rectangle; press onto bottom and ¾ in. up sides of a greased 13x9-in. baking dish. Seal seams and perforations. Top with half of the ham; layer with Swiss cheese, pepperoni, provolone cheese and remaining ham. Top with red peppers.
2. In a small bowl, whisk eggs, Parmesan cheese and salad dressing mix; reserve ¼ cup. Pour remaining egg mixture over peppers.
3. On a lightly floured surface, roll out remaining crescent dough into a 13x9-in. rectangle; seal seams and perforations. Place over filling; pinch edges to seal.
4. Bake, covered, for 30 minutes. Uncover; brush with reserved egg mixture. Bake until crust is golden brown, 20-25 minutes longer. Cool on a wire rack for 5 minutes. Cut into triangles. Serve warm.
1 PIECE: 165 cal., 10g fat (4g sat. fat), 50mg chol., 485mg sod., 8g carb. (2g sugars, 0 fiber), 8g pro.

GREEN CHILI ADOBADO POUTINE

HOT BACON CHEESE DIP

SLOW COOKER

HOT BACON CHEESE DIP

I've tried assorted appetizers before, but this one is a surefire people-pleaser. The thick dip has lots of bacon flavor and keeps my guests happily munching as long as it lasts. I serve it with tortilla chips or sliced French bread.
—Suzanne Whitaker, Knoxville, TN

PREP: 15 MIN. • **COOK:** 2 HOURS • **MAKES:** 4 CUPS

- **2 pkg. (8 oz. each) cream cheese, cubed**
- **4 cups shredded cheddar cheese**
- **1 cup half-and-half cream**
- **2 tsp. Worcestershire sauce**
- **1 tsp. dried minced onion**
- **1 tsp. prepared mustard**
- **16 bacon strips, cooked and crumbled**
- **Tortilla chips or French bread slices**

1. In a 1½-qt. slow cooker, combine the first six ingredients. Cover and cook on low for 2-3 hours or until cheeses are melted, stirring occasionally.
2. Just before serving, stir in crumbled bacon. Serve warm with tortilla chips or bread.
¼ CUP: 261 cal., 23g fat (14g sat. fat), 77mg chol., 417mg sod., 3g carb. (1g sugars, 0 fiber), 11g pro.
BAKED BACON CHEESE DIP: Preheat oven to 375°. Transfer cheese mixture to a 1½-qt. baking dish. Bake, uncovered, 20-25 minutes or until bubbly. Stir in bacon.

FAST FIX

QUICK WHITE SANGRIA

Using white instead of red wine makes my version of sangria a bit lighter, yet with the same wonderful sweetness. Frozen fruit allows me to serve this refreshing sipper any time of year.
—Sharon Tipton, Casselberry, FL

TAKES: 15 MIN. • **MAKES:** 6 SERVINGS

- **¼ cup sugar**
- **¼ cup brandy**
- **1 cup sliced peeled fresh or frozen peaches, thawed**
- **1 cup sliced fresh or frozen sliced strawberries, thawed**
- **1 medium lemon, sliced**
- **1 medium lime, sliced**
- **1 bottle (750 ml) dry white wine, chilled**
- **1 can (12 oz.) lemon-lime soda, chilled**
- **Ice cubes**

In a pitcher, mix sugar and brandy until sugar is dissolved. Add remaining ingredients; stir gently to combine. Serve over ice.
¾ CUP: 196 cal., 0 fat (0 sat. fat), 0 chol., 12mg sod., 23g carb. (19g sugars, 1g fiber), 1g pro.

REUBEN ROLLS

I wanted the flavor of a classic Reuben in a fun-to-eat appetizer. The empty platter at my party signaled that these rolls were a hit!
—Darlene Abney, Muenster, TX

PREP: 30 MIN. + CHILLING • **MAKES:** ABOUT 8 DOZEN

- **1 pkg. (8 oz.) cream cheese, softened**
- **3 Tbsp. spicy brown mustard**
- **¼ tsp. prepared horseradish**
- **5 flour tortillas (10 in.), room temperature**
- **7 pkg. (2 oz. each) thinly sliced deli corned beef**
- **15 thin slices Swiss cheese**
- **1 can (14 oz.) sauerkraut, rinsed and well drained**

1. In a small bowl, beat the cream cheese, mustard and horseradish until blended. Spread a heaping tablespoonful of cream cheese mixture over each tortilla.
2. Layer each tortilla with eight slices of corned beef, three slices of cheese, another heaping tablespoonful of cream cheese mixture and ½ cup sauerkraut. Roll up tightly. Chill for 1 hour. Cut each roll-up into ½-in. slices.
1 APPETIZER: 31 cal., 2g fat (1g sat. fat), 6mg chol., 118mg sod., 2g carb. (0 sugars, 0 fiber), 2g pro.

REUBEN ROLLS

QUICK WHITE SANGRIA

BBQ CHICKEN GRITS BITES

EAT SMART

PARTY SHRIMP

The marinade for this dish makes the shrimp so flavorful, you won't even need a dipping sauce. Even those who claim they don't like shellfish really dig this appetizer.
—Kendra Doss, Colorado Springs, CO

PREP: 15 MIN. + MARINATING
BROIL: 10 MIN. • **MAKES:** ABOUT 2½ DOZEN

- **1 Tbsp. olive oil**
- **1½ tsp. brown sugar**
- **1½ tsp. lemon juice**
- **1 garlic clove, thinly sliced**
- **½ tsp. paprika**
- **½ tsp. Italian seasoning**
- **½ tsp. dried basil**
- **¼ tsp. pepper**
- **1 lb. uncooked large shrimp, peeled and deveined**

1. In a bowl or shallow dish, combine the first eight ingredients. Add shrimp and turn to coat. Cover and refrigerate 2 hours.
2. Drain shrimp, discarding marinade from bowl. Place shrimp on an ungreased baking sheet. Broil 4 in. from heat until the shrimp turn pink, 3-4 minutes on each side.
1 SHRIMP: 14 cal., 0 fat (0 sat. fat), 18mg chol., 18mg sod., 0 carb. (0 sugars, 0 fiber), 2g pro.

PARTY SHRIMP

BBQ CHICKEN GRITS BITES

I love grits and barbecued chicken, so I decided to combine them into a jaunty appetizer. You can also use shredded pork instead of chicken.
—Jamie Jones, Madison, GA

PREP: 30 MIN. • **BAKE:** 15 MIN.
MAKES: 2½ DOZEN

- **2 cups 2% milk**
- **¾ cup quick-cooking grits**
- **¼ tsp. salt**
- **⅛ tsp. pepper**
- **4 oz. crumbled goat cheese, divided**
- **¼ cup apricot preserves**
- **¼ cup barbecue sauce**
- **1½ cups chopped rotisserie chicken**
- **3 green onions, thinly sliced**

1. Preheat the oven to 350°. Grease 30 mini-muffin cups.
2. In a large saucepan, bring milk to a boil. Slowly stir in grits, salt and pepper. Reduce heat to medium-low; cook, covered, until thickened, about 5 minutes, stirring occasionally. Stir in half of the cheese. Spoon 1 Tbsp. mixture into each prepared muffin cup.
3. In a medium bowl, mix the preserves and barbecue sauce; toss with chicken. Spoon about 1 tsp. chicken mixture into each cup; press lightly into grits.
4. Bake until heated through, 15-20 minutes. Top with remaining cheese; sprinkle with green onions. Cool 5 minutes before removing from pans. Serve warm.
1 APPETIZER: 56 cal., 2g fat (1g sat. fat), 12mg chol., 76mg sod., 7g carb. (3g sugars, 0 fiber), 4g pro.

NUTTY STUFFED MUSHROOMS

APPETIZER BLUE CHEESE LOGS

Three kinds of cheese and some curry powder make this cheese log a little more lively than most. Swipe it on your favorite cracker with a drizzle of honey for a sensational snack.
—Ethel Johnson, North Saanich, BC

PREP: 15 MIN. • **COOK:** 5 MIN. + CHILLING • **MAKES:** 2 CHEESE LOGS

- **1 pkg. (8 oz.) cream cheese, softened**
- **1 cup shredded sharp cheddar cheese**
- **½ cup crumbled blue cheese**
- **1 Tbsp. butter**
- **1½ tsp. curry powder**
- **½ cup finely chopped pecans**
- **2 Tbsp. minced fresh parsley**
- **Assorted crackers**

1. Beat cream cheese until smooth. Fold in cheddar and blue cheeses. Refrigerate, covered, at least 2 hours.
2. In a small skillet, heat butter over medium heat. Add curry powder; saute 1-2 minutes. Stir in pecans; cook and stir 1 minute. Stir in parsley. Cool slightly. Roll cheese mixture into two logs, each about 5 in. long. Roll in pecan mixture; refrigerate. Serve with crackers.
2 TBSP.: 196 cal., 19g fat (9g sat. fat), 45mg chol., 243mg sod., 2g carb. (1g sugars, 1g fiber), 6g pro.

APPETIZER BLUE CHEESE LOGS

FAST FIX

NUTTY STUFFED MUSHROOMS

Basil, Parmesan cheese and mushroom blend together well, while buttery pecans give these treats unexpected crunch. Our children, grandchildren and great-grandchildren always ask for them!
—Mildred Eldred, Union City, MI

TAKES: 30 MIN. • **MAKES:** 20 SERVINGS

- **20 large fresh mushrooms**
- **3 Tbsp. butter**
- **1 small onion, chopped**
- **¼ cup dry bread crumbs**
- **¼ cup finely chopped pecans**
- **3 Tbsp. grated Parmesan cheese**
- **¼ tsp. salt**
- **¼ tsp. dried basil**
- **Dash cayenne pepper**

1. Preheat oven to 400°. Remove stems from mushrooms; set caps aside. Finely chop stems. In a large skillet, heat butter over medium heat. Add chopped mushrooms and onion; saute until liquid has evaporated, about 5 minutes. Remove from the heat; set aside.
2. Meanwhile, combine remaining ingredients; add mushroom mixture. Stuff firmly into mushroom caps. Bake, uncovered, in a greased 15x10x1-in. baking pan until tender, 15-18 minutes. Serve warm.
1 STUFFED MUSHROOM: 44 cal., 3g fat (1g sat. fat), 5mg chol., 67mg sod., 3g carb. (0 sugars, 0 fiber), 2g pro.

HOT CHIPOTLE SPINACH & ARTICHOKE DIP WITH LIME

FAST FIX

HOT CHIPOTLE SPINACH & ARTICHOKE DIP WITH LIME

I make spinach and artichoke dip for party guests all the time, but I wanted to give it a Mexican twist. I amped up this app with smoky chipotle chilies and tangy lime for an unexpected kick.
—Joseph A. Sciascia, San Mateo, CA

TAKES: 30 MIN. • **MAKES:** 4 CUPS

- **2 cups shredded mozzarella cheese**
- **1 pkg. (8 oz.) cream cheese, softened**
- **½ cup mayonnaise**
- **½ cup grated Parmesan cheese, divided**
- **2 chipotle peppers in adobo sauce, finely minced**
- **1 Tbsp. grated lime zest**
- **¼ cup lime juice**
- **¼ tsp. kosher salt**
- **¼ tsp. pepper**
- **1 can (14 oz.) water-packed artichoke hearts, drained and coarsely chopped**
- **1 pkg. (10 oz.) frozen chopped spinach, thawed and squeezed dry**
- **3 green onions, chopped**
- **1 large garlic clove, finely chopped**
- **Optional accompaniments: baked pita chips, tortilla chips, sliced French bread baguette or assorted crackers**

1. Preheat oven to 400°. Combine mozzarella cheese, cream cheese, mayonnaise and ¼ cup grated Parmesan cheese; stir in next nine ingredients. Spoon into a deep-dish pie plate; sprinkle with remaining Parmesan.
2. Bake until golden brown and bubbly, 20-25 minutes. Serve as desired with pita or tortilla chips, baguette slices or crackers.
¼ CUP: 164 cal., 14g fat (6g sat. fat), 28mg chol., 318mg sod., 4g carb. (1g sugars, 1g fiber), 6g pro.

TEST KITCHEN TIP

Got a crowd coming? You can extend this dip even more by adding shredded rotisserie chicken. Also try it as a delicious sandwich spread, or as a schmear on bagels.

EAT SMART FAST FIX

CURRY CARROT DIP

The flavors of sweet carrots, mustard and curry blend deliciously in this appetizing dip. Raw veggies are the perfect partner.
—Louise Weyer, Marietta, GA

TAKES: 30 MIN. • **MAKES:** 1 CUP

- **1 small onion, chopped**
- **2 tsp. canola oil**
- **4 medium carrots, sliced**
- **⅓ cup water**
- **¼ tsp. salt**
- **¼ tsp. pepper**
- **¼ tsp. curry powder**
- **2 Tbsp. reduced-fat mayonnaise**
- **2 tsp. prepared mustard**
- **Assorted raw vegetables**

1. In a nonstick skillet, saute onion in oil. Add the carrots, water, salt, pepper and curry. Bring to a boil. Reduce heat; cover and simmer for 6 minutes or until vegetables are tender. Uncover; cook for 8 minutes or until liquid has evaporated. Cool.
2. Transfer to a food processor or blender; cover and process until smooth. Add mayonnaise and mustard; mix well. Serve with vegetables.
2 TBSP.: 40 cal., 3g fat (0 sat. fat), 1mg chol., 133mg sod., 4g carb. (2g sugars, 1g fiber), 0 pro.

CURRY CARROT DIP

KING OF WINGS

Denver cook Nick Iverson has a knack for making crowd-pleasing chicken wings, plus sticky-finger sauces made for slathering. Pick your favorite or serve all three.

BEST EVER FRIED CHICKEN WINGS

For game days, I shake things up with these saucy chicken wings. Whenever I run out, friends hover around the snack table until I bring out more. You'll be glad these chicken wings are so easy, because you'll be making a lot of them.
—Nick Iverson, Denver, CO

PREP: 10 MIN. + CHILLING • **COOK:** 20 MIN.
MAKES: ABOUT 4 DOZEN

- 4 **lbs. chicken wings**
- 2 **tsp. kosher salt**
- **Oil for deep-fat frying**

BUFFALO WING SAUCE

- ¾ **cup Louisiana-style hot sauce**
- ¼ **cup unsalted butter, cubed**
- 2 **Tbsp. molasses**
- ¼ **tsp. cayenne pepper**

SPICY THAI SAUCE

- 1 **Tbsp. canola oil**
- 1 **tsp. grated fresh gingerroot**
- 1 **garlic clove, minced**
- 1 **minced Thai chili pepper or ¼ tsp. crushed red pepper flakes**
- ¼ **cup packed dark brown sugar**
- 2 **Tbsp. lime juice**
- 2 **Tbsp. minced fresh cilantro**
- 1 **Tbsp. fish sauce**

SPICY BBQ SAUCE

- ¾ **cup barbecue sauce**
- 2 **chipotle peppers in adobo sauce, finely chopped**
- 2 **Tbsp. honey**
- 1 **Tbsp. cider vinegar**
- **Thinly sliced green onions, optional**

1. Using a sharp knife, cut through the two wing joints; discard wing tips. Pat chicken dry with paper towels. Toss wings with kosher salt. Place on a wire rack in a 15x10x1-in. baking pan. Refrigerate at least 1 hour or overnight.
2. In an electric skillet or deep-fat fryer, heat oil to 375°. Fry wings in batches until skin is crisp and meat is tender, 8-10 minutes. Drain on paper towels.
3. For Buffalo wing sauce, bring hot sauce just to a boil in a small saucepan. Remove from heat; whisk in butter one piece at a time. Stir in molasses and cayenne pepper.
4. For Thai sauce, heat oil in a small saucepan over medium heat. Add ginger, garlic and chili pepper; cook and stir until fragrant, 2 minutes. Stir in brown sugar and lime juice. Bring to a boil; cook until slightly thickened, about 5 minutes. Stir in cilantro and fish sauce.
5. For spicy BBQ sauce, heat prepared barbecue sauce in a small saucepan over medium heat. Stir in chipotle peppers, honey and vinegar. Bring to a boil; cook and stir until slightly thickened, about 5 minutes.
6. Toss wings with one of the sauces. If desired, sprinkle with green onion slices.
NOTE: Uncooked chicken wing sections (wingettes) may be substituted for whole chicken wings.

1 PIECE WITH BUFFALO SAUCE: 87 cal., 8g fat (2g sat. fat), 15mg chol., 218mg sod., 1g carb. (1g sugars, 0 fiber), 4g pro.

1 PIECE WITH THAI SAUCE: 82 cal., 7g fat (1g sat. fat), 12mg chol., 121mg sod., 1g carb. (1g sugars, 0 fiber), 4g pro.

1 PIECE WITH SPICY BBQ SAUCE: 85 cal., 7g fat (1g sat. fat), 12mg chol., 136mg sod., 2g carb. (1g sugars, 0 fiber), 4g pro.

CORNED BEEF PIZZA SWIRLS

CORNED BEEF PIZZA SWIRLS

You don't have to wait until St. Patrick's Day to enjoy this easy Reuben appetizer. Deli meat and cheese make it doable year-round.
—Colleen Delawder, Herndon, VA

PREP: 30 MIN. + RISING • **BAKE:** 35 MIN. • **MAKES:** 12 SERVINGS

- **2 tsp. granulated sugar**
- **1 tsp. active dry yeast**
- **1 cup warm whole milk (110° to 115°)**
- **1 Tbsp. olive oil**
- **2 tsp. kosher salt**
- **2 tsp. caraway seeds**
- **2½ cups all-purpose flour**

THOUSAND ISLAND SAUCE
- **½ cup mayonnaise**
- **3 Tbsp. finely diced dill pickles**
- **2 Tbsp. ketchup**
- **1 tsp. brown sugar**
- **½ tsp. onion powder**
- **¼ tsp. pepper**
- **2 dashes Louisiana-style hot sauce**
- **Dash garlic powder**

PIZZA SWIRLS
- **¾ lb. thinly sliced corned beef**
- **½ lb. thinly sliced lacy Swiss cheese**

1. Add sugar and yeast to warm milk; let stand 15 minutes. Beat yeast mixture, oil, kosher salt and caraway seeds until blended. Beat in flour, ½ cup at a time, just until combined. With oiled hands, place dough in a greased bowl, turning once to grease the top. Cover and let rise in a warm place until doubled, about 2 hours.
2. Meanwhile, mix all of the ingredients for the Thousand Island sauce; refrigerate.
3. Punch down dough. To assemble pizza swirls, turn dough onto a well-floured surface; roll into a 15x10-in. rectangle. Arrange corned beef and cheese slices to within ¾ in. of edges. Roll up jelly-roll style, starting with a long side; pinch seam to seal and tuck ends under. Cut crosswise into 1-in. slices. Place slices, sides touching, on a parchment paper-lined baking sheet.
4. Preheat oven to 375°. Cover pizza swirls with greased foil; let stand 20 minutes. Bake, covered, 20 minutes; remove foil and bake until golden brown, 15-20 minutes longer. Serve warm with Thousand Island sauce.

1 PIZZA SWIRL: 290 cal., 16g fat (6g sat. fat), 36mg chol., 807mg sod., 23g carb. (3g sugars, 1g fiber), 13g pro.

EAT SMART

SPICY MIXED NUTS

Cumin and chili powder give extra oomph to the classic homemade nut mix. It's a smart solution for holiday snacking and gift giving.
—Delores Hill, Helena, MT

PREP: 5 MIN. • **COOK:** 10 MIN. + COOLING • **MAKES:** 3 CUPS

- **3 Tbsp. butter**
- **1 can (15 to 16 oz.) mixed nuts**
- **¼ tsp. Worcestershire sauce**
- **½ tsp. salt**
- **¼ tsp. paprika**
- **¼ tsp. cayenne pepper**
- **¼ tsp. chili powder**
- **⅛ tsp. ground cumin**

In a large skillet, melt butter over low heat. Add nuts and Worcestershire sauce; cook and stir 5-7 minutes. Drain on paper towels. Place nuts in a large bowl. Combine remaining ingredients; sprinkle over nuts, tossing to coat. Cool. Store nuts in an airtight container at room temperature.

¼ CUP: 225 cal., 19g fat (2g sat. fat), 0 chol., 232mg sod., 10g carb. (2g sugars, 3g fiber), 7g pro.

SPICY MIXED NUTS

FAST FIX

STUFFED CHERRY TOMATOES

I adapted this tomato appetizer from a stuffed mushroom recipe that I've used for years. The tasty little treats always win compliments—they're outstanding at parties or for potlucks and salad luncheons.
—Donna Smith, Grey Cliff, MT

TAKES: 30 MIN. • **MAKES:** ABOUT 2 DOZEN

1 pint cherry tomatoes

FILLING

3 oz. cream cheese, softened
¼ cup ranch salad dressing
2 Tbsp. thinly sliced green onion
2 Tbsp. finely chopped water chestnuts
2 Tbsp. finely chopped walnuts
Whole chives, optional

Make an "X" in the top of each tomato, cutting two-thirds of the way to the bottom. Scoop out pulp with the tip of a knife. Drain tomatoes, upside down, on a paper towel. Combine filling ingredients in small bowl. Stuff tomatoes with filling. Keep refrigerated until serving. If desired, garnish with chives for flower stems.
1 STUFFED TOMATO: 29 cal., 3g fat (1g sat. fat), 4mg chol., 36mg sod., 1g carb. (1g sugars, 0 fiber), 0 pro.

STUFFED CHERRY TOMATOES

DANA HINCK
Pensacola, FL

PEACH-BASIL COOLER

5 INGREDIENTS

PEACH-BASIL COOLER

Tired of lemonade? Mix delicious peaches and aromatic basil with club soda for a cool and refreshing mocktail.
—Dana Hinck, Pensacola, FL

PREP: 25 MIN. + CHILLING
MAKES: 12 SERVINGS (1 CUP EACH)

2 cups sugar
4 cups chopped peeled fresh peaches or 1 lb. frozen unsweetened sliced peaches
1 pkg. (¾ oz.) fresh basil leaves
2 cups cold water
1½ cups fresh lemon juice
Additional cold water
Ice cubes
Club soda or champagne
Additional fresh basil leaves

1. In a large saucepan, combine sugar, peaches, basil and water; bring to a boil. Reduce heat; simmer, uncovered, for 5 minutes. Remove from heat; let stand 30 minutes. Discard basil; stir in lemon juice. Refrigerate until cooled completely.
2. Place peach mixture in a blender; cover and process until blended. Strain into a pitcher; add additional cold water to reach desired consistency. To serve, fill glasses with ice. Pour peach mixture halfway up the glass; top with club soda or, if desired, champagne. Serve with additional basil.
1 CUP: 157 cal., 0 fat (0 sat. fat), 0 chol., 1mg sod., 41g carb. (38g sugars, 1g fiber), 1g pro.

GARLIC-DILL DEVILED EGGS

EAT SMART

GARLIC-DILL DEVILED EGGS

In my family, Easter isn't complete without deviled eggs. Fresh dill and garlic perk up the flavor of these irresistible appetizers you'll want to eat on every occasion.
—Kami Horch, Calais, ME

PREP: 20 MIN. + CHILLING • **MAKES:** 2 DOZEN

- **12 hard-boiled large eggs**
- **⅔ cup mayonnaise**
- **4 tsp. dill pickle relish**
- **2 tsp. snipped fresh dill**
- **2 tsp. Dijon mustard**
- **1 tsp. coarsely ground pepper**
- **¼ tsp. garlic powder**
- **⅛ tsp. paprika or cayenne pepper**

1. Cut eggs lengthwise in half. Remove yolks, reserving whites. In a bowl, mash yolks. Stir in all remaining ingredients except paprika. Spoon or pipe mixture into egg whites.
2. Refrigerate, covered, at least 30 minutes before serving. Sprinkle with paprika.
1 STUFFED EGG HALF: 81 cal., 7g fat (1g sat. fat), 94mg chol., 81mg sod., 1g carb. (0 sugars, 0 fiber), 3g pro.

(5) INGREDIENTS

SNACK CRACKERS

When the children were at home, our daughter, Dana, loved making this crunchy and flavorful snack for us. Her four older brothers would finish off a batch in no time.
—Sue Manel, Milladore, WI

PREP: 5 MIN. + STANDING • **MAKES:** 12 CUPS

- **¾ cup canola oil**
- **1½ tsp. dill weed**
- **1 envelope (1 oz.) ranch salad dressing mix**
- **2 pkg. (10 oz. each) oyster crackers**

In a small bowl, whisk the oil, dill and salad dressing mix. Place the crackers in a large bowl; pour dressing mixture over crackers and toss gently to coat. Allow to stand at least 1 hour before serving.
⅓ CUP: 237 cal., 16g fat (2g sat. fat), 0 chol., 780mg sod., 20g carb. (0 sugars, 1g fiber), 2g pro.

FAST FIX

SALMON MOUSSE ENDIVE LEAVES

I recently made this simple but elegant appetizer and everyone raved. The creamy salmon mousse is lovely for special occasions.
—Doreen Matthew, San Marcos, CA

TAKES: 20 MIN. • **MAKES:** 2 DOZEN

- **2 pkg. (3 oz. each) smoked salmon or lox**
- **6 oz. cream cheese, softened**
- **1 Tbsp. dill weed**
- **1 Tbsp. lemon juice**
- **½ tsp. onion powder**
- **½ tsp. prepared horseradish**
- **24 endive leaves**
- **Watercress and diced pimientos, optional**

Place the first six ingredients in a food processor; cover and process until smooth. Pipe or spoon about 1 Tbsp. filling onto each endive leaf. Garnish with watercress and pimientos if desired.
1 SERVING: 45 cal., 3g fat (2g sat. fat), 9mg chol., 177mg sod., 3g carb. (0 sugars, 2g fiber), 3g pro.

SMOKED SALMON CREAM CHEESE

THE TASTY 10

SAY CREAM CHEESE

HERE ARE 10 WAYS TO CELEBRATE YOUR GO-TO APPETIZER INGREDIENT. PIPE IT INTO DATES, TOP IT WITH SMOKED SALMON OR DOUSE IT IN SWEET-HOT RASPBERRY SAUCE.

RASPBERRY CREAM CHEESE SPREAD

STUFFED DATES

1 RASPBERRY CREAM CHEESE SPREAD
Never fails! Pull the tines of a fork lengthwise on a block of cream cheese, then top with bottled raspberry chipotle sauce. The ridges keep the sauce on top, and the contrast of colors is eye-appealing. This is devoured, always.
—Claudia Dixon Caplinger, Houston, TX

2 3-2-1 DIP
Heat three bricks cream cheese, two cans Ro-Tel tomatoes and a package of browned hot sausage in a slow cooker. Serve with crackers or tortilla chips.
—Amy Surface Parsons, Odessa, MO

3 CRUNCHY PEANUT BUTTER CHEESE BALL
Mix cream cheese, a dab of peanut butter, powdered sugar and vanilla. Add Heath toffee bits and serve with graham crackers.
—Sherre Hannum Zink, Bloomington, IN

4 SWEET CREAM CHEESE
I like to sweeten cream cheese with honey to taste, spread it over toasted baguettes, and top with sliced apples and chopped walnuts or pecans.
—Brieanne Oliver, Longmont, CO

5 PIZZA BITES
Mix a block of cream cheese, a cup of grated Parmesan and chopped pepperoni. Divide between two cans of crescent rolls laid out in rectangles. Roll up jelly-roll style, pinching seams to seal. Cut into eight slices each and bake at 375° until golden brown. Good hot or cold!
—Dawn Crum, Canal Fulton, OH

6 FRUIT FLUFF DIP
Whip softened cream cheese with 1 Tbsp. of orange juice concentrate. Add a jar of marshmallow fluff. Serve in the center of a tray of assorted fruit.
—Kathi Morris Mayberry, Streator, IL

7 CRAB CREAM CHEESE DIP
One 6-oz. can lump crabmeat, a block of cream cheese, 1 cup shredded mozzarella, 1 tsp. hot sauce and a few scallions bake up into a creamy, irresistible dip. Yummy with tortilla chips or baked wonton crisps.
—Carol Bancroft, Clinton Corners, NY

8 SMOKED SALMON CREAM CHEESE
Spread cream cheese on multigrain crackers and top with smoked salmon, thinly sliced red onion and capers. It tastes like a deconstructed lox bagel.
—Niki Henry, Cloverdale, IN

9 STUFFED DATES
Slice pockets into dried dates; stuff with cream cheese and an almond. Wrap in thinly sliced bacon, secure with a toothpick and bake at 400° until bacon is crispy.
—Nikki Ward, Nampa, ID

10 DANISH BLUE CHEESE SPREAD
Mix a block of cream cheese, blue cheese crumbles to taste, chopped green olives, softened butter and a sprinkle of garlic salt to spreading consistency. Pimiento-stuffed olives make this a pretty spread for the holiday season.
—Debra Falasco, Milliken, CO

SUMMER SALAD BY THE LAKE
PAGE 39

SALADS & DRESSINGS

Look here for fresh meal solutions. Discover satisfying grain salads, fun dinner bowls, crowd-pleasing sides, homemade dressings and on-the-go salads in a jar.

CRAN-ORANGE COUSCOUS SALAD

EAT SMART
CRAN-ORANGE COUSCOUS SALAD

I often create salads for summer using a variety of healthy, filling grains. This version with tender couscous is amped up by the bright flavors of oranges, cranberries, basil and a touch of fennel.
—Kristen Heigl, Staten Island, NY

PREP: 25 MIN. • **COOK:** 15 MIN.
MAKES: 12 SERVINGS

- **3 cups uncooked pearl (Israeli) couscous**
- **2 cans (14 oz. each) garbanzo beans or chickpeas, rinsed and drained**
- **2 large navel oranges, peeled and chopped**
- **2 cups fresh baby spinach**
- **1 cup crumbled goat cheese**
- **1 small red onion, chopped**
- **¾ cup dried cranberries**
- **½ cup fennel bulb, thinly sliced, fronds reserved**
- **½ cup chopped pecans, toasted**
- **8 fresh basil leaves, chopped, plus more for garnish**

VINAIGRETTE
- **½ cup olive oil**
- **¼ cup orange juice**
- **¼ cup balsamic vinegar**
- **1 Tbsp. grated orange zest**
- **2 tsp. honey**
- **1 tsp. salt**
- **½ tsp. pepper**

Prepare couscous according to package directions. Fluff with a fork; cool. In a bowl, combine couscous and the next nine ingredients. In a small bowl, whisk together vinaigrette ingredients until blended. Pour over the salad; toss to coat. Garnish with additional chopped basil and reserved fennel fronds.

¾ CUP: 403 cal., 16g fat (3g sat. fat), 12mg chol., 335mg sod., 57g carb. (15g sugars, 5g fiber), 10g pro.

EAT SMART
KOHLRABI, CUCUMBER & TOMATO SALAD

This refreshing salad is wonderful on hot days. It has a nice crunch and a delicious balance of sweet and spicy flavors.
—Kristina Segarra, Yonkers, NY

PREP: 20 MIN. + CHILLING • **COOK:** 10 MIN.
MAKES: 6 SERVINGS

- **2 Tbsp. olive oil**
- **1 medium red onion, finely chopped**
- **2 pickled hot cherry peppers, seeded and finely chopped**
- **2 garlic cloves, minced**
- **2 Tbsp. cider vinegar**
- **1 tsp. salt**
- **1 kohlrabi, peeled and cut into ½-in. pieces**
- **2 large yellow tomatoes, seeded and chopped**
- **2 mini cucumbers, cut into ½-in. pieces**
- **2 Tbsp. minced fresh cilantro**

1. In a small skillet, heat oil over medium-high heat. Add onion; cook and stir for 2-3 minutes or until crisp-tender. Add the peppers and garlic; cook 2 minutes longer. Stir in vinegar and salt; remove from heat.
2. In a large bowl, combine the kohlrabi, tomatoes and cucumbers. Pour in the onion mixture; gently toss to coat. Chill 1 hour. Sprinkle the salad with cilantro before serving.

¾ CUP: 59 cal., 4g fat (1g sat. fat), 0 chol., 372mg sod., 6g carb. (2g sugars, 2g fiber), 2g pro. **Diabetic exchanges:** 1 vegetable, ½ fat.

TEST KITCHEN TIP
Kirby cucumbers are a good choice in this recipe. The pickled peppers don't add a lot of heat, but you can cut them back or even eliminate them. You can use cherry tomatoes or other favorite vegetables you may have in the garden.

SHAVED BRUSSELS SPROUTS SALAD

EAT SMART

SHAVED BRUSSELS SPROUT SALAD

The first time my friends tasted my new side dish, they said it was phenomenal. The longer you let it chill in the fridge, the more tender the sprouts will become.
—Nick Iverson, Denver, CO

PREP: 20 MIN. + CHILLING • **MAKES:** 6 SERVINGS

- **1 Tbsp. cider vinegar**
- **1 Tbsp. Dijon mustard**
- **2 tsp. honey**
- **1 small garlic clove, minced**
- **2 Tbsp. olive oil**
- **1 lb. Brussels sprouts, halved and thinly sliced**
- **1 small red onion, halved and thinly sliced**
- **⅓ cup dried cherries, chopped**
- **⅓ cup chopped pecans, toasted**

1. Whisk together the first four ingredients; gradually whisk in oil until blended.
2. Place Brussels sprouts, onion and cherries in a large bowl; toss with dressing. Refrigerate, covered, at least 1 hour. Stir in pecans just before serving.
NOTE: To toast nuts, cook in a skillet over low heat until lightly browned, stirring occasionally.
¾ CUP: 156 cal., 9g fat (1g sat. fat), 0 chol., 79mg sod., 18g carb. (10g sugars, 4g fiber), 3g pro. **Diabetic exchanges:** 2 fat, 1 vegetable, ½ starch.

EAT SMART

THAI CHICKEN & SLAW

Because of the hint of sweetness from the honey, this recipe has become very popular with my friends and family. I make it whenever I have visitors.
—Karen Norris, Philadelphia, PA

PREP: 25 MIN. + MARINATING • **COOK:** 30 MIN. • **MAKES:** 8 SERVINGS

- **½ cup canola oil**
- **½ cup white wine vinegar**
- **½ cup honey**
- **2 Tbsp. minced fresh gingerroot**
- **2 Tbsp. reduced-sodium soy sauce**
- **2 garlic cloves, minced**
- **1 tsp. sesame oil**
- **8 boneless skinless chicken thighs (about 2 lbs.)**

SLAW

- **6 cups coleslaw mix**
- **1 cup frozen shelled edamame, thawed**
- **1 medium sweet pepper, chopped**
- **1 Tbsp. creamy peanut butter**
- **½ tsp. salt**
- **4 green onions, sliced**

1. In a small bowl, whisk the first seven ingredients until blended. Pour 1 cup marinade into a bowl or shallow dish. Add chicken and turn to coat. Refrigerate overnight. Cover and refrigerate remaining marinade.
2. Preheat oven to 350°. Drain chicken, discarding marinade from the bowl. Place in a 13x9-in. baking dish coated with cooking spray. Bake, uncovered, 30-40 minutes or until a thermometer reads 170°.
3. Meanwhile, place coleslaw mix, edamame and pepper in a large bowl. Add peanut butter and salt to reserved marinade; whisk until blended. Pour over coleslaw mixture; toss to coat. Refrigerate until serving. Serve chicken with slaw. Sprinkle with green onions.
3 OZ. COOKED CHICKEN WITH ⅔ CUP SLAW: 326 cal., 18g fat (3g sat. fat), 76mg chol., 171mg sod., 16g carb. (12g sugars, 2g fiber), 24g pro. **Diabetic exchanges:** 3 lean meat, 2 fat, 1 vegetable, ½ starch.

THAI CHICKEN & SLAW

WARM CABBAGE, FENNEL & PEAR SALAD

FAST FIX

WARM CABBAGE, FENNEL & PEAR SALAD

This crunchy salad makes an elegant first course or side, but it's hearty enough to be an entree when paired with a crusty artisan bread. We love it served warm.
—Grace Voltolina, Westport, CT

TAKES: 25 MIN. • **MAKES:** 4 SERVINGS

- **2 firm medium pears**
- **¼ cup brandy or Cognac, optional**
- **3 Tbsp. olive oil**
- **1 large fennel bulb, halved, cored and thinly sliced**
- **4 cups shredded or thinly sliced cabbage**
- **¼ cup water**
- **3 Tbsp. lemon juice**
- **2 tsp. honey or agave nectar**
- **1 tsp. kosher salt**
- **½ tsp. pepper**
- **¾ cup crumbled or sliced Gorgonzola cheese (about 4 oz.)**
- **½ cup chopped walnuts, toasted**

1. Peel and core pears; cut into ½-in. slices. If desired, toss with brandy. Set pears aside.
2. In a large skillet, heat oil over medium-high heat. Add fennel; saute until crisp-tender, 2-3 minutes. Add cabbage; toss with fennel. Cook until both are tender, 2-3 minutes longer. Add pears, water, lemon juice, honey, salt and pepper to skillet, gently combining ingredients. Cook until liquid is evaporated, 6-8 minutes. Transfer to a serving bowl. Top with Gorgonzola cheese and toasted walnuts. Serve warm or at room temperature.
NOTE: To toast nuts, bake in a shallow pan in a 350° oven for 5-10 minutes or cook in a skillet over low heat until lightly browned, stirring occasionally.
1 CUP: 391 cal., 26g fat (7g sat. fat), 19mg chol., 810mg sod., 28g carb. (14g sugars, 8g fiber), 9g pro.

ALMOND-APRICOT CHICKEN SALAD

My one-of-a-kind pasta salad combines tender chicken, sweet apricots, and crunchy vegetables and almonds. The lemony dressing can't be beat.
—Susan Voigt, Plymouth, MN

PREP: 20 MIN. + CHILLING • **MAKES:** 10 SERVINGS

- **1 pkg. (8 oz.) spiral pasta**
- **1 pkg. (6 oz.) dried apricots, thinly sliced**
- **3 cups coarsely chopped fresh broccoli**
- **2½ cups diced cooked chicken**
- **½ cup chopped green onions**
- **½ cup chopped celery**
- **1 cup sour cream**
- **¾ cup mayonnaise**
- **1 Tbsp. lemon juice**
- **2 tsp. grated lemon zest**
- **2 tsp. Dijon mustard**
- **1½ tsp. salt**
- **¾ tsp. dried savory**
- **½ tsp. pepper**
- **¾ cup sliced almonds, toasted**

1. Cook pasta according to package directions, adding apricots during the last 4 minutes. Drain and rinse with cold water; place in a large bowl. Add broccoli, chicken, onions and celery.
2. In a small bowl, combine the next eight ingredients. Pour over salad and toss to coat. Cover and chill until serving; fold in almonds.
1 SERVING: 411 cal., 24g fat (6g sat. fat), 52mg chol., 524mg sod., 31g carb. (10g sugars, 4g fiber), 17g pro.

ALMOND-APRICOT CHICKEN SALAD

EAT SMART FAST FIX

MANGO BARLEY SALAD

I made this colorful mango salad on the fly and it was a big hit! The bright flavor is perfect for a spring or summer picnic, served right away or chilled.
—Dan Wellberg, Elk River, MN

TAKES: 25 MIN. • **MAKES:** 6 SERVINGS

- **1¾ cups water**
- **1 cup quick-cooking barley**
- **2 medium limes**
- **¼ cup olive oil**
- **1 Tbsp. Dijon mustard**
- **1 Tbsp. honey**
- **½ tsp. salt**
- **¼ tsp. ground cumin**
- **¼ tsp. pepper**
- **½ cup chopped sweet red pepper**
- **½ cup chopped green pepper**
- **¼ cup chopped red onion**
- **1 medium mango, peeled and chopped**
- **¼ cup minced fresh cilantro**

1. In a small saucepan, bring water to a boil. Stir in barley. Reduce the heat; simmer, covered, until barley is tender, 10-12 minutes. Remove from heat; let stand 5 minutes.

2. Finely grate enough zest from limes to measure 1 tsp. Cut limes crosswise in half; squeeze juice from limes. In a small bowl, whisk the lime juice, lime zest, oil, mustard, honey, salt, cumin and pepper until blended.

3. In a large bowl, combine barley, peppers, onion, mango and cilantro. Add dressing; toss to coat. Refrigerate until serving.

¾ CUP: 185 cal., 10g fat (1g sat. fat), 0 chol., 261mg sod., 25g carb. (9g sugars, 5g fiber), 2g pro. **Diabetic exchanges:** 2 fat, 1½ starch.

TEST KITCHEN TIP

Fresh pineapple or papaya can be used to replace some or all of the mango. Just because we call for barley doesn't mean you can't try this salad made with quinoa, farro or another grain. It's all going to be delicious!

LIGHT STRAWBERRY-SPINACH SALAD

EAT SMART FAST FIX

LIGHT STRAWBERRY-SPINACH SALAD

This salad makes a wonderful light summer meal. The ingredients go together in a snap, and all of the flavors and colors complement one another very nicely. Farmers here in Washington grow a lot of strawberries—and they're the sweetest ones I've ever tasted. I'm always looking for new and different ways to use them.
—Perlene Hoekema, Lynden, WA

TAKES: 20 MIN. • **MAKES:** 8 SERVINGS

- **2 Tbsp. sesame seeds**
- **1½ lbs. fresh spinach**
- **⅓ cup canola oil**
- **⅓ cup red wine vinegar**
- **1 Tbsp. sugar**
- **2 tsp. minced green onion**
- **½ tsp. paprika**
- **¼ tsp. Worcestershire sauce**
- **2 cups fresh strawberries, washed, hulled & halved**

In a small skillet over medium heat, stir sesame seeds until golden; set aside. Wash spinach thoroughly; dry on paper towels and tear into bite-sized pieces. Blend oil, vinegar, sugar, green onion, paprika and Worcestershire sauce. In a large bowl, mix together spinach, strawberries, dressing and seeds. Serve immediately.

¾ CUP: 127 cal., 10g fat (1g sat. fat), 0 chol., 113mg sod., 8g carb. (4g sugars, 2g fiber), 2g pro. **Diabetic exchanges:** 2 fat, 1 vegetable.

CRYSTAL SCHLUETER
Babbitt, MN

FLAMBOYANT FLAMENCO SUMMER SALAD

EAT SMART **FAST FIX**

FLAMBOYANT FLAMENCO SUMMER SALAD

I came up with this salad simply by choosing the best-looking vegetables at a local farmers market—the colors are so beautiful! Turn it into a full vegetarian meal by adding roasted garbanzo beans or cooked white beans.
—Crystal Schlueter, Babbitt, MN

TAKES: 25 MIN. • **MAKES:** 8 SERVINGS

- **3 medium rainbow carrots**
- **4 medium blood oranges, peeled and segmented**
- **½ small red onion, thinly sliced**
- **½ medium fresh beet, thinly sliced**
- **½ medium watermelon radish, thinly sliced**
- **2 radishes, thinly sliced**
- **2 Tbsp. chopped pistachios, toasted**
- **2 Tbsp. chopped oil-packed sun-dried tomatoes**
- **1 Tbsp. capers, drained**
- **¼ tsp. salt**
- **¼ tsp. pepper**
- **¼ cup white balsamic vinaigrette**
- **4 cups torn leaf lettuce**
- **¼ cup shaved Manchego or Parmesan cheese**

Using a vegetable peeler, shave carrots into very thin ribbons; place in a large bowl. Add oranges, red onion, beet, radishes, pistachios, tomatoes, capers, salt and pepper. Drizzle with dressing; lightly toss. Place lettuce on a platter; top with vegetables and cheese.
1 CUP: 103 cal., 6g fat (1g sat. fat), 4mg chol., 203mg sod., 12g carb. (8g sugars, 3g fiber), 2g pro. **Diabetic exchanges:** 1 vegetable, 1 fat, ½ fruit.

FAST FIX

APPLE CAMEMBERT SALAD

I like to serve this refreshing salad with thinly sliced pork roast or diced chicken breast.
—Trisha Kruse, Eagle, ID

TAKES: 15 MIN. • **MAKES:** 4 SERVINGS

- **3 cups torn Boston lettuce**
- **½ cup chopped apple**
- **2 oz. Camembert cheese, cubed**
- **2 Tbsp. dried cherries**
- **2 Tbsp. glazed pecans**

DRESSING

- **2 Tbsp. mayonnaise**
- **1 Tbsp. white wine vinegar**
- **1 Tbsp. canola oil**
- **1 Tbsp. maple syrup**
- **Dash each sugar, salt and pepper**

In a large bowl, combine the first five ingredients. In a small bowl, whisk the dressing ingredients. Pour over salad and toss to coat.
¾ CUP: 182 cal., 14g fat (3g sat. fat), 13mg chol., 210mg sod., 11g carb. (9g sugars, 1g fiber), 4g pro.

EAT SMART **FAST FIX**

GINGER GREEN BEANS

The bright, gingery sauce on these green beans is delicious and so simple to whip up. It's perfection on either hot or cold beans, but I also really love it tossed with cooked shrimp.
—Marina Castle Kelley, Canyon Country, CA

TAKES: 30 MIN. • **MAKES:** 8 SERVINGS

- **1½ lbs. fresh green beans, trimmed**
- **1 tangerine, peeled, segmented, seeds removed**
- **¼ cup chopped green onions**
- **¼ cup soy sauce**
- **1 Tbsp. lemon juice**
- **1 Tbsp. olive oil**
- **1 Tbsp. minced fresh gingerroot**
- **1 garlic clove, peeled and halved**
- **1 tsp. packed brown sugar**
- **½ tsp. salt**
- **¼ tsp. pepper**
- **¼ tsp. white vinegar**

In a 6-qt. stockpot, bring 12 cups water to a boil. Add green beans; cook, uncovered, 2-3 minutes or just until crisp-tender and bright green. Quickly remove and immediately drop into ice water. Drain and pat dry. In a blender or food processor, combine the remaining ingredients; process until well blended. Pour dressing mixture over beans; toss to coat. Refrigerate until serving.
¾ CUP: 59 cal., 2g fat (0 sat. fat), 0 chol., 614mg sod., 9g carb. (4g sugars, 3g fiber), 3g pro. **Diabetic exchanges:** 1 vegetable, ½ fat.

GINGER GREEN BEANS

MEDITERRANEAN SHRIMP SALAD IN A JAR

MEDITERRANEAN SHRIMP SALAD IN A JAR

This Greek salad to go is packed with so much freshness, it instantly brightens up your day. Just layer it all in a jar and pack it up—then serve and enjoy.
—Taste of Home *Test Kitchen*

PREP: 20 MIN. • **COOK:** 15 MIN.
MAKES: 4 SERVINGS

- ¾ **cup uncooked orzo pasta**
- ¾ **cup Greek vinaigrette**
- ½ **cup minced fresh parsley**
- ⅓ **cup chopped fresh dill**
- ¾ **lb. peeled and deveined cooked shrimp (31-40 per lb.)**
- 1 **can (14 oz.) water-packed quartered artichoke hearts, rinsed and drained**
- 1 **medium sweet red pepper, chopped**
- 1 **medium green pepper, chopped**
- 1 **small red onion, thinly sliced**
- ½ **cup pitted Greek olives, sliced**
- ½ **cup crumbled feta cheese**
- 8 **cups fresh arugula**

1. Cook orzo according to the package directions. Drain; rinse with cold water and drain well. Combine orzo with Greek vinaigrette and herbs.
2. In each of four 1-qt. wide-mouth canning jars, divide and layer ingredients in the following order: orzo mixture, shrimp, artichokes, red pepper, green pepper, red onion, Greek olives, feta cheese and arugula. Cover and refrigerate until serving. Transfer salads into bowls; toss to combine.
1 SERVING: 548 cal., 26g fat (5g sat. fat), 137mg chol., 1287mg sod., 47g carb. (5g sugars, 4g fiber), 29g pro.

EAT SMART

CURRIED QUINOA SALAD

Quinoa is such a fantastic salad base—it's full of protein, it adds a nutty flavor, and it's the perfect vehicle to soak up any kind of dressing. If you like a little more heat, add more cayenne or curry to the dressing.
—Shannon Dobos, Calgary, AB

PREP: 20 MIN. + CHILLING
COOK: 15 MIN. + STANDING
MAKES: 6 SERVINGS

- 1 **cup quinoa, rinsed**
- 1 **tsp. ground turmeric**
- ¼ **tsp. ground cumin**
- 1 **can (14½ oz.) vegetable or chicken broth**
- 1½ **cups grape tomatoes, halved**
- 1 **small cucumber, diced**
- ⅓ **cup diced red onion**

DRESSING

- 2 **Tbsp. lemon juice**
- 2 **Tbsp. olive oil**
- 1 **Tbsp. honey**
- 1 **tsp. yellow mustard**
- ½ **tsp. curry powder**
- ¼ **tsp. salt**
- ⅛ **tsp. cayenne pepper**

1. In a small saucepan, combine first four ingredients; bring to a boil. Reduce heat; simmer, covered, until liquid is absorbed, 12-15 minutes. Remove from heat; let stand, covered, 15 minutes. Transfer to a large bowl; cool slightly.
2. Add tomatoes, cucumber and onion to quinoa. In a small bowl, whisk together dressing ingredients; toss with salad. Refrigerate, covered, until cold, about 2 hours. Stir before serving.
¾ CUP: 176 cal., 6g fat (1g sat. fat), 0 chol., 320mg sod., 25g carb. (5g sugars, 3g fiber), 5g pro. **Diabetic exchanges:** 1½ starch, 1 fat.

CURRIED QUINOA SALAD

RASPBERRY-WALNUT PORK SALAD

EAT SMART

RASPBERRY-WALNUT PORK SALAD

Combine raspberry, rosemary, Gorgonzola and walnuts to make a pork dish that's bursting with flavor.
—Virginia Anthony, Jacksonville, FL

PREP: 30 MIN. • **COOK:** 20 MIN. • **MAKES:** 6 SERVINGS

1½ lbs. pork tenderloins, cut into 1-in. slices
⅓ cup ground walnuts
2 Tbsp. all-purpose flour
½ tsp. salt, divided
½ tsp. coarsely ground pepper, divided
4½ tsp. walnut oil
⅓ cup chopped shallot
1 medium pear, chopped
¾ cup reduced-sodium chicken broth
¾ cup seedless raspberry preserves
½ cup raspberry vinegar
2 tsp. minced fresh rosemary or ½ tsp. dried rosemary, crushed
2 tsp. minced fresh sage
2 pkg. (6 oz. each) fresh baby spinach
½ cup crumbled Gorgonzola cheese
½ cup chopped walnuts, toasted

1. Flatten pork slices to ½-in. thickness. In a shallow dish, combine the ground walnuts, flour, ¼ tsp. salt and ¼ tsp. pepper. Add pork, a few pieces at a time, and turn to coat.
2. In a large skillet over medium heat, cook pork in oil in batches for 2-3 minutes on each side or until the meat is no longer pink. Remove and keep warm.
3. In the same skillet, saute shallot until tender. Add pear; cook 1 minute longer. Add the broth, preserves and vinegar. Bring to a boil; cook for 6-8 minutes or until slightly thickened. Stir in the rosemary, sage and remaining salt and pepper. Remove from the heat.
4. Place spinach in a large bowl. Add pear mixture; toss to coat. Divide among six plates; top each with pork. Sprinkle with cheese and chopped walnuts.
1 SERVING: 398 cal., 17g fat (4g sat. fat), 71mg chol., 415mg sod., 34g carb. (25g sugars, 2g fiber), 30g pro.

EAT SMART FAST FIX

CRUNCHY LEMON-PESTO GARDEN SALAD

I love using fresh vegetables straight from the garden to prepare this salad. If I pick the squash and cucumbers early enough, their skins are so tender that there's no need to remove them. Best yet, it's easily adaptable—any fresh veggie from the garden can be swapped in with delicious results!
—Carmell Childs, Clawson, UT

TAKES: 25 MIN. • **MAKES:** 6 SERVINGS

5 Tbsp. prepared pesto
1 Tbsp. lemon juice
2 tsp. grated lemon zest
1½ tsp. Dijon mustard
¼ tsp. garlic salt
¼ tsp. pepper
2½ cups yellow summer squash, thinly sliced
1¾ cups mini cucumber, thinly sliced
¾ cup fresh peas
½ cup shredded Parmesan cheese
¼ cup thinly sliced green onions
5 thick-sliced bacon strips, cooked and crumbled

In a bowl, whisk together the first six ingredients until blended. In another bowl, combine squash, cucumber, peas, Parmesan and green onions. Pour dressing over salad; toss to coat. Top with bacon to serve.
¾ CUP: 159 cal., 11g fat (3g sat. fat), 13mg chol., 586mg sod., 8g carb. (4g sugars, 2g fiber), 8g pro. **Diabetic exchanges:** 2 fat, 1 vegetable.

CRUNCHY LEMON-PESTO GARDEN SALAD

TOMATO, AVOCADO & GRILLED CORN SALAD

EAT SMART

TOMATO, AVOCADO & GRILLED CORN SALAD

With ripe tomatoes, fresh basil and grilled corn off the cob, this sunny salad tastes just like summertime!
—Angela Spengler, Tampa, FL

PREP: 20 MIN. • **GRILL:** 10 MIN. + COOLING • **MAKES:** 8 SERVINGS

- **1 medium ear sweet corn, husks removed**
- **3 large red tomatoes, sliced**
- **3 large yellow tomatoes, sliced**
- **¾ tsp. kosher salt, divided**
- **½ tsp. pepper, divided**
- **2 medium ripe avocados, peeled and sliced**
- **¼ cup olive oil**
- **2 Tbsp. red wine vinegar**
- **1 Tbsp. minced fresh basil, plus more for garnish**
- **⅓ cup crumbled feta cheese**

1. Grill corn, covered, over medium heat 10-12 minutes or until lightly browned and tender, turning occasionally. Cool slightly. Cut corn from cob.
2. Arrange tomatoes on a large serving platter. Sprinkle with ½ tsp. salt and ¼ tsp. pepper. Top with avocado slices. Whisk together oil, vinegar, basil and the remaining salt and pepper; drizzle half over the tomatoes and avocados. Top with grilled corn and feta; drizzle remaining dressing over top. Garnish with additional chopped basil.
1 SERVING: 164 cal., 13g fat (2g sat. fat), 3mg chol., 237mg sod., 11g carb. (4g sugars, 4g fiber), 3g pro. **Diabetic exchanges:** 2 fat, 1 vegetable, ½ starch.

TEST KITCHEN TIP

This dish is spectacular with fresh heirloom tomatoes, and all that flavor means you can use less salt. To turn this into a quick, healthy main dish, top the salad with grilled chicken.

EAT SMART FAST FIX

WARM RICE & PINTOS SALAD

During my undergrad years, my roommate taught me how to cook vegetarian dishes like brown rice with pintos. It's so versatile; you can serve it over lettuce like this, in a wrap or as a warm dish.
—Natalie Van Apeldoorn, Vancouver, BC

TAKES: 30 MIN. • **MAKES:** 4 SERVINGS

- **1 Tbsp. olive oil**
- **1 cup frozen corn**
- **1 small onion, chopped**
- **2 garlic cloves, minced**
- **1½ tsp. chili powder**
- **1½ tsp. ground cumin**
- **1 can (15 oz.) pinto beans, rinsed and drained**
- **1 pkg. (8.8 oz.) ready-to-serve brown rice**
- **1 can (4 oz.) chopped green chilies**
- **½ cup salsa**
- **¼ cup chopped fresh cilantro**
- **1 bunch romaine, quartered lengthwise through the core**
- **¼ cup finely shredded cheddar cheese**

1. In a large skillet, heat oil over medium-high heat. Add corn and onion; cook and stir 4-5 minutes or until onion is tender. Stir in garlic, chili powder and cumin; cook and stir 1 minute longer.
2. Add beans, rice, green chilies, salsa and cilantro; heat through, stirring occasionally.
3. Serve over romaine wedges. Sprinkle with cheese.
1 SERVING: 331 cal., 8g fat (2g sat. fat), 7mg chol., 465mg sod., 50g carb. (5g sugars, 9g fiber), 12g pro. **Diabetic exchanges:** 2½ starch, 2 vegetable, 1 lean meat, ½ fat.

WARM RICE & PINTO SALAD

EAT SMART FAST FIX

RADISH ASPARAGUS SALAD

Lemon zest and mustard in the dressing add the perfect punch to crisp asparagus and spicy radishes in this fun spring salad. My family loves it!
—Nancy Latulippe, Simcoe, ON

TAKES: 25 MIN. • **MAKES:** 6 SERVINGS

- **1 lb. fresh asparagus, trimmed and cut into 2-in. pieces**
- **7 radishes, thinly sliced**
- **2 Tbsp. sesame seeds**

DRESSING

- **2 Tbsp. olive oil**
- **2 Tbsp. thinly sliced green onion**
- **1 Tbsp. white wine vinegar**
- **1 Tbsp. lemon juice**
- **2 tsp. honey**
- **1 tsp. Dijon mustard**
- **¼ tsp. garlic powder**
- **¼ tsp. grated lemon zest**
- **¼ tsp. pepper**

1. In a large saucepan, bring 6 cups water to a boil. Add asparagus; cover and boil for 3 minutes. Drain and immediately place asparagus in ice water. Drain and pat dry.
2. Transfer to a large bowl; add radishes and sesame seeds. Place the dressing ingredients in a jar with a tight-fitting lid; shake well. Pour over salad; toss to coat.
⅔ CUP: 73 cal., 6g fat (1g sat. fat), 0 chol., 28mg sod., 5g carb. (3g sugars, 1g fiber), 2g pro. **Diabetic exchanges:** 1 vegetable, 1 fat.

SHRIMP & SPINACH SALAD WITH HOT BACON DRESSING

EAT SMART FAST FIX

SHRIMP & SPINACH SALAD WITH HOT BACON DRESSING

When I meet former co-workers for lunch at our favorite restaurant, we always order this salad. I wanted to share it with my husband, so I made it my mission to re-create it. Mission accomplished!
—Lisa L. Bynum, Brandon, MS

TAKES: 30 MIN. • **MAKES:** 6 SERVINGS

- **1½ lbs. uncooked shrimp (31-40 per lb.), peeled and deveined**
- **1 tsp. Montreal steak seasoning**
- **4 bacon strips, chopped**
- **1 shallot, finely chopped**
- **⅓ cup cider vinegar**
- **1 Tbsp. olive oil**
- **1 tsp. Dijon mustard**
- **½ tsp. sugar**
- **½ tsp. salt**
- **¼ tsp. pepper**
- **1 pkg. (10 oz.) fresh spinach**
- **¾ cup roasted sweet red peppers**
- **¼ cup sliced almonds**

1. Sprinkle shrimp with steak seasoning. On four metal or soaked wooden skewers, thread shrimp. Grill, covered, over medium heat or broil 4 in. from heat until shrimp turn pink, 2-3 minutes on each side.
2. Meanwhile, in a large skillet, cook bacon over medium heat until crisp, stirring occasionally. Remove with a slotted spoon; drain on paper towels. Discard all but 1 Tbsp. drippings. Add shallot; cook and stir over medium heat until tender, 1-2 minutes. Stir in next six ingredients; bring to a boil. Remove from heat.
3. In a large serving bowl, combine spinach and dressing; toss to coat. Layer with shrimp and pepper slices; top with cooked bacon pieces and sliced almonds.
1½ CUPS: 212 cal., 10g fat (2g sat. fat), 145mg chol., 739mg sod., 6g carb. (2g sugars, 1g fiber), 22g pro. **Diabetic exchanges:** 3 lean meat, 2 vegetable, 2 fat.

SKINNY COBB SALAD

EAT SMART FAST FIX

SKINNY COBB SALAD

This skinny version of Cobb salad has all the taste and creaminess with half the fat and calories. You can skip the coleslaw mix and do all lettuce, but I like the crunch you get with cabbage.
—Taylor Kiser, Brandon, FL

TAKES: 25 MIN. • **MAKES:** 4 SERVINGS

- **¼ cup fat-free plain Greek yogurt**
- **2 Tbsp. reduced-fat ranch salad dressing**
- **1 to 2 tsp. cold water**

SALAD

- **3 cups coleslaw mix**
- **3 cups chopped lettuce**
- **1 large apple, chopped**
- **½ cup crumbled reduced-fat feta or blue cheese**
- **1 cup cubed cooked chicken breast**
- **2 green onions, chopped**
- **4 turkey bacon strips, chopped and cooked**
- **1 can (15 oz.) garbanzo beans or chickpeas, rinsed and drained**
- **1 small ripe avocado, peeled and cubed**

1. Mix yogurt and dressing; thin with water as desired. Toss coleslaw mix with lettuce; divide among four plates.

2. Arrange remaining ingredients in rows over top. Drizzle with yogurt mixture.

1 SERVING: 324 cal., 13g fat (3g sat. fat), 48mg chol., 646mg sod., 31g carb. (11g sugars, 9g fiber), 23g pro. **Diabetic exchanges:** 2 lean meat, 2 fat, 1½ starch, 1 vegetable.

TEST KITCHEN TIP

Combining classic Cobb salad flavors with healthy ingredients—like Greek yogurt, chopped apple and garbanzo beans—makes this main-dish salad a win-win.

MEXICAN ROASTED POTATO SALAD

My husband usually doesn't like potato salad, but he loves this one! It makes a fabulous side dish for grilled chicken or burgers. Although I usually serve it warm, the leftovers are truly outstanding straight from the fridge.
—Elisabeth Larsen, Pleasant Grove, UT

PREP: 20 MIN. • **BAKE:** 25 MIN.
MAKES: 10 SERVINGS

- **4 lbs. potatoes, peeled and cut into ½-in. cubes (about 8 cups)**
- **1 Tbsp. canola oil**
- **1½ tsp. salt, divided**
- **½ tsp. pepper**
- **1 can (15 oz.) black beans, rinsed and drained**
- **1 can (4 oz.) chopped green chilies**
- **2 Tbsp. minced fresh cilantro**
- **¾ cup sour cream**
- **¾ cup mayonnaise**
- **2 tsp. lime juice**
- **1 tsp. ground chipotle pepper or 2 tsp. chili powder**
- **½ tsp. ground cumin**
- **¼ tsp. garlic powder**

1. Preheat oven to 425°. Place potatoes in a greased 15x10x1-in. baking pan. Drizzle with oil; sprinkle with 1 tsp. salt and the pepper. Toss to coat. Roast 25-30 minutes or until tender, stirring occasionally.

2. In a large bowl, mix potatoes, beans, chilies and cilantro. In a small bowl, combine sour cream, mayonnaise, lime juice, chipotle pepper, cumin, garlic powder and the remaining salt. Pour dressing over potato mixture; toss to coat. Serve warm.

¾ CUP: 334 cal., 17g fat (4g sat. fat), 5mg chol., 588mg sod., 39g carb. (2g sugars, 6g fiber), 6g pro.

MINTY WATERMELON SALAD

EAT SMART 5 INGREDIENTS

MINTY WATERMELON SALAD

My 4-year-old twin grandchildren love to cook in the kitchen with me. Last summer, the three of us were experimenting with watermelon and cheese, and that's where this recipe began. It's ideal for picnics or neighborhood gatherings or as a healthy snack on a hot summer day.
—Gwendolyn Vetter, Rogers, MN

PREP: 20 MIN. + CHILLING • **MAKES:** 8 SERVINGS

- **6 cups cubed watermelon**
- **½ cup thinly sliced fennel bulb**
- **⅓ cup crumbled feta cheese**
- **2 Tbsp. minced fresh mint**
- **2 Tbsp. thinly sliced pickled onions**
- **½ tsp. pepper**

In a large bowl, combine all ingredients. Refrigerate, covered, at least 1 hour.

¾ CUP: 45 cal., 1g fat (1g sat. fat), 2mg chol., 65mg sod., 11g carb. (10g sugars, 1g fiber), 1g pro. **Diabetic exchanges:** ½ fruit.

EAT SMART

SUMMER SALAD BY THE LAKE

I came up with this recipe to show appreciation to all the teachers at my son's school. The dish had to be as special as the teachers, who always go the extra mile for their students. I think this salad did the trick! It's hearty, earthy, sweet and loaded with good stuff.
—Ramya Ramamurthy, Fremont, CA

PREP: 35 MIN. • **COOK:** 15 MIN. + STANDING • **MAKES:** 10 SERVINGS

- **15 garlic cloves, peeled and halved lengthwise**
- **2 medium sweet peppers, sliced**
- **2 Tbsp. olive oil**
- **½ tsp. salt**
- **½ tsp. pepper**

SALAD

- **2½ cups water**
- **1 Tbsp. olive oil**
- **1½ tsp. salt**
- **1 cup uncooked pearl (Israeli) couscous**
- **½ cup red quinoa, rinsed**
- **2 large tomatoes, cut into 1-in. pieces**
- **2 cups fresh arugula or baby spinach**
- **1 cup cubed fresh pineapple**
- **½ cup fresh shelled peas or frozen peas**
- **½ cup crumbled feta cheese**
- **½ cup sunflower kernels, toasted**
- **¼ cup minced fresh parsley**

DRESSING

- **¼ cup olive oil**
- **3 Tbsp. balsamic vinegar**
- **2 tsp. honey**
- **1 tsp. grated lemon zest**
- **½ tsp. salt**
- **½ tsp. pepper**

1. Preheat oven to 425°. Toss together garlic, sweet peppers, oil, salt and pepper; transfer to a parchment paper-lined 15x10x1-in. baking pan. Bake until dark golden brown, about 15 minutes. Transfer to a large bowl.

2. Meanwhile, in a small saucepan, bring water, oil and salt to a boil. Stir in couscous and quinoa. Reduce heat; simmer, covered, for 15 minutes or until liquid is absorbed. Remove from heat; let stand, covered, 5 minutes.

3. Transfer the couscous and quinoa to the large bowl. Stir in the remaining salad ingredients. In a small bowl, whisk dressing ingredients until blended. Pour over salad; gently toss to coat.

¾ CUP: 269 cal., 15g fat (2g sat. fat), 3mg chol., 700mg sod., 29g carb. (7g sugars, 3g fiber), 7g pro. **Diabetic exchanges:** 2 starch, 2 fat.

SUMMER SALAD BY THE LAKE

BLUEBERRY, CORN & FETA SALAD

EAT SMART

BLUEBERRY, CORN & FETA SALAD

I'm not typically a huge fan of ears of corn, but when it comes to this sweet, salty, refreshing salad, I can't put my fork down. I find that grilling the corn inside of the husk makes it easier to remove all the corn silk from each cob.
—Colleen Delawder, Herndon, VA

PREP: 30 MIN. + SOAKING • **GRILL:** 20 MIN. • **MAKES:** 10 SERVINGS

- 8 **medium ears sweet corn**
- 3 **Tbsp. olive oil**
- 3 **Tbsp. white balsamic vinegar**
- 1 **Tbsp. minced fresh chives, plus more for garnish**
- ¾ **tsp. kosher salt**
- ¼ **tsp. pepper**
- 1 **cup fresh blueberries**
- ½ **cup crumbled feta cheese**

1. Carefully peel back corn husks to within 1 in. of bottoms; remove silk. Rewrap corn in husks; secure with kitchen string. Place in a stockpot; cover with cold water. Soak 20 minutes; drain.
2. Grill corn, covered, over medium heat about 20 minutes or until tender, turning often. Cut string and peel back husks. Cool slightly. Cut corn from cobs; transfer to a large bowl.
3. In a small bowl, whisk the oil, vinegar, chives, salt and pepper. Pour over corn; toss to coat. Gently fold in blueberries and feta. Garnish with additional chives as desired.

¾ CUP: 133 cal., 6g fat (1g sat. fat), 3mg chol., 210mg sod., 19g carb. (8g sugars, 2g fiber), 4g pro. **Diabetic exchanges:** 1 starch, 1 fat.

EAT SMART FAST FIX

CHICKEN TZATZIKI CUCUMBER BOATS

I've tended a garden for decades, and these colorful boats made from cucumbers hold my fresh tomatoes, peas and dill. It's absolute garden greatness.
—Ronna Farley, Rockville, MD

TAKES: 15 MIN. • **MAKES:** 2 SERVINGS

- 2 **medium cucumbers**
- ½ **cup fat-free plain Greek yogurt**
- 2 **Tbsp. mayonnaise**
- ½ **tsp. garlic salt**
- 3 **tsp. snipped fresh dill, divided**
- 1 **cup chopped cooked chicken breast**
- 1 **cup chopped seeded tomato (about 1 large), divided**
- ½ **cup fresh or frozen peas, thawed**

1. Cut each cucumber lengthwise in half; scoop out pulp, leaving a ¼-in. shell. In a bowl, mix yogurt, mayonnaise, garlic salt and 1 tsp. dill; gently stir in chicken, ¾ cup tomato and peas.
2. Spoon into cucumber shells. Top with the remaining tomato and dill.

2 FILLED CUCUMBER HALVES: 312 cal., 12g fat (2g sat. fat), 55mg chol., 641mg sod., 18g carb. (10g sugars, 6g fiber), 34g pro. **Diabetic exchanges:** 4 lean meat, 2 vegetable, 2 fat, ½ starch.

CHICKEN TZATZIKI CUCUMBER BOATS

FAST FIX

FAJITA IN A BOWL

Pull out the skewers and take a stab at grilling peppers, onions and corn for an awesome steak salad that's all summer and smoke.
—Peggy Woodward, Shullsburg, WI

TAKES: 30 MIN. • **MAKES:** 4 SERVINGS

- **1 Tbsp. brown sugar**
- **1 Tbsp. chili powder**
- **½ tsp. salt**
- **1 beef flank steak (1 lb.)**
- **12 miniature sweet peppers, halved and seeded**
- **1 medium red onion, cut into thin wedges**
- **2 cups cherry tomatoes**
- **2 medium ears sweet corn, husks removed**

SALAD

- **12 cups torn mixed salad greens**
- **1 cup fresh cilantro leaves**
- **½ cup reduced-fat lime vinaigrette**
  Optional ingredients: cotija cheese, lime wedges and tortillas

1. In a small bowl, mix brown sugar, chili powder and salt. Rub onto both sides of the steak.
2. Place peppers and onion on a grilling grid; place on grill rack over medium heat. Grill, covered, 9-11 minutes or until crisp-tender, stirring occasionally; add tomatoes during the last 2 minutes. Remove from grill.
3. Place steak and corn directly on grill rack; close lid. Grill steak 8-10 minutes on each side or until a thermometer reads 135° for medium-rare; grill corn 10-12 minutes or until lightly charred, turning occasionally.
4. Divide greens and cilantro among four bowls. Cut corn from cobs and thinly slice steak across the grain; place in bowls. Top with vegetables; drizzle with vinaigrette. If desired, serve with cotija cheese, lime and tortillas.
NOTE: If you do not have a grilling grid, use a disposable foil pan with holes poked into the bottom with a meat fork.
1 SERVING: 351 cal., 14g fat (5g sat. fat), 54mg chol., 862mg sod., 33g carb. (16g sugars, 7g fiber), 28g pro.

FAJITA IN A BOWL

JALAPENO POPPER CORN SALAD

I created this recipe for a wedding I was catering, and it's a good thing I made buckets of it, because I couldn't stop eating it! This chilled creamy salad combines all the best flavors of jalapeno poppers with the delicate sweetness of fresh corn.
—Amanda Miller, Hutchinson, KS

PREP: 25 MIN. • **COOK:** 15 MIN. + COOLING
MAKES: 8 SERVINGS

- **1 medium onion, quartered**
- **2 jalapeno peppers**
- **1 cup sour cream**
- **1 cup mayonnaise**
- **2 oz. cream cheese, softened**
- **2 tsp. ground cumin**
- **1 tsp. garlic powder**
- **1 tsp. chili powder**
- **1 tsp. smoked paprika**
- **¼ tsp. salt**
- **¼ tsp. pepper**
- **4 cups fresh corn (about 8 ears), cooked and cooled**
- **1 cup shredded sharp cheddar cheese**
- **1 cup shredded pepper jack cheese**
- **½ cup crumbled cooked bacon, divided**

1. Grill the onion and jalapenos, covered, over medium-high heat or broil 4 in. from the heat 3-5 minutes on each side or until lightly charred. Cool completely; chop into ½-in. pieces.
2. Combine the next nine ingredients. Stir in corn, cheeses, half the bacon, and the grilled vegetables. Top with the remaining bacon to serve.
¾ CUP: 476 cal., 40g fat (14g sat. fat), 47mg chol., 616mg sod., 18g carb. (7g sugars, 2g fiber), 14g pro.

STRAWBERRY-CHICKEN PASTA SALAD

EAT SMART FAST FIX

STRAWBERRY POPPY SEED DRESSING

In the wonderful world of vinegars, strawberry is the new raspberry, giving you a fresh way to put those ruby-red gems to good use.
—Taste of Home *Test Kitchen*

TAKES: 10 MIN. • **MAKES:** 1 CUP

- **⅓ cup confectioners' sugar**
- **¼ cup strawberry or raspberry vinegar**
- **2 Tbsp. orange juice**
- **½ tsp. onion powder**
- **¼ tsp. salt**
- **¼ tsp. ground ginger**
- **⅓ cup canola oil**
- **½ tsp. poppy seeds**

In a blender, combine the first six ingredients; cover and process until blended. While processing, gradually add oil in a steady stream. Stir in poppy seeds. Chill until serving.

2 TBSP.: 108 cal., 9g fat (1g sat. fat), 0 chol., 74mg sod., 6g carb. (5g sugars, 0 fiber), 0 pro. **Diabetic exchanges:** 1½ fat, ½ starch.

STRAWBERRY-CHICKEN PASTA SALAD

When I figured out how to re-create this restaurant dish at home, my family was so excited. For a different spin, use raspberries or peaches instead of strawberries.
—Jane Ozment, Purcell, OK

PREP: 25 MIN. • **GRILL:** 15 MIN.
MAKES: 4 SERVINGS

- **½ cup sliced fresh strawberries**
- **1 Tbsp. sugar**
- **1 Tbsp. balsamic vinegar**
- **½ tsp. salt, divided**
- **¼ tsp. pepper, divided**
- **3 Tbsp. olive oil**
- **4 boneless skinless chicken breast halves (6 oz. each)**

ASSEMBLY

- **1 pkg. (10 oz.) hearts of romaine salad mix**
- **1 cup cooked gemelli or spiral pasta**
- **1 small red onion, halved and thinly sliced**
- **1 cup sliced fresh strawberries**
- **½ cup glazed pecans**

1. Place strawberries, sugar, vinegar, ¼ tsp. salt and ⅛ tsp. pepper in a blender; cover and process until smooth. While processing, gradually add oil in a steady stream. Refrigerate until serving.

2. Sprinkle chicken with remaining salt and pepper; grill, covered, on an oiled rack over medium heat until a thermometer reads 165°, 6-8 minutes on each side.

3. Cut chicken into slices. Divide salad mix among four plates; top with pasta, onion, chicken and strawberries. Drizzle with vinaigrette; sprinkle with pecans.

1 SERVING: 450 cal., 20g fat (3g sat. fat), 94mg chol., 492mg sod., 29g carb. (13g sugars, 4g fiber), 39g pro.

STRAWBERRY POPPY SEED DRESSING

PESTO BUTTERMILK DRESSING

EAT SMART

PESTO BUTTERMILK DRESSING

A good dressing is hard to beat; a great one is brilliant. My family loves a tangy blend of buttermilk and Greek yogurt.
—Liz Bellville, Jacksonville, NC

PREP: 10 MIN. + CHILLING • **MAKES:** 1¾ CUPS

- **⅔ cup buttermilk**
- **½ cup fat-free plain Greek yogurt**
- **½ cup prepared pesto**
- **¼ cup shredded Parmesan cheese**
- **1 Tbsp. white wine vinegar**
- **1 Tbsp. grated lemon zest**
- **1 garlic clove, minced**
- **½ tsp. coarsely ground pepper**
- **⅛ tsp. salt**

Place all ingredients in a jar with a tight-fitting lid; shake well. Refrigerate 1 hour. Just before serving, shake dressing again.
2 TBSP.: 50 cal., 4g fat (1g sat. fat), 2mg chol., 165mg sod., 2g carb. (1g sugars, 0 fiber), 2g pro. **Diabetic exchanges:** 1 fat.

(5) INGREDIENTS FAST FIX

GARLIC MAPLE DRESSING

Here's my go-to dressing for pretty much any salad (or veggie!) under the sun. It stores beautifully, so make it ahead—or leave the shaking to the kids while you finish up last-minute dinner details. They'll do you proud.
—Emily Tyra, Traverse City, MI

TAKES: 5 MIN. • **MAKES:** ¾ CUP

- **⅓ cup olive oil**
- **¼ cup maple syrup**
- **Juice of 1 medium lemon**
- **2 to 3 garlic cloves, minced**
- **1 to 2 tsp. Dijon mustard**
- **⅛ tsp. salt**
- **⅛ tsp. coarsely ground pepper**

Combine all ingredients in a jar with a tight-fitting lid; shake well.
2 TBSP.: 145 cal., 12g fat (2g sat. fat), 0 chol., 71mg sod., 10g carb. (9g sugars, 0 fiber), 0 pro.

EAT SMART

SOUTH-OF-THE-BORDER CITRUS SALAD

Orange, grapefruit and jicama add color and texture to this out-of-the-ordinary fruit salad. Sometimes I'll toss in slices of mango and cucumber for extra fun.
—Mary Fuller, SeaTac, WA

PREP TIME: 20 MIN. + CHILLING • **MAKES:** 6 SERVINGS

- **3 medium pink grapefruit**
- **3 medium oranges**
- **1 cup julienned peeled jicama**
- **2 Tbsp. minced fresh cilantro**
- **2 Tbsp. lime juice**
- **¼ tsp. ground cinnamon**

1. Cut a thin slice from the top and bottom of each grapefruit and orange; stand fruit upright on a cutting board. With a knife, cut off peel and outer membrane from fruit. Cut fruit crosswise into slices; place in a large bowl.
2. Add remaining ingredients; toss to combine. Transfer to a platter; refrigerate, covered, until serving.
¾ CUP: 70 cal., 0 fat (0 sat. fat), 0 chol., 2mg sod., 17g carb. (13g sugars, 3g fiber), 1g pro. **Diabetic exchanges:** 1 fruit.

SOUTH-OF-THE-BORDER CITRUS SALAD

CHEESEBURGER BOWL

EAT SMART

CALIFORNIA ROLL IN A JAR

I'm a big sushi fan, but it can be tricky to make at home. This jar has sushi flavor without the fuss.
—James Schend, Pleasant Prairie, WI

PREP: 20 MIN. • **COOK:** 15 MIN. + STANDING • **MAKES:** 4 SERVINGS

- **1 cup uncooked sushi rice**
- **1 cup water**
- **½ tsp. salt**
- **1 Tbsp. rice vinegar**
- **1 Tbsp. sugar**
- **2 medium ripe avocados, peeled and cubed**
- **1 cup lump crabmeat, drained**
- **1 cup chopped cucumber**
- **2 nori sheets, thinly sliced**
- **Pickled ginger slices, soy sauce and toasted sesame seeds, optional**

1. Wash rice in a colander until water runs clear. Combine rice, 1 cup water and salt in a large saucepan; bring to a boil. Reduce heat; cover. Simmer until water is absorbed and rice is tender, 15-20 minutes. Remove from heat. Let stand 10 minutes. Combine rice vinegar and sugar, stirring until sugar is dissolved. Stir into rice.
2. Place ⅓ cup rice into each of four 1-pint wide-mouth canning jars. Layer half of the avocados, crabmeat, cucumber and nori among the four jars. Top with remaining rice and repeat layers. Cover and refrigerate until serving. Transfer into bowls; toss to combine. If desired, serve with optional ingredients.
1 SERVING: 349 cal., 11g fat (2g sat. fat), 33mg chol., 562mg sod., 52g carb. (6g sugars, 7g fiber), 11g pro.

CALIFORNIA ROLL IN A JAR

CHEESEBURGER BOWL

This recipe is a unique and lighter way to enjoy an American summer staple. You can also make the dressing with ranch dressing and a tablespoon each of yellow mustard and ketchup.
—Laurie Rogerson, Ellington, CT

PREP: 25 MIN. • **GRILL:** 10 MIN. • **MAKES:** 4 SERVINGS

- **1 lb. lean ground beef (90% lean)**
- **½ tsp. salt**
- **¼ tsp. pepper**
- **½ cup reduced-fat ranch salad dressing**
- **2 Tbsp. ketchup**
- **4 cups shredded lettuce**
- **4 cups torn romaine**
- **1 medium cucumber, finely chopped**
- **1 medium tomato, finely chopped**
- **½ cup chopped dill pickles**
- **¼ cup finely chopped red onion**
- **¾ cup shredded cheddar cheese**
- **Crushed potato chips, optional**

1. In a small bowl, combine beef, salt and pepper, mixing lightly but thoroughly. Shape into four ½-in.-thick patties.
2. Grill burgers, covered, over medium heat 4-5 minutes on each side or until a thermometer reads 160°.
3. Meanwhile, whisk salad dressing and ketchup. In a large bowl, toss lettuces with half the dressing mixture; divide among four plates. Top with burger, cucumber, tomato, pickles, onion and cheese. Serve with remaining dressing. Top with potato chips if desired.
2 CUPS SALAD MIXTURE WITH 2 TBSP. DRESSING: 374 cal., 21g fat (8g sat. fat), 95mg chol., 1099mg sod., 11g carb. (7g sugars, 3g fiber), 29g pro.

EAT SMART

EGGPLANT SALAD WITH TOMATO & GOAT CHEESE

Hearty grilled eggplant helps make this colorful salad feel like a meal. The balsamic dressing adds so much depth and a burst of extra flavor.
—Susan Leiser, Hammonton, NJ

PREP: 25 MIN. • **GRILL:** 10 MIN.
MAKES: 8 SERVINGS

- **1 large eggplant, cut into 8 slices**
- **¼ cup extra virgin olive oil, divided**
- **1¼ tsp. salt, divided**
- **½ tsp. pepper, divided**
- **4 plum tomatoes, chopped**
- **¼ cup chopped red onion**
- **2 Tbsp. chopped fresh basil**
- **2 Tbsp. chopped fresh parsley**
- **4 tsp. balsamic vinegar**
- **4 cups fresh arugula or baby spinach**
- **½ cup crumbled goat cheese**

1. Brush both sides of eggplant slices with 2 Tbsp. oil. Sprinkle with ¾ tsp. salt and ¼ tsp. pepper.
2. Broil eggplant 3-4 in. from heat or grill, covered, over medium heat, until tender, 4-5 minutes per side.
3. Meanwhile, in a small bowl, combine tomatoes, onion, basil, parsley, vinegar, 1 Tbsp. oil and remaining salt and pepper. Toss arugula with remaining oil and divide among eight plates. Top each with eggplant, tomato mixture, and goat cheese.
1 SERVING: 115 cal., 9g fat (2g sat. fat), 9mg chol., 410mg sod., 8g carb. (5g sugars, 3g fiber), 3g pro. **Diabetic exchanges:** 2 fat, 1 vegetable.

TEST KITCHEN TIP

Try this salad with portobello mushrooms instead of eggplant. Serve with toasted flatbread or pita chips.

EGGPLANT SALAD WITH TOMATO & GOAT CHEESE

FAST FIX

VEGGIE-SESAME CHICKEN SALAD

Sweet, crisp, sunshine-packed and fun, this delightful salad has it all. It's perfect for those nights you don't want to cook.
—Betty Slivon, Sun City, AZ

TAKES: 10 MIN. • **MAKES:** 4 SERVINGS

- **1 pkg. (5 oz.) spring mix salad greens**
- **2½ cups shredded rotisserie chicken**
- **1 can (8 oz.) unsweetened pineapple chunks, drained**
- **½ cup shredded carrots**
- **½ cup frozen shelled edamame, thawed**
- **½ cup chopped sweet red pepper**
- **2 green onions, chopped**
- **½ cup sesame ginger salad dressing**
- **½ cup wonton strips**

Combine the first seven ingredients in a large bowl. Drizzle with dressing; toss to coat. Sprinkle with wonton strips.
2 CUPS: 386 cal., 18g fat (3g sat. fat), 78mg chol., 458mg sod., 25g carb. (15g sugars, 3g fiber), 30g pro.

FAST FIX

CREAMY FRENCH DRESSING

This creamy classic is always anticipated at family get-togethers. It's been a favorite for years.
—Monika Rahn, Dillsburg, PA

TAKES: 15 MIN. • **MAKES:** 2½ CUPS

- **½ cup lemon juice**
- **½ cup sugar**
- **½ cup ketchup**
- **¼ cup chopped onion**
- **1½ tsp. salt**
- **1½ tsp. Worcestershire sauce**
- **⅛ tsp. garlic powder**
- **1 cup canola oil**

In a blender or food processor, combine the first seven ingredients; cover and process until smooth. While processing, gradually add oil in a steady stream. Process until thickened. Transfer to a bowl or jar; cover and store in the refrigerator.
2 TBSP.: 127 cal., 11g fat (1g sat. fat), 0 chol., 253mg sod., 7g carb. (6g sugars, 0 fiber), 0 pro. **Diabetic exchanges:** 1½ fat, ½ starch.

GOURMET GRILLED CHEESE
WITH DATE-BACON JAM
PAGE 54

SOUPS & SANDWICHES

We all love soups and sandwiches, whether we want to warm up on a wintry day, tuck them into a lunchbox or just enjoy the ultimate comfort-food combo. On the following pages, you'll discover dozens of heartwarming inspirations...all from home cooks like you!

FRENCH LENTIL & CARROT SOUP

FAST FIX

BART'S BLACK BEAN SOUP

For a superfast dinner, try my 10-minute soup! If you want more kick to it, just use a hotter salsa.
—Sharon Ullyot, London, ON

TAKES: 10 MIN. • **MAKES:** 4 SERVINGS

- **1 can (15 oz.) black beans, rinsed and drained**
- **1½ cups chicken broth**
- **¾ cup chunky salsa**
- **½ cup canned whole kernel corn, drained**
- **Dash hot pepper sauce**
- **2 tsp. lime juice**
- **1 cup shredded cheddar cheese**
- **2 Tbsp. chopped green onions**

In a microwave-safe bowl, combine the first five ingredients. Cover and microwave on high for 2 minutes or until heated through. Pour into four serving bowls; drizzle each with lime juice. Sprinkle with cheese and green onions.

1 CUP: 229 cal., 8g fat (6g sat. fat), 32mg chol., 1004mg sod., 23g carb. (4g sugars, 5g fiber), 12g pro.

EAT SMART SLOW COOKER

FRENCH LENTIL & CARROT SOUP

It's crazy how just a few ingredients can make such a difference. Using finely chopped rotisserie chicken in this recipe makes it perfect for a busy weeknight meal, but you can leave the chicken out altogether if you prefer.
—Colleen Delawder, Herndon, VA

PREP: 15 MIN. • **COOK:** 6¼ HOURS • **MAKES:** 6 SERVINGS

- **5 large carrots, peeled and sliced**
- **1½ cups dried green lentils, rinsed**
- **1 shallot, finely chopped**
- **2 tsp. Herbes de Provence**
- **½ tsp. pepper**
- **¼ tsp. kosher salt**
- **6 cups reduced-sodium chicken broth**
- **2 cups cubed rotisserie chicken**
- **¼ cup heavy whipping cream**

1. Combine the first seven ingredients in a 5- or 6-qt. slow cooker; cover. Cook on low until lentils are tender, 6-8 hours.

2. Stir in chicken and cream. Cover and continue cooking until heated through, about 15 minutes.

1½ CUPS: 338 cal., 8g fat (3g sat. fat), 53mg chol., 738mg sod., 39g carb. (5g sugars, 7g fiber), 29g pro. **Diabetic exchanges:** 3 lean meat, 2 starch, 1 vegetable.

BART'S BLACK BEAN SOUP

WASABI MONTE CRISTO

FAST FIX

WASABI MONTE CRISTO

I love Monte Cristo sandwiches, but I wanted to use a few tricks to make them healthy and delicious. The spicy wasabi and sweet mango make a tasty twist on the traditional sandwich.
—Susan Riley, Allen, TX

TAKES: 15 MIN. • **MAKES:** 2 SERVINGS

- **2 Tbsp. reduced-fat mayonnaise**
- **½ to 1 tsp. prepared wasabi**
- **1 medium mango, peeled and chopped, or ⅔ cup frozen mango chunks, thawed**
- **2 tsp. light brown sugar**
- **4 slices multigrain bread**
- **2 oz. thinly sliced deli turkey**
- **2 oz. thinly sliced smoked deli ham**
- **2 oz. sliced baby Swiss cheese**
- **Mango chutney, optional**
- **2 large egg whites, beaten**
- **1½ tsp. confectioners' sugar**
- **Fresh mint leaves, optional**

1. Combine mayonnaise and wasabi; set aside. In another bowl, combine mango and brown sugar; puree with an immersion blender or in batches in a regular blender. Set aside.
2. Spread two slices of bread with the mayonnaise mixture. Layer slices evenly with turkey, ham and cheese. If desired, spread the remaining bread with chutney. Top the meat and cheese with the remaining bread. Dip sandwiches in egg whites.
3. In a large oiled nonstick skillet, brown the sandwiches over medium-high heat for about 2-3 minutes on each side. Before serving, dust with confectioners' sugar; halve sandwiches. Serve with mango mixture for dipping and, if desired, mint leaves.
1 SANDWICH: 499 cal., 17g fat (6g sat. fat), 54mg chol., 954mg sod., 58g carb. (34g sugars, 7g fiber), 31g pro.

SLOW COOKER

ITALIAN SAUSAGE PIZZA SOUP

My mom's friend shared this recipe with her over 50 years ago. I've tweaked it over the years, and it's still a family favorite. Warm garlic bread is heavenly on the side.
—Joan Hallford, North Richland Hills, TX

PREP: 15 MIN. • **COOK:** 6 HOURS • **MAKES:** 12 SERVINGS (3 QT.)

- **1 pkg. (1 lb.) Italian turkey sausage links**
- **1 medium onion, chopped**
- **1 medium green pepper, cut into strips**
- **1 medium sweet red or yellow pepper, cut into strips**
- **1 can (15 oz.) great northern or cannellini beans, rinsed and drained**
- **1 can (14½ oz.) diced tomatoes, undrained**
- **1 jar (14 oz.) pizza sauce**
- **2 tsp. Italian seasoning**
- **2 garlic cloves, minced**
- **2 cans (14½ oz. each) beef broth**
- **1 pkg. (5 oz.) Caesar salad croutons**
- **Shredded part-skim mozzarella cheese**

1. Remove casings from sausage. In a large skillet over medium-high heat, cook and crumble sausage until no longer pink. Add onion and peppers; cook until crisp-tender. Drain and transfer to a 6-qt. slow cooker.
2. Add the next five ingredients; pour in broth. Cook, covered, on low until vegetables are tender, 6-8 hours. Serve with croutons and cheese.
1 CUP: 158 cal., 5g fat (1g sat. fat), 15mg chol., 828mg sod., 19g carb. (4g sugars, 4g fiber), 9g pro.

ITALIAN SAUSAGE PIZZA SOUP

GRILLED CHEESE & TOMATO SOUP

Our food stylist Josh Rink reveals the secrets to taking a classic comfort-food combo from simple to simply amazing.

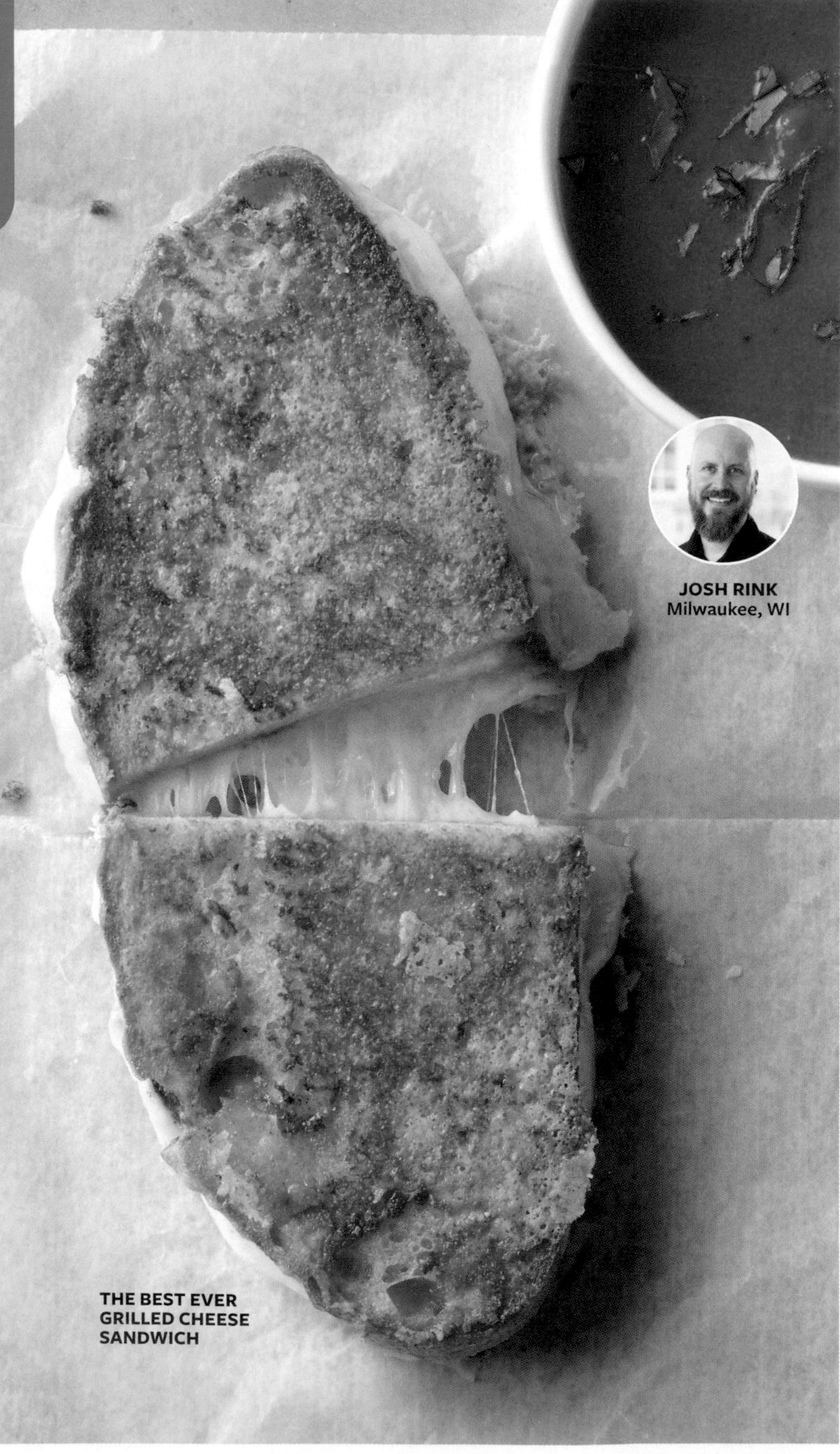

JOSH RINK
Milwaukee, WI

THE BEST EVER GRILLED CHEESE SANDWICH

EAT SMART

THE BEST EVER TOMATO SOUP

Creamy, rich and bursting with brightness, this soup is the ultimate sidekick to a grilled cheese sandwich.
—Josh Rink, Milwaukee, WI

PREP: 20 MIN. • **COOK:** 30 MIN.
MAKES: 16 SERVINGS (4 QT.)

- 3 Tbsp. olive oil
- 3 Tbsp. butter
- ¼ to ½ tsp. crushed red pepper flakes
- 3 large carrots, peeled and chopped
- 1 large onion, chopped
- 2 garlic cloves, minced
- 2 tsp. dried basil
- 3 cans (28 oz. each) whole peeled tomatoes
- 1 container (32 oz.) chicken stock
- 2 Tbsp. tomato paste
- 3 tsp. sugar
- 1 tsp. salt
- ½ tsp. pepper
- 1 cup heavy whipping cream, optional
- Fresh basil leaves, thinly sliced, optional

1. In a 6-qt. stockpot or Dutch oven, heat oil, butter and pepper flakes over medium heat until butter is melted. Add carrots and onion; cook, uncovered, stirring frequently, until vegetables are softened, 8-10 minutes. Add garlic and dried basil; cook and stir 1 minute longer. Stir in tomatoes, chicken stock, tomato paste, sugar, salt and pepper; stir well. Bring to a boil. Reduce heat; simmer, uncovered, to blend flavors, 20-25 minutes.
2. Remove pan from heat. Using a blender, puree soup in batches until smooth. If desired, slowly add heavy cream, stirring continuously to incorporate; return to stove to heat through. If desired, top with fresh basil.

1 CUP: 104 cal., 5g fat (2g sat. fat), 6mg chol., 572mg sod., 15g carb. (10g sugars, 2g fiber), 3g pro. **Diabetic exchanges:** 1 starch, 1 fat.

THE BEST EVER TOMATO SOUP

FAST FIX

THE BEST EVER GRILLED CHEESE SANDWICH

Spreading the bread with a mix of mayo and butter creates an exceptional crispy crust and delivers the buttery richness we expect.
—Josh Rink, Milwaukee, WI

TAKES: 30 MIN. • **MAKES:** 4 SERVINGS

- **6 Tbsp. butter, softened, divided**
- **8 slices sourdough bread**
- **3 Tbsp. mayonnaise**
- **3 Tbsp. finely shredded Manchego or Parmesan cheese**
- **⅛ tsp. onion powder**
- **½ cup shredded sharp white cheddar cheese**
- **½ cup shredded Monterey Jack cheese**
- **½ cup shredded Gruyere cheese**
- **4 oz. Brie cheese, rind removed and sliced**

1. Spread 3 Tbsp. butter on one side of bread slices. Toast bread, butter side down, in a large skillet or electric griddle over medium-low heat until golden brown, 2-3 minutes; remove from pan. In a small bowl, mix together mayonnaise, Manchego cheese, onion powder and the remaining 3 Tbsp. butter. In another bowl, combine cheddar, Monterey Jack and Gruyere.

2. Top toasted side of four bread slices with sliced Brie. Sprinkle the cheddar cheese mixture evenly over the Brie. Top with the remaining bread slices, toasted side facing inward. Spread the mayonnaise mixture on the outside of each sandwich. Place in same skillet and cook until golden brown and cheese is melted, 5-6 minutes on each side. Serve immediately.

1 SANDWICH: 659 cal., 49g fat (27g sat. fat), 122mg chol., 1017mg sod., 30g carb. (3g sugars, 1g fiber), 24g pro.

SUCCESS TIPS

In the food world, few pairings are as iconic as grilled cheese and tomato soup. Here are are Josh's tips to help you nail this duo at home:

- Tomatoes and basil are one of those "best friends" flavor combinations, and that's why basil is called for in the soup. (Josh chose dried basil because it's almost always on hand.)
- If you have fresh basil, it makes a pretty garnish atop each serving.
- Carrots in the soup lend a subtle sweetness. They balance out the acidity of the tomatoes, creating a well-rounded and satisfying soup.
- A mixture of butter and mayo on the sandwiches creates a delightfully crispy crust with all the wonderful butter flavor you'd expect on a grilled cheese sandwich.
- Rustic bread like sourdough from the bakery will stand up the gooey cheese inside each sandwich. And sourdough's robust flavor won't get lost when it's paired with the rich cheeses.
- For the ideal melt, Josh chose a blend of cheeses. Each brings something unique to the party.

Manchego has a low moisture content that makes for those lovely crispy bits on the outer edge of the sandwich.

Sharp white cheddar provides the perfect amount of tangy flavor.

Monterey Jack adds an irresistible ooey-gooey effect when the sandwich is sliced and pulled apart.

Gruyere gives the sandwich a nutty boost of flavor.

Brie has a creamy texture that makes it melty and slightly sophisticated.

SLOW-COOKER CUBANO SANDWICHES

SLOW COOKER

SLOW-COOKER CUBANO SANDWICHES

This recipe came about when I didn't have pepperoncinis for my usual Italian pork recipe, so I used pickles instead. It reminded me so much of a Cuban that I added ham and Swiss cheese to complete the dish. Instead of adding cheese to the slow cooker, you can also build the sandwiches and top them with sliced cheese—just place them under the broiler to melt.
—Kristie Schley, Severna Park, MD

PREP: 15 MIN. • **COOK:** 6½ HOURS • **MAKES:** 8 SERVINGS

2 lbs. pork tenderloin
7 Tbsp. stone-ground mustard, divided
1 tsp. pepper, freshly ground
1 lb. fully cooked boneless ham steak, cut into ½-in. cubes
1 jar (16 oz.) whole baby dill pickles, undrained, sliced thick
2 cups shredded Swiss cheese
8 submarine buns, split

1. Rub pork with 3 Tbsp. mustard, season with pepper and place in a 5- or 6-qt. slow cooker. Add ham and pickles, including pickle juice. Cover and cook on low until tender, turning halfway through, about 6 hours.
2. Shred pork with two forks. Sprinkle cheese over meat mixture; cover and cook until cheese melts, about 30 minutes.
3. When ready to serve, slice rolls and toast lightly in a toaster oven or broiler. Spread the remaining mustard evenly over both sides of the rolls. Using a slotted spoon, top rolls with meat mixture. Serve immediately.
1 SANDWICH: 420 cal., 12g fat (4g sat. fat), 93mg chol., 1891mg sod., 35g carb. (4g sugars, 3g fiber), 41g pro.

SLOW COOKER

SAUERBRATEN SOUP

Sauerbraten and soup are both family favorites. This combines the two, without the long marinating time the traditional beef dish requires. You can substitute spaetzle or gnocchi for the egg noodles.
—Jennifer Yerkes, Franklin Square, NY

PREP: 15 MIN. • **COOK:** 4 HOURS • **MAKES:** 11 CUPS

2 Tbsp. olive oil
2 lbs. beef stew meat, cut into 1-in. pieces
1 Tbsp. mixed pickling spices
1 bay leaf
6 cups beef broth, divided
1 medium onion, chopped
1 jar (16 oz.) shredded sweet-and-sour red cabbage
½ tsp. ground ginger
¼ tsp. ground cloves
8 gingersnap cookies, crushed
Cooked wide egg noodles

1. In a large skillet, heat oil over medium-high heat; brown meat in batches. Transfer meat to a 4- or 5-qt. slow cooker. Place pickling spices and bay leaf on a double thickness of cheesecloth. Gather corners of cloth to enclose seasonings; tie securely with kitchen string. Add spice bag, 4 cups broth, onion, cabbage, ginger and cloves to slow cooker. Cook, covered, on high for 3 hours.
2. Meanwhile, in a saucepan, heat remaining broth and gingersnaps over medium heat; cook and stir until thickened, about 10 minutes. Transfer to slow cooker; cook, covered, until meat is tender, about 1 hour. Discard spice bag. Serve with noodles.
1¾ CUPS: 371 cal., 16g fat (5g sat. fat), 94mg chol., 1226mg sod., 22g carb. (13g sugars, 1g fiber), 32g pro.

SAUERBRATEN SOUP

THAI-STYLE CHICKEN CHILI

FAST FIX

THAI-STYLE CHICKEN CHILI

I love this Asian take on the classic one-pot meal. It's quick, easy, nutritious and delicious.
—Roxanne Chan, Albany, CA

TAKES: 30 MIN. • **MAKES:** 6 SERVINGS

- **2 Tbsp. sesame oil**
- **1 lb. boneless skinless chicken thighs, cut into 1-in. pieces**
- **1 medium carrot, diced**
- **1 celery rib, chopped**
- **1 tsp. minced fresh gingerroot**
- **1 large garlic clove, minced**
- **1 can (28 oz.) diced tomatoes**
- **1 can (13.66 oz.) light coconut milk**
- **1 Tbsp. red curry paste**
- **¾ tsp. salt**
- **¼ tsp. pepper**
- **1 cup frozen shelled edamame, thawed**
- **2 cups fresh baby spinach**
- **1 green onion, minced**
- **½ tsp. grated lemon zest**
- **Fresh cilantro leaves**
- **Dry roasted peanuts**

1. In a large saucepan, heat sesame oil over medium heat. Add chicken, carrot and celery; cook and stir until the vegetables are slightly softened, 3-4 minutes. Add ginger and garlic; cook 1 minute more.

2. Stir in tomatoes, coconut milk, curry paste, salt and pepper. Bring to a boil. Reduce heat; simmer, covered, 10 minutes. Add edamame; cook 5 minutes more. Stir in spinach, green onion and lemon zest until the spinach wilts. Remove from heat; top with cilantro and peanuts.

1⅓ CUPS: 270 cal., 16g fat (6g sat. fat), 50mg chol., 635mg sod., 12g carb. (7g sugars, 4g fiber), 18g pro.

5 INGREDIENTS FAST FIX

WISCONSIN BUTTER-BASTED BURGERS

It's no secret Wisconsinites love their dairy—in fact, they love it so much they top their burgers with a generous pat of butter! My recipe is a lot like the butter burgers you'll find in popular restaurants all over the state.
—Becky Carver, North Royalton, OH

TAKES: 30 MIN. • **MAKES:** 4 SERVINGS

- **1 lb. lean ground beef (90% lean)**
- **½ tsp. seasoned salt**
- **½ tsp. pepper**
- **½ pound fresh mushrooms**
- **2 Tbsp. plus 4 tsp. butter, divided**
- **4 hamburger buns, split**
- **Optional toppings: tomato slices, lettuce leaves, dill pickle slices, ketchup and mustard**

1. Sprinkle ground beef with seasoned salt and pepper. Pulse mushrooms in a food processor until finely chopped. Add to seasoned beef, mixing lightly but thoroughly. Shape into four ½-in.-thick patties.

2. In a large skillet, heat 2 Tbsp. butter over medium heat. Add burgers; cook 6-8 minutes on each side, basting with butter, until a thermometer reads 160°. Remove from heat; keep warm. Add bun tops to skillet; toast until golden brown.

3. Transfer burgers to bun bottoms. Top each burger with 1 tsp. butter. Replace bun tops. Serve with toppings.

1 BURGER: 400 cal., 21g fat (10g sat. fat), 96mg chol., 543mg sod., 24g carb. (3g sugars, 1g fiber), 28g pro.

WISCONSIN BUTTER-BASTED BURGERS

SLOW-COOKER CORDON BLEU SOUP

FREEZE IT SLOW COOKER

SLOW-COOKER CORDON BLEU SOUP

I've taken this creamy slow cooker soup to potlucks and teacher luncheons, and brought home an empty crock every time. When my son's school recently created a cookbook, this was the first recipe he asked me to submit, and his teachers were glad he did.
—Erica Winkel, Ada, MI

PREP: 40 MIN. + COOLING • **COOK:** 3 HOURS
MAKES: 8 SERVINGS

- 3 **Tbsp. butter, melted**
- ¼ **tsp. garlic powder**
- ¼ **tsp. pepper**
- 4 **cups cubed French bread**

SOUP

- 1 **small onion, diced**
- 1 **celery rib, diced**
- 1 **garlic clove, minced**
- ¼ **tsp. salt**
- ¼ **tsp. pepper**
- 3 **cans (14½ oz. each) reduced-sodium chicken broth**
- ⅓ **cup all-purpose flour**
- ⅓ **cup water**
- ¼ **cup white wine or additional reduced-sodium chicken broth**
- 8 **oz. reduced-fat cream cheese, cubed**
- 1½ **cups Swiss cheese, shredded**
- ½ **cup shredded cheddar cheese**
- ½ **lb. diced rotisserie chicken**
- ½ **lb. diced deli ham**

1. For croutons, preheat oven to 375°. In a large bowl, mix the melted butter, garlic powder and pepper. Add bread cubes; toss to coat. Transfer croutons to a 15x10x1-in. baking pan; bake, stirring every 5 minutes, until golden brown, 15-20 minutes. Remove to wire racks to cool completely.
2. Meanwhile, combine next five ingredients in a 4- or 5-qt. slow cooker; pour in broth. Cook, covered, on low until the vegetables are tender, about 2 hours.
3. Increase setting to high. Mix flour and water until smooth; whisk the flour mixture into broth. Cook until thickened, 30-40 minutes. Stir in wine. Whisk in cheeses until melted. Add chicken and ham; heat through. Serve with croutons.

FREEZE OPTION: Before adding croutons, freeze cooled soup in freezer containers. Freeze croutons separately. To use, partially thaw soup in refrigerator overnight. Heat soup through in a saucepan, stirring occasionally and adding a little broth or water if necessary. While soup is heating, thaw croutons at room temperature; sprinkle over soup.

1¼ CUPS PLUS ½ CUP CROUTONS: 384 cal., 23g fat (13g sat. fat), 100mg chol., 1112mg sod., 15g carb. (3g sugars, 1g fiber), 29g pro.

GOURMET GRILLED CHEESE WITH DATE-BACON JAM

(SHOWN ON PAGE 46)

This sandwich doubles up on melty cheese, but the star of the show is the sweet and salty jam. It makes for a truly grown-up version of grilled cheese.
—Kathy Cooper, Tucson, AZ

PREP: 1 HOUR + COOLING • **COOK:** 5 MIN.
MAKES: 4 SERVINGS

- ½ **lb. bacon strips, diced**
- 1 **cup finely chopped sweet onion**
- 1 **garlic clove, minced**
- 6 **oz. pitted dates, chopped**
- ¾ **cup water**
- ¼ **cup cider vinegar**
- ⅛ **tsp. salt**
- ⅛ **tsp. pepper**

SANDWICHES

- ½ **cup shredded cheddar cheese**
- 1 **round (8 oz.) Brie cheese, rind removed, softened**
- 8 **slices sourdough bread**
- 2 **Tbsp. butter, softened**

1. In a large skillet, cook bacon over medium heat until crisp, stirring occasionally. Remove from pan with a slotted spoon; drain on paper towels. Discard all but 2 Tbsp. of the drippings.
2. Add onion to skillet with drippings; cook and stir over medium heat until softened. Reduce heat to medium-low; cook, stirring occasionally, until onion is deep golden brown and caramelized, 35-40 minutes. Add garlic during last 5 minutes of cooking.
3. Return the bacon to skillet; add the next five ingredients. Stir well. Reduce heat; simmer, covered, about 30 minutes, stirring occasionally. Cool.
4. For sandwiches, combine cheeses, mixing well. Layer four slices of bread with the cheese mixture, 2 Tbsp. date-bacon jam and the remaining bread. Spread the outsides of the sandwiches with butter. In a nonstick skillet, toast sandwiches over medium-low heat until golden brown and the cheese is melted, 2-3 minutes per side. Cover and refrigerate the remaining jam; save for another use.

1 SANDWICH: 572 cal., 33g fat (19g sat. fat), 97mg chol., 1015mg sod., 45g carb. (14g sugars, 3g fiber), 25g pro.

SLOW COOKER

MOROCCAN CAULIFLOWER & ALMOND SOUP

This soup tastes rich and decadent, but is really very healthy! Bonus—it's vegan, and also makes your house smell amazing!
—Barbara Marynowski, Hutto, TX

PREP: 20 MIN. • **COOK:** 6 HOURS
MAKES: 8 SERVINGS

- **1 large head cauliflower (about 3½ lbs.), broken into florets**
- **6 cups vegetable stock**
- **¾ cup sliced almonds, toasted and divided**
- **½ cup plus 2 Tbsp. minced fresh cilantro, divided**
- **2 Tbsp. olive oil**
- **1 to 3 tsp. harissa chili paste or hot pepper sauce**
- **½ tsp. ground cinnamon**
- **½ tsp. ground cumin**
- **½ tsp. ground coriander**
- **1¼ tsp. salt**
- **½ tsp. pepper**
- **Additional harissa chili paste, optional**

1. In a 5- or 6-qt. slow cooker, combine cauliflower, vegetable stock, ½ cup almonds, ½ cup cilantro and the next seven ingredients. Cook, covered, on low until the cauliflower is tender, 6-8 hours.
2. Puree soup using an immersion blender. Or, cool slightly and puree in batches in a blender; return to slow cooker and heat through. Serve with remaining almonds and cilantro and, if desired, additional harissa.
1¼ CUPS: 116 cal., 8g fat (1g sat. fat), 0 chol., 835mg sod., 9g carb. (2g sugars, 3g fiber), 4g pro.

TEST KITCHEN TIP

Harissa chili paste is a blend of different types of chilies, garlic, herbs and spices. You can find it in jars in the spice section of your supermarket. This soup freezes well for up to three months, so it's perfect to have on hand for quick dinners or lunches. Don't skip toasting the nuts; it brings out their flavor, so a little can go a long way.

BROCCOLI CHEESEBURGERS WITH SPICY SWEET POTATOES

BROCCOLI CHEESEBURGERS WITH SPICY SWEET POTATOES

These faux burgers are so packed with flavor that nobody notices they're also packed with protein, fiber and vitamins.
—Pamela Vachon, Astoria, NY

PREP: 10 MIN. • **COOK:** 35 MIN.
MAKES: 4 SERVINGS

- **2 medium sweet potatoes, cut into 12 wedges each**
- **Cooking spray**
- **1 tsp. salt-free spicy seasoning blend or reduced-sodium Creole seasoning**
- **4 tsp. extra virgin olive oil, divided**
- **1 shallot, minced**
- **1 cup fresh broccoli florets, cut into ¾-in. pieces**
- **1 large egg, beaten**
- **1 cup white kidney or cannellini beans, rinsed and drained**
- **1 cup ready-to-serve quinoa**
- **¾ cup shredded reduced-fat cheddar cheese**
- **4 whole wheat hamburger buns, split**
- **Optional toppings: lettuce leaves, tomato slices, ketchup, mustard and reduced-fat mayonnaise**

1. Preheat oven to 450°. Spritz sweet potato wedges with cooking spray until lightly coated. Sprinkle with seasoning mix; toss to coat. Arrange in a single layer on a 15x10x1-in. baking sheet. Bake, turning wedges halfway through cooking, until tender and lightly spotted, 30-35 minutes.
2. Meanwhile, in a large nonstick skillet, heat 2 tsp. olive oil over medium heat. Add shallot; cook until translucent, about 2 minutes. Add broccoli; cook just until it turns bright green, about 3 minutes longer.
3. Transfer broccoli mixture to a food processor. Add egg and beans; pulse until the ingredients are blended but not pureed. Pour the broccoli mixture into a large bowl. Add the quinoa and cheddar cheese; mix lightly but thoroughly. Shape into four ½-in.-thick patties.
4. In a large nonstick skillet, heat the remaining oil over medium-high heat. Add burger patties to skillet; cook until golden and heated through, about 3 minutes on each side.
5. Serve immediately on whole wheat buns with sweet potato wedges on the side. If desired, add optional toppings.
1 BURGER WITH SIX SWEET POTATO WEDGES: 457 cal., 14g fat (4g sat. fat), 62mg chol., 550mg sod., 65g carb. (14g sugars, 11g fiber), 18g pro.

GRUYERE & EGG BURGERS

GRUYERE & EGG BURGERS

These burgers were a huge hit with our friends during football season. Regular mayo can easily be substituted for the garlic aioli if desired.
—Melissa Pelkey Hass, Waleska, GA

PREP: 30 MIN. • **COOK:** 20 MIN.
MAKES: 8 SERVINGS

- ½ **cup mayonnaise**
- 2 **garlic cloves, minced**
- 1 **tsp. lemon juice**
- ½ **tsp. grated lemon zest**

CHEESEBURGERS

- 2 **lbs. lean ground beef (90% lean)**
- 1 **Tbsp. stone-ground mustard**
- 1 **Tbsp. olive oil**
- 1 **tsp. dried thyme**
- ½ **tsp. salt**
- ½ **tsp. pepper**
- 8 **slices Gruyere or aged Swiss cheese**
- 8 **mini pretzel buns, split**

FRIED EGGS

- 2 **Tbsp. butter**
- 8 **large eggs**

TOPPINGS

- **Fresh arugula**
- 2 **medium tomatoes, sliced**
- **Additional stone-ground mustard, optional**

1. Whisk mayonnaise, garlic, lemon juice and lemon zest until blended. Refrigerate.
2. Combine the next six ingredients, mixing lightly but thoroughly (do not overmix). Shape into eight patties. Grill, covered, over medium direct heat until a thermometer reads 160°, 5-7 minutes on each side. Top with cheese; grill, covered, until the cheese is melted, 1-2 minutes longer. Place burgers on bun bottoms. Keep warm.
3. Melt 1 Tbsp. butter over medium heat in each of two large skillets (on grill or stovetop). Break eggs, one at a time, into a custard cup or saucer, then gently slide into pans. Immediately reduce heat to low. To prepare eggs sunny-side up, cover pan and cook until yolks thicken but are not hard. To make basted eggs, spoon butter in pan over eggs while cooking. For over-easy, carefully turn eggs to cook both sides but do not cover pan.
4. To serve, spread mayonnaise mixture over bun tops. Add arugula, tomatoes and, if desired, additional mustard to burgers. Top with fried eggs. Replace bun tops.
1 BURGER: 595 cal., 38g fat (13g sat. fat), 289mg chol., 729mg sod., 23g carb. (3g sugars, 1g fiber), 39g pro.

(5) INGREDIENTS

SAUSAGE & PEPPER SHEET-PAN SANDWICHES

Sausage with peppers was always on the table when I was growing up. Here's how I do it the easy way. Just grab a sheet pan and the ingredients, then let your oven do the work.
—Debbie Glasscock, Conway, AR

PREP: 20 MIN. • **BAKE:** 35 MIN.
MAKES: 6 SERVINGS

- 1 **lb. uncooked sweet Italian turkey sausage links, roughly chopped**
- 3 **medium sweet red peppers, seeded and sliced**
- 1 **large onion, halved and sliced**
- 1 **Tbsp. olive oil**
- 6 **hot dog buns, split**
- 6 **slices provolone cheese**

1. Preheat oven to 375°. Place sausage pieces in a 15x10x1-in. sheet pan, arranging peppers and onions around the sausage. Drizzle olive oil over the sausage and vegetables; bake, stirring mixture after 15 minutes, until sausage is no longer pink and vegetables are tender, 30-35 minutes.
2. During the last 5 minutes of baking, arrange buns cut side up in a second sheet pan; top each bun bottom with a cheese slice. Bake until the buns are golden brown and the cheese is melted. Spoon sausage and pepper mixture onto the bun bottoms. Replace tops.
1 SANDWICH: 315 cal., 15g fat (5g sat. fat), 43mg chol., 672mg sod., 28g carb. (7g sugars, 2g fiber), 18g pro.

SAUSAGE & PEPPER SHEET-PAN SANDWICHES

CHICKEN & BROCCOLI RABE SOUP WITH TORTELLINI

With chicken, pasta and a bold tomato broth, this hearty and inviting soup is like a big, comforting hug in a bowl!
—Cyndy Gerken, Naples, FL

PREP: 15 MIN. • **COOK:** 45 MIN.
MAKES: 10 SERVINGS

- 1 lb. broccoli rabe
- ½ tsp. ground nutmeg
- ½ tsp. salt, divided
- ¼ tsp. pepper, divided
- 2 Tbsp. olive oil
- ¼ lb. diced pancetta or 4 bacon strips, chopped
- 1 large onion, chopped
- 4 garlic cloves, minced
- 2 cartons (32 oz. each) chicken stock
- 1 can (15 oz.) tomato sauce
- 3 fresh thyme sprigs
- 3 Tbsp. minced fresh parsley
- 1 bay leaf
- ¼ cup grated Parmesan cheese
- 1 package (19 oz.) frozen cheese tortellini
- Additional grated Parmesan cheese

1. Fill a Dutch oven two-thirds full with water; bring to a boil. Cut ½ in. off ends of broccoli rabe; trim woody stems. Coarsely chop stems and leaves; add to boiling water. Cook, uncovered, just until crisp-tender, 1-2 minutes. Drain; sprinkle with nutmeg, ¼ tsp. salt and ⅛ tsp. pepper.

2. In the same Dutch oven, heat olive oil over medium heat. Add pancetta; cook until brown and crisp, 4-5 minutes. Add onion and the remaining salt and pepper; cook until tender, 3-4 minutes. Stir in garlic; cook 1 minute more. Add the next six ingredients and broccoli rabe; bring to a boil. Reduce heat; simmer, covered, 30 minutes. Discard bay leaf and thyme sprigs. Add chicken; heat through.

3. Cook tortellini according to package directions. To serve, spoon tortellini into individual bowls; pour soup into bowls. Sprinkle with additional Parmesan.

1⅓ CUPS: 328 cal., 13g fat (4g sat. fat), 72mg chol., 1176mg sod., 24g carb. (3g sugars, 3g fiber), 28g pro.

TERI RASEY
Cadillac, MI

BEEF & BEAN TACO CHILI

BEEF & BEAN TACO CHILI

This chili recipe can be a lifesaver when I'm cooking on the fly. It's loaded with convenience ingredients, but you can pile on the veggies if you're in the mood for a fresh crunch.
—Teri Rasey, Cadillac, MI

PREP: 10 MIN. • **COOK:** 40 MIN.
MAKES: 12 SERVINGS

- 1 Tbsp. canola oil
- 1 lb. lean ground beef (90% lean)
- 2 large onions, diced
- 2 envelopes reduced-sodium taco seasoning
- 3 cans (15 to 16 oz. each) black beans, undrained
- 3 cans (15 to 16 oz. each) pinto beans, rinsed and drained
- 2 cans (15 oz. each) no-salt-added tomato sauce
- 1 tsp. reduced-sodium beef bouillon granules
- Optional toppings: sour cream, shredded Mexican cheese, chopped tomatoes and crushed tortilla chips

In a Dutch oven, heat oil over medium heat; add beef and onions. Cook until beef is no longer pink and onions are tender, 6-8 minutes. Drain. Stir in the remaining ingredients; bring to a boil. Reduce heat; simmer, uncovered, stirring occasionally, until flavors are blended, about 30 minutes. If desired, serve with toppings.

1⅓ CUPS: 282 cal., 5g fat (1g sat. fat), 24mg chol., 1131mg sod., 44g carb. (8g sugars, 13g fiber), 20g pro.

TEST KITCHEN TIP

This chili freezes well, so you can make a double batch and freeze half of it for a warm and hearty meal another time.

BUTTERNUT SQUASH CHILI

EAT SMART

BUTTERNUT SQUASH CHILI

Add butternut squash to chili for a tasty, satisfying, energy-packed dish your whole family will love. Mine does!
—Jeanne Larson, Rancho Santa Margarita, CA

PREP: 20 MIN. • **COOK:** 30 MIN. • **MAKES:** 8 SERVINGS (2 QT.)

- **1 lb. ground beef or turkey**
- **¾ cup chopped red onion**
- **5 garlic cloves, minced**
- **3 Tbsp. tomato paste**
- **1 Tbsp. chili powder**
- **1 tsp. ground cumin**
- **½ to 1 tsp. salt**
- **1¾ to 2 cups water**
- **1 can (15 oz.) black beans, rinsed and drained**
- **1 can (15 oz.) pinto beans, rinsed and drained**
- **1 can (14½ oz.) diced tomatoes**
- **1 can (14½ to 15 oz.) tomato sauce**
- **3 cups peeled butternut squash, cut into ½-in. cubes**
- **2 Tbsp. cider vinegar**
- **Chopped avocado, plain Greek yogurt and shredded mozzarella cheese, optional**

1. In a Dutch oven over medium heat, cook beef and onion, crumbling meat, until beef is no longer pink and onion is tender, 6-8 minutes.
2. Add the next five ingredients; cook 1 minute longer. Stir in water, both types of beans, diced tomatoes and tomato sauce. Bring to a boil; reduce heat. Stir in squash; simmer, covered, until squash is tender, 20-25 minutes. Stir in vinegar.
3. If desired, serve with chopped avocado, Greek yogurt and shredded mozzarella cheese.
1 CUP: 261 cal., 8g fat (3g sat. fat), 35mg chol., 704mg sod., 32g carb. (6g sugars, 8g fiber), 18g pro. **Diabetic exchanges:** 2 starch, 2 lean meat.

EAT SMART

LENTIL, BACON & BEAN SOUP

This quick soup feels extra cozy with lots of lentils and a touch of smoky, bacony goodness. You might want to cook up extra—I think it's even better the next day!
—Janie Zirbser, Mullica Hill, NJ

PREP: 15 MIN. • **COOK:** 30 MIN. • **MAKES:** 8 SERVINGS

- **4 bacon strips, chopped**
- **6 medium carrots, chopped**
- **2 small onions, diced**
- **Olive oil, optional**
- **2 Tbsp. tomato paste**
- **2 garlic cloves, minced**
- **1 tsp. minced fresh thyme**
- **½ tsp. pepper**
- **5 cups chicken stock**
- **1 cup dry white wine or additional chicken stock**
- **2 cans (15 to 16 oz. each) butter beans, rinsed and drained**
- **2 cans (15 oz. each) cooked lentils, rinsed and drained**
- **6 fresh thyme sprigs**

1. In a Dutch oven, cook bacon over medium heat until crisp, stirring occasionally. Remove with a slotted spoon; drain on paper towels. Cook and stir carrots and onions in bacon drippings, adding olive oil if necessary, until crisp-tender, 3-4 minutes. Add tomato paste, garlic, thyme and pepper; cook 1 minute longer.
2. Add stock and wine; increase heat to medium-high. Cook for 2 minutes, stirring to loosen browned bits from pan. Stir in butter beans, lentils and bacon. Bring to a boil. Reduce heat; simmer, covered, 5 minutes. Uncover; continue simmering until vegetables are tender, 15-20 minutes. Serve with thyme sprigs.
1 CUP: 271 cal., 6g fat (2g sat. fat), 9mg chol., 672mg sod., 41g carb. (7g sugars, 13g fiber), 18g pro. **Diabetic exchanges:** 3 starch, 1 medium-fat meat.

LENTIL, BACON & BEAN SOUP

GREEK GRILLED CHICKEN PITAS

GREEK GRILLED CHICKEN PITAS

I switched up my mom's recipe to create this tasty variation. It's delicious and perfect for warm days. It takes advantage of fresh summer veggies and keeps my kitchen cool.
—Blair Lonergan, Rochelle, VA

PREP: 20 MIN. + MARINATING • **GRILL:** 10 MIN. • **MAKES:** 4 SERVINGS

- **1 lb. boneless skinless chicken breast halves**
- **½ cup balsamic vinaigrette**

CUCUMBER SAUCE

- **1 cup plain Greek yogurt**
- **½ cup finely chopped cucumber**
- **¼ cup finely chopped red onion**
- **1 Tbsp. minced fresh parsley**
- **1 Tbsp. lime juice**
- **1 garlic clove, minced**
- **¼ tsp. salt**
- **⅛ tsp. pepper**

PITAS

- **8 pita pocket halves**
- **½ cup sliced cucumber**
- **½ cup grape tomatoes, chopped**
- **½ cup sliced red onion**
- **½ cup crumbled feta cheese**

1. Marinate chicken in vinaigrette, covered, in refrigerator for at least 4 hours or overnight. In a small bowl, combine the sauce ingredients; chill until serving.
2. Drain and discard marinade. If grilling the chicken, lightly oil the grill rack. Grill chicken, covered, over medium heat or broil 4 in. from the heat until a thermometer reads 170°, 4-7 minutes on each side.
3. Cut chicken into strips. Fill each pita half with chicken, cucumber, tomatoes, onion and cheese; drizzle with sauce.
NOTE: If Greek yogurt is not available in your area, line a strainer with a coffee filter and place over a bowl. Place 2 cups fat-free yogurt in the prepared strainer; refrigerate overnight. Discard liquid from bowl; proceed as directed
2 FILLED PITA HALVES: 428 cal., 14g fat (6g sat. fat), 85mg chol., 801mg sod., 41g carb. (7g sugars, 3g fiber), 33g pro.

SLOW COOKER

GENERAL TSO'S SOUP

I love Asian food and wanted a chili-like soup with the distinctive flavors of General Tso's chicken. The slow cooker makes this super easy, and you can use any meat you like. It's a great with turkey, ground meats or leftover pork.
—Lori McLain, Denton, TX

PREP: 10 MIN. • **COOK:** 4 HOURS • **MAKES:** 6 SERVINGS

- **1 cup tomato juice**
- **½ cup pickled cherry peppers, chopped**
- **2 Tbsp. soy sauce**
- **2 Tbsp. hoisin sauce**
- **1 Tbsp. peanut oil**
- **1 to 2 tsp. crushed red pepper flakes**
- **1 lb. shredded cooked chicken**
- **1½ cups chopped onion**
- **1 cup chopped fresh broccoli**
- **¼ cup chopped green onions**
- **1 tsp. sesame seeds, toasted**

In a 4- or 5-qt. slow cooker, combine the first six ingredients. Stir in chicken, onion and broccoli. Cook, covered, on low until vegetables are tender, about 2 hours. Top with green onions and sesame seeds to serve.
1 CUP: 222 cal., 9g fat (2g sat. fat), 67mg chol., 791mg sod., 10g carb. (5g sugars, 2g fiber), 25g pro.

GENERAL TSO'S SOUP

HOW TO MAKE

FRENCH ONION SOUP

Coax every bit of flavor from a heap of onions in this soup. Be whisked away to a Paris cafe without leaving the kitchen.

CLASSIC FRENCH ONION SOUP

Pick Your Fave

Almost any onion variety will give you the rich flavor of this classic soup. Try Spanish, yellow or white onions—leeks will work, too—but use sweet onions sparingly, as their sweetness can overpower the finished product.

Low & Slow

Patience is key—if you brown the onions too quickly, you won't extract the natural sugars and the soup will end up thin, flat and boring. For intense flavor, cook the onions over low heat for a long time, stirring often.

Freeze It

Caramelized onions freeze beautifully, so why not double the batch and store half for a meal later on? Completely cooked soup can be frozen up to six months. Omit the bread and cheese, cool and freeze.

CLASSIC FRENCH ONION SOUP

Enjoy my signature soup the same way my granddaughter Becky does. I make it for her in a French onion soup bowl complete with garlic croutons and gobs of melted Swiss cheese on top.
—Lou Sansevero, Ferron, UT

PREP: 20 MIN. • **COOK:** 2 HOURS + BROILING
MAKES: 12 SERVINGS

- **5 Tbsp. olive oil, divided**
- **1 Tbsp. butter**
- **8 cups thinly sliced onions (about 3 lbs.)**
- **3 garlic cloves, minced**
- **½ cup port wine**
- **2 cartons (32 oz. each) beef broth**
- **½ tsp. pepper**
- **¼ tsp. salt**
- **24 slices French bread baguette (½ in. thick)**
- **2 large garlic cloves, peeled and halved**
- **¾ cup shredded Gruyere or Swiss cheese**

1. In a Dutch oven, heat 2 Tbsp. oil and butter over medium heat. Add onions; cook and stir until softened, 10-13 minutes. Reduce heat to medium-low; cook, stirring occasionally, until deep golden brown, 30-40 minutes. Add minced garlic; cook 2 minutes longer.
2. Stir in wine. Bring to a boil; cook until liquid is reduced by half. Add broth, pepper and salt; return to a boil. Reduce heat. Simmer, covered, stirring occasionally, for 1 hour.
3. Meanwhile, preheat oven to 400°. Place baguette slices on a baking sheet; brush both sides with the remaining oil. Bake until toasted, 3-5 minutes on each side. Rub toasts with halved garlic.
4. To serve, place twelve 8-oz. broiler-safe bowls or ramekins on baking sheets. Place one toast in each. Ladle with soup; top with cheese. Broil 4 in. from heat until the cheese is melted.

¾ CUP SOUP WITH 2 SLICES BREAD AND 1 TBSP. CHEESE: 195 cal., 10g fat (3g sat. fat), 9mg chol., 805mg sod., 20g carb. (4g sugars, 2g fiber), 6g pro.

HOW-TO

To-Do's (and Ta-Da's)

- The onions are the backbone of this dish, so don't skimp on them. It may look as if you have too many, but don't let that fool you. They'll cook way down during caramelizing.

- A hearty, full-bodied wine adds complex flavor to this soup. Port, a slightly sweet fortified wine, pairs well with onion and Gruyere cheese.

- Ladling soup over the baguettes keeps them moist. If you prefer a crispy topping, top soup with bread and cheese (shown opposite page), then broil.

ARTICHOKE CHICKEN PASTA
PAGE 71

QUICK FIXES

Even the busiest people can eat right—every night—thanks to the genius dinners in this breezy chapter. Every dish you find here is table-ready in half an hour or less.

FAJITA-STYLE SHRIMP & GRITS

FAST FIX

FAJITA-STYLE SHRIMP & GRITS

I combined two of my favorite dishes—fajitas and shrimp with cheesy grits—into this spicy one-dish meal. For more heat, use pepper jack cheese instead of Mexican cheese blend.
—Arlene Erlbach, Morton Grove, IL

TAKES: 30 MIN. • **MAKES:** 4 SERVINGS

- **1 lb. uncooked shrimp (16-20 per lb.), peeled and deveined**
- **2 Tbsp. fajita seasoning mix**
- **1 cup quick-cooking grits**
- **4 cups boiling water**
- **1½ cups shredded Mexican cheese blend**
- **3 Tbsp. 2% milk**
- **2 Tbsp. canola oil**
- **3 medium sweet peppers, seeded and cut into 1-in. strips**
- **1 medium sweet onion, cut into 1-in. strips**
- **1 jar (15½ to 16 oz.) medium chunky salsa**
- **¼ cup orange juice**
- **¼ cup plus 1 Tbsp. fresh cilantro leaves, divided**

1. Sprinkle shrimp with fajita seasoning; toss to coat. Set aside.
2. Slowly stir the grits into boiling water. Reduce heat to medium; cook, covered, stirring occasionally, until thickened, 5-7 minutes. Remove from heat. Stir in cheese until melted; stir in milk. Keep warm.
3. In a large skillet, heat oil over medium-high heat. Add peppers and onion; cook and stir until tender and pepper edges are slightly charred. Add salsa, orange juice and shrimp. Cook, stirring constantly, until the shrimp turn pink, 4-6 minutes. Stir in ¼ cup cilantro. Remove from heat.
4. Spoon the grits into serving bowls; top with the shrimp mixture. Sprinkle with the remaining cilantro.

1 SERVING: 561 cal., 23g fat (8g sat. fat), 176mg chol., 1324mg sod., 55g carb. (12g sugars, 4g fiber), 33g pro.

5 INGREDIENTS FAST FIX

CHEESY SUMMER SQUASH FLATBREADS

When you want a meatless meal with Mediterranean style, these flatbreads deliver the goods!
—Matthew Hass, Franklin, WI

TAKES: 30 MIN. • **MAKES:** 4 SERVINGS

- **3 small yellow summer squash, sliced ¼ in. thick**
- **1 Tbsp. olive oil**
- **½ tsp. salt**
- **2 cups fresh baby spinach, coarsely chopped**
- **2 naan flatbreads**
- **⅓ cup roasted red pepper hummus**
- **1 carton (8 oz.) fresh mozzarella cheese pearls**
- **Pepper**

1. Preheat oven to 425°. Toss squash with oil and salt; spread evenly in a 15x10x1-in. baking pan. Roast 8-10 minutes or until tender. Transfer to a bowl; stir in spinach.
2. Place naan on a baking sheet; spread with hummus. Top with squash mixture and cheese. Bake on a lower oven rack just until cheese melts, 4-6 minutes. Sprinkle with pepper.

½ TOPPED FLATBREAD: 332 cal., 20g fat (9g sat. fat), 47mg chol., 737mg sod., 24g carb. (7g sugars, 3g fiber), 15g pro.

CHEESY SUMMER SQUASH FLATBREADS

EAT SMART FAST FIX

CHICKEN WITH PEACH-CUCUMBER SALSA

To keep our kitchen cool, we grill chicken outdoors and serve it with a minty peach salsa that can easily be made ahead.
—Janie Colle, Hutchinson, KS

TAKES: 25 MIN. • **MAKES:** 4 SERVINGS

- **1½ cups chopped peeled fresh peaches (about 2 medium)**
- **¾ cup chopped cucumber**
- **4 Tbsp. peach preserves, divided**
- **3 Tbsp. finely chopped red onion**
- **1 tsp. minced fresh mint**
- **¾ tsp. salt, divided**
- **4 boneless skinless chicken breast halves (6 oz. each)**
- **¼ tsp. pepper**

1. For the salsa, combine peaches, cucumber, 2 Tbsp. preserves, onion, mint and ¼ tsp. salt.
2. Sprinkle chicken with pepper and the remaining salt. On a lightly greased grill rack, grill chicken, covered, over medium heat for 5 minutes. Turn; grill 7-9 minutes longer or until a thermometer reads 165°, brushing tops occasionally with remaining preserves. Serve with salsa.
1 CHICKEN BREAST HALF WITH ½ CUP SALSA: 261 cal., 4g fat (1g sat. fat), 94mg chol., 525mg sod., 20g carb. (17g sugars, 1g fiber), 35g pro. Diabetic exchanges: 5 lean meat, ½ starch, ½ fruit.

(5) INGREDIENTS FAST FIX

BAKED SALMON

I often make this very moist and flavorful salmon for company because I can have it ready in less than half an hour. I like to serve it with rice, or a green vegetable and a tossed salad.
—Emily Chaney, Blue Hill, ME

TAKES: 30 MIN. • **MAKES:** 8 SERVINGS

- **1 salmon fillet (2 lbs.)**
- **2 Tbsp. butter, softened**
- **¼ cup white wine or chicken broth**
- **2 Tbsp. lemon juice**
- **½ tsp. pepper**
- **½ tsp. dried tarragon**

1. Pat salmon dry. Place in a greased 13x9-in. baking dish. Brush with butter. Combine remaining ingredients; pour over salmon.
2. Bake, uncovered, at 425° for 15-20 minutes or until fish flakes easily with a fork.
3 OZ. COOKED SALMON: 209 cal., 13g fat (4g sat. fat), 64mg chol., 78mg sod., 1g carb. (0 sugars, 0 fiber), 19g pro. **Diabetic exchanges:** 3 lean meat, 1 fat.

CHICKEN WITH PEACH-CUCUMBER SALSA

JANIE COLLE
Hutchinson, KS

WHOLE GRAIN CHOW MEIN

FAST FIX

WHOLE GRAIN CHOW MEIN

My kids are picky eaters, but a little sweet hoisin works wonders. They love this dish, and I love the healthy goodness of whole grain pasta. —*Kelly Shippey, Orange, CA*

TAKES: 30 MIN. • **MAKES:** 6 SERVINGS

- **6 oz. uncooked whole wheat spaghetti**
- **2 Tbsp. canola oil**
- **2 cups small fresh broccoli florets**
- **2 bunches baby bok choy, trimmed and cut into 1-in. pieces (about 2 cups)**
- **¾ cup fresh baby carrots, halved diagonally**
- **½ cup reduced-sodium chicken broth, divided**
- **3 Tbsp. reduced-sodium soy sauce, divided**
- **¼ tsp. pepper**
- **4 green onions, diagonally sliced**
- **12 oz. refrigerated fully cooked teriyaki and pineapple chicken meatballs or frozen fully cooked turkey meatballs, thawed**
- **2 Tbsp. hoisin sauce**
- **1 cup bean sprouts**
- **Additional sliced green onions**

1. Cook spaghetti according to package directions; drain.
2. In a large nonstick skillet, heat oil over medium-high heat. Add broccoli, bok choy and carrots; stir-fry 4 minutes. Stir in ¼ cup broth, 1 Tbsp. soy sauce and the pepper; reduce heat to medium. Cook, covered, 3-5 minutes or until vegetables are crisp-tender. Stir in green onions; remove from pan.
3. In same skillet, mix hoisin sauce and the remaining broth and soy sauce; add meatballs. Cook, covered, over medium-low heat 4-5 minutes or until heated through, stirring occasionally.
4. Add bean sprouts, spaghetti and broccoli mixture; heat through, tossing to combine. Top with additional green onions.
1⅓ CUPS: 304 cal., 14g fat (3g sat. fat), 54mg chol., 759mg sod., 31g carb. (4g sugars, 5g fiber), 18g pro.

FAST FIX

CREAMY RANCH MAC & CHEESE

I came up with the recipe for this creamy macaroni and cheese with a special ranch-flavored twist. Now it's one of my husband's favorites. —*Michelle Rotunno, Independence, MO*

TAKES: 30 MIN. • **MAKES:** 8 SERVINGS

- **1 pkg. (16 oz.) elbow macaroni**
- **1 cup 2% milk**
- **2 Tbsp. butter**
- **4½ tsp. ranch salad dressing mix**
- **1 tsp. garlic pepper blend**
- **1 tsp. lemon-pepper seasoning**
- **½ tsp. garlic powder**
- **1 cup shredded Monterey Jack cheese**
- **1 cup shredded Colby cheese**
- **1 cup reduced-fat sour cream**
- **½ cup crushed saltines**
- **⅓ cup grated Parmesan cheese**

1. Cook macaroni according to package directions. Meanwhile, in a Dutch oven, combine the milk, butter, dressing mix and seasonings; heat through. Stir in Monterey Jack and Colby cheeses until melted. Stir in sour cream.
2. Drain the macaroni; stir into the cheese sauce with the saltines. Sprinkle with Parmesan cheese.
1 CUP: 433 cal., 17g fat (10g sat. fat), 49mg chol., 766mg sod., 51g carb. (6g sugars, 2g fiber), 19g pro.

CREAMY RANCH MAC & CHEESE

EAT SMART FAST FIX

PINEAPPLE SHRIMP FRIED RICE

My husband often ordered pineapple fried rice at Thai restaurants, so I surprised him by tweaking some similar recipes to come up with a version that's simple and delicious. —Bonnie Brien, Pacific Grove, CA

TAKES: 30 MIN. • **MAKES:** 4 SERVINGS

- 2 **Tbsp. reduced-sodium soy sauce**
- 1 **tsp. curry powder**
- ½ **tsp. sugar**
- 2 **Tbsp. peanut or canola oil, divided**
- 1 **lb. uncooked shrimp (31-40 per lb.), peeled and deveined**
- 2 **tsp. minced fresh gingerroot**
- 1 **garlic clove, minced**
- 1 **medium sweet red pepper, chopped**
- 1 **medium carrot, finely chopped**
- ½ **cup chopped onion**
- 1 **can (20 oz.) unsweetened pineapple tidbits, drained**
- 2 **cups cooked rice, room temperature**
- 6 **green onions, chopped**
- ½ **cup finely chopped salted peanuts**
- **Lime wedges**

1. Mix soy sauce, curry powder and sugar. In a large skillet, heat 1 Tbsp. oil over medium-high heat; stir-fry shrimp until it turns pink, 2-3 minutes. Remove from pan.

2. In same pan, heat the remaining oil over medium-high heat. Add ginger and garlic; cook just until fragrant, about 10 seconds. Add pepper, carrot and onion; stir-fry for 2 minutes. Stir in the pineapple and shrimp. Add rice and the soy sauce mixture; heat through over medium heat, tossing to combine and break up any clumps of rice. Stir in green onions. Sprinkle with peanuts; serve with lime wedges.

1½ CUPS: 491 cal., 18g fat (3g sat. fat), 138mg chol., 513mg sod., 54g carb. (22g sugars, 5g fiber), 28g pro.

PINEAPPLE SHRIMP FRIED RICE

★★★★★ **READER REVIEW**

"This was great! I halved the recipe for the two of us, except for using the full amount of the soy-curry-sugar mixture. I microwaved the jasmine rice and added a bit of hot chili sesame oil to it in place of butter. We will be having this dish again before very long."

BROWNS19FAN
TASTEOFHOME.COM

CHORIZO SPAGHETTI SQUASH SKILLET

EAT SMART FAST FIX

CHORIZO SPAGHETTI SQUASH SKILLET

Get your noodle fix minus the pasta with this spicy one-dish meal. It's a fill-you-up dinner that's low in calories—a weeknight winner!
—Sherrill Oake, Springfield, MA

TAKES: 30 MIN. • **MAKES:** 4 SERVINGS

- **1 small spaghetti squash (about 2 lbs.)**
- **1 Tbsp. canola oil**
- **1 pkg. (12 oz.) fully cooked chorizo chicken sausage links or flavor of choice, sliced**
- **1 medium sweet yellow pepper, chopped**
- **1 medium sweet onion, halved and sliced**
- **1 cup sliced fresh mushrooms**
- **1 can (14½ oz.) no-salt-added diced tomatoes, undrained**
- **1 Tbsp. reduced-sodium taco seasoning**
- **¼ tsp. pepper**
- **Chopped green onions, optional**

1. Halve squash lengthwise; discard seeds. Place the squash halves on a microwave-safe plate, cut side down; microwave on high until tender, about 15 minutes. Cool slightly.
2. Meanwhile, in a large skillet, heat 1 Tbsp. oil over medium-high heat; saute sausage, yellow pepper, onion and mushrooms until onion is tender, about 5 minutes.
3. Separate the strands of squash with a fork; add to skillet. Stir in tomatoes and seasonings; bring to a boil. Reduce heat; simmer, uncovered, until flavors are blended, about 5 minutes. If desired, top with green onions.
1½ CUPS: 299 cal., 12g fat (3g sat. fat), 65mg chol., 725mg sod., 34g carb. (12g sugars, 6g fiber), 18g pro. **Diabetic exchanges:** 2 starch, 2 lean meat, 1 vegetable, 1 fat.

FAST FIX

CHICKEN FLORENTINE PIZZA

On pizza night, we like to switch things up with this chicken and spinach version. One taste of the ricotta cheese base and you won't miss traditional sauce one bit. For a fun appetizer, cut the baked pizza into bite-sized pieces. Feel free to add a few of your favorite toppings; fresh tomatoes are great on this!
—Pam Corder, Monroe, LA

TAKES: 25 MIN. • **MAKES:** 8 SERVINGS

- **1 tsp. Italian seasoning**
- **½ tsp. garlic powder**
- **3 cups cooked chicken breasts (about 1 lb.), cubed**
- **1 cup ricotta cheese**
- **1 prebaked 12-in. pizza crust**
- **1 pkg. (10 oz.) frozen chopped spinach, thawed and squeezed dry**
- **2 Tbsp. oil-packed sun-dried tomatoes, drained and chopped**
- **½ cup whole milk mozzarella cheese, shredded**
- **¼ cup grated Parmesan cheese**

Preheat oven to 425°. Stir together Italian seasoning and garlic powder; toss with chicken. Spread ricotta cheese on pizza crust. Top with chicken, spinach and tomatoes. Sprinkle with mozzarella and Parmesan cheese. Bake until crust is golden and cheese is melted, 10-15 minutes.
1 SLICE: 311 cal., 11g fat (5g sat. fat), 65mg chol., 423mg sod., 26g carb. (3g sugars, 2g fiber), 28g pro.

FAST FIX

SUPER EASY SPAGHETTI SAUCE

At my house, we never know how many we'll have for dinner. That's why this spaghetti sauce is one of my favorites—it's flavorful, filling and fast. Italian sausage gives it depth, and salsa adds the kick.
—Bella Anderson, Chester, SC

TAKES: 30 MIN. • **MAKES:** 2½ QT.

- **1 lb. ground beef**
- **1 lb. Italian sausage links, cut into ¼-in. slices**
- **2 jars (24 oz. each) spaghetti sauce with mushrooms**
- **1 jar (16 oz.) chunky salsa**
- **Hot cooked pasta**
- **Shredded or shaved Parmesan cheese, optional**

1. In a Dutch oven, cook beef over medium heat until no longer pink; drain and set aside. In the same pan, cook sausage over medium heat until browned and no longer pink.
2. Stir in spaghetti sauce, salsa and beef; heat through. Serve with pasta; if desired, sprinkle with cheese.
1 CUP: 284 cal., 16g fat (5g sat. fat), 53mg chol., 874mg sod., 19g carb. (12g sugars, 2g fiber), 15g pro.

CHICKEN FLORENTINE PIZZA

COD & ASPARAGUS BAKE

EAT SMART FAST FIX

SALMON WITH HORSERADISH PISTACHIO CRUST

Impress everyone at your table with this elegant but easy salmon dish that's delicious and nutritious. You can substitute scallions for the shallots if you like.
—Linda Press Wolfe, Cross River, NY

TAKES: 30 MIN. • **MAKES:** 6 SERVINGS

- **6 salmon fillets (4 oz. each)**
- **⅓ cup sour cream**
- **⅔ cup dry bread crumbs**
- **⅔ cup chopped pistachios**
- **½ cup minced shallots**
- **2 Tbsp. olive oil**
- **1 to 2 Tbsp. prepared horseradish**
- **1 Tbsp. snipped fresh dill or 1 tsp. dill weed**
- **½ tsp. grated lemon or orange zest**
- **¼ tsp. crushed red pepper flakes**
- **1 garlic clove, minced**

Preheat oven to 350°. Place salmon, skin side down, in an ungreased 15x10x1-in. baking pan. Spread sour cream over each fillet. Combine the remaining ingredients. Pat the crumb-nut mixture onto tops of salmon fillets, pressing to help coating adhere. Bake until fish just begins to flake easily with a fork, 12-15 minutes.

1 SALMON FILLET: 376 cal., 25g fat (5g sat. fat), 60mg chol., 219mg sod., 15g carb. (3g sugars, 2g fiber), 24g pro. **Diabetic exchanges:** 3 lean meat, 2 fat.

TEST KITCHEN TIP

You can substitue any nuts for the pistachios in this recipe. Some of our favorites are almonds and pecans. This nutty coating also adds a nice crunch to chicken and pork.

EAT SMART 5 INGREDIENTS FAST FIX

COD & ASPARAGUS BAKE

This one-dish meal is so flavorful and healthy! The fresh taste of lemon holds it all together. You can also use grated Parmesan cheese if you prefer.
—Thomas Faglon, Somerset, NJ

TAKES: 30 MIN. • **MAKES:** 4 SERVINGS

- **4 cod fillets (4 oz. each)**
- **1 lb. fresh thin asparagus, trimmed**
- **1 pint cherry tomatoes, halved**
- **2 Tbsp. lemon juice**
- **1½ tsp. grated lemon zest**
- **¼ cup grated Romano cheese**

1. Preheat oven to 375°. Place cod and asparagus on a 15x10x1-in. baking sheet brushed with oil. Add tomatoes, cut side down. Brush fish with lemon juice; sprinkle with lemon zest. Sprinkle the fish and vegetables with Romano cheese. Bake until fish just begins to flake easily with a fork, about 12 minutes.

2. Remove pan from oven; preheat the broiler. Broil cod mixture 3-4 in. from heat until vegetables are lightly browned, 2-3 minutes.

1 SERVING: 141 cal., 3g fat (2g sat. fat), 45mg chol., 184mg sod., 6g carb. (3g sugars, 2g fiber), 23g pro. **Diabetic exchanges:** 3 lean meat, 1 vegetable.

PEANUTTY ASIAN LETTUCE WRAPS

FAST FIX

PEANUTTY ASIAN LETTUCE WRAPS

This recipe packs so much flavor into a beautiful, healthy presentation. I usually serve it with a little extra hoisin sauce on the side.
—Mandy Rivers, Lexington, SC

TAKES: 30 MIN. • **MAKES:** 6 SERVINGS

- **⅓ cup reduced-sodium teriyaki sauce**
- **¼ cup hoisin sauce**
- **3 Tbsp. creamy peanut butter**
- **1 Tbsp. rice vinegar**
- **1 Tbsp. sesame oil**
- **1½ lbs. lean ground turkey**
- **½ cup shredded carrot**
- **2 Tbsp. minced fresh gingerroot**
- **4 garlic cloves, minced**
- **1 can (8 oz.) whole water chestnuts, drained and chopped**
- **½ cup chopped fresh snow peas**
- **4 green onions, chopped**
- **12 Bibb lettuce leaves**
- **Additional hoisin sauce, optional**

1. Whisk together the first five ingredients until smooth. In a large skillet, cook and crumble turkey with carrot over medium-high heat until no longer pink, 6-8 minutes; drain. Add ginger and garlic; cook and stir for 1 minute. Stir in sauce mixture, water chestnuts, snow peas and green onions; heat through.
2. Serve in lettuce leaves. If desired, drizzle wraps with additional hoisin sauce.
2 WRAPS: 313 cal., 16g fat (4g sat. fat), 90mg chol., 613mg sod., 18g carb. (9g sugars, 3g fiber), 24g pro. **Diabetic exchanges:** 3 lean meat, 2 vegetable, 2 fat, ½ starch.

EAT SMART FAST FIX

ARTICHOKE CHICKEN PASTA

Here's a colorful, delicious chicken dish that's easy enough for weeknights but special enough for guests. Oregano, garlic and a light wine sauce add lovely flavor.
—Cathy Dick, Roanoke, VA

TAKES: 30 MIN. • **MAKES:** 4 SERVINGS

- **6 oz. uncooked fettuccine**
- **2 tsp. all-purpose flour**
- **⅓ cup dry white wine or broth**
- **¼ cup reduced-sodium chicken broth**
- **3 tsp. olive oil, divided**
- **1 lb. boneless skinless chicken breasts, cut into thin strips**
- **½ cup fresh broccoli florets**
- **½ cup sliced fresh mushrooms**
- **½ cup cherry tomatoes, halved**
- **2 garlic cloves, minced**
- **1 can (14 oz.) water-packed artichoke hearts, drained and halved**
- **½ tsp. salt**
- **½ tsp. dried oregano**
- **1 Tbsp. minced fresh parsley**
- **1 Tbsp. shredded Parmesan cheese**

1. Cook fettuccine according to package directions; drain.
2. Meanwhile, in a small bowl, mix flour, wine and broth until smooth. In a large nonstick skillet coated with cooking spray, heat 2 tsp. oil over medium heat. Add chicken; cook and stir 2-4 minutes or until no longer pink. Remove from pan.
3. In the same skillet, heat the remaining oil over medium-high heat. Add broccoli; cook and stir 2 minutes. Add mushrooms, tomatoes and garlic; cook and stir 2 minutes longer. Stir in artichoke hearts, salt, oregano and flour mixture. Bring to a boil; cook and stir for 1-2 minutes or until thickened.
4. Add fettuccine, chicken and parsley; heat through, tossing to combine. Sprinkle with cheese.
2 CUPS: 378 cal., 8g fat (2g sat. fat), 64mg chol., 668mg sod., 41g carb. (2g sugars, 2g fiber), 33g pro. **Diabetic exchanges:** 3 lean meat, 2 starch, 2 vegetable, 1 fat.

ARTICHOKE CHICKEN PASTA

FAST FIX

LEMONY GREEK BEEF & VEGETABLES

I love the lemon in this recipe, which is the latest addition to my collection of quick, healthy dinners. I'm sensitive to cow's milk, so I use goat cheese crumbles on my portion instead of the Parmesan.
—Alice Neff, Lake Worth, FL

TAKES: 30 MIN. • **MAKES:** 4 SERVINGS

- **1 bunch baby bok choy**
- **2 Tbsp. olive oil, divided**
- **1 lb. ground beef**
- **5 medium carrots, sliced**
- **3 garlic cloves, minced**
- **¼ cup plus 2 Tbsp. white wine, divided**
- **1 can (15 to 16 oz.) navy beans, rinsed and drained**
- **2 Tbsp. minced fresh oregano or 2 tsp. dried**
- **¼ tsp. salt**
- **2 Tbsp. lemon juice**
- **½ cup shredded Parmesan cheese**

1. Trim and discard the root end of the bok choy. Coarsely chop leaves. Cut stalks into 1-in. pieces. Set aside.
2. In a large skillet, heat 1 Tbsp. olive oil over medium-high heat. Add ground beef; cook, crumbling meat, until no longer pink, 5-7 minutes; drain. Remove from skillet and set aside.
3. In same skillet, heat the remaining oil. Add carrots and the bok choy stalks; cook and stir until crisp-tender, 5-7 minutes. Stir in garlic, bok choy leaves and ¼ cup wine; increase heat to medium-high. Cook, stirring to loosen browned bits from pan, until the greens wilt, 3-5 minutes.
4. Stir in ground beef, beans, oregano, salt and enough of the remaining wine to keep mixture moist. Reduce heat; simmer about 3 minutes. Stir in lemon juice; sprinkle with Parmesan cheese.
1½ CUPS: 503 cal., 24g fat (8g sat. fat), 77mg chol., 856mg sod., 36g carb. (7g sugars, 10g fiber), 36g pro.

LEMONY GREEK BEEF & VEGETABLES

APPLE & SWEET POTATO QUINOA

EAT SMART FAST FIX

APPLE & SWEET POTATO QUINOA

When feeding three hungry boys, I rely on quick, filling and tasty meals. My boys aren't usually big quinoa fans, but the sweet potatoes and apples in this dish won them over.
—Cheryl Beadle, Plymouth, MI

TAKES: 30 MIN. • **MAKES:** 6 SERVINGS

- **2¼ cups chicken or vegetable stock**
- **1 cup quinoa, rinsed**
- **2 Tbsp. canola oil**
- **2 lbs. sweet potatoes (about 3 medium), peeled and cut into ½-in. pieces**
- **2 shallots, finely chopped**
- **3 medium Gala or Honeycrisp apples, cut into ¼-in. slices**
- **½ cup white wine or additional stock**
- **½ tsp. salt**
- **1 can (15 oz.) black beans, rinsed and drained**

1. In a large saucepan, combine stock and quinoa; bring to a boil. Reduce heat; simmer, covered, 15-20 minutes or until liquid is almost absorbed. Remove from heat.
2. Meanwhile, in a 6-qt. stockpot, heat oil over medium heat. Add sweet potatoes and shallots; cook and stir 5 minutes. Add apples; cook and stir 6-8 minutes longer until the potatoes and apples are tender.
3. Stir in wine and salt. Bring to a boil; cook, uncovered, until the wine has evaporated, about 1 minute. Stir in black beans and quinoa; heat through.
1⅓ CUPS: 423 cal., 7g fat (1g sat. fat), 0 chol., 541mg sod., 76g carb. (23g sugars, 10g fiber), 12g pro.

EAT SMART ⑤ INGREDIENTS FAST FIX

GINGER-GLAZED GRILLED SALMON

Our family loves this salmon, and it's a real treat to grill out on a warm summer evening. These fillets also may be baked at 450° for 18 minutes, basting occasionally.
—Wanda Toews, Cromer, MB

TAKES: 15 MIN. • **MAKES:** 4 SERVINGS

- 2 **Tbsp. reduced-sodium soy sauce**
- 2 **Tbsp. maple syrup**
- 2 **tsp. minced fresh gingerroot**
- 2 **garlic cloves, minced**
- 4 **salmon fillets (6 oz. each)**

1. For glaze, mix first four ingredients.
2. Place salmon on an oiled grill rack over medium heat, skin side up. Grill, covered, until fish just begins to flake easily with a fork, 4-5 minutes per side; brush top with half of the glaze after turning. Brush with the remaining glaze before serving.
1 FILLET: 299 cal., 16g fat (3g sat. fat), 85mg chol., 374mg sod., 8g carb. (6g sugars, 0 fiber), 29g pro. **Diabetic exchanges:** 4 lean meat, ½ starch.

GINGER-GLAZED GRILLED SALMON

PEAR & FENNEL PORK

PEAR & FENNEL PORK

Fresh fennel has a large bulbous base and pale green stems with wispy foliage. Often mislabeled as sweet anise, it has a sweeter and more delicate flavor than anise.
—Taste of Home Test Kitchen

TAKES: 25 MIN. • **MAKES:** 4 SERVINGS

- 4 **boneless butterflied pork chops (½ in. thick and 6 oz. each)**
- ½ **tsp. salt**
- ¼ **tsp. pepper**
- 1 **Tbsp. olive oil**
- 1 **cup sliced onion**
- 1 **cup sliced fennel bulb**
- 1 **Tbsp. butter**
- 2 **Tbsp. cornstarch**
- 2 **cups pear nectar**
- 3 **Tbsp. maple syrup**
- ½ **to 1 tsp. ground nutmeg**

1. Sprinkle pork chops with salt and pepper. In a large skillet, cook the chops in oil over medium-high heat until juices run clear, 4-5 minutes on each side; drain. Set chops aside and keep warm.
2. In the same skillet, saute the onion and fennel in butter until crisp-tender. In a small bowl, combine the cornstarch, pear nectar, syrup and nutmeg until smooth; add to the skillet. Bring to a boil; cook and stir until thickened, about 2 minutes. Serve over pork chops.
1 SERVING: 431 cal., 16g fat (6g sat. fat), 90mg chol., 390mg sod., 38g carb. (30g sugars, 2g fiber), 33g pro.

FAST FIX

POTATO KIELBASA SKILLET

Smoky kielbasa steals the show in this hearty home-style meal. It's especially soothing on those cold late fall and early winter nights.
—Taste of Home *Test Kitchen*

TAKES: 30 MIN. • **MAKES:** 4 SERVINGS

- **1 lb. red potatoes (3-4 medium), cut into 1-in. pieces**
- **3 Tbsp. water**
- **2 Tbsp. brown sugar**
- **2 Tbsp. cider vinegar**
- **1 Tbsp. Dijon mustard**
- **1½ tsp. minced fresh thyme or ½ tsp. dried thyme**
- **¼ tsp. pepper**
- **1 Tbsp. olive oil**
- **½ cup chopped onion**
- **¾ lb. smoked kielbasa or Polish sausage, cut into ¼-in. slices**
- **4 cups fresh baby spinach**
- **5 bacon strips, cooked and crumbled**

1. Place potatoes and water in a microwave-safe dish. Microwave, covered, on high until the potatoes are tender, 3-4 minutes; drain.
2. Meanwhile, mix brown sugar, vinegar, mustard, thyme and pepper. In a large skillet, heat oil over medium-high heat; saute onion and kielbasa until the onion is tender.
3. Add potatoes; cook and stir until lightly browned, 3-5 minutes. Stir in brown sugar mixture; bring to a boil. Reduce heat; simmer, uncovered, 2 minutes, stirring occasionally. Stir in spinach until wilted. Stir in bacon.
1½ CUPS: 472 cal., 31g fat (10g sat. fat), 66mg chol., 873mg sod., 31g carb. (10g sugars, 3g fiber), 17g pro.

FAST FIX

HONEY WALLEYE

Our state is known as the Land of 10,000 Lakes, so fishing is a favorite recreational activity here. This recipe is a quick way to prepare all the fresh walleye hooked by the anglers in our family!
—Kitty McCue, St. Louis Park, MN

TAKES: 20 MIN. • **MAKES:** 6 SERVINGS

- **1 large egg**
- **2 tsp. honey**
- **2 cups crushed Ritz crackers (about 45 to 50)**
- **½ tsp. salt**
- **1½ lbs. walleye fillets**
- **⅓ to ½ cup canola oil**
- **Lemon wedge and minced fresh parsley, optional**

1. In a shallow bowl, beat egg; add honey. In a plastic bag, combine crackers and salt. Dip fish in egg mixture, then shake in bag until coated.
2. Heat oil in a large skillet over medium heat. Cook fillets for 3-5 minutes per side or until golden and fish flakes easily with a fork. Top with parsley and serve with lemon wedges if desired.
3 OZ. COOKED FISH: 389 cal., 22g fat (3g sat. fat), 133mg chol., 514mg sod., 23g carb. (5g sugars, 1g fiber), 25g pro.

CURRIED CHICKEN SKILLET

EAT SMART FAST FIX

CURRIED CHICKEN SKILLET

This protein-packed skillet dish is loaded with bright flavor. A little curry and fresh ginger make the veggies, chicken and quinoa pop.
—Ruth Hartunian-Alumbaugh, Willimantic, CT

TAKES: 30 MIN. • **MAKES:** 4 SERVINGS

- **1⅓ cups plus ½ cup reduced-sodium chicken broth**
- **⅔ cup quinoa, rinsed**
- **1 Tbsp. canola oil**
- **1 medium sweet potato, diced**
- **1 medium onion, chopped**
- **1 celery rib, chopped**
- **1 cup frozen peas**
- **2 garlic cloves, minced**
- **1 tsp. minced fresh gingerroot**
- **3 tsp. curry powder**
- **¼ tsp. salt**
- **2 cups shredded cooked chicken**

1. In a small saucepan, bring 1⅓ cups broth to a boil. Add quinoa. Reduce heat; simmer, covered, until the liquid is absorbed, 12-15 minutes.

2. In a large skillet, heat oil over medium-high heat; saute sweet potato, onion and celery until potato is tender, 10-12 minutes. Add peas, garlic, ginger and seasonings; cook and stir 2 minutes. Stir in chicken and remaining broth; heat through. Stir in quinoa.

2 CUPS: 367 cal., 11g fat (2g sat. fat), 62mg chol., 450mg sod., 39g carb. (8g sugars, 6g fiber), 29g pro. **Diabetic exchanges:** 3 lean meat, 2½ starch, ½ fat.

FAST FIX

MEATBALL PIZZA

I always keep meatballs and pizza crusts in the freezer to make this specialty on the spur of the moment. Add a tossed salad, and you have a delicious dinner.
—Mary Humeniuk-Smith, Perry Hall, MD

TAKES: 25 MIN. • **MAKES:** 8 SLICES

- **1 prebaked 12-in. pizza crust**
- **1 can (8 oz.) pizza sauce**
- **1 tsp. garlic powder**
- **1 tsp. Italian seasoning**
- **¼ cup grated Parmesan cheese**
- **1 small onion, halved and sliced**
- **12 frozen fully cooked Italian meatballs (½ oz. each), thawed and halved**
- **1 cup shredded part-skim mozzarella cheese**
- **1 cup shredded cheddar cheese**

1. Preheat oven to 350°. Place crust on an ungreased 12-in. pizza pan or baking sheet.

2. Spread sauce over crust; sprinkle with garlic powder, Italian seasoning and Parmesan cheese. Top with onion and meatballs; sprinkle with remaining cheeses. Bake 12-17 minutes or until cheese is melted.

1 SLICE: 321 cal., 16g fat (8g sat. fat), 36mg chol., 755mg sod., 28g carb. (3g sugars, 2g fiber), 17g pro.

MEATBALL PIZZA

ROSEMARY-THYME LAMB CHOPS

(5) INGREDIENTS FAST FIX

ROSEMARY-THYME LAMB CHOPS

My father loves lamb, so I make this dish whenever he visits. It's the perfect main course for holidays or get-togethers.
—Kristina Mitchell, Clearwater, FL

TAKES: 30 MIN. • **MAKES:** 4 SERVINGS

- **8 lamb loin chops (3 oz. each)**
- **½ tsp. pepper**
- **¼ tsp. salt**
- **3 Tbsp. Dijon mustard**
- **1 Tbsp. minced fresh rosemary**
- **1 Tbsp. minced fresh thyme**
- **3 garlic cloves, minced**

1. Sprinkle lamb chops with pepper and salt. In a small bowl, mix mustard, rosemary, thyme and garlic.
2. Grill chops, covered, on an oiled rack over medium heat for 6 minutes. Turn; spread herb mixture over chops. Grill 6-8 minutes longer or until the meat reaches desired doneness (for medium-rare, a thermometer should read 135°; medium, 140°; medium-well, 145°).
2 LAMB CHOPS: 231 cal., 9g fat (4g sat. fat), 97mg chol., 493mg sod., 3g carb. (0 sugars, 0 fiber), 32g pro. **Diabetic exchanges:** 4 lean meat.

EAT SMART FAST FIX

CHICKEN WITH FIRE-ROASTED TOMATOES

My skillet chicken with the colors and flavors of Italy is so easy to make. The fire-roasted tomatoes sound complicated, but all you have to do is open a can!
—Margaret Wilson, San Bernardino, CA

TAKES: 30 MIN. • **MAKES:** 4 SERVINGS

- **2 Tbsp. salt-free garlic herb seasoning blend**
- **½ tsp. salt**
- **¼ tsp. Italian seasoning**
- **¼ tsp. pepper**
- **⅛ tsp. crushed red pepper flakes, optional**
- **4 boneless skinless chicken breast halves (6 oz. each)**
- **1 Tbsp. olive oil**
- **1 can (14½ oz.) fire-roasted diced tomatoes, undrained**
- **¾ lb. fresh green beans, trimmed**
- **2 Tbsp. water**
- **1 Tbsp. butter**
- **Hot cooked pasta, optional**

1. Mix seasoning ingredients; sprinkle over both sides of chicken breasts. In a large skillet, heat oil over medium heat. Brown chicken on both sides. Add tomatoes; bring to a boil. Reduce heat; simmer, covered, 10-12 minutes or until a thermometer inserted in chicken reads 165°.
2. Meanwhile, in a 2-qt. microwave-safe dish, combine green beans and water; microwave, covered, on high for 3-4 minutes or just until tender. Drain.
3. Remove chicken from skillet; keep warm. Stir butter and beans into tomato mixture. Serve with chicken and, if desired, pasta.
1 CHICKEN BREAST HALF WITH 1 CUP BEAN MIXTURE: 294 cal., 10g fat (3g sat. fat), 102mg chol., 681mg sod., 12g carb. (5g sugars, 4g fiber), 37g pro. **Diabetic exchanges:** 5 lean meat, 1 vegetable, 1 fat.

CHICKEN WITH FIRE-ROASTED TOMATOES

EAT SMART FAST FIX

BROCCOLI-PORK STIR-FRY WITH NOODLES

I combined several recipes to come up with this dish that my family loves. It is not only quick and delicious but healthy as well. I sometimes substitute boneless, skinless chicken breasts for the pork.
—Joan Hallford, North Richland Hills, TX

TAKES: 30 MIN. • **MAKES:** 4 SERVINGS

- **6 oz. uncooked whole wheat linguine**
- **2 Tbsp. cornstarch**
- **3 Tbsp. reduced-sodium soy sauce**
- **1½ cups reduced-sodium chicken broth**
- **3 green onions, chopped**
- **1½ tsp. canola oil**
- **1 pork tenderloin (1 lb.), cut into bite-sized pieces**
- **1 Tbsp. minced fresh gingerroot**
- **3 garlic cloves, minced**
- **1½ lbs. fresh broccoli florets (about 10 cups)**
- **1 Tbsp. sesame seeds, toasted**

1. Cook linguine according to package directions; drain and keep warm. Whisk cornstarch into soy sauce and broth until smooth; stir in green onions.
2. In a large nonstick skillet, heat oil over medium-high heat; stir-fry pork 3 minutes. Add ginger and garlic; cook and stir until the pork is browned, 2 minutes. Remove from pan.
3. Add the broth mixture to skillet; bring to a boil. Cook and stir until thickened, 1-2 minutes. Add broccoli; reduce heat. Simmer, covered, until the broccoli is crisp-tender, 5-8 minutes. Stir in the pork; heat through, 2-3 minutes.
4. Serve over linguine; sprinkle with sesame seeds.

1 SERVING: 376 cal., 8g fat (2g sat. fat), 64mg chol., 595mg sod., 47g carb. (4g sugars, 9g fiber), 35g pro. **Diabetic exchanges:** 3 lean meat, 2 starch, 2 vegetable, ½ fat.

TEST KITCHEN TIP

Try this as a cold noodle salad for lunch. Don't limit your veggie choices. Carrots, snap peas and sprouts would all be great in this!

JOAN HALLFORD
North Richland Hills, TX

BROCCOLI-PORK STIR-FRY WITH NOODLES

FAST FIX

TORTELLINI WITH TOMATO-CREAM SAUCE

Put frozen food and pantry staples to mouthwatering use in this warm and satisfying meatless meal.
—Barbra Stanger, West Jordan, UT

TAKES: 25 MIN. • **MAKES:** 6 SERVINGS

- **1 pkg. (16 oz.) frozen cheese tortellini**
- **1 small onion, chopped**
- **2 Tbsp. olive oil**
- **3 garlic cloves, minced**
- **1 can (14½ oz.) diced tomatoes, undrained**
- **1 pkg. (10 oz.) frozen chopped spinach, thawed and squeezed dry**
- **1½ tsp. dried basil**
- **1 tsp. salt**
- **½ tsp. pepper**
- **1½ cups heavy whipping cream**
- **½ cup grated Parmesan cheese**
- **Additional grated Parmesan cheese, optional**

1. Cook tortellini according to package directions. Meanwhile, in a large skillet, saute onion in oil until tender. Add garlic; cook 1 minute longer. Add the tomatoes, spinach, basil, salt and pepper. Cook and stir over medium heat until the liquid is absorbed, about 3 minutes.
2. Stir in cream and cheese. Bring to a boil. Reduce heat; simmer, uncovered, until thickened, 8-10 minutes.
3. Drain tortellini; toss with sauce. Sprinkle with additional cheese if desired.

1 CUP: 459 cal., 33g fat (18g sat. fat), 99mg chol., 835mg sod., 29g carb. (4g sugars, 4g fiber), 13g pro.

PEAR & POMEGRANATE
LAMB TAGINE, PAGE 80

MAIN DISHES

The memorable main dishes you'll find on these pages are ready to star at the dinner table. This chapter is brimming with dozens of mealtime choices for weekdays, holidays and every day in between.

SHEET-PAN CHIPOTLE LIME SHRIMP BAKE

SHEET-PAN CHIPOTLE LIME SHRIMP BAKE

I like to make this seafood dinner for company because it tastes amazing, yet it takes very little effort to throw together. Use asparagus, Broccolini or a mix of the two. It's all about what's available for a decent price.
—Colleen Delawder, Herndon, VA

PREP: 10 MIN. • **BAKE:** 40 MIN.
MAKES: 4 SERVINGS

- **1½ lbs. baby red potatoes, cut into ¾-in. cubes**
- **1 Tbsp. extra virgin olive oil**
- **¾ tsp. sea salt, divided**
- **3 medium limes**
- **¼ cup unsalted butter, melted**
- **1 tsp. ground chipotle pepper**
- **½ lb. fresh asparagus, trimmed**
- **½ lb. Broccolini or broccoli cut into small florets**
- **1 lb. uncooked shrimp (16-20 per lb.), peeled and deveined**
- **2 Tbsp. minced fresh cilantro**

1. Preheat oven to 400°. Place potatoes in a greased 15x10x1-in. sheet pan; drizzle with olive oil. Sprinkle with ¼ tsp. sea salt; stir to combine. Bake 30 minutes. Meanwhile, squeeze ⅓ cup juice from limes, reserving fruit. Combine lime juice, melted butter, chipotle and remaining sea salt.
2. Remove sheet pan from oven; stir potatoes. Arrange asparagus, Broccolini, shrimp and reserved limes on top of potatoes. Pour lime juice mixture over vegetables and shrimp.
3. Bake until shrimp turn pink and vegetables are tender, about 10 minutes. Sprinkle with minced cilantro.
1 SERVING: 394 cal., 17g fat (8g sat. fat), 168mg chol., 535mg sod., 41g carb. (4g sugars, 6g fiber), 25g pro.

EAT SMART SLOW COOKER

PEAR & POMEGRANATE LAMB TAGINE

(SHOWN ON PAGE 78)
Pomegranate, pear, and orange go so well together, I decided to use these ingredients to prepare a Middle Eastern-themed tagine with lamb. This dish is absolutely terrific over couscous, polenta, or cauliflower mashed with some feta cheese.
—Arlene Erlbach, Morton Grove, IL

PREP: 20 MIN. • **COOK:** 6 HOURS
MAKES: 4 SERVINGS

- **2½ lbs. lamb shanks**
- **2 large pears, finely chopped**
- **3 cups thinly sliced shallots**
- **½ cup orange juice, divided**
- **½ cup pomegranate juice, divided**
- **1 Tbsp. honey**
- **1½ tsp. ground cinnamon**
- **1 tsp. salt**
- **1 tsp. ground allspice**
- **1 tsp. ground cardamom**
- **¼ cup pomegranate seeds**
- **¼ cup minced fresh parsley**
- **Cooked couscous, optional**

1. Place lamb in a 5- or 6-qt. oval slow cooker. Add pears and shallots. Combine ¼ cup orange juice, ¼ cup pomegranate juice, honey and seasonings; pour over the shallots.
2. Cook, covered, on low for 6-8 hours or until meat is tender. Remove lamb to a rimmed serving platter; keep warm. Stir remaining orange and pomegranate juices into cooking liquid; pour over lamb. Sprinkle with pomegranate seeds and parsley. If desired, serve over couscous.
½ LAMB SHANK WITH 1 CUP VEGETABLES: 438 cal., 13g fat (5g sat. fat), 99mg chol., 680mg sod., 52g carb. (28g sugars, 5g fiber), 31g pro.

ZUCCHINI-CRUSTED PIZZA

EAT SMART

ZUCCHINI-CRUSTED PIZZA

It's flavorful, nutritious, easy to prep ahead and freeze, and fun to make with kids—and it quadruples nicely. What's not to like?
—Ruth Hartunian-Alumbaugh, Willimantic, CT

PREP: 20 MIN. • **BAKE:** 25 MIN.
MAKES: 6 SERVINGS

- **2 large eggs, lightly beaten**
- **2 cups shredded zucchini (about 1½ medium), squeezed dry**
- **½ cup shredded part-skim mozzarella cheese**
- **½ cup grated Parmesan cheese**
- **¼ cup all-purpose flour**
- **1 Tbsp. olive oil**
- **1 Tbsp. minced fresh basil**
- **1 tsp. minced fresh thyme**

TOPPINGS

- **1 jar (12 oz.) roasted sweet red peppers, julienned**
- **1 cup shredded part-skim mozzarella cheese**
- **½ cup sliced turkey pepperoni**

1. Preheat oven to 450°. Mix first eight ingredients; transfer to a 12-in. pizza pan coated generously with cooking spray. Spread mixture to an 11-in. circle.

2. Bake until light golden brown, 13-16 minutes. Reduce the oven setting to 400°. Add toppings. Bake until the cheese is melted, 10-12 minutes longer.

1 SLICE: 219 cal., 12g fat (5g sat. fat), 95mg chol., 680mg sod., 10g carb. (4g sugars, 1g fiber), 14g pro. **Diabetic exchanges:** 2 medium-fat meat, ½ starch, ½ fat.

SLOW COOKER

EASY SLOW-COOKER CHICKEN ROPA VIEJA

When discussing various methods of cooking ropas, a friend of mine told me her sister adds apple juice. I thought a Granny Smith apple might give it a tangy kick— and it does.
—Arlene Erlbach, Morton Grove, IL

PREP: 20 MIN. • **COOK:** 5 HOURS • **MAKES:** 6 SERVINGS

- **2 medium sweet red peppers, sliced**
- **1 medium Granny Smith apple, peeled chopped**
- **1 cup fresh cilantro leaves**
- **1 cup chunky salsa**
- **2 Tbsp. tomato paste**
- **1 garlic clove, minced**
- **1 tsp. ground cumin**
- **5 tsp. adobo seasoning, divided**
- **1½ lbs. boneless skinless chicken thighs**
- **3 to 6 tsp. lime juice**
- **¼ cup butter**
- **3 ripe plantains, peeled and thinly sliced into thin rounds**
- **Lime wedges and additional fresh cilantro leaves, optional**

1. Place the first seven ingredients and 1 tsp. adobo in a 5- or 6-qt. slow cooker. Rub the remaining adobo seasoning over chicken; add to slow cooker. Cook, covered, on low until chicken is tender, 5-6 hours. Using two forks, shred chicken. Stir in lime juice to taste; heat through.

2. Meanwhile, heat butter in a large skillet over medium heat. Cook plantains in batches until tender and golden brown, about 3 minutes each side. Drain on paper towels.

3. Serve chicken with a slotted spoon over plantains. If desired, serve with lime wedges and cilantro.

1 SERVING: 387 cal., 16g fat (7g sat. fat), 96mg chol., 1428mg sod., 39g carb. (20g sugars, 4g fiber), 23g pro.

EASY SLOW-COOKER CHICKEN ROPA VIEJA

CORNED BEEF HASH RUSTIC PIE

CORNED BEEF HASH RUSTIC PIE

This suppertime pie has all the yummies: homemade crust, seasoned potatoes, and lots and lots of corned beef and cheese. How could you not fall in love with it? I know we have.
—Colleen Delawder, Herndon, VA

PREP: 25 MIN. + CHILLING • **BAKE:** 55 MIN. • **MAKES:** 8 SERVINGS

- **1¾ cups all-purpose flour**
- **1 tsp. kosher salt**
- **1 tsp. sugar**
- **½ cup plus 2 Tbsp. cold unsalted butter, cubed**
- **2 to 4 Tbsp. cold lager beer or beef broth**

POTATOES

- **2 medium red potatoes, cut into ¼-in. cubes**
- **½ tsp. kosher salt**
- **3 green onions, chopped**
- **2 Tbsp. unsalted butter, cubed**
- **1 Tbsp. stone-ground Dijon mustard**
- **½ tsp. pepper**

RUSTIC PIE

- **½ lb. thinly sliced deli corned beef**
- **¼ lb. sliced provolone cheese**
- **1 Tbsp. cold whole milk or heavy whipping cream**

1. Whisk flour, salt and sugar; cut in butter until mixture resembles small peas. Gradually add beer, tossing with a fork until dough holds together when pressed. Shape into a disk; wrap and refrigerate 1 hour or overnight.

2. Meanwhile, place potatoes and salt in a small saucepan; add water to cover. Bring to a boil. Reduce heat; simmer, uncovered, until potatoes are crisp-tender, 6-8 minutes. Drain. Return to saucepan; add green onions, butter, mustard and pepper. Cook over medium heat, stirring frequently, until potatoes are tender and browned, 6-8 minutes. Remove from heat; cool.

3. Roll dough between two pieces of waxed paper to a ⅛-in.-thick, 12-in.-diameter circle. Remove top piece of waxed paper; place a 9-in. pie plate upside down over crust. Lifting with waxed paper, carefully invert crust into pan. Remove waxed paper. Trim to ½ in. beyond rim of plate; flute edge. Refrigerate 30 minutes.

4. Preheat oven to 400°. Prick bottom and sides of crust with a fork; line with a double thickness of foil. Fill with pie weights, dried beans or uncooked rice. Bake on a lower oven rack until edges are light golden brown, 15-20 minutes. Remove foil and weights; bake until bottom is golden brown, 3-6 minutes longer. Cool slightly.

5. To assemble the rustic pie, layer half the corned beef, half the cheese and three-fourths of potato mixture in baked crust. Repeat corned beef and cheese layers; sprinkle with remaining potato mixture. Reroll dough trimmings; use a heart-shaped cookie cutter to make shamrock petals and a knife to cut out a stem. Brush dough trimmings with milk. Bake until crust and cheese are golden brown, 35-40 minutes.

1 SLICE: 356 cal., 23g fat (14g sat. fat), 72mg chol., 827mg sod., 27g carb. (1g sugars, 1g fiber), 12g pro.

SHEET-PAN TILAPIA & VEGETABLE MEDLEY

Unlike some one-pan dinners that require some precooking in a skillet or pot, this one, with fish and spring veggies, uses just the sheet pan, period.
—Judy Batson, Tampa, FL

PREP: 15 MIN. • **BAKE:** 25 MIN.
MAKES: 2 SERVINGS

- **2 medium Yukon Gold potatoes, cut into wedges**
- **3 large fresh Brussels sprouts, thinly sliced**
- **3 large radishes, thinly sliced**
- **1 cup fresh sugar snap peas, cut into ½-in. pieces**
- **1 small carrot, thinly sliced**
- **2 Tbsp. butter, melted**
- **½ tsp. garlic salt**
- **½ tsp. pepper**
- **2 tilapia fillets (6 oz. each)**
- **2 tsp. minced fresh tarragon or ½ tsp. dried tarragon**
- **⅛ tsp. salt**
- **1 Tbsp. butter, softened**
- **Lemon wedges and tartar sauce, optional**

1. Preheat oven to 450°. Line a 15x10x1-in. sheet pan with foil; grease foil.

2. In a large bowl, combine the first five ingredients. Add melted butter, garlic salt and pepper; toss to coat. Place vegetables in a single layer in prepared pan; bake until potatoes are tender, about 20 minutes.

3. Remove from oven; preheat broiler. Arrange vegetables on one side of sheet pan. Add fish to other side. Sprinkle fillets with tarragon and salt; dot with softened butter. Broil 4-5 in. from heat until fish flakes easily with a fork, about 5 minutes. If desired, serve with lemon wedges and tartar sauce.

1 SERVING: 555 cal., 20g fat (12g sat. fat), 129mg chol., 892mg sod., 56g carb. (8g sugars, 8g fiber), 41g pro.

TEST KITCHEN TIP

Feel free to try any mild herb, such as dill, chervil or parsley, instead of tarragon.

SHEET-PAN TILAPIA & VEGETABLE MEDLEY

SHRIMP WITH WARM GERMAN-STYLE COLESLAW

EAT SMART FAST FIX

SHRIMP WITH WARM GERMAN-STYLE COLESLAW

We love anything that's tangy or bacony. With fennel and tarragon, this is a super savory dish. I use the medley from Minute Rice if I don't have time to make my own.
—Ann Sheehy, Lawrence, MA

TAKES: 30 MIN. • **MAKES:** 4 SERVINGS

- 6 **bacon strips**
- 2 **Tbsp. canola oil, divided**
- 3 **cups finely shredded green cabbage**
- ½ **cup finely shredded carrot (1 medium carrot)**
- 1 **cup finely shredded red cabbage, optional**
- ½ **cup finely shredded fennel bulb, optional**
- 6 **green onions, finely chopped**
- 3 **Tbsp. minced fresh parsley**
- 2 **Tbsp. minced fresh tarragon or 2 tsp. dried tarragon**
- ¼ **tsp. salt**
- ⅛ **tsp. pepper**
- ¼ **cup red wine vinegar**
- 1 **lb. uncooked shrimp (26-30 per lb.), peeled and deveined**
- 3 **cups hot cooked rice or multigrain medley**

1. In a large skillet, cook bacon over medium heat until crisp. Remove to paper towels to drain. Pour off drippings, discarding all but 2 Tbsp. Crumble bacon.
2. In same skillet, heat 1 Tbsp. drippings with 1 Tbsp. oil over medium heat. Add green cabbage and carrot and, if desired, red cabbage and fennel; cook and stir until vegetables are just tender, 1-2 minutes. Remove to a bowl. Stir in green onions, parsley, tarragon, salt and pepper; toss with vinegar. Keep warm.
3. Add remaining 1 Tbsp. drippings and remaining oil to skillet. Add shrimp; cook and stir over medium heat until the shrimp turn pink, 2-3 minutes. Remove from heat.
4. To serve, spoon rice and coleslaw into soup bowls. Top with shrimp; sprinkle with crumbled bacon.

1 SERVING: 472 cal., 20g fat (5g sat. fat), 156mg chol., 546mg sod., 44g carb. (2g sugars, 3g fiber), 28g pro.

SLOW COOKER

ZA'ATAR CHICKEN

It's hard to find a dinner that my husband and kids will both enjoy—and even harder to find one that's fast and easy. This is it! No matter how much I make of this dish, it's gone to the last bite.
—Esther Erani, Brooklyn, NY

PREP: 20 MIN. • **COOK:** 5 HOURS
MAKES: 6 SERVINGS

- ¼ **cup za'atar seasoning**
- ¼ **cup olive oil**
- 3 **tsp. dried oregano**
- 1 **tsp. salt**
- ½ **tsp. ground cumin**
- ½ **tsp. ground turmeric**
- 3 **lbs. bone-in chicken thighs**
- 1 **cup pimiento-stuffed olives**
- ½ **cup dried apricots**
- ½ **cup pitted dried plums**
- ¼ **cup water**
- **Hot cooked basmati rice, optional**

1. In a large bowl, combine the first six ingredients. Add chicken; toss to coat.
2. Arrange olives, apricots and plums on the bottom of a 4- or 5-qt. slow cooker. Top with chicken and water. Cook, covered, on low 5-6 hours or until chicken is tender. If desired, serve with rice.

1 SERVING: 484 cal., 32g fat (7g sat. fat), 107mg chol., 1367mg sod., 18g carb. (10g sugars, 2g fiber), 30g pro.

TEST KITCHEN TIP

Za'atar seasoning may become your new favorite spice. Add it to melted butter and toss with popcorn, mix it with olive oil for a dipping sauce or toss it with potatoes before roasting.

GARDEN-STUFFED ZUCCHINI BOATS

GARDEN-STUFFED ZUCCHINI BOATS

These boats are not only healthy, they're basically a one-dish meal that covers all the bases—just grab your favorite garden goodies and add any spices or mix-ins you like.
—Janie Zirbser, Mullica Hill, NJ

PREP: 40 MIN. + COOLING • **BAKE:** 25 MIN. • **MAKES:** 3 SERVINGS

3 medium zucchini
¾ lb. ground beef
¾ cup chopped onion
½ cup chopped green pepper
2 garlic cloves, minced
1½ cups water, divided
¾ cup fire-roasted diced tomatoes or chopped fresh tomatoes (with seeds and juices)
½ cup chopped roasted sweet red peppers, drained
⅓ cup chopped fresh mushrooms
¼ cup ditalini or other small pasta
2 tsp. minced fresh thyme or 1 tsp. dried thyme
½ tsp. minced fresh oregano or ¼ tsp. dried oregano
¼ tsp. salt
¼ tsp. pepper
¼ cup grated Parmesan cheese
1 cup shredded Italian cheese blend, divided
Pasta sauce, optional

1. Preheat oven to 350°. Halve zucchini lengthwise; place cut side down in an ungreased 13x9-in. baking dish. Bake 10 minutes. When cool enough to handle, scoop out seeds, leaving a ¼-in. shell.
2. Meanwhile, in a large skillet, cook beef, onion, green pepper and garlic over medium heat 8-10 minutes or until beef is no longer pink, breaking up beef into crumbles; drain. Stir in 1 cup water, tomatoes, red peppers, mushrooms, pasta, thyme, oregano, salt and pepper. Cook until mixture is thickened and pasta is al dente, 12-15 minutes. Stir in Parmesan cheese.
3. Spoon mixture into zucchini shells. Place in an ungreased 13x9-in. baking dish; sprinkle with ¾ cup Italian cheese blend. Pour remaining water into bottom of dish. Bake, covered, 20 minutes. Sprinkle with remaining cheese. Bake, uncovered, until zucchini is tender and cheese is melted, about 5 minutes longer. Serve with pasta sauce if desired.
2 STUFFED ZUCCHINI HALVES: 489 cal., 24g fat (12g sat. fat), 103mg chol., 992mg sod., 28g carb. (10g sugars, 4g fiber), 36g pro.

SANTA FE CHICKEN PIZZA PIE

Give your pie a Southwest twist when you slather on the taco sauce and top with black beans, green chilies and kicked-up chicken strips.
—Taste of Home *Test Kitchen*

PREP: 15 MIN. • **BAKE:** 25 MIN. • **MAKES:** 6 SERVINGS

1 tube (13.8 oz.) refrigerated pizza crust
1 bottle (16 oz.) taco sauce
1 can (15 oz.) black beans, rinsed and drained
1 large tomato, chopped
½ cup chopped green pepper
½ cup chopped red onion
1 can (4 oz.) chopped green chilies, drained
1 pkg. (6 oz.) ready-to-use southwestern chicken strips, chopped
1½ cups shredded Mexican cheese blend

1. Press pizza dough into a greased 15x10x1-in. baking pan, building up edges slightly. Prick dough thoroughly with a fork. Bake at 400° until lightly browned, 8-9 minutes.
2. Spread with taco sauce; top with beans, tomato, green pepper, onion, chilies and chicken. Sprinkle with cheese. Bake until crust is golden brown, 15-18 minutes.
1 SERVING: 434 cal., 12g fat (5g sat. fat), 44mg chol., 1218mg sod., 52g carb. (12g sugars, 5g fiber), 21g pro.

SANTA FE CHICKEN PIZZA PIE

PRIME TIME

For the holiday headliner, Kathryn Conrad of Wisconsin roasts prime rib low and slow and offers both gravy and a glorious glaze.

KATHRYN CONRAD
MILWAUKEE, WI

BEST EVER MUSTARD-CRUSTED PRIME RIB WITH MADEIRA GLAZE

EAT SMART (5) INGREDIENTS

BEST EVER APPLE GRAVY

You might want to make a double batch of this rich apple gravy. Yep, it's sensational with beef, but you've gotta try it on mashed potatoes, chops, roasted veggies—pretty much anything goes.
—Kathryn Conrad, Milwaukee, WI

PREP: 20 MIN. • **COOK:** 25 MIN.
MAKES: 1 CUP

- 1 **Tbsp. plus 2 tsp. butter, divided**
- 1 **large apple (Jonagold or Honeycrisp), peeled and chopped**
- ¼ **cup apple brandy**
- 1 **cup beef broth**
- ⅛ **tsp. salt**
- ¼ **tsp. coarsely ground pepper, optional**

1. In a small saucepan, heat 1 Tbsp. butter over medium heat. Add apple; saute until dark brown, adding 1 tsp. butter to prevent scorching. Remove from heat; add brandy. Cook over medium-high heat, stirring to loosen browned bits from pan.
2. Add broth and salt. Reduce heat; simmer 15 minutes. Using a blender or an immersion blender, puree apple mixture. Return to saucepan; simmer until liquid is reduced to 1 cup. Remove from the heat. Whisk in remaining butter. If desired, add pepper.
2 TBSP.: 36 cal., 2g fat (1g sat. fat), 5mg chol., 163mg sod., 3g carb. (2g sugars, 0 fiber), 0 pro.

BEST EVER MUSTARD-CRUSTED PRIME RIB WITH MADEIRA GLAZE

This juicy prime rib is spectacular on its own, but the rich Madeira glaze takes it up a notch to wow at special dinners. What's even better is that it roasts with a bed of tender veggies, so you have the whole holiday meal covered in one pan.
—Kathryn Conrad, Milwaukee, WI

PREP: 20 MIN.
BAKE: 2½ HOURS + STANDING
MAKES: 8 SERVINGS

- 1 **bone-in beef rib roast (about 5 lbs.)**
- ½ **cup stone-ground mustard**
- 6 **small garlic cloves, minced**
- 1 **Tbsp. brown sugar**
- ½ **tsp. salt**
- ½ **tsp. coarsely ground pink peppercorns, optional**

VEGETABLES

- 2 **lbs. medium Yukon Gold potatoes, cut into eighths (about 2-in. chunks)**
- 4 **medium carrots, halved lengthwise and cut into 2-in. pieces**
- 1 **medium red onion, cut into eighths (but with root end intact)**
- 1 **medium fennel bulb, cut into eighths**
- 3 **Tbsp. olive oil**
- 1 **Tbsp. balsamic vinegar**
- 1 **tsp. brown sugar**
- ¾ **tsp. salt**
- ½ **tsp. pepper**

MADEIRA GLAZE

- 1 **cup balsamic vinegar**
- ½ **cup Madeira wine**
- 1 **tsp. brown sugar**
- **Cracked pink peppercorns and fennel fronds, optional**

1. Let roast stand at room temperature for 1 hour. Preheat oven to 450°. Combine mustard, garlic, brown sugar, salt and, if desired, peppercorns; brush evenly over top and sides of roast but not over bones (mixture may seem loose but will adhere). Place bone side down on a rack in a shallow roasting pan. Place pan on middle oven rack; immediately reduce heat to 350°. Roast 1 hour.
2. Toss potatoes, carrots, onion and fennel with next five ingredients. Arrange the vegetables in a single layer in a 15x10x1-in. baking pan on lowest rack of oven. Roast meat and vegetables, stirring vegetables midway through baking, until meat reaches desired doneness (a thermometer should read 135° for medium-rare, 140° for medium and 145° for medium-well), about 1½ hours. Cover roast loosely with foil during the last 30 minutes to prevent overbrowning. Let stand 15 minutes before carving.
3. Meanwhile, for glaze, combine balsamic vinegar, Madeira wine and brown sugar in a small saucepan. Bring to a boil over medium-high heat; cook until reduced to ½ cup, about 15 minutes. Let glaze cool to room temperature. Serve roast with vegetables and glaze and, if desired, pink peppercorns and fennel fronds.
1 SERVING: 575 cal., 25g fat (8g sat. fat), 0 chol., 828mg sod., 44g carb. (18g sugars, 5g fiber), 42g pro.

SUCCESS TIPS

- Roast the prime rib fat side up. Gravity will help bathe the roast in flavorful juices as it cooks.
- No roasting rack? Coarsely chop all the vegetables and place the roast on top of them in the pan.
- Prime rib is actually a rib roast. Don't confuse "prime" for the grade of beef, which will likely be choice.

PASTA PIZZA

EAT SMART

PASTA PIZZA

My family often requests this meatless main dish, a tempting cross between pizza and spaghetti.
—Andrea Quick, Columbus, OH

PREP: 25 MIN. • **BAKE:** 10 MIN. • **MAKES:** 4 SERVINGS

- **8 oz. uncooked angel hair pasta**
- **4 tsp. olive oil, divided**
- **2 cups sliced fresh mushrooms**
- **½ cup chopped green pepper**
- **¼ cup chopped onion**
- **1 can (15 oz.) pizza sauce**
- **¼ cup sliced ripe olives**
- **½ cup shredded part-skim mozzarella cheese**
- **¼ tsp. Italian seasoning**

1. Preheat oven to 400°. Cook pasta according to the package directions; drain.
2. In a large ovenproof skillet, heat 1 tsp. oil over medium heat. Add mushrooms, green pepper and onion; saute until tender. Remove with a slotted spoon and keep warm. Increase heat to medium-high. In same skillet, heat remaining oil. Spread pasta evenly in skillet to form a crust. Cook until lightly browned, 5-7 minutes.
3. Turn crust onto a large plate. Reduce heat to medium; slide crust back into skillet. Top with pizza sauce, sauteed vegetables and olives; sprinkle with cheese and Italian seasoning. Bake until the cheese is melted, 10-12 minutes.
1 SERVING: 374 cal., 10g fat (3g sat. fat), 9mg chol., 532mg sod., 56g carb. (7g sugars, 5g fiber), 14g pro.

CHICKEN GARDEN MEDLEY

After my family sampled this dish at a friend's house, it quickly became a favorite—especially with our teenage daughters, who request it at least once a week!
—Dohreen Winkler, Howell, MI

PREP: 25 MIN. • **BAKE:** 20 MIN. • **MAKES:** 4 SERVINGS

- **1 lb. boneless skinless chicken breasts, cut into strips**
- **1 garlic clove, minced**
- **¼ cup butter, divided**
- **1 small yellow squash, halved lengthwise and sliced**
- **1 small zucchini, halved lengthwise and sliced**
- **½ cup julienned sweet red pepper**
- **½ cup julienned green pepper**
- **¼ cup thinly sliced onion**
- **2 Tbsp. all-purpose flour**
- **½ tsp. salt**
- **¼ tsp. pepper**
- **¾ cup chicken broth**
- **½ cup half-and-half cream**
- **8 oz. angel hair pasta, cooked and drained**
- **2 Tbsp. shredded Parmesan cheese**

1. In a large skillet, saute chicken and garlic in 2 Tbsp. butter for 10-12 minutes or until chicken juices run clear. Add vegetables. Cook until crisp-tender; remove from skillet and set aside.
2. In the same skillet, melt remaining butter. Add flour, salt and pepper; stir to form a smooth paste. Gradually add broth. Bring to a boil; cook and stir for 2 minutes or until thickened. Stir in cream and heat through. Add chicken and vegetables; stir until well mixed.
3. Place pasta in a greased 2-qt. baking dish. Pour chicken mixture over top. Sprinkle with Parmesan cheese. Cover and bake at 350° for 15 minutes; uncover and bake 5 minutes longer.
1½ cups: 404 cal., 19g fat (11g sat. fat), 111mg chol., 690mg sod., 26g carb. (4g sugars, 2g fiber), 30g pro.

CHICKEN GARDEN MEDLEY

(5) INGREDIENTS

MOM'S ROAST CHICKEN

This is the best way to cook a whole chicken. It roasts up juicy with crisp, golden skin. It's simply seasoned, yet packs so much flavor.
—James Schend, Pleasant Prairie, WI

PREP: 15 MIN. + CHILLING • **BAKE:** 35 MIN. + STANDING • **MAKES:** 6 SERVINGS

- **1 broiler/fryer chicken (4 to 5 lbs.)**
- **2 tsp. kosher salt**
- **1 tsp. coarsely ground pepper**
- **2 tsp. olive oil**
- **Minced fresh thyme or rosemary, optional**

1. Rub outside of chicken with salt and pepper. Transfer chicken to a rack in a rimmed baking sheet. Refrigerate, uncovered, overnight.
2. Preheat oven to 450°. Remove chicken from refrigerator while oven heats. Heat a 12-in. cast-iron or ovenproof skillet in the oven for 15 minutes.
3. Place chicken on a work surface, neck side down. Cut through skin where legs connect to body. Press thighs down so joints pop and legs lie flat.
4. Carefully place chicken, breast side up, into hot skillet; press legs down so they lie flat on bottom of pan. Brush with oil. Roast until a thermometer inserted in thickest part of thigh reads 170°-175°, 35-40 minutes. Remove chicken from oven; let stand for 10 minutes before carving. If desired, top with herbs before serving.
5 OZ. COOKED CHICKEN: 405 cal., 24g fat (6g sat. fat), 139mg chol., 760mg sod., 0 carb. (0 sugars, 0 fiber), 44g pro.

BEEF STEW SKILLET PIE

BEEF STEW SKILLET PIE

Puff pastry makes a pretty topping for this homey skillet potpie.
—Josh Rink, Milwaukee, WI

PREP: 1½ HOURS
BAKE: 30 MIN. + STANDING
MAKES: 6 SERVINGS

- **6 Tbsp. all-purpose flour, divided**
- **1½ tsp. salt**
- **½ tsp. pepper**
- **1 lb. boneless beef round steak, cut into 1-in. pieces**
- **2 Tbsp. canola oil**
- **1 large onion, chopped**
- **2 garlic cloves, minced**
- **¼ cup dry red wine**
- **2 cups beef broth, divided**
- **1 Tbsp. tomato paste**
- **½ tsp. Italian seasoning**
- **½ tsp. dried basil**
- **1 bay leaf**
- **2 medium potatoes, cubed**
- **3 large carrots, peeled and sliced**
- **½ cup frozen peas**
- **2 Tbsp. minced fresh parsley**
- **1 sheet frozen puff pastry, thawed**
- **1 large egg, beaten**

1. In a large resealable container, combine 3 Tbsp. flour, salt and pepper. Add beef in batches; shake to coat. Invert a 10-in. ovenproof skillet onto parchment paper; trace circle around pan ¼ in. larger than rim. Cut out circle and set aside. In same skillet, saute beef in oil until browned. Add onion and garlic; cook and stir until onion is tender. Add wine, stirring to loosen browned bits.
2. Combine 1½ cups broth, tomato paste, Italian seasoning and basil; stir into skillet. Add bay leaf. Bring to a boil. Reduce heat; cover and simmer until meat is tender, about 45 minutes. Add the potatoes and carrots; cook until vegetables are tender, 20-25 minutes longer.
3. Meanwhile, roll out puff pastry to fit skillet using parchment circle as guide; cut venting slits in pastry. Keep chilled until ready to use.
4. Combine remaining flour and broth until smooth; gradually stir into skillet. Bring to a boil; cook and stir for 2 minutes or until thickened and bubbly. Discard bay leaf. Stir in peas and parsley.
5. Brush beaten egg around edge of skillet to help pastry adhere; carefully place pastry over filling. Using a fork, press pastry firmly onto rim of pan; brush with egg. Bake pie at 425° until pastry is cooked through and dark golden brown, 30-35 minutes. Let stand for 10 minutes before serving.
1 SERVING: 473 cal., 19g fat (4g sat. fat), 73mg chol., 1088mg sod., 49g carb. (4g sugars, 6g fiber), 25g pro.

BISTRO CHICKEN FETTUCCINE

BISTRO CHICKEN FETTUCCINE

This is one of my go-to weeknight meals made from pantry ingredients. Every bite makes me think of France.
—Devon Delaney, Westport, CT

PREP: 20 MIN. • **COOK:** 15 MIN.
MAKES: 4 SERVINGS

- **½ lb. uncooked spinach fettuccine**
- **2 Tbsp. extra virgin olive oil, divided**
- **1 lb. boneless skinless chicken breasts, cut into ½-in. strips**
- **¼ tsp. salt**
- **¼ tsp. pepper**
- **2 plum tomatoes, chopped**
- **¼ lb. prosciutto, julienned**
- **1 shallot, minced (about 2 Tbsp.)**
- **2 Tbsp. finely chopped dried apricots**
- **⅛ tsp. crushed red pepper flakes**
- **¼ cup white wine or chicken broth**
- **1 Tbsp. Dijon mustard**
- **½ cup crumbled goat cheese**
- **¼ tsp. dried tarragon or ½ tsp. minced fresh tarragon**
- **¼ cup chopped walnuts, toasted**

1. Cook fettuccine according to package directions for al dente; drain, reserving ½ cup pasta water. Transfer to a serving platter; keep warm.
2. In a large skillet, heat 1 Tbsp. oil over medium heat. Sprinkle chicken with salt and pepper. Add to pan; cook and stir until no longer pink, 4-6 minutes. Remove chicken. Add remaining oil to skillet; stir in next five ingredients and saute 4-6 minutes. Return chicken to skillet.
3. Stir in wine and mustard. Bring to a boil; cook until the liquid is reduced slightly, 2-4 minutes. Pour chicken mixture over fettuccine; add cheese and tarragon. Toss to combine, adding enough reserved pasta water to moisten pasta. Top with toasted walnuts.

1½ CUPS: 561 cal., 22g fat (6g sat. fat), 116mg chol., 942mg sod., 45g carb. (4g sugars, 4g fiber), 42g pro.

MAMA'S PUERTO RICAN CHICKEN

My mom has a vast repertoire of recipes, and this extra-crispy, spiced-up chicken is the best one of the bunch. We love it served with a side of traditional red beans and rice.
—Edwin Robles Jr., Milwaukee, WI

PREP: 20 MIN. • **COOK:** 45 MIN.
MAKES: 8 SERVINGS

- **1 broiler/fryer chicken (about 4 lbs.), cut up**
- **1 tsp. ground cumin**
- **1 tsp. dried oregano**
- **1 tsp. garlic powder, divided**
- **1 tsp. salt, divided**
- **1 tsp. coarsely ground pepper, divided**
- **1 cup dry bread crumbs**
- **¾ cup all-purpose flour**
- **2 large eggs, beaten**
- **¼ cup canola oil**
- **¼ cup butter**

1. Preheat oven to 350°. Sprinkle chicken with cumin, oregano, ½ tsp. garlic powder, ½ tsp. salt and ½ tsp. pepper. In a shallow bowl, mix bread crumbs with remaining garlic powder, salt and pepper. Place flour and eggs in separate shallow bowls. Dip chicken pieces in flour to coat all sides; shake off excess. Dip in eggs, then in crumb mixture, patting to help coating adhere.
2. In a large skillet, heat oil over medium heat. Stir in butter. Add chicken in batches; cook until golden brown, 2-3 minutes per side. Place chicken on a rack in a shallow roasting pan. Bake, uncovered, until chicken is no longer pink, 30-35 minutes.

1 SERVING: 421 cal., 20g fat (6g sat. fat), 152mg chol., 507mg sod., 19g carb. (1g sugars, 1g fiber), 38g pro.

NEW ZEALAND ROSEMARY LAMB SHANKS

EAT SMART SLOW COOKER

NEW ZEALAND ROSEMARY LAMB SHANKS

When I was young, my family lived in New Zealand for two years. One item that was always available was lamb shanks. Mother cooked them all the time with root vegetables, and to this day I love lamb!
—Nancy Heishman, Las Vegas, NV

PREP: 25 MIN. • **COOK:** 6 HOURS • **MAKES:** 8 SERVINGS

- 1 **tsp. salt**
- ¾ **tsp. pepper**
- 4 **lamb shanks (about 20 oz. each)**
- 1 **Tbsp. butter**
- ½ **cup white wine**
- 3 **medium parsnips, peeled and cut into 1-in. chunks**
- 2 **large carrots, peeled and cut into 1-in. chunks**
- 2 **medium turnips, peeled and cut into 1-in. chunks**
- 2 **large tomatoes, chopped**
- 1 **large onion, chopped**
- 4 **garlic cloves, minced**
- 2 **cups beef broth**
- 1 **pkg. (10 oz.) frozen peas, thawed**
- ⅓ **cup chopped fresh parsley**
- 2 **Tbsp. minced fresh rosemary**

1. Rub salt and pepper over lamb. In a large skillet, heat butter over medium-high heat; brown meat. Transfer meat to a 6- or 7-qt. slow cooker. Add wine to skillet; cook and stir 1 minute to loosen brown bits. Pour over lamb. Add the parsnips, carrots, turnips, tomatoes, onion, garlic and broth. Cook, covered, on low until meat is tender, 6-8 hours.
2. Remove lamb; keep warm. Stir in peas, parsley and rosemary; heat through. Serve lamb with vegetables.
½ LAMB SHANK WITH 1 CUP VEGETABLES: 350 cal., 15g fat (6g sat. fat), 103mg chol., 668mg sod., 22g carb. (8g sugars, 6g fiber), 31g pro. **Diabetic exchanges:** 4 lean meat, 1 starch, 1 vegetable, ½ fat.

EAT SMART

PRESSURE-COOKER FABULOUS FAJITAS

When friends call to ask for new recipes to try, suggest these tasty fajitas. Top as you like to add healthy color and extra flavor.
—Taste of Home *Test Kitchen*

PREP: 20 MIN. • **COOK:** 25 MIN. + RELEASING
MAKES: 8 SERVINGS

- 1½ **lbs. beef top sirloin steak, cut into thin strips**
- 1½ **tsp. ground cumin**
- ½ **tsp. seasoned salt**
- ½ **tsp. chili powder**
- ¼ **to ½ tsp. crushed red pepper flakes**
- 2 **Tbsp. canola oil**
- 2 **Tbsp. lemon juice**
- 1 **garlic clove, minced**
- 1 **large sweet red pepper, thinly sliced**
- 1 **large onion, thinly sliced**
- 8 **flour tortillas (8 in.), warmed**
  Optional toppings: sliced avocado and jalapeno peppers, shredded cheddar cheese and chopped tomatoes

1. In a bowl, toss steak with cumin, salt, chili powder and red pepper flakes. On a 6-qt. electric pressure cooker, select saute setting and adjust for high heat. Heat oil; brown meat in batches and remove. Add lemon juice and garlic to cooker; stir to loosen browned bits. Return beef to cooker. Lock lid; make sure vent is closed. Select manual setting; adjust pressure to high, and set time for 20 minutes.
2. When finished cooking, allow pressure to naturally release for 10 minutes, then quick-release any remaining pressure according to the manufacturer's directions. Remove steak; keep warm.
3. Add red pepper and onion to cooker; lock lid. Select steam setting; cook for 5 minutes. When finished cooking, quick-release pressure according to manufacturer's directions. Serve vegetables and steak with tortillas and desired optional toppings.
1 FAJITA: 314 cal., 11g fat (2g sat. fat), 34mg chol., 374mg sod., 31g carb. (1g sugars, 2g fiber), 23g pro. **Diabetic exchanges:** 3 lean meat, 2 starch, 1 fat.

PRESSURE-COOKER FABULOUS FAJITAS

SLOW-COOKER CHICKEN TIKKA MASALA

SLOW COOKER

SLOW-COOKER CHICKEN TIKKA MASALA

Just a small dash of garam marsala adds lots of flavor. The bright red sauce coats the caramelized chicken beautifully.
—Anwar Khan, Irving, TX

PREP: 25 MIN. • **COOK:** 3 HOURS 10 MIN. • **MAKES:** 4 SERVINGS

- **1 can (15 oz.) tomato puree**
- **1 small onion, grated**
- **3 garlic cloves, minced**
- **2 Tbsp. tomato paste**
- **1 tsp. grated lemon peel**
- **1 Tbsp. lemon juice**
- **1 tsp. hot pepper sauce**
- **1 Tbsp. canola oil**
- **1 tsp. curry powder**
- **1 tsp. salt**
- **¼ tsp. pepper**
- **¼ tsp. garam masala**
- **4 bone-in chicken thighs**
- **3 Tbsp. plain Greek yogurt, plus more for topping**
- **1 Tbsp. unsalted butter, melted**
- **chopped cilantro, optional**
- **Grated lemon peel, optional**
- **Hot cooked rice**

1. Combine first 12 ingredients in a 3- or 4-qt. slow cooker. Add chicken thighs and stir gently to coat. Cook, covered, on low for 3-4 hours or until chicken is tender.
2. Preheat broiler. Using a slotted spoon, transfer chicken to a broiler-safe baking pan lined with foil. Broil 4-6 in. from heat for 3-4 minutes on each side or until lightly charred.
3. Meanwhile, transfer cooking juices from slow cooker to saucepan. Cook, uncovered, over medium-high heat until slightly thickened, 6-8 minutes. Remove from heat and gently stir in butter and yogurt. Serve chicken with sauce. If desired, garnish with chopped cilantro, lemon zest and additional yogurt. Serve with rice.
1 CHICKEN THIGH WITH SAUCE: 364 cal., 22g fat (7g sat. fat), 91mg chol., 705mg sod., 12g carb. (4g sugars, 3g fiber), 25g pro.

ARIZONA CHICKEN IN ACORN SQUASH

Give stuffed acorn squash a taste of the Southwest with this comforting recipe. We love the crunch of the toasted almonds, heat of the green chilies, and creamy texture of the avocado.
—Martha Sparlin, Albuquerque, NM

PREP: 50 MIN. • **BAKE:** 20 MIN. • **MAKES:** 6 SERVINGS

- **3 medium acorn squash**
- **6 tsp. butter**
- **2 cups cubed cooked chicken**
- **1¼ cups (5 oz.) shredded cheddar cheese**
- **1 can (4 oz.) chopped green chilies**
- **½ cup chopped celery**
- **½ cup sour cream**
- **⅓ cup chopped green onions**
- **1 can (2¼ oz.) sliced ripe olives, drained**
- **½ tsp. paprika**
- **¼ tsp. pepper**
- **1 medium ripe avocado, peeled and cut into 12 slices**
- **6 Tbsp. slivered almonds, toasted**

1. Preheat oven to 350°. Cut each squash crosswise in half; discard seeds. Cut a thin slice from bottom of each squash half to allow them to lie flat. Place on a 15x10-in. baking sheet, cut side up; fill each with 1 tsp. butter. Bake until fork-tender, 35-40 minutes.
2. In a large bowl, combine chicken, cheese, chilies, celery, sour cream, green onions, olives, paprika and pepper; spoon into squash.
3. Bake until filling is heated through and the squash is tender, 20-25 minutes. Top with avocado and nuts.
1 STUFFED SQUASH HALF: 492 cal., 28g fat (11g sat. fat), 80mg chol., 404mg sod., 43g carb. (9g sugars, 9g fiber), 25g pro.

ARIZONA CHICKEN IN ACORN SQUASH

SPICED GRILLED CHICKEN WITH CILANTRO LIME BUTTER

This grilled chicken gets a lovely pop of color and flavor from the lime butter—don't skip it!
—Diane Halferty, Corpus Christi, TX

PREP: 20 MIN. • **GRILL:** 35 MIN.
MAKES: 6 SERVINGS

- **1 Tbsp. chili powder**
- **1 Tbsp. brown sugar**
- **2 tsp. ground cinnamon**
- **1 tsp. baking cocoa**
- **½ tsp. salt**
- **½ tsp. pepper**
- **3 Tbsp. olive oil**
- **1 Tbsp. balsamic vinegar**
- **6 bone-in chicken breast halves (8 oz. each)**

CILANTRO LIME BUTTER

- **⅓ cup butter, melted**
- **¼ cup minced fresh cilantro**
- **2 Tbsp. finely chopped red onion**
- **1 Tbsp. lime juice**
- **1 serrano pepper, finely chopped**
- **⅛ tsp. pepper**

1. In a small bowl, combine the first eight ingredients. Brush over chicken.
2. Place chicken skin side down on grill rack. Grill, covered, over indirect medium heat for 15 minutes. Turn; grill 20-25 minutes longer or until a thermometer reads 165°.
3. Meanwhile, in a small bowl, combine the butter ingredients. Drizzle over chicken before serving.
NOTE: Wear disposable gloves when cutting hot peppers; the oils can burn skin. Avoid touching your face.
1 CHICKEN BREAST HALF WITH 1 TBSP. LIME BUTTER: 430 cal., 27g fat (10g sat. fat), 138mg chol., 411mg sod., 5g carb. (3g sugars, 1g fiber), 40g pro.

SPICED GRILLED CHICKEN WITH CILANTRO LIME BUTTER

SLOW COOKER

SLOW-COOKER CARIBBEAN MOO SHU CHICKEN

A tropical twist on a takeout favorite, this slow-cooker creation is simple, satisfying and destined to become a new family favorite!
—Shannon Kohn, Simpsonville, SC

PREP: 10 MIN. • **COOK:** 3 HOURS
MAKES: 8 SERVINGS

- **6 boneless skinless chicken breast halves (about 6 oz. each)**
- **1½ cups chopped onions (about 2 medium)**
- **1 cup chopped sweet red pepper**
- **⅔ cup chopped dried pineapple**
- **½ cup chopped dried mango**
- **1 can (14½ oz.) fire-roasted diced tomatoes, drained**
- **⅔ cup hoisin sauce**
- **3 Tbsp. hot pepper sauce**
- **16 flour tortillas (6 in.), warmed**
- **4 cups coleslaw mix**
- **½ cup chopped dry roasted peanuts**

1. In a 4- or 5-qt. slow cooker, combine first five ingredients. In a small bowl, stir together tomatoes, hoisin sauce and hot pepper sauce. Pour tomato mixture over chicken mixture. Cook, covered, on low until chicken is tender, 3-4 hours. Remove meat. When cool enough to handle, shred with two forks; return to slow cooker. Heat through.
2. To serve, divide mixture evenly among tortillas. Top with coleslaw and peanuts.
2 FILLED TORTILLAS: 552 cal., 15g fat (4g sat. fat), 71mg chol., 1122mg sod., 66g carb. (24g sugars, 7g fiber), 35g pro.

TEST KITCHEN TIP

An equal amount of dried apricots may be substituted for either the dried pineapple or the mango.

BAKED TERIYAKI PORK & VEGGIES

SLOW COOKER

GERMAN SCHNITZEL & POTATOES WITH GORGONZOLA CREAM

I lived in Germany for five years and ate a lot of schnitzel. I developed this recipe so it wasn't so time-consuming to make. I am asked for the recipe every time I make it.
—Beth Taylor, Pleasant Grove, UT

PREP: 20 MIN. • **COOK:** 4 HOURS
MAKES: 4 SERVINGS

- **1 pork tenderloin (1 lb.)**
- **1 cup dry bread crumbs**
- **2 lbs. medium Yukon Gold potatoes, peeled and cut into ¼-in. slices**
- **2 cups heavy whipping cream**
- **⅔ cup crumbled Gorgonzola cheese**
- **1 tsp. salt**
- **¼ cup minced fresh Italian parsley**
- **Lemon wedges**

1. Cut tenderloin into 12 slices. Pound with a meat mallet to ¼-in. thickness. Place four slices in a 3- or 4-qt. slow cooker. Layer with ¼ cup bread crumbs and a third of the potatoes. Repeat the layers twice; top with remaining bread crumbs.
2. In a small bowl, combine the cream, Gorgonzola and salt. Pour over the pork mixture; cook on low, covered, until meat and potatoes are tender, 4-6 hours. Sprinkle with parsley; serve with lemon wedges.
3 SLICES PORK WITH 1 CUP POTATO MIXTURE: 926 cal., 54g fat (33g sat. fat), 216mg chol., 1132mg sod., 73g carb. (9g sugars, 5g fiber), 38g pro.

GERMAN SCHNITZEL & POTATOES WITH GORGONZOLA CREAM

BAKED TERIYAKI PORK & VEGGIES

Minimal preparation makes this dish easy. I use precut broccoli and pork chops to save time. Sometimes I throw in multicolored carrots for extra prettiness. Try it served over rice or noodles.
—Billie Davis, Spring Creek, NV

PREP: 15 MIN. • **BAKE:** 30 MIN.
MAKES: 4 SERVINGS

- **2 cups fresh broccoli florets**
- **1 lb. fresh baby carrots, halved lengthwise**
- **1 Tbsp. olive oil**
- **1 tsp. minced fresh gingerroot**
- **½ tsp. pepper**
- **¼ tsp. salt**
- **4 boneless pork loin chops (6 oz. each)**
- **4 Tbsp. reduced-sodium teriyaki sauce**
- **Toasted sesame seeds, optional**

1. Preheat oven to 375°. Line a 15x10x1-in. pan with foil; add broccoli and carrots. Toss with olive oil, ginger, pepper and salt; spread out into a single layer.
2. Place pork chops on top of vegetables; drizzle with teriyaki sauce. Bake until a thermometer inserted in pork reads 145°, about 30 minutes. If desired, preheat broiler; broil chops and vegetables 2-4 in. from heat until browned, 1-2 minutes. Top with sesame seeds if desired.
1 PORK CHOP WITH 1 CUP VEGETABLES: 322 cal., 13g fat (4g sat. fat), 82mg chol., 613mg sod., 14g carb. (9g sugars, 3g fiber), 35g pro. **Diabetic exchanges:** 5 lean meat, 2 vegetable, ½ fat.

SLOW-COOKER MALAYSIAN CHICKEN

SLOW COOKER

SLOW-COOKER MALAYSIAN CHICKEN

Malaysian food has influences from the Malays, Chinese, Indians, Thai, Portuguese and British. In this dish, Asian ingredients combine for maximum flavor, and the sweet potatoes help to thicken the sauce as the dish slowly cooks.
—Suzanne Banfield, Basking Ridge, NJ

PREP: 20 MIN. • **COOK:** 5 HOURS • **MAKES:** 6 SERVINGS

- **1 cup coconut milk**
- **2 Tbsp. brown sugar**
- **2 Tbsp. soy sauce**
- **2 Tbsp. creamy peanut butter**
- **1 Tbsp. fish sauce**
- **2 tsp. curry powder**
- **2 garlic cloves, minced**
- **½ tsp. salt**
- **½ tsp. pepper**
- **1 can (14½ oz.) diced tomatoes, undrained**
- **2 medium sweet potatoes, peeled and cut into ½-in. thick slices**
- **2 lbs. boneless skinless chicken thighs**
- **2 Tbsp. cornstarch**
- **2 Tbsp. water**

1. In a bowl, whisk together the first nine ingredients; stir in tomatoes. Place sweet potatoes in a 5- or 6-qt. slow cooker; top with chicken. Pour tomato mixture over top. Cook, covered, on low until chicken is tender and a thermometer reads 170°, 5-6 hours.
2. Remove chicken and sweet potatoes; keep warm. Transfer cooking juices to a saucepan. In a small bowl, mix cornstarch and water until smooth; stir into cooking juices. Bring to a boil; cook and stir 1-2 minutes or until thickened. Serve with chicken and potatoes.
1 SERVING: 425 cal., 20g fat (10g sat. fat), 101mg chol., 964mg sod., 28g carb. (14g sugars, 4g fiber), 33g pro.

EAT SMART SLOW COOKER

NORTH AFRICAN CHICKEN & RICE

I'm always looking to try recipes from different cultures and this one is a huge favorite. We love the spice combinations. This cooks equally well in a slow cooker or a pressure cooker.
—Courtney Stultz, Weir, KS

PREP: 10 MIN. • **COOK:** 4 HOURS • **MAKES:** 8 SERVINGS

- **1 medium onion, diced**
- **1 Tbsp. olive oil**
- **8 boneless skinless chicken thighs (about 2 lbs.)**
- **1 Tbsp. minced fresh cilantro**
- **1 tsp. ground turmeric**
- **1 tsp. paprika**
- **1 tsp. sea salt**
- **½ tsp. pepper**
- **½ tsp. ground cinnamon**
- **½ tsp. chili powder**
- **1 cup golden raisins**
- **½ to 1 cup chopped pitted green olives**
- **1 medium lemon, sliced**
- **2 garlic cloves, minced**
- **½ cup chicken broth or water**
- **4 cups hot cooked brown rice**

In a 3- or 4-qt. slow cooker, combine onion and oil. Place chicken thighs on top of onion; sprinkle with next seven ingredients. Top with raisins, olives, lemon and garlic. Add broth. Cook, covered, on low until chicken is tender, 4-5 hours. Serve with hot cooked rice.
1 SERVING: 386 cal., 13g fat (3g sat. fat), 76mg chol., 556mg sod., 44g carb. (12g sugars, 3g fiber), 25g pro.

NORTH AFRICAN CHICKEN & RICE

TANGERINE CHICKEN TAGINE

SLOW COOKER

TANGERINE CHICKEN TAGINE

My family and friends love foods from around the world, especially Moroccan entrees, so I created this flavorful dish. Cooking it in the slow cooker keeps each morsel moist and rich in flavor.
—Brenda Watts, Gaffney, SC

PREP: 20 MIN. • **COOK:** 6 HOURS • **MAKES:** 8 SERVINGS

- **2 Tbsp. brown sugar**
- **1 tsp. curry powder**
- **1 tsp. ground cinnamon**
- **1 tsp. cumin seeds**
- **½ tsp. ground ginger**
- **1 roasting chicken (5 to 6 lbs.), patted dry**
- **1 lb. carrots, peeled and thinly sliced**
- **1 lb. parsnips, peeled and thinly sliced**
- **2 large tangerines, peeled and sliced**
- **1 cup chopped dried apricots**
- **½ cup slivered almonds**
- **½ cup chicken broth**

Combine first five ingredients; rub spice mixture over chicken until well coated. Arrange carrots, parsnips, tangerines, apricots and almonds in bottom of a 6-qt. slow cooker. Place chicken breast side up on vegetables; pour in broth. Cook, covered, on low until a thermometer inserted in thigh reads 170° and chicken is tender, 6-8 hours. Remove chicken, vegetables and fruits to a serving platter; let stand 5 to 10 minutes before carving chicken.
1 SERVING: 503 cal., 24g fat (6g sat. fat), 112mg chol., 232mg sod., 35g carb. (20g sugars, 6g fiber), 39g pro.

HOISIN SRIRACHA SHEET-PAN CHICKEN

The convenience and simplicity of this chicken dinner make it extra awesome. Change up the veggies throughout the year—the sticky-spicy-sweet sauce is good on all of them!
—Julie Peterson, Crofton, MD

PREP: 20 MIN. • **BAKE:** 40 MIN. • **MAKES:** 4 SERVINGS

- **⅓ cup hoisin sauce**
- **⅓ cup reduced-sodium soy sauce**
- **2 Tbsp. maple syrup**
- **2 Tbsp. Sriracha Asian hot chili sauce**
- **1 Tbsp. rice vinegar**
- **2 tsp. sesame oil**
- **2 garlic cloves, minced**
- **½ tsp. minced fresh gingerroot**
- **4 bone-in chicken thighs (6 oz. each)**
- **¼ tsp. salt**
- **¼ tsp. pepper**
- **1 medium sweet potato, cut into ¾-in. cubes**
- **2 Tbsp. olive oil, divided**
- **4 cups fresh cauliflowerets**
- **1 medium sweet red pepper, cut into ¾-in. pieces**
- **Sesame seeds, optional**

1. Preheat oven to 400°. Whisk together the first eight ingredients. Set aside.
2. Sprinkle both sides of chicken with salt and pepper. Place chicken and sweet potato in a single layer in a foil-lined 15x10x1-in. sheet pan. Drizzle with 1 Tbsp. olive oil and a third of hoisin mixture; toss to coat.
3. Bake 15 minutes; turn chicken and potatoes. Add cauliflower and red pepper; drizzle with another third of hoisin mixture and remaining olive oil. Bake until a thermometer inserted in chicken reads 170°-175°, about 25 minutes longer. Drizzle with remaining sauce. If desired, sprinkle with sesame seeds.
1 SERVING: 490 cal., 24g fat (5g sat. fat), 81mg chol., 1665mg sod., 40g carb. (23g sugars, 5g fiber), 28g pro.

HOISIN SRIRACHA SHEET-PAN CHICKEN

EAT SMART

LOADED CHICKEN CARBONARA CUPS

Spaghetti cupcakes with a chicken carbonara twist make for a tasty, fun family dinner. Whole wheat pasta and reduced-fat ingredients make these quick and easy little pasta cakes nutritional winners, too.
—Jeanne Holt, Mendota Heights, MN

PREP: 30 MIN. • **BAKE:** 15 MIN.
MAKES: 6 SERVINGS

- **4 oz. uncooked whole wheat spaghetti**
- **1 large egg, lightly beaten**
- **5 oz. frozen chopped spinach, thawed and squeezed dry (about ½ cup)**
- **½ cup 2% cottage cheese**
- **½ cup shredded Parmesan cheese, divided**
- **¼ tsp. lemon-pepper seasoning**
- **6 bacon strips, cooked and crumbled, divided**
- **½ cup reduced-fat reduced-sodium condensed cream of chicken soup, undiluted**
- **¼ cup reduced-fat spreadable chive and onion cream cheese**
- **1 cup chopped cooked chicken breast**
- **⅓ cup shredded part-skim mozzarella cheese**
- **¼ cup finely chopped oil-packed sun-dried tomatoes**

1. Preheat oven to 350°. In a large saucepan, cook spaghetti according to package directions; drain, reserving ⅓ cup of pasta water.
2. In a large bowl, mix egg, spinach, cottage cheese, ¼ cup Parmesan cheese, lemon pepper and half of the bacon. Add spaghetti; toss to combine. Divide among 12 greased muffin cups. Using a greased tablespoon, make an indentation in the center of each.
3. In a large bowl, whisk together soup, cream cheese and reserved pasta water. Stir in chicken, mozzarella cheese and tomatoes; spoon into cups. Sprinkle with the remaining bacon and Parmesan cheese.
4. Bake until set, about 15 minutes. Cool 5 minutes before removing from pan.
2 PASTA CUPS: 266 cal., 12g fat (5g sat. fat), 74mg chol., 553mg sod., 20g carb. (4g sugars, 3g fiber), 21g pro. **Diabetic exchanges:** 2 lean meat, 1½ fat, 1 starch.

LOADED CHICKEN CARBONARA CUPS

EAT SMART

PASTA WITH CREAMY FENNEL SAUCE

When pureeing fennel one day, I realized its velvety texture would make for a creamy, delicious pasta sauce—without all the guilt. My experiment worked, and now I enjoy this good-for-you pasta all the time.
—Deb Schwab, Moraga, CA

PREP: 20 MIN. • **COOK:** 40 MIN.
MAKES: 6 SERVINGS

- **2 large fennel bulbs**
- **1 medium potato**
- **1 shallot**
- **2 garlic cloves**
- **2 cups 2% milk**
- **1 cup chicken broth**
- **3 Tbsp. cream cheese, softened**
- **2 Tbsp. grated Parmesan cheese**
- **½ tsp. salt**
- **¼ tsp. pepper**
- **1 Tbsp. minced fresh parsley**
- **2 pkg. (10 oz. each) fresh butternut squash ravioli**
- **Additional grated Parmesan cheese, optional**

1. Chop enough fennel fronds to measure 1 Tbsp.; reserve, discarding the rest of the tops or saving for another use. Core and slice fennel bulbs. Peel and cube potato. Slice shallot; smash garlic cloves and peel.
2. Place vegetables, milk and broth in a Dutch oven. Bring to a boil. Reduce heat; simmer, covered, until tender, 25-30 minutes. Drain, reserving ¼ cup cooking liquid; cool slightly. Stir in reserved cooking liquid, cream cheese, Parmesan, salt and pepper.
3. Process in a blender or food processor until pureed. Stir in parsley and reserved fennel fronds; keep warm.
4. Cook ravioli according to package directions. Drain. Toss with sauce. If desired, top with additional Parmesan.
1 SERVING: 309 cal., 7g fat (3g sat. fat), 19mg chol., 690mg sod., 51g carb. (11g sugars, 5g fiber), 12g pro.

ELISABETH LARSEN
Pleasant Grove, UT

CHICKEN POTPIE GALETTE WTH
CHEDDAR-THYME CRUST

CHICKEN POTPIE GALETTE WITH CHEDDAR-THYME CRUST

This gorgeous galette takes traditional chicken potpie and gives it a fun open-faced spin. The rich filling and flaky cheddar-flecked crust make it taste so homey.
—Elisabeth Larsen, Pleasant Grove, UT

PREP: 45 MIN. + CHILLING • **BAKE:** 30 MIN. + COOLING
MAKES: 8 SERVINGS

- **1¼ cups all-purpose flour**
- **½ cup shredded sharp cheddar cheese**
- **2 Tbsp. minced fresh thyme**
- **¼ tsp. salt**
- **½ cup cold butter, cubed**
- **¼ cup ice water**

FILLING

- **3 Tbsp. butter**
- **2 large carrots, sliced**
- **1 celery rib, diced**
- **1 small onion, diced**
- **8 oz. sliced fresh mushrooms**
- **3 cups julienned Swiss chard**
- **3 garlic cloves, minced**
- **1 cup chicken broth**
- **3 Tbsp. all-purpose flour**
- **½ tsp. salt**
- **¼ tsp. pepper**
- **2 cups shredded cooked chicken**
- **½ tsp. minced fresh oregano**
- **2 Tbsp. minced fresh parsley**

1. Combine flour, cheese, thyme and salt; cut in butter until crumbly. Gradually add ice water, tossing with a fork until dough holds together when pressed. Shape into a disk; refrigerate 1 hour.
2. For filling, melt butter in a large saucepan over medium-high heat. Add carrots, celery and onion; cook and stir until slightly softened, 5-7 minutes. Add mushrooms; cook 3 minutes longer. Add Swiss chard and garlic; cook until wilted, 2-3 minutes.
3. Whisk together broth, flour, salt and pepper; slowly pour over vegetables, stirring constantly. Cook until thickened, 2-3 minutes. Stir in chicken and oregano.
4. Preheat oven to 400°. On a floured sheet of parchment paper, roll dough into a 12-in. circle. Transfer to a baking sheet. Spoon filling over pastry to within 2 in. of edge. Fold pastry edge over filling, pleating as you go, leaving center uncovered. Bake on a lower oven rack until crust is golden brown and filling bubbly, 30-35 minutes. Cool 15 minutes before slicing. Sprinkle with parsley.
1 PIECE: 342 cal., 21g fat (12g sat. fat), 81mg chol., 594mg sod., 22g carb. (2g sugars, 2g fiber), 16g pro.

CHICKEN FRANCESE

I grew up on this tender, lemony chicken Francese dish that's a classic in Italian cooking. It's delicious as is, but we sometimes add sauteed mushrooms. Serve it with pasta or crusty bread to mop up all that delicious pan sauce.
—Joe Losardo, New York, NY

PREP: 20 MIN. • **COOK:** 20 MIN. • **MAKES:** 4 SERVINGS

- **1 lb. boneless skinless chicken breasts**
- **1 large egg, beaten**
- **¾ cup dry bread crumbs**
- **3 Tbsp. grated Parmesan cheese**
- **1 tsp. dried parsley flakes**
- **½ tsp. garlic powder**
- **½ tsp. salt**
- **½ tsp. pepper**
- **¼ cup olive oil**

LEMON SAUCE

- **1 cup water**
- **⅓ cup lemon juice**
- **2 chicken bouillon cubes**
- **Lemon slices**

1. Pound chicken breasts with a meat mallet to ¼-in. thickness; slice into cutlets 1½ in. wide. Place beaten eggs in a shallow bowl; in a separate shallow bowl, combine the next six ingredients. Dip chicken in egg, then in crumb mixture, patting to help coating adhere.
2. In a large skillet, heat 2 Tbsp. oil over medium heat. Brown chicken in batches, adding oil as needed, until golden brown, 2-3 minutes per side. Remove; drain on paper towels.
3. For lemon sauce, add water, lemon juice and bouillon to skillet, stirring to loosen browned bits from pan. Bring to a boil over medium-high heat. Reduce heat; simmer, uncovered, until liquid is reduced by half, 8-10 minutes. Return chicken to pan; toss to coat. Cook until heated through, 4-6 minutes. Serve with lemon slices.
1 SERVING: 318 cal., 19g fat (3g sat. fat), 111mg chol., 806mg sod., 10g carb. (2g sugars, 1g fiber), 27g pro.

CHICKEN FRANCESE

FIERY STUFFED POBLANOS

EAT SMART

FIERY STUFFED POBLANOS

I love Southwest-inspired cuisine, but the dishes are often unhealthy. As a dietitian, I try to come up with nutritious twists on recipes, which is how my stuffed chili dish was born.
—Amber Massey, Argyle, TX

PREP: 50 MIN. + STANDING • **BAKE:** 20 MIN.
MAKES: 8 SERVINGS

- 8 **poblano peppers**
- 1 **can (15 oz.) black beans, rinsed and drained**
- 1 **medium zucchini, chopped**
- 1 **small red onion, chopped**
- 4 **garlic cloves, minced**
- 1 **can (15¼ oz.) whole kernel corn, drained**
- 1 **can (14½ oz.) fire-roasted diced tomatoes, undrained**
- 1 **cup cooked brown rice**
- 1 **Tbsp. ground cumin**
- 1 **to 1½ tsp. ground ancho chili pepper**
- ¼ **tsp. salt**
- ¼ **tsp. pepper**
- 1 **cup shredded reduced-fat Mexican cheese blend, divided**
- 3 **green onions, chopped**
- ½ **cup reduced-fat sour cream**

1. Broil peppers 3 in. from heat until skins blister, about 5 minutes. With tongs, rotate peppers a quarter turn. Broil and rotate until all sides are blistered and blackened. Immediately place peppers in a large bowl; cover and let stand for 20 minutes.

2. Meanwhile, in a small bowl, coarsely mash beans; set aside. In a large nonstick skillet, cook and stir zucchini and onion until tender. Add garlic; cook 1 minute longer. Add corn, tomatoes, rice, seasonings and beans. Remove from the heat; stir in ½ cup cheese. Set aside.

3. Preheat oven to 375°. Peel charred skins from poblanos and discard. Cut a lengthwise slit through each pepper, leaving stem intact; discard membranes and seeds. Spoon ⅔ cup filling into each pepper.

4. Place peppers in a 13x9-in. baking dish coated with cooking spray. Bake until heated through, 18-22 minutes, sprinkling with green onions and remaining cheese during last 5 minutes of baking. Serve peppers with sour cream.

1 STUFFED PEPPER: 223 cal., 5g fat (2g sat. fat), 15mg chol., 579mg sod., 32g carb. (9g sugars, 7g fiber), 11g pro. **Diabetic exchanges:** 2 vegetable, 1 starch, 1 lean meat, 1 fat.

SLOW COOKER

MEAT LOAF & MASHED RED POTATOES

Satisfy the meat-and-potatoes eaters in your house with this satisfying dish that cooks up in one pot! Talk about classic comfort food.
—Faith Cromwell, San Francisco, CA

PREP: 30 MIN. • **COOK:** 4 HOURS + STANDING • **MAKES:** 8 SERVINGS

- **3 lbs. small red potatoes, quartered**
- **1½ cups beef stock, divided**
- **3 slices white bread, torn into small pieces**
- **2 large portobello mushrooms (about 6 oz.), cut into chunks**
- **1 medium onion, cut into wedges**
- **1 medium carrot, cut into chunks**
- **1 celery rib, cut into chunks**
- **3 garlic cloves, halved**
- **2 large eggs, lightly beaten**
- **1¼ lbs. ground beef**
- **¾ lb. ground pork**
- **2 Tbsp. Worcestershire sauce**
- **2 tsp. salt, divided**
- **1 tsp. pepper, divided**

GLAZE

- **½ cup ketchup**
- **2 Tbsp. tomato paste**
- **2 Tbsp. brown sugar**

POTATOES

- **3 Tbsp. butter**

1. In a large microwave-safe bowl, combine potatoes and 1 cup stock. Microwave, covered, on high just until softened, 12-15 minutes. Transfer mixture to a 6-qt. slow cooker. Combine bread and remaining stock in a large bowl; let stand until liquid is absorbed.
2. Meanwhile, pulse mushrooms, onion, carrot, celery and garlic in a food processor until finely chopped. Add vegetable mixture, eggs, beef, pork, Worcestershire sauce, 1¼ tsp. salt and ¾ tsp. pepper to bread mixture; mix lightly but thoroughly. Place meat mixture on an 18x12-in. piece of heavy-duty foil; shape into a 10x6-in. oval loaf. Lifting with foil, place in slow cooker on top of potatoes; press foil up sides and over edges of slow cooker, creating a bowl to contain meat loaf juices. Mix together glaze ingredients; spread over loaf.
3. Cook, covered, on low until a thermometer reads 160°, 4-5 hours. Using a turkey baster, remove and discard liquid contained in foil; lifting with foil, remove meat loaf to a platter (or carefully remove meat loaf using foil, draining liquid into a small bowl). Let stand 10 minutes before cutting.
4. Drain potatoes, reserving cooking liquid; transfer potatoes to a large bowl. Mash, gradually adding butter, remaining salt and pepper and enough reserved cooking liquid to reach desired consistency. Serve with meat loaf.

1 SLICE WITH ⅔ CUP MASHED POTATOES: 485 cal., 21g fat (9g sat. fat), 130mg chol., 1107mg sod., 46g carb. (12g sugars, 4g fiber), 28g pro.

LEHMEJUN (ARMENIAN PIZZA)

This pizza-style recipe came from my friend Ruby's mom, who is a crazy-good cook. I added my own flair and tweaked it by using flour tortillas instead of making a dough.
—Tamar Yacoubian, Ketchum, ID

PREP: 20 MIN. • **COOK:** 15 MIN. • **MAKES:** 8 SERVINGS

- **1 lb. ground beef**
- **1 lb. ground lamb**
- **1 medium onion, halved and sliced**
- **1 can (6 oz.) tomato paste**
- **2 jalapeno peppers, seeded and diced**
- **¼ cup minced fresh parsley**
- **2 Tbsp. harissa chili paste**
- **2 Tbsp. dry red wine**
- **1 Tbsp. ground sumac**
- **½ tsp. ground cinnamon**
- **¼ tsp. salt**
- **¼ tsp. pepper**
- **8 flour tortillas (6 in.)**
- **Cooking spray**
- **1 medium lemon, cut in wedges**

1. Preheat broiler. In a large skillet, cook and crumble the beef and lamb with onion over medium-high heat until meat is no longer pink, 5-7 minutes; drain.
2. Mix together next nine ingredients. Add to meat mixture; cook, stirring occasionally, until well blended and heated through. Remove from heat.
3. In batches, spritz both sides of tortillas with cooking spray and place on a baking sheet; broil 4-5 in. from heat until crisp and lightly browned, 45-60 seconds per side. Spread meat mixture over tortillas. Serve with lemon wedges.

1 FILLED TORTILLA: 371 cal., 19g fat (7g sat. fat), 72mg chol., 464mg sod., 24g carb. (3g sugars, 3g fiber), 24g pro.

LEHMEJUN (ARMENIAN PIZZA)

SLOW-COOKER SHREDDED BEEF LETTUCE CUPS

EAT SMART SLOW COOKER

SLOW-COOKER SHREDDED BEEF LETTUCE CUPS

The slow cooker is our summertime go-to for cool kitchen cooking. After swim lessons and outdoor activities, it's so nice to come back to a tasty, light dinner. If you can't find Bibb or Boston, green leaf lettuce is less sturdy but can work in a pinch.
—Elisabeth Larsen, Pleasant Grove, UT

PREP: 20 MIN. • **COOK:** 6 HOURS • **MAKES:** 8 SERVINGS

- **1 boneless beef chuck roast (2 lbs.)**
- **3 medium carrots, peeled and chopped**
- **2 medium sweet red peppers, chopped**
- **1 medium onion, chopped**
- **1 can (8 oz.) unsweetened crushed pineapple, undrained**
- **½ cup reduced-sodium soy sauce**
- **2 Tbsp. packed brown sugar**
- **2 Tbsp. white vinegar**
- **1 garlic clove, minced**
- **½ tsp. pepper**
- **3 Tbsp. cornstarch**
- **3 Tbsp. water**
- **24 Bibb or Boston lettuce leaves**
- **Sliced green onions, optional**

1. In a 4- or 5-qt. slow cooker, combine roast, carrots, peppers and onion. Stir together next six ingredients in small bowl; pour over roast. Cook, covered, on low until roast is tender, 6-8 hours.
2. Remove roast from slow cooker. Cool slightly; shred with two forks. Skim fat from cooking juices; transfer juices and vegetables to a small saucepan. Bring to a boil over high heat. In a small bowl, combine cornstarch and water. Gradually stir cornstarch mixture into juices; cook until the sauce is thickened, 3-4 minutes. Return beef, sauce and vegetables to slow cooker; cook until heated through, 10-15 minutes.
3. Serve beef in lettuce leaves. If desired, sprinkle with green onions.
3 LETTUCE CUPS: 271 cal., 11g fat (4g sat. fat), 74mg chol., 642mg sod., 18g carb. (11g sugars, 2g fiber), 24g pro. **Diabetic exchanges:** 3 lean meat, 1 starch.

MILE-HIGH CHICKEN POTPIE

Classic chicken potpie gets extra homey when it's loaded with a creamy filling and baked tall in a springform pan. This deep-dish marvel is perfect for Sunday dinners.
—Shannon Roum, Cudahy, WI

PREP: 40 MIN. + CHILLING • **BAKE:** 50 MIN. + STANDING
MAKES: 6 SERVINGS

- **1 large egg, separated**
- **4 to 6 Tbsp. cold water, divided**
- **2 cups all-purpose flour**
- **¼ tsp. salt**
- **⅔ cup cold butter, cubed**

FILLING

- **3 Tbsp. butter**
- **2 medium potatoes, peeled and cut into ½-in. cubes**
- **4 medium carrots, thinly sliced**
- **2 celery ribs, finely chopped**
- **¼ cup finely chopped onion**
- **3 Tbsp. all-purpose flour**
- **2 Tbsp. chicken bouillon granules**
- **1½ tsp. dried tarragon**
- **½ tsp. coarsely ground pepper**
- **1½ cups half-and-half cream**
- **2½ cups cubed cooked chicken**
- **1½ cups fresh peas or frozen peas**
- **½ to 1 tsp. celery seed**

1. In a small bowl, beat egg yolk with 2 Tbsp. water. In a large bowl, combine flour and salt; cut in butter until crumbly. Gradually add yolk mixture, tossing with a fork; add additional water, 1 Tbsp. at a time, until dough forms a ball. Divide dough into two portions, one with three-quarters of the dough and one with the remainder. Shape each into a disk; wrap in plastic. Refrigerate 1 hour or overnight.
2. For filling, in a Dutch oven, melt butter. Saute potatoes, carrots, celery and onion until crisp-tender, 5-7 minutes. Stir in flour, bouillon, tarragon and pepper. Gradually stir in cream. Bring to a boil; cook and stir until thickened, about 2 minutes. Stir in chicken and peas; set aside to cool completely. On a lightly floured surface, roll out larger portion of dough to fit bottom and up the sides of an 8-in. springform pan. Add cooled filling. Roll remaining dough to fit over the top. Place over filling. Trim, seal and flute edge. Cut slits in top. Chill for at least 1 hour.
3. Lightly beat egg white with 1 tsp. water. Brush over the top crust; sprinkle with celery seed. Place pie on a rimmed baking tray. Bake at 400° until crust is golden brown and filling is bubbly, 50-55 minutes. Cool on a wire rack at least 30 minutes before cutting.
1 PIECE: 700 cal., 38g fat (22g sat. fat), 183mg chol., 1282mg sod., 58g carb. (8g sugars, 6g fiber), 29g pro.

SLOW COOKER

SPICY KALE & HERB PORCHETTA

Serve this classic Italian specialty as a main dish or on crusty artisan bread as a sandwich. Use the liquid from the slow cooker with your favorite seasonings to make a sauce or gravy.
—Sandi Sheppard, Norman, OK

PREP: 30 MIN. + CHILLING • **COOK:** 5 HOURS
MAKES: 12 SERVINGS

- **1½ cups packed fresh kale leaves, torn and stems removed**
- **¼ cup chopped fresh sage**
- **¼ cup chopped fresh rosemary**
- **¼ cup chopped fresh parsley**
- **2 Tbsp. kosher salt**
- **1 Tbsp. crushed fennel seed**
- **1 tsp. crushed red pepper flakes**
- **4 garlic cloves, halved**
- **1 boneless pork shoulder roast (about 6 lbs.), butterflied**
- **2 tsp. grated lemon zest**
- **1 large sweet onion, thickly sliced**
- **¼ cup white wine or chicken broth**
- **1 Tbsp. olive oil**
- **3 Tbsp. cornstarch**
- **3 Tbsp. water**

1. In a blender or food processor, pulse the first eight ingredients until finely chopped. In a 15x10x1-in. baking pan, open roast flat. Spread herb mixture evenly over meat to within ½ in. of edges; sprinkle lemon zest over herb mixture.
2. Starting at a long side, roll up jelly-roll style. Using a sharp knife, score fat on outside of roast. Tie at 2-in. intervals with kitchen string. Secure ends with toothpicks. Refrigerate, covered, for at least 4 hours or overnight.
3. In a 6-qt. slow cooker, combine onion and wine. Place porchetta seam side down on top of onion. Cook, covered, on low until tender, 5-6 hours. Remove toothpicks. Reserve cooking juices.
4. In a large skillet, heat oil over medium heat. Brown porchetta on all sides; remove from heat. Tent with foil. Let stand for 15 minutes.
5. Meanwhile, strain and skim fat from cooking juices. Transfer to a large saucepan; bring to a boil. In a small bowl mix cornstarch and water until smooth; stir into juices. Return to a boil, stirring constantly; cook and stir until thickened, 1-2 minutes. Cut string on roast and slice. Serve with gravy.

1 SERVING: 402 cal., 24g fat (8g sat. fat), 135mg chol., 1104mg sod., 5g carb. (1g sugars, 1g fiber), 39g pro.

SAUSAGE & PUMPKIN PASTA

Pumpkin for dinner? Yes! This quick, healthy skillet is made for busy weeknights.
—Katherine Wollgast, Troy, MO

PREP: 20 MIN. • **COOK:** 15 MIN.
MAKES: 4 SERVINGS

- **2 cups uncooked multigrain bow tie pasta**
- **½ lb. Italian turkey sausage links, casings removed**
- **½ lb. sliced fresh mushrooms**
- **1 medium onion, chopped**
- **4 garlic cloves, minced**
- **1 cup reduced-sodium chicken broth**
- **1 cup canned pumpkin**
- **½ cup white wine or additional reduced-sodium chicken broth**
- **½ tsp. rubbed sage**
- **¼ tsp. salt**
- **¼ tsp. garlic powder**
- **¼ tsp. pepper**
- **¼ cup grated Parmesan cheese**
- **1 Tbsp. dried parsley flakes**

1. Cook pasta according to the package directions.
2. Meanwhile, in a large nonstick skillet coated with cooking spray, cook the sausage, mushrooms and onion over medium heat until meat is no longer pink. Add garlic; cook 1 minute longer. Stir in the broth, pumpkin, wine, sage, salt, garlic powder and pepper. Bring to a boil. Reduce heat; simmer, uncovered, for 5-6 minutes or until slightly thickened.
3. Drain pasta; add to the skillet and heat through. Just before serving, sprinkle with cheese and parsley.

1¾ CUPS: 348 cal., 9g fat (2g sat. fat), 38mg chol., 733mg sod., 42g carb. (7g sugars, 7g fiber), 23g pro. **Diabetic exchanges:** 2½ starch, 2 lean meat, 1 vegetable, ½ fat.

TEST KITCHEN TIP

Sneak in some greens by tossing a handful or two of baby spinach into the skillet just before serving. The residual heat will wilt the greens.

SPICY KALE & HERB PORCHETTA

KOREAN SAUSAGE BOWL

KOREAN SAUSAGE BOWL

When we hosted a student from South Korea, she shared some of her favorite Korean dishes. We especially liked her bibimbap. *I created a variation on the dish with Italian sausage.*
—Michal Riege, Cedarburg, WI

PREP: 15 MIN. + MARINATING
COOK: 25 MIN. • **MAKES:** 4 SERVINGS

- **1 pkg. (19 oz.) Italian sausage links, cut into 1-in. pieces**
- **¾ cup Korean barbecue sauce, divided**
- **1 tsp. plus 1 Tbsp. canola oil, divided**
- **1 large egg**
- **2 medium carrots, julienned**
- **1 medium sweet red pepper, julienned**
- **3 green onions, thinly sliced**
- **2 garlic cloves, minced**
- **½ tsp. salt**
- **¼ tsp. crushed red pepper flakes**
- **¼ tsp. pepper**
- **8 oz. uncooked angel hair pasta**
- **Additional sliced green onions, optional**

1. In a large bowl, toss sausage pieces with ½ cup barbecue sauce; refrigerate, covered, 4 hours.
2. In a large skillet, heat 1 tsp. oil over medium heat. Break egg into pan; cook until yolk is set, turning once. Remove from pan; cut into thin strips.
3. In same pan, heat remaining oil over medium-high heat. Add carrots and red pepper; cook and stir until crisp-tender. Stir in green onions, garlic and seasonings; cook 1 minute longer. Remove from pan.
4. Drain sausage, discarding marinade. In same pan, cook and stir sausage until no longer pink, 12-15 minutes.
5. Cook pasta according to package directions; drain, reserving ¼ cup pasta water. Add pasta, pasta water, carrot mixture and remaining barbecue sauce to sausage. Toss to combine. Divide among four bowls; top with egg strips and, if desired, additional green onions.
1¾ CUPS: 672 cal., 39g fat (10g sat. fat), 119mg chol., 1620mg sod., 56g carb. (9g sugars, 4g fiber), 25g pro.

CREAMY GREEN CHILI CHICKEN COBBLER

Rotisserie chickens are so convenient. This dish, which combines shredded chicken with diced green chilies, green enchilada sauce, creams and cheeses, is a family go-to that everyone raves about.
—Johnna Johnson, Scottsdale, AZ

PREP: 25 MIN. • **BAKE:** 45 MIN.
MAKES: 8 SERVINGS

- **2 cups all-purpose flour**
- **½ cup grated Parmesan cheese**
- **2 tsp. baking powder**
- **6 Tbsp. cold butter, cubed**
- **¾ cup plus 2 Tbsp. heavy whipping cream**
- **3 oz. cream cheese, softened**
- **½ cup sour cream**
- **1 can (10½ oz.) condensed cream of chicken soup, undiluted**
- **1 can (10 oz.) green enchilada sauce**
- **2 cans (4 oz. each) chopped green chilies**
- **2½ cups shredded rotisserie chicken (about 10 oz.)**
- **1½ cups shredded Colby-Monterey Jack cheese**

1. Preheat oven to 450°. For crumb topping, whisk together flour, cheese and baking powder. Cut in butter until the mixture resembles coarse crumbs. Add cream; stir just until moistened. On a lightly greased 15x10x1-in. pan, crumble the mixture into ½- to 1-in. pieces.
2. Bake on an upper oven rack until light golden brown, 8-10 minutes. Reduce oven setting to 350°.
3. In a large bowl, mix cream cheese and sour cream until smooth. Stir in soup, enchilada sauce, green chilies and chicken. Transfer to an 11x7-in. baking dish; sprinkle with cheese. Add crumb topping (dish will be full).
4. Place dish on a baking sheet. Bake, uncovered, on a lower oven rack until topping is deep golden brown and filling is bubbly, 35-40 minutes.
1¼ CUPS: 581 cal., 39g fat (22g sat. fat), 132mg chol., 1076mg sod., 33g carb. (3g sugars, 2g fiber), 25g pro.

UPPER PENINSULA PASTIES

I grew up in Michigan's Upper Peninsula, where many people are of English ancestry. Pasties—traditional meat pies often eaten by hand—are popular there.
—Carole Derifield, Valdez, AK

PREP: 35 MIN. + CHILLING • **BAKE:** 1 HOUR • **MAKES:** 12 SERVINGS

- **2 cups shortening**
- **2 cups boiling water**
- **5½ to 6 cups all-purpose flour**
- **2 tsp. salt**

FILLING

- **6 medium red potatoes (about 3 lbs.), peeled**
- **2 small rutabagas (about 1½ lbs.), peeled**
- **1 lb. ground beef**
- **½ lb. ground pork**
- **2 medium onions, chopped into ¼-in. pieces**
- **3 tsp. salt**
- **2 tsp. pepper**
- **2 tsp. garlic powder**
- **¼ cup butter**
- **Half-and-half cream or a lightly beaten large egg, optional**

1. In a large bowl, stir shortening and water until shortening is melted. Gradually stir in flour and salt until a very soft dough is formed; cover and refrigerate for 1½ hours.
2. Cut potatoes and rutabagas into ⅛- or ¼-in. cubes; do not make cubes too large or they will not cook properly. Gently combine ground pork and beef; break into small crumbles. In a large bowl, combine potatoes, rutabagas, onions, meat mixture and seasonings.
3. Divide dough into 12 equal portions. On a floured surface, roll out one portion at a time into a 8-in. circle. Mound 1½-2 cups filling on half of each circle; dot with 1 tsp. butter. Moisten edges with water; carefully fold dough over filling and press edges with a fork to seal.
4. Place on ungreased baking sheets. Cut several slits in top of pasties. If desired, brush with cream or beaten egg. Bake at 350° until golden brown, about 1 hour. Cool on wire racks. Serve hot or cold. Store in the refrigerator.
1 PASTY: 757 cal., 44g fat (13g sat. fat), 46mg chol., 1060mg sod., 69g carb. (5g sugars, 5g fiber), 19g pro.

UPPER PENINSULA PASTIES

BRAISED PORK WITH TOMATILLOS

BRAISED PORK WITH TOMATILLOS

A pork braise is a sure way to make people's mouths water. The tomatillos offer a subtle lightness. For ultimate flavor, make the dish one day ahead and reheat.
—Matthew Lawrence, Vashon, WA

PREP: 25 MIN. • **BAKE:** 3 HOURS • **MAKES:** 6 SERVINGS

- **1 Tbsp. coriander seeds**
- **1 Tbsp. cumin seeds**
- **1 bone-in pork shoulder roast (3 to 4 lbs.)**
- **¼ tsp. salt**
- **¼ tsp. pepper**
- **1 Tbsp. canola oil**
- **15 tomatillos, husks removed, chopped**
- **1 medium onion, chopped**
- **2 garlic cloves, peeled and halved**
- **1 cup white wine**
- **8 cups chicken broth**

POLENTA

- **4 cups chicken broth**
- **1 cup yellow cornmeal**

1. In a small dry skillet over medium heat, toast coriander and cumin seeds until aromatic, 1-2 minutes. Remove from skillet. Crush seeds using a spice grinder or mortar and pestle; set aside.
2. Sprinkle pork with salt and pepper. In an ovenproof Dutch oven, brown roast in oil on all sides. Remove and set aside. Add tomatillos and onion to the pan; saute until tomatillos are tender and lightly charred. Add the garlic and crushed spices; cook 1 minute longer.
3. Add wine, stirring to loosen browned bits from pan. Stir in 8 cups broth and return roast to pan. Bring to a boil. Cover and bake at 350° until pork is tender, 3-3½ hours.
4. Meanwhile, in a large heavy saucepan, bring broth to a boil. Reduce heat to a gentle boil; slowly whisk in cornmeal. Cook and stir with a wooden spoon until polenta is thickened and pulls away cleanly from the sides of the pan, 15-20 minutes. Serve with pork.
1 SERVING: 514 cal., 24g fat (7g sat. fat), 120mg chol., 1160mg sod., 30g carb. (6g sugars, 3g fiber), 41g pro.

SHEET-PAN CHICKEN PARMESAN

SHEET-PAN CHICKEN PARMESAN

Saucy chicken, melty mozzarella and crisp-tender broccoli, all in one pan. What could be better?
—Becky Hardin, Saint Peters, MO

PREP: 15 MIN. • **BAKE:** 20 MIN. + BROILING • **MAKES:** 4 SERVINGS

- **1 large egg**
- **½ cup panko (Japanese) bread crumbs**
- **½ cup grated Parmesan cheese**
- **½ tsp. salt**
- **1 tsp. pepper**
- **1 tsp. garlic powder**
- **4 boneless skinless chicken breast halves (6 oz. each)**
- **Olive oil-flavored cooking spray**
- **4 cups fresh or frozen broccoli florets (about 10 oz.)**
- **1 cup marinara sauce**
- **1 cup shredded mozzarella cheese**
- **¼ cup minced fresh basil, optional**

1. Preheat oven to 400°. Lightly coat a 15x10x1-in. sheet pan with cooking spray.
2. In a shallow bowl, whisk egg. In a separate shallow bowl, stir together the next five ingredients. Dip chicken breast in egg; allow excess to drip off. Then dip in crumb mixture, patting to help coating adhere. Repeat with remaining chicken. Place chicken breasts in center third of baking sheet. Spritz with cooking spray.
3. Bake 10 minutes. Remove from oven. Spread broccoli in a single layer along both sides of sheet pan (if broccoli is frozen, break pieces apart). Return to oven; bake 10 minutes longer. Remove from oven.
4. Preheat broiler. Spread marinara sauce over chicken; top with shredded cheese. Broil chicken and broccoli 3-4 in. from heat until cheese is golden brown and vegetables are tender, 3-5 minutes. If desired, sprinkle with basil.
1 SERVING: 504 cal., 17g fat (7g sat. fat), 147mg chol., 1151mg sod., 27g carb. (10g sugars, 8g fiber), 52g pro.

EAT SMART

MUSHROOM & SWEET POTATO POTPIE

The last time I was in the U.S., I had an amazing mushroom and beer potpie at a small brew pup. It was so rich and comforting. I tried numerous versions when I got home, and I think this one comes pretty close!
—Iben Ravn, Copenhagen, Denmark

PREP: 15 MIN. • **COOK:** 1 HOUR • **MAKES:** 8 SERVINGS

- **⅓ cup olive oil, divided**
- **1 lb. sliced fresh shiitake mushrooms**
- **1 lb. sliced baby portobello mushrooms**
- **2 large onions, chopped**
- **2 garlic cloves, minced**
- **1 tsp. minced fresh rosemary, plus more for topping**
- **1 bottle (12 oz.) porter or stout beer**
- **1½ cups mushroom broth or vegetable broth, divided**
- **2 bay leaves**
- **1 Tbsp. balsamic vinegar**
- **2 Tbsp. reduced-sodium soy sauce**
- **¼ cup cornstarch**
- **3 to 4 small sweet potatoes, peeled and thinly sliced**
- **¾ tsp. coarsely ground pepper**
- **½ tsp. salt**

1. Preheat oven to 400°. In a Dutch oven, heat 1 Tbsp. oil over medium heat. Add shiitake mushrooms and cook in batches until dark golden brown, 8-10 minutes; remove with a slotted spoon. Repeat with 1 Tbsp. oil and the portobello mushrooms.
2. In same pan, heat 1 Tbsp. oil over medium heat. Add onions; cook and stir 8-10 minutes or until tender. Add garlic and 1 tsp. rosemary; cook 30 seconds longer. Stir in beer, 1 cup broth, bay leaves, vinegar, soy sauce and sauteed mushrooms.
3. Bring to a boil. Reduce heat; simmer, uncovered, 10 minutes. In a small bowl, mix cornstarch and remaining broth until smooth; stir into mushroom mixture. Return to a boil, stirring constantly; cook and stir until thickened, 1-2 minutes. Remove and discard bay leaves; transfer mushroom mixture to eight greased 8-oz. ramekins.
4. Layer sweet potatoes in a circular pattern on top of each ramekin; brush with remaining oil and sprinkle with pepper, salt and additional rosemary. Bake, covered, until potatoes are tender, 20-25 minutes. Remove cover and bake until potatoes are lightly browned, 8-10 minutes. Let stand 5 minutes before serving.
1 SERVING: 211 cal., 10g fat (1g sat. fat), 0 chol., 407mg sod., 26g carb. (10g sugars, 4g fiber), 5g pro.

SLOW COOKER

FILIPINO ADOBO AROMATIC CHICKEN

This saucy chicken packs a wallop of flavor—salty, sweet, sour, slightly spicy and even a little umami. It can be made on the stove, too. Any way I make it, I think it tastes even better the next day served over warm rice.
—Loanne Chiu, Fort Worth, TX

PREP: 30 MIN. • **COOK:** 3 HOURS 20 MIN.
MAKES: 6 SERVINGS

- **8 bacon strips, chopped**
- **3 lbs. boneless skinless chicken thighs**
- **1 large onion, chopped**
- **4 garlic cloves, minced**
- **2 medium limes**
- **¼ cup dry sherry**
- **3 Tbsp. soy sauce**
- **3 Tbsp. molasses**
- **2 Tbsp. minced fresh gingerroot**
- **3 bay leaves**
- **1 tsp. pepper**
- **½ tsp. chili garlic sauce**
- **Minced fresh cilantro and toasted sesame seeds**
- **Hot cooked rice**
- **Lime wedges, optional**

1. In a large skillet, cook bacon over medium heat until crisp, stirring occasionally. Remove with a slotted spoon; drain on paper towels. Discard drippings, reserving 1 Tbsp. in pan. Brown chicken in bacon drippings in batches. Transfer chicken to a 4- or 5-qt. slow cooker.
2. Add onion to the same pan; cook and stir until tender, 3-5 minutes. Add garlic; cook and stir 1 minute longer. Finely grate enough zest from limes to measure 2 tsp. Cut limes crosswise in half; squeeze juice from limes. Add the lime juice and zest, sherry, soy sauce, molasses, ginger, bay leaves, pepper and chili sauce to pan; cook and stir to loosen browned bits. Pour over chicken. Cook, covered, on high until a thermometer reads 170°, 3-4 hours.
3. Remove chicken; keep warm. If desired, slightly thicken juices by cooking in a saucepan over medium-high heat about 20 minutes. Remove bay leaves. Stir in bacon. Pour over chicken; sprinkle with cilantro and sesame seeds. Serve with rice and, if desired, lime wedges.

6 OZ. COOKED CHICKEN WITH ¼ CUP SAUCE: 474 cal., 23g fat (7g sat. fat), 164mg chol., 865mg sod., 15g carb. (9g sugars, 1g fiber), 47g pro.

FILIPINO ADOBO AROMATIC CHICHEN

PRESSURE-COOKER CAJUN PORK & RICE

I created this recipe after returning home from a trip and finding little food in the house. I used ingredients already available in the refrigerator and pantry. My husband loves this pork dish because it's tasty, and I love it because it's easy.
—Allison Gapinski, Cary, NC

PREP: 20 MIN. • **COOK:** 20 MIN. + RELEASING
MAKES: 4 SERVINGS

- **1 tsp. olive oil**
- **1 medium green pepper, julienned**
- **1½ tsp. ground cumin**
- **1½ tsp. chili powder**
- **1½ lbs. boneless pork loin chops**
- **1 can (14½ oz.) petite diced tomatoes, undrained**
- **1 small onion, finely chopped**
- **1 celery rib, chopped**
- **1 small carrot, julienned**
- **1 garlic cloves, minced**
- **½ tsp. Louisiana-style hot sauce**
- **¼ tsp. salt**
- **¾ cup reduced-sodium chicken broth**
- **1½ cups uncooked instant rice**

1. Select saute setting on a 6-qt. electric pressure cooker and adjust for high heat; add oil. Add green pepper; cook and stir 4-5 minutes or until crisp-tender. Remove pepper and set aside. Select cancel setting to turn off saute function.
2. Mix cumin and chili powder; sprinkle pork chops with 2 tsp. spice mixture. Place pork in pressure cooker. In a small bowl, mix tomatoes, onion, celery, carrot, garlic, hot sauce, salt and remaining spice mixture; pour over pork. Lock lid; make sure vent is closed. Select manual setting; adjust pressure to high and set time for 6 minutes. When cooking finishes, allow pressure to naturally release for 5 minutes, then quick-release any remaining pressure according to the manufacturer's instructions.
3. Stir in chicken broth, breaking up pork into pieces. Select saute setting and adjust for normal heat; bring to a boil. Add rice. Cook until rice is tender, 5 minutes longer. Serve with sauteed green pepper.

1 SERVING: 423cal., 12g fat (4g sat. fat), 82mg chol., 573mg sod., 40g carb. (6g sugars, 4g fiber), 38g pro. **Diabetic exchanges:** 5 lean meat, 2 starch, 1 vegetable.

HOW TO MAKE

GRILLED PIZZA

Grilling your own pizza is easier than you think. Follow these steps for a crisp crust with smoky-good flavor.

SMOKY GRILLED PIZZA WITH GREENS & TOMATOES

Prep First

Grilling pizza is a very quick process, so have all your tools ready to go beforehand. If any toppings need to be cooked longer than two to four minutes, cook them first.

Fire It Up!

You can use a gas or charcoal grill to make grilled pizza. If using gas, preheat it to medium temperature. For charcoal, the fire should be moderately hot. If you can hold your hand 4 inches above the fire for a max of three seconds, that's about right.

Pile On Flavor

Heirloom tomatoes' seeds have been passed down through generations because of the fruits' color, flavor and nutritional value. Find heirloom tomatoes at farmers markets in the summer and in many specialty grocery stores. You can substitute regular sun-ripened tomatoes if heirloom varieties aren't available.

SMOKY GRILLED PIZZA WITH GREENS & TOMATOES

This smoky grilled pizza scores big with me for two reasons: It encourages my husband and son to eat greens, and it showcases fresh summer produce.
—Sarah Gray, Erie, CO

PREP: 15 MIN. + RISING • **GRILL:** 10 MIN
MAKES: 2 PIZZAS (4 SLICES EACH)

- **3 cups all-purpose flour**
- **2 tsp. kosher salt**
- **1 tsp. active dry yeast**
- **3 Tbsp. olive oil, divided**
- **1¼ to 1½ cups warm water (120° to 130°)**

TOPPING

- **2 Tbsp. olive oil**
- **10 cups beet greens, coarsely chopped**
- **4 garlic cloves, minced**
- **2 Tbsp. balsamic vinegar**
- **¾ cup prepared pesto**
- **¾ cup shredded Italian cheese blend**
- **½ cup crumbled feta cheese**
- **2 medium heirloom tomatoes, thinly sliced**
- **¼ cup fresh basil leaves, chopped**

1. Place flour, salt and yeast in a food processor; pulse until blended. While processing, add 2 Tbsp. oil and enough water in a steady stream for dough to form a ball. Turn dough onto a floured surface; knead until smooth and elastic, 6-8 minutes.
2. Place in a greased bowl, turning once to grease the top. Cover with plastic wrap and let rise in a warm place until almost doubled, about 1½ hours.
3. Punch down dough. On a lightly floured surface, divide dough into two portions. Press or roll each portion into a 10-in. circle; place each on a piece of greased foil (about 12 in. square). Brush tops with remaining oil; cover with plastic wrap and let rest for 10 minutes.
4. For topping, in a 6-qt. stockpot, heat oil over medium-high heat. Add beet greens; cook and stir until tender, 3-5 minutes. Add garlic; cook 30 seconds longer. Remove from heat; stir in vinegar.
5. Carefully invert pizza crusts onto oiled grill rack; remove foil. Grill, covered, over medium heat until bottoms are lightly browned, 3-5 minutes. Turn; grill until second side begins to brown, 1-2 minutes.
6. Remove from grill. Spread with pesto; top with beet greens, cheeses and tomatoes. Return pizzas to grill. Cook, covered, over medium heat until cheese is melted, 2-4 minutes. Sprinkle with basil.

1 SLICE: 407 cal., 20g fat (5g sat. fat), 11mg chol., 1007mg sod., 44g carb. (3g sugars, 4g fiber), 11g pro.

HOW-TO

To-Dos (and Ta-Da's)

- Before placing dough on the grill, brush it generously with olive oil to ensure that the crust doesn't stick to the grill grate.
- Make sure the grate is clean, oiled and preheated. Gently place the dough over direct heat and cover. After several minutes, lift an edge to check for browning.
- When the underside is light brown and the dough starts to bubble and puff up like a pancake, it's time to turn it over. Flip the crust using tongs or a large spatula.
- Once the second side is golden brown, use tongs to slide the crust onto a baking sheet (or a pizza peel if you have one).
- Add toppings before returning the pizza to the grill. Don't overload it or the crust will char before the toppings heat through.

STUFFED SPAGHETTI SQUASH
PAGE 116

EVERYDAY FRESH

Comfort food gets a modern upgrade when it's prepared with a rainbow of fresh, nutrient-rich ingredients. These easy-to-follow recipes—some even boasting bold global flavors—take the guesswork out of meal planning and help keep your healthy lifestyle on track.

FILIPINO CHICKEN ADOBO

FILIPINO CHICKEN ADOBO

My mother always makes her saucy chicken adobo when I come home to visit. It's even better the next day as leftovers—Mom says it's because of the vinegar.
—Michael Moya, New York, NY

PREP: 10 MIN. + MARINATING
COOK: 30 MIN. • **MAKES:** 6 SERVINGS

- **1 cup white vinegar**
- **¼ cup soy sauce**
- **1 whole garlic bulb, smashed and peeled**
- **2 tsp. kosher salt**
- **1 tsp. coarsely ground pepper**
- **1 bay leaf**
- **2 lbs. bone-in chicken thighs or drumsticks**
- **1 Tbsp. canola oil**
- **1 cup water**

1. Combine the first six ingredients. Add the chicken; refrigerate, covered, for 20-30 minutes. Drain, reserving marinade. Pat chicken dry.
2. In a large skillet, heat oil over medium-high heat; brown chicken. Stir in water and reserved marinade. Bring to a boil. Reduce heat; simmer, uncovered, until chicken is no longer pink and sauce is slightly reduced, 20-25 minutes. If desired, serve chicken with cooking sauce.
1 SERVING: 234 cal., 15g fat (4g sat. fat), 71mg chol., 1315mg sod., 2g carb. (0 sugars, 0 fiber), 22g pro.

EAT SMART FAST FIX

SALMON WITH ROOT VEGETABLES

This cozy hash is loaded with protein and healthy fats that keep you going on hectic days. We've been known to devour it at breakfast, lunch and dinner!
—Courtney Stultz, Weir, KS

TAKES: 25 MIN. • **MAKES:** 6 SERVINGS

- **2 Tbsp. olive oil**
- **2 medium sweet potatoes, peeled and cut into ¼-in. cubes**
- **2 medium red potatoes, cut into ¼-in. cubes**
- **2 medium turnips, peeled and diced**
- **2 medium carrots, peeled and diced**
- **1 tsp. sea salt, divided**
- **1 tsp. chili powder**
- **¾ tsp. pepper, divided**
- **½ tsp. ground cinnamon**
- **½ tsp. ground cumin**
- **6 salmon fillets (6 oz. each)**

1. Preheat oven to 400°. In a large skillet, heat oil over medium heat. Add potatoes, turnips and carrots. Combine ½ tsp. salt, chili powder, ½ tsp. pepper, cinnamon and cumin; sprinkle over vegetables. Cook, stirring frequently, until vegetables are tender, 15-20 minutes.
2. Meanwhile, place salmon, skin side down, in a foil-lined 15x10x1-in. baking pan. Sprinkle with remaining salt and pepper. Bake 10 minutes. Preheat broiler; broil until fish just begins to flake easily, 2-5 minutes. Serve salmon with vegetables.
1 SERVING: 417 cal., 21g fat (4g sat. fat), 85mg chol., 464mg sod., 26g carb. (9g sugars, 4g fiber), 31g pro. **Diabetic exchanges:** 4 lean meat, 2 starch, 1 fat.

GOES **GREAT** WITH

Fennel Spinach Saute

2 tsp. olive oil • 2 tsp. butter • 1 cup thinly sliced fennel bulb • ¼ cup thinly sliced red onion • 1 garlic clove, minced • 6 cups fresh baby spinach • ¼ cup minced fresh basil • ¼ tsp. salt • ¼ tsp. pepper • In a large skillet, heat the oil and butter over medium-high heat. Add fennel and onion; cook and stir until tender. Add garlic; cook 1 minute longer. Add remaining ingredients; cook and stir just until the spinach is wilted, 4-5 minutes. **Makes 4 servings.**
—Noelle Myers, Grand Forks, ND

COURTNEY STULTZ
Weir, KS

FENNEL SPINACH SAUTE

SALMON WITH ROOT VEGETABLES

SHIITAKE-CHICKEN SLIDERS

My husband and I love Asian cuisine. One of our favorite items to order at Thai restaurants is chicken satay skewers with spicy peanut sauce. These sliders are a fun variation. They're moist and flavorful with the addition of shiitake mushrooms, and topped with the spicy-sweet peanut sauce and tangy cucumber slices.
—Julie Hession, Las Vegas, NV

PREP: 35 MIN. • **GRILL:** 10 MIN. • **MAKES:** 18 SLIDERS

- **⅓ cup rice vinegar**
- **4½ tsp. sugar**
- **1¼ cups thinly sliced cucumber**

BURGERS

- **½ lb. sliced fresh shiitake mushrooms**
- **1 Tbsp. canola oil**
- **3 garlic cloves, minced**
- **1 Tbsp. minced fresh gingerroot**
- **3 Tbsp. reduced-sodium soy sauce**
- **2 tsp. sesame oil**
- **⅓ cup green onions**
- **½ tsp. kosher salt**
- **½ tsp. crushed red pepper flakes**
- **2 lbs. ground chicken**

SPICY PEANUT SAUCE

- **1 cup water**
- **½ cup creamy peanut butter**
- **2 Tbsp. brown sugar**
- **2 Tbsp. rice vinegar**
- **2 Tbsp. reduced-sodium soy sauce**
- **1 Tbsp. cornstarch**
- **1 Tbsp. Sriracha Asian hot chili sauce or 1½ tsp. hot pepper sauce**
- **18 dinner rolls, split and toasted**

1. In a small bowl, combine the vinegar and sugar. Add cucumber and toss to coat; set aside.
2. In a large skillet, saute mushrooms in canola oil until tender. Add garlic and ginger; cook 1 minute longer. Remove from the heat.
3. In a large bowl, combine the soy sauce, sesame oil, onions, salt, pepper flakes and mushrooms. Crumble chicken over mixture and mix well. Shape into 18 patties.
4. Grill burgers, covered, on a greased grill rack over medium heat until a thermometer reads 165° and juices run clear, 3-4 minutes on each side.
5. For sauce, in a small saucepan, combine the water, peanut butter, brown sugar, rice vinegar, soy sauce, cornstarch and chili sauce until smooth. Bring to a boil; cook and stir until thickened, about 2 minutes.
6. Serve burgers on rolls with sauce and sliced cucumber.
1 SLIDER: 246 cal., 11g fat (3g sat. fat), 51mg chol., 504mg sod., 24g carb. (4g sugars, 2g fiber), 14g pro

GOES **GREAT** WITH

Peas with Shallots

1 Tbsp. butter • ½ lb. fresh sugar snap peas, trimmed • 1 cup frozen peas • 2 shallots, thinly sliced • ½ tsp. salt • ¼ tsp. pepper • In a large skillet, heat butter over medium-high heat. Add snap peas and frozen peas; cook and stir until crisp-tender, 4-5 minutes. Add shallots, salt and pepper; cook 1 minute longer. **Makes 4 servings.**
—Rosemary Schirm, Avondale, PA

EAT SMART **FAST FIX**

PRESSURE-COOKED RISOTTO WITH SHRIMP & ASPARAGUS

This speedy method of cooking risotto works every time!
—Kim Gray, Davie, FL

TAKES: 30 MIN • **MAKES:** 8 SERVINGS

- **3 Tbsp. unsalted butter**
- **1 small onion, finely diced**
- **9 garlic cloves, minced, divided**
- **1⅔ cups uncooked arborio rice**
- **1 cup white wine**
- **4 cups reduced-sodium chicken broth**
- **½ cup shredded Parmesan cheese, divided**
- **2 Tbsp. olive oil**
- **2 lbs. uncooked shrimp (26-30 per lb.), peeled and deveined**
- **1 Tbsp. unsalted butter**
- **½ cup Italian salad dressing**
- **1 lb. fresh asparagus, trimmed**
- **Salt and pepper to taste**

1. Select saute setting on a 6-qt. electric pressure cooker and adjust for high heat; warm butter until melted. Add onion; cook 4-5 minutes. Add six minced garlic cloves; cook 1 minute. Add rice; cook and stir 2 minutes. Stir in ½ cup wine; cook and stir until absorbed. Add remaining wine, broth and ¼ cup cheese. Lock lid; make sure vent is closed. Select manual setting; adjust pressure to high. Set the time for 8 minutes. When finished cooking, quick-release pressure according to manufacturer's directions; stir.
2. Meanwhile, heat oil in a large skillet over medium-high heat. Add remaining garlic; cook 1 minute. Add shrimp; cook and stir until shrimp begin to turn pink, about 5 minutes. Add butter and dressing; stir until butter melts. Reduce heat. Add asparagus; cook until tender, 3-5 minutes. Serve over risotto. Season with salt and pepper. Sprinkle with remaining cheese.
1 SERVING: 424 cal., 15g fat (6g sat. fat), 157mg chol., 661mg sod., 39g carb. (3g sugars, 1g fiber), 26g pro.

PRESSURE-COOKED RISOTTO WITH SHRIMP & ASPARAGUS

RHUBARB PORK CHOP CASSEROLE

RHUBARB PORK CHOP CASSEROLE

The usual reaction to this dish is that it's a nice mix of sweet and tart—and a unique use of rhubarb! I love that this recipe offers a savory, nondessert way to enjoy the popular summer fruit.
—Jeanie Castor, Decatur, IL

PREP: 20 MIN. • **BAKE:** 35 MIN. • **MAKES:** 4 SERVINGS

- **4 boneless pork loin chops (¾ in. thick and 4 oz. each)**
- **1 Tbsp. canola oil**
- **Salt and pepper to taste**
- **2 Tbsp. butter**
- **3 cups soft bread crumbs**
- **3 cups sliced fresh or frozen rhubarb (1-in. pieces)**
- **½ cup packed brown sugar**
- **¼ cup all-purpose flour**
- **1 tsp. ground cinnamon**

1. In a large skillet, brown pork chops in oil; sprinkle with salt and pepper. Remove and keep warm. Add butter to the drippings to melt; mix with bread crumbs. Remove from heat.
2. In a large bowl, combine the rhubarb, sugar, flour and cinnamon; spoon mixture into a greased 11x7-in. baking dish. Sprinkle crumbs over top.
3. Cover with foil and bake at 350° for 25-30 minutes. Remove the foil. Arrange the pork chops on top. Bake, uncovered, until heated through, 10-15 minutes.
1 SERVING: 477 cal., 17g fat (7g sat. fat), 70mg chol., 254mg sod., 54g carb. (30g sugars, 3g fiber), 26g pro.

CARIBBEAN CURRIED CHICKEN

EAT SMART **SLOW COOKER**

CARIBBEAN CURRIED CHICKEN

Having grown up in the Virgin Islands, I've eaten my fair share of authentic curried chicken. This recipe hits the mark with big, bold flavors. It's delicious served over rice.
—Sharon Gibson, Hendersonville, NC

PREP: 20 MIN. • **COOK:** 4 HOURS
MAKES: 8 SERVINGS

- **1 Tbsp. Madras curry powder**
- **1 tsp. garlic powder**
- **1 tsp. pepper**
- **8 boneless skinless chicken thighs (about 4 oz. each)**
- **1 medium onion, thinly sliced**
- **1½ cups Goya mojo criollo marinade, well-shaken**
- **2 Tbsp. canola oil**
- **2 Tbsp. all-purpose flour**
- **Hot cooked rice, green onions and fresh cilantro leaves, optional**

1. Combine curry powder, garlic powder and pepper; sprinkle over chicken, pressing to help it adhere. Place chicken in a 3-qt. slow cooker. Sprinkle with onion. Carefully pour mojo criollo marinade along the sides of slow cooker, avoiding chicken to keep coating intact. Cook, covered, on low until a thermometer reads 170°, 4-6 hours. Remove chicken; keep warm.

2. Pour cooking juices from slow cooker into a measuring cup; skim fat. In a large saucepan, heat oil over medium heat; whisk in flour until smooth. Gradually whisk in cooking juices. Bring to a boil, stirring constantly; cook and stir until thickened, 1-2 minutes. Reduce heat; add chicken and simmer about 5 minutes. If desired, serve with rice, green onions and cilantro.

1 CHICKEN THIGH WITH 6 TBSP. SAUCE: 249 cal., 13g fat (3g sat. fat), 76mg chol., 514mg sod., 11g carb. (5g sugars, 1g fiber), 22g pro. **Diabetic exchanges:** 3 lean meat, 1 fat.

TEST KITCHEN TIP

Mojo criollo (pronounced *mo-ho cree-OH-yo*) is a citrus-based marinade commonly used in Latin American and Caribbean cooking. You'll find it in large bottles in most supermarkets. Chop up leftovers of this curried chicken and scoop into warmed tortillas for burritos. Yum!

EAT SMART **FAST FIX**

STUFFED SPAGHETTI SQUASH

(SHOWN ON PAGE 110)

I've been working on developing healthy recipes that both taste delicious and keep me satisfied. This squash tossed with beef, beans and kale has so much flavor, it's easy to forget it's good for you!
—Charlotte Cravins, Opelousas, LA

TAKES: 30 MIN. • **MAKES:** 4 SERVINGS

- **1 medium spaghetti squash**
- **1 cup water**
- **¾ lb. lean ground beef (90% lean)**
- **½ cup chopped red onion**
- **2 Tbsp. yellow mustard**
- **2 to 3 tsp. Louisiana-style hot sauce**
- **4 small garlic cloves, minced**
- **1 can (15 oz.) no-salt-added black beans, rinsed and drained**
- **2 cups chopped fresh kale**
- **¼ cup plain Greek yogurt**

1. Trim ends of spaghetti squash and halve lengthwise; discard seeds. Place squash, cut side down, on the trivet in a 6-qt. electric pressure cooker. Add water to cooker. Lock lid; make sure vent is closed. Select steam setting; adjust pressure to high and set time for 7 minutes. When squash is finished cooking, quickly release pressure according to the manufacturer's directions. Set squash aside; remove water from cooker. In a large skillet, crumble beef and cook with onion over medium heat until no longer pink, 4-6 minutes; drain. Add mustard, hot sauce and garlic; cook 1 minute more. Stir in black beans and kale; cook just until wilted, 2-3 minutes.

2. Using a fork, separate strands of spaghetti squash; combine with meat mixture. Dollop servings with Greek yogurt.

1½ CUPS: 401 cal., 12g fat (4g sat. fat), 57mg chol., 314mg sod., 51g carb. (2g sugars, 13g fiber), 26g pro.

FAST FIX

PORK PIPERADE

I spice up my meat dishes with peppers. My recipe for Basque piperade—adapted from a Spanish recipe—is a family favorite.
—Hyacinth Rizzo, Buffalo, NY

TAKES: 30 MIN. • **MAKES:** 4 SERVINGS

- **¼ cup all-purpose flour**
- **1 envelope (1¼ oz.) reduced-sodium taco seasoning, divided**
- **1 lb. boneless pork, cut into 1½x⅛-in. strips**
- **2 Tbsp. canola oil**

PIPERADE

- **3 Tbsp. olive oil**
- **1 medium Spanish onion, thinly sliced**
- **2 medium sweet red peppers, julienned**
- **2 cups canned plum tomatoes, drained (reserve juices)**

1. In a shallow bowl, combine flour and half of seasoning mix. Add pork, a few pieces at a time, and toss to coat; shake off excess.
2. In a large skillet, heat the canola oil over medium-high heat. Add pork; stir-fry until browned, 3-4 minutes. Remove with a slotted spoon; cover and keep warm.
3. In the same skillet, heat olive oil. Stir-fry onion and peppers until crisp-tender. Chop the tomatoes; add to skillet. In a small bowl, combine the remaining taco seasoning and reserved tomato juices. Add sauce to skillet. Bring to a boil; cook and stir until thickened. Reduce heat to medium-low. Return pork to skillet; heat through.

1 SERVING: 414 cal., 24g fat (4g sat. fat), 67mg chol., 720mg sod., 23g carb. (10g sugars, 4g fiber), 26g pro.

GOES **GREAT** WITH

Lemon Rice Pilaf

1 cup uncooked jasmine or long grain white rice • 1 cup sliced celery • 1 cup thinly sliced green onions • 2 Tbsp. butter • 1 Tbsp. grated lemon zest • 1 tsp. salt • ¼ tsp. pepper • Cook rice according to package directions. Meanwhile, in a skillet over medium heat, saute celery and onions in butter until tender. Add the rice, lemon zest, salt and pepper; toss lightly. Cook and stir until heated through. **Makes 6 servings.**
—Taste of Home *Test Kitchen*

CAJUN SIRLOIN WITH MUSHROOM LEEK SAUCE

ASPARAGUS, SQUASH & RED PEPPER SAUTE

FAST FIX

CAJUN SIRLOIN WITH MUSHROOM LEEK SAUCE

In 30 minutes, you'll have restaurant-quality steak with a bold Cajun flair. The best part? You can skip the drive, the wait and the bill!
—Joshua Keefer, Delaware, OH

TAKES: 30 MIN. • **MAKES:** 4 SERVINGS

- 1 beef top sirloin steak (1¼ lbs.)
- 2 Tbsp. Cajun seasoning
- 2 Tbsp. olive oil
- ½ lb. sliced assorted fresh mushrooms
- 1 medium leek (white portion only), halved and sliced
- 1 Tbsp. butter
- 1 tsp. minced garlic
- 1½ cups dry red wine or reduced-sodium beef broth
- ¼ tsp. pepper
- ⅛ tsp. salt

1. Rub steak with Cajun seasoning; let stand for 5 minutes.
2. In a large skillet, cook steak in oil over medium-high heat for 7-10 minutes on each side or until meat reaches desired doneness (for medium-rare, a thermometer should read 135°; medium, 140°; medium-well, 145°). Remove and keep warm.
3. In the same skillet, saute mushrooms and leek in butter until tender. Add garlic; cook 1 minute longer. Add the wine, pepper and salt, stirring to loosen browned bits from pan. Bring to a boil; cook until liquid is reduced by half. Slice steak; serve with mushroom sauce.

4 OZ. COOKED BEEF WITH ¼ CUP SAUCE: 325 cal., 16g fat (5g sat. fat), 65mg chol., 976mg sod., 7g carb. (2g sugars, 1g fiber), 32g pro.

GOES **GREAT** WITH

Asparagus, Squash & Red Pepper Saute

2 medium sweet red peppers, julienned • 2 medium yellow summer squash, halved lengthwise and cut into ¼-in. slices • 6 oz. fresh asparagus, trimmed and cut into 1½-in. pieces • ¼ cup white wine or vegetable broth • 4½ tsp. olive oil • ¼ tsp. salt • ¼ tsp. pepper • In a large skillet, saute the peppers, squash and asparagus in wine and oil until crisp-tender. Sprinkle with salt and pepper. **Makes 4 servings.**
—Deirdre Cox, Kansas City, MO

ROXANNE CHAN
Albany, CA

CASABLANCA CHICKEN COUSCOUS

EAT SMART

CASABLANCA CHICKEN COUSCOUS

Risotto has always been one of my favorite Italian comfort foods. For a fun spin, I used lively North African-inspired flavors that still pack all the creamy goodness of the original.
—Roxanne Chan, Albany, CA

PREP: 20 MIN. • **COOK:** 15 MIN. + STANDING
MAKES: 6 SERVINGS

- 1 Tbsp. olive oil
- 1 medium onion, chopped
- 1 lb. boneless skinless chicken thighs, cut into 1-in. pieces
- 1 pkg. (8.8 oz.) uncooked Israeli couscous
- ½ tsp. salt
- ¼ tsp. pepper
- ¼ tsp. crushed red pepper flakes
- 2 cans (14½ oz. each) reduced-sodium chicken broth
- ⅔ cup dried tropical fruit
- 1 can (15 to 15½ oz.) garbanzo beans or chickpeas, rinsed and drained
- ½ cup plain yogurt
- 1 small carrot, grated
- ¼ cup minced fresh parsley
- 1 medium lemon

1. In a large skillet, heat the olive oil over medium-high heat. Add onion; saute until softened, 3-4 minutes. Add the chicken, couscous, salt, pepper and pepper flakes; cook and stir until chicken begins to brown, 3-5 minutes. Add broth and dried fruit; cook, uncovered, until the chicken and couscous are tender and the fruit is moist, 8-10 minutes.
2. Stir in the remaining ingredients; heat through. Remove from the heat. Let stand, covered, 10 minutes. Meanwhile, zest the lemon peel into strips; cut lemon into six wedges. Top couscous with zest strips and serve with lemon wedges.

1⅓ CUPS: 448 cal., 11g fat (3g sat. fat), 53mg chol., 715mg sod., 63g carb. (17g sugars, 4g fiber), 25g pro.

CREOLE SHRIMP PIZZA

EAT SMART

PORK & ASPARAGUS SHEET-PAN DINNER

When time is of the essence, it's nice to have a quick and easy recipe in your back pocket. Not only is this sheet-pan meal delicious, but you can clean it up in a flash.
—Joan Hallford, North Richland Hills, TX

PREP: 20 MIN. • **BAKE:** 20 MIN.
MAKES: 4 SERVINGS

- **¼ cup olive oil, divided**
- **3 cups diced new potatoes**
- **3 cups fresh asparagus, cut into 1-in. pieces**
- **¼ tsp. salt**
- **¼ tsp. pepper**
- **1 large Gala or Honeycrisp apple, peeled and cut into ½-in. slices**
- **2 tsp. brown sugar**
- **1 tsp. ground cinnamon**
- **¼ tsp. ground ginger**
- **4 boneless pork loin chops (1 in. thick and about 6 oz. each)**
- **2 tsp. southwest seasoning**

1. Preheat oven to 425°. Line a 15x10x1-in. sheet pan with foil; brush with 2 tsp. olive oil.
2. In a large bowl, toss potatoes with 1 Tbsp. olive oil. Place in one section of prepared sheet pan. In same bowl, toss asparagus with 1 Tbsp. olive oil; place in another section of pan. Sprinkle salt and pepper over potatoes and asparagus.
3. In same bowl, toss apple with 1 tsp. olive oil. Mix brown sugar, cinnamon and ginger; sprinkle over apples and toss to coat. Transfer to a different section of pan.
4. Brush pork chops with remaining olive oil; sprinkle both sides with southwest seasoning. Place chops in remaining section of pan. Bake until a thermometer inserted in pork reads 145° and potatoes and apples are tender, 20-25 minutes. Let stand for 5 minutes before serving.

1 SERVING: 486 cal., 23g fat (5g sat. fat), 82mg chol., 447mg sod., 32g carb. (10g sugars, 5g fiber), 37g pro.

CREOLE SHRIMP PIZZA

The flavors of Creole cuisine put a fun twist on a traditional pizza. If you like yours spicy, add more hot sauce to boost the heat.
—Robin Haas, Cranston, RI

PREP: 15 MIN. • **BAKE:** 25 MIN.
MAKES: 6 SLICES

- **1 prebaked 12-in. pizza crust**
- **1 Tbsp. olive oil, divided**
- **1½ cups shredded part-skim mozzarella cheese, divided**
- **1 Tbsp. lemon juice**
- **1½ tsp. reduced-sodium Creole seasoning, divided**
- **1 lb. uncooked shrimp (31-40 per lb.), peeled and deveined**
- **1 large onion, chopped**
- **½ tsp. coarsely ground pepper**
- **¼ tsp. celery seed**
- **2 garlic cloves, minced**
- **1 cup pizza sauce**
- **¼ tsp. Louisiana-style hot sauce**
- **1 large green pepper, thinly sliced**

1. Preheat oven to 425°. Place crust on an ungreased baking sheet. Brush with 1½ tsp. oil; sprinkle with ½ cup mozzarella cheese. Set aside. Combine lemon juice and ½ tsp. Creole seasoning. Add shrimp; toss to coat.
2. In a small skillet, heat remaining oil over medium heat. Add the onion, pepper, celery seed and remaining Creole seasoning; saute until onion is tender. Add the garlic; cook 1 minute longer. Stir in pizza sauce and hot sauce. Remove from heat.
3. Drain shrimp. Spread sauce mixture over crust. Top with shrimp and green pepper; sprinkle with remaining cheese. Bake until shrimp turn pink and cheese is melted, 25-30 minutes.

NOTE: The following spices may be substituted for 1 tsp. Creole seasoning: ¼ tsp. each salt, garlic powder and paprika; and a pinch each of dried thyme, ground cumin and cayenne pepper.

1 SLICE: 378 cal., 13g fat (4g sat. fat), 110mg chol., 969mg sod., 39g carb. (6g sugars, 3g fiber), 27g pro.

EAT SMART FAST FIX

SHRIMP ORZO WITH FETA

Tender, hearty and flavorful, this dish is one of my favorites. Garlic and a splash of lemon add to the fresh taste, and the benefits of heart-healthy shrimp can't be beat.
—Sarah Hummel, Moon Township, PA

TAKES: 25 MIN. • **MAKES:** 4 SERVINGS

- **1¼ cups uncooked whole wheat orzo pasta**
- **2 Tbsp. olive oil**
- **2 garlic cloves, minced**
- **2 medium tomatoes, chopped**
- **2 Tbsp. lemon juice**
- **1¼ lbs. uncooked shrimp (26-30 per lb.), peeled and deveined**
- **2 Tbsp. minced fresh cilantro**
- **¼ tsp. pepper**
- **½ cup crumbled feta cheese**

1. Cook orzo according to the package directions. Meanwhile, in a large skillet, heat oil over medium heat. Add garlic; cook and stir 1 minute. Add tomatoes and lemon juice. Bring to a boil. Stir in shrimp. Reduce heat; simmer, uncovered, 4-5 minutes or until shrimp turn pink.
2. Drain orzo. Add the orzo, cilantro and pepper to shrimp mixture; heat through. Sprinkle with feta cheese.

1 CUP: 406 cal., 12g fat (3g sat. fat), 180mg chol., 307mg sod., 40g carb. (2g sugars, 9g fiber), 33g pro. **Diabetic exchanges:** 4 lean meat, 2 starch, 1 fat.

SHRIMP ORZO WITH FETA

SMOKY CAULIFLOWER BITES

CRANBERRY TURKEY BURGERS WITH ARUGULA SALAD

EAT SMART FAST FIX

CRANBERRY TURKEY BURGERS WITH ARUGULA SALAD

Enjoy a taste of the holidays in every bite with these healthy turkey burgers. They're perfect for those on a gluten-restricted diet, but don't be surprised if everyone at the table asks for seconds.
—Nicole Stevens, Mount Pleasant, SC

TAKES: 25 MIN. • **MAKES:** 4 SERVINGS

- **¾ lb. ground turkey**
- **⅓ cup dried cranberries**
- **⅓ cup gluten-free soft bread crumbs**
- **3 green onions, finely chopped**
- **2 to 3 Tbsp. crumbled goat cheese**
- **2 Tbsp. pepper jelly**
- **3 garlic cloves, minced**
- **1 large egg yolk**
- **¼ tsp. salt**
- **¼ tsp. pepper**
- **4 cups fresh arugula**
- **1 Tbsp. grapeseed oil or olive oil**
- **1 Tbsp. honey**

1. Preheat oven to 375°. Combine the first 10 ingredients, mixing lightly but thoroughly. Shape into four ½-in. thick patties; transfer to a greased baking sheet. Bake until no longer pink, 10-12 minutes. Heat broiler; broil until a thermometer inserted in burgers reads 165°, about 5 minutes.
2. Meanwhile, toss arugula with oil. Drizzle with honey; toss to combine. Top salad with turkey burgers.

1 BURGER WITH 1 CUP SALAD: 281 cal., 12g fat (3g sat. fat), 107mg chol., 240mg sod., 26g carb. (21g sugars, 2g fiber), 19g pro.

GOES **GREAT** WITH

Smoky Cauliflower Bites

¼ cup olive oil • ¾ tsp. sea salt • 1 tsp. paprika • ½ tsp. ground cumin • ¼ tsp. ground turmeric • ⅛ tsp. chili powder • 1 medium head cauliflower, broken into florets • Preheat oven to 450°. Mix first six ingredients. Add cauliflower florets; toss to coat. Transfer to a 15x10x1-in. baking pan. Roast until tender, 15-20 minutes, stirring halfway. **Makes 4 servings.**
—Courtney Stultz, Weir, KS

EAT SMART

PRESSURE-COOKER CHICKEN THIGHS IN WINE SAUCE

I adore this recipe because it has amazing flavor, and everyone who has tried it loves it. For an easy meal, pair it with mashed potatoes and your favorite vegetable.
—Heike Annucci, Hudson, NC

PREP: 15 MIN. • **COOK:** 20 MIN. + RELEASING • **MAKES:** 4 SERVINGS

- **2 Tbsp. butter, divided**
- **1 cup sliced fresh mushrooms**
- **6 bone-in chicken thighs, skin removed (about 2¼ lbs.)**
- **¼ tsp. salt**
- **¼ tsp. pepper**
- **¼ tsp. Italian seasoning**
- **¼ tsp. paprika**
- **⅓ cup all-purpose flour**
- **½ cup chicken broth**
- **½ cup white wine or additional chicken broth**
- **3 green onions, thinly sliced**

1. Select saute setting and adjust for medium heat in a 6-qt. electric pressure cooker; heat 1 Tbsp. butter. Add mushrooms; cook until tender, 3-4 minutes. Remove. Sprinkle chicken with salt, pepper, Italian seasoning and paprika. Place flour in a shallow bowl. Add chicken, a few pieces at a time, and toss to coat; shake off excess.

2. Heat remaining butter in pressure cooker; brown chicken on both sides. Remove. Add broth and wine to cooker; increase heat to medium-high. Cook 2-3 minutes, stirring to loosen browned bits from pan.

3. Return chicken and mushrooms to cooker; add green onions. Lock lid; make sure vent is closed. Select manual setting; adjust pressure to high, and set time for 10 minutes. When finished cooking, allow pressure to naturally release for 10 minutes; then quick-release any remaining pressure according to manufacturer's directions.

1 SERVING: 243 cal., 13g fat (5g sat. fat), 97mg chol., 284mg sod., 3g carb. (1g sugars, 0 fiber), 25g pro. **Diabetic exchanges:** 3 lean meat, 1½ fat.

GOES **GREAT** WITH

Balsamic-Glazed Zucchini

1 Tbsp. olive oil • 3 medium zucchini, cut into ½-in. slices • 2 garlic cloves, minced • ¼ tsp. salt • ¼ cup balsamic vinegar
In a large skillet, heat oil over medium-high heat. Add zucchini; cook and stir 5-7 minutes or until tender. Add garlic and salt; cook 1 minute longer. Remove from pan. Add vinegar to same pan; bring to a boil. Cook until reduced by half. Add zucchini; toss to coat.
Makes 4 servings.
—Joe Cherry, Metuchen, NJ

LINGUINE WITH FRIED EGGS & GARLIC

My egg-topped pasta is perfect for those days when you need something quick and have only a handful of everyday ingredients to work with. The result is a healthy, satisfying meal.
—E. Gelesky, Bala Cynwyd, PA

PREP: 20 MIN. • **COOK:** 15 MIN. • **MAKES:** 6 SERVINGS

- **1 pkg. (16 oz.) linguine**
- **4 Tbsp. olive oil, divided**
- **2 Tbsp. butter, divided**
- **6 garlic cloves, thinly sliced**
- **½ tsp. crushed red pepper flakes**
- **8 large eggs, divided use**
- **2 Tbsp. freshly grated Parmigiano-Reggiano cheese, plus additional for sprinkling**
- **½ tsp. salt**
- **¼ tsp. pepper**
- **Fresh parsley, optional**

1. Cook linguine according to package directions for al dente. Meanwhile, in a large skillet, heat 2 Tbsp. oil and 1 Tbsp. butter over medium heat until butter melts. Stir in garlic; cook until golden, about 1 minute. Add pepper flakes.
2. Break two eggs, one at a time, into a custard cup or saucer; slip into skillet on top of garlic and pepper flakes. Reduce heat to low; cook until whites are completely set.
3. Drain linguine; return to pan. Add cooked egg mixture; stir in 2 Tbsp. cheese, salt and pepper, tossing to coat. Keep warm. In the same skillet, heat remaining oil and butter over medium heat. Break remaining eggs, one at a time, into a custard cup or saucer; slip into skillet. Reduce heat to low; cook until whites are set and yolks begin to thicken, turning once if desired.
4. Serve pasta in individual bowls. Top with fried eggs, additional cheese for sprinkling and, if desired, parsley.
1 SERVING: 492 cal., 21g fat (6g sat. fat), 260mg chol., 356mg sod., 57g carb. (3g sugars, 3g fiber), 19g pro.

LINGUINE WITH FRIED EGGS & GARLIC

SOUP-BOWL CABBAGE ROLLS

SOUP-BOWL CABBAGE ROLLS

Try this fun twist on traditional stuffed cabbage rolls. It's handy for busy weeknights—and it will warm you from head to toe.
– Terri Pearce, Houston, TX

PREP: 15 MIN. • **COOK:** 35 MIN. • **MAKES:** 4 SERVINGS

- **1 lb. lean ground beef (90% lean)**
- **1 garlic clove, minced**
- **1 small head cabbage, chopped**
- **2½ cups water**
- **⅔ cup uncooked long grain rice**
- **1 Tbsp. Worcestershire sauce**
- **1 tsp. onion powder**
- **1 tsp. dried basil**
- **¼ tsp. cayenne pepper**
- **¼ tsp. pepper**
- **1 can (28 oz.) crushed tomatoes**
- **½ tsp. salt**
- **Grated Parmesan cheese, optional**

In a nonstick Dutch oven, cook beef and garlic over medium heat until meat is no longer pink; drain. Stir in next eight ingredients; bring to a boil. Reduce heat; simmer, covered, until rice is tender, 25-30 minutes. Stir in tomatoes and salt; heat through. If desired, sprinkle with cheese.
2¼ CUPS: 397 cal., 9g fat (4g sat. fat), 56mg chol., 707mg sod., 51g carb. (6g sugars, 9g fiber), 30g pro.

HERBED PORTOBELLO PASTA

EAT SMART FAST FIX

CHILI STEAK & PEPPERS

Bright and loaded with flavor, this is a delicious dish you'll be proud to serve.
—Taste of Home *Test Kitchen*

TAKES: 30 MIN. • **MAKES:** 4 SERVINGS

- 2 **Tbsp. chili sauce**
- 1 **Tbsp. lime juice**
- 1 **tsp. brown sugar**
- ½ **tsp. crushed red pepper flakes**
- ½ **tsp. salt, divided**
- 1 **beef top sirloin steak (1¼ lbs.)**
- 1 **medium onion, halved and sliced**
- 1 **medium green pepper, cut into strips**
- 1 **medium sweet yellow pepper, cut into strips**
- 2 **tsp. olive oil**
- 1 **small garlic clove, minced**
- ⅛ **tsp. pepper**
- ¼ **cup reduced-fat sour cream**
- 1 **tsp. prepared horseradish**

1. Combine the chili sauce, lime juice, brown sugar, pepper flakes and ¼ tsp. salt; brush over steak. Broil steak 4-6 in. from the heat for 5-7 minutes on each side or until meat reaches desired doneness (for medium-rare, a thermometer should read 135°; medium, 140°; medium-well, 145°).
2. Meanwhile, in a large skillet, saute the onion and green and yellow peppers in oil until tender. Add the garlic, pepper and remaining salt; cook 1 minute longer. In a small bowl, combine sour cream and horseradish. Slice steak and serve with pepper mixture and sauce.

4 OZ. COOKED BEEF WITH ⅓ CUP PEPPER MIXTURE AND 1 TBSP. SAUCE: 265 cal., 9g fat (3g sat. fat), 62mg chol., 491mg sod., 12g carb. (8g sugars, 2g fiber), 32g pro. **Diabetic exchanges:** 4 lean meat, 1 vegetable, 1 fat.

GOES GREAT WITH

Baked Chili-Lime Corn

¼ cup melted butter • 2 Tbsp. lime juice • 1½ tsp. lime zest • 1 tsp. chili powder • ¾ tsp. seasoned pepper • ¼ tsp. salt • 4 ears sweet corn, cut into 3-in. pieces
Combine the first six ingredients. Place corn in a greased 13x9-in. baking dish. Brush corn with half the butter mixture. Cover and bake at 400° for 30 minutes. Uncover; brush corn with the remaining butter mixture. Bake, uncovered, until tender, about 5 minutes. **Makes 4 servings.**
—Lawrence Davis, St. Louis, MO

EAT SMART

HERBED PORTOBELLO PASTA

Meaty mushrooms make this light pasta taste hearty and filling. It's my fast and fresh go-to weeknight dinner.
—Laurie Trombley, Stonyford, CA

PREP: 20 MIN. • **COOK:** 15 MIN
MAKES: 4 SERVINGS

- ½ **lb. uncooked multigrain angel hair pasta**
- 4 **large portobello mushrooms (¾ lb.), stems removed**
- 1 **Tbsp. olive oil**
- 2 **garlic cloves, minced**
- 4 **plum tomatoes, chopped**
- ¼ **cup pitted Greek olives**
- ¼ **cup minced fresh basil**
- 1 **tsp. minced fresh rosemary or ¼ tsp. dried rosemary, crushed**
- 1 **tsp. minced fresh thyme or ¼ tsp. dried thyme**
- ¼ **tsp. salt**
- ⅛ **tsp. pepper**
- ⅔ **cup crumbled feta cheese**
- ¼ **cup shredded Parmesan cheese**

1. Cook pasta according to the package directions for al dente. Meanwhile, cut mushrooms in half and thinly slice. In a large skillet, heat oil over medium heat. Add the mushrooms; saute until tender, 8-10 minutes. Add garlic; cook 1 minute longer. Stir in tomatoes and olives. Reduce heat to low; cook, uncovered, until slightly thickened, about 5 minutes. Stir in herbs, salt and pepper.
2. Drain pasta, reserving ¼ cup pasta water. Toss pasta with mushroom mixture, adjusting consistency with reserved pasta water. Sprinkle with cheeses.

1½ CUPS: 375 cal., 12g fat (4g sat. fat), 14mg chol., 585mg sod., 48g carb. (5g sugars, 7g fiber), 18g pro. **Diabetic exchanges:** 3 starch, 2 medium-fat meat, 2 fat, 1 vegetable.

CHILI STEAK
& PEPPERS
BAKED
CHILI-LIME
CORN

(5) INGREDIENTS

PANCETTA & MUSHROOM-STUFFED CHICKEN BREAST

I was inspired by a stuffed chicken Marsala dish I had at a restaurant and wanted to come up with my own version using a different flavor profile. This is the delicious result!
—Ashley Laymon, Lititz, PA

PREP: 15 MIN. • **BAKE:** 30 MIN.
MAKES: 4 SERVINGS

- **4 slices pancetta**
- **1 Tbsp. olive oil**
- **1 shallot, finely chopped**
- **¾ cup chopped fresh mushrooms**
- **¼ tsp. salt, divided**
- **¼ tsp. pepper, divided**
- **4 boneless skinless chicken breast halves (6 oz. each)**
- **½ cup prepared pesto**

1. Preheat oven to 350°. In a large skillet, cook pancetta over medium heat until partially cooked but not crisp; drain on paper towels.

2. In same skillet, heat oil over medium-high heat. Add shallot; cook and stir until lightly browned, 1-2 minutes. Stir in mushrooms; cook until tender, 1-2 minutes. Add ⅛ tsp. salt and ⅛ tsp. pepper.

3. Pound chicken breasts with a meat mallet to ¼-in. thickness. Spread each with 2 Tbsp. pesto; layer with one slice pancetta and a fourth of the mushroom mixture. Fold chicken in half, enclosing filling; secure with toothpicks. Sprinkle with remaining salt and pepper.

4. Transfer to a greased 13x9-in. baking dish. Bake until a thermometer inserted in chicken reads 165°, 30-35 minutes. Discard toothpicks before serving.

1 STUFFED CHICKEN BREAST HALF: 420 cal., 25g fat (6g sat. fat), 112mg chol., 1013mg sod., 5g carb. (2g sugars, 1g fiber), 41g pro.

GOES **GREAT** WITH

Ginger Beets & Carrots

1½ cups thinly sliced fresh carrots • 1½ cups thinly sliced fresh beets • 4 tsp. olive oil • 1½ tsp. honey • 1½ tsp. ground ginger • ¾ tsp. soy sauce • ½ tsp. sea salt • ½ tsp. chili powder • Preheat oven to 400°. Place vegetables in a greased 15x10x1-in. baking pan. Whisk remaining ingredients; drizzle over vegetables. Toss to coat. Bake until carrots and beets are crisp-tender, 15-20 minutes. **Makes 4 servings.**
—Courtney Stultz, Weir, KS

EAT SMART **FAST FIX**

WEEKNIGHT CHICKEN CHOP SUEY

If you'd like a little extra crunch with this colorful chop suey, serve it with chow mein noodles.
—George Utley, South Hill, VA

TAKES: 30 MIN. • **MAKES:** 6 SERVINGS

- **4 tsp. olive oil**
- **1 lb. boneless skinless chicken breasts, cut into 1-in. cubes**
- **½ tsp. dried tarragon**
- **½ tsp. dried basil**
- **½ tsp. dried marjoram**
- **½ tsp. grated lemon zest**
- **1½ cups chopped carrots**
- **1 cup unsweetened pineapple tidbits, drained (reserve juice)**
- **1 can (8 oz.) sliced water chestnuts, drained**
- **1 tart medium apple, chopped**
- **½ cup chopped onion**
- **1 cup cold water, divided**
- **3 Tbsp. unsweetened pineapple juice**
- **3 Tbsp. reduced-sodium teriyaki sauce**
- **2 Tbsp. cornstarch**
- **3 cups hot cooked brown rice**

1. In a large nonstick skillet, heat oil over medium heat. Add chicken, herbs and lemon zest; saute until lightly browned. Add next five ingredients. Stir in ¾ cup water, pineapple juice and teriyaki sauce; bring to a boil. Reduce the heat; simmer, covered, until chicken juices run clear and carrots are tender, 10-15 minutes.
2. Combine cornstarch and remaining water. Gradually stir into chicken mixture. Bring to a boil; cook and stir until thickened, about 2 minutes. Serve with rice.
1 CUP CHOP SUEY WITH ½ CUP RICE: 330 cal., 6g fat (1g sat. fat), 42mg chol., 227mg sod., 50g carb. (14g sugars, 5g fiber), 20g pro. **Diabetic exchanges:** 3 vegetable, 3 lean meat, 1 fruit, 1 fat.

SANTA MARIA ROAST BEEF

EAT SMART

SANTA MARIA ROAST BEEF

A simple dry rub is enough to turn plain roast beef into something special. Pair the slightly spicy meat with mashed potatoes, or enjoy it as leftovers, stacked between slices of bread.
—Allison Ector, Ardmore, PA

PREP: 20 MIN. + MARINATING
GRILL: 1 HOUR + STANDING
MAKES: 6 SERVINGS

- **4 Tbsp. paprika**
- **3 Tbsp. brown sugar**
- **2 Tbsp. chili powder**
- **1 Tbsp. garlic powder**
- **1 Tbsp. white pepper**
- **1 Tbsp. celery salt**
- **1 Tbsp. ground cumin**
- **1 Tbsp. dried oregano**
- **1 Tbsp. pepper**
- **2 tsp. cayenne pepper**
- **1 tsp. ground mustard**
- **1 beef tri-tip roast or beef sirloin tip roast (2 to 3 lbs.)**
- **2 cups soaked hickory wood chips or chunks**
- **2 Tbsp. canola oil**

1. Combine the first 11 ingredients; rub desired amount over roast. Wrap and refrigerate overnight. Store leftover dry rub in an airtight container for up to 6 months.
2. Remove roast from the refrigerator 1 hour before grilling. Prepare grill for indirect heat, using a drip pan. Add wood chips according to the manufacturer's directions.
3. Unwrap roast and brush with oil; place over drip pan. Grill, covered, over medium-low indirect heat for 1-1½ hours or until meat reaches desired doneness (for medium-rare, a thermometer should read 135°; medium, 140°; medium-well, 145°). Let stand for 10-15 minutes before slicing.
4 OZ. COOKED BEEF: 294 cal., 16g fat (4g sat. fat), 91mg chol., 324mg sod., 5g carb. (3g sugars, 1g fiber), 32g pro. **Diabetic exchanges:** 4 lean meat, 1 fat.
BAKED SANTA MARIA ROAST BEEF: Prepare roast and refrigerate as directed. Unwrap roast and brush with oil and ½ tsp. liquid smoke. Place on a rack in a shallow roasting pan. Bake, uncovered, at 425° until meat reaches desired doneness, 55-75 minutes.

SKILLET PLUM CHICKEN TENDERS

EAT SMART

SKILLET PLUM CHICKEN TENDERS

Plum lovers, this recipe is for you! I combine the fruit with chicken tenders for a quick and easy flavorful meal. Serve with brown rice or orzo pasta.
—Nancy Heishman, Las Vegas, NV

PREP: 20 MIN. • **COOK:** 15 MIN. • **MAKES:** 4 SERVINGS

- **½ tsp. garlic salt**
- **½ tsp. lemon-pepper seasoning**
- **1½ lbs. chicken tenderloins**
- **1 Tbsp. extra virgin olive oil**
- **2 cups sliced fresh plums**
- **½ cup diced red onion**
- **⅓ cup apple jelly**
- **1 Tbsp. grated fresh gingerroot**
- **1 Tbsp. balsamic vinegar**
- **2 tsp. reduced-sodium soy sauce**
- **1 tsp. minced fresh thyme or ½ tsp. dried thyme**
- **1 Tbsp. cornstarch**
- **2 Tbsp. white wine**
- **1 Tbsp. sesame seeds, toasted**

1. Combine garlic salt and lemon pepper; sprinkle mixture over chicken. In a large nonstick skillet, heat oil over medium-high heat; brown chicken tenderloins. Add plums and red onion; cook and stir 1-2 minutes.
2. Reduce heat. Stir in next five ingredients. Mix cornstarch and wine until smooth; gradually stir into pan. Cook, covered, until chicken juices run clear and plums are tender, about 10 minutes. Just before serving, sprinkle with toasted sesame seeds.
1 SERVING: 343 cal., 6g fat (1g sat. fat), 83mg chol., 483mg sod., 33g carb. (26g sugars, 2g fiber), 41g pro.

EAT SMART

SPICY SHRIMP WITH RICE

No one will doubt that light cooking can be tasty when you put a helping of this zippy shrimp in front of them. The seafood is seasoned with just the right amount of garlic, pepper and hot sauce.
—Jeannie Klugh, Lancaster, PA

PREP: 15 MIN. • **COOK:** 25 MIN. • **MAKES:** 8 SERVINGS

- **1 large onion, finely chopped**
- **1 large green pepper, chopped**
- **1 Tbsp. olive oil**
- **3 garlic cloves, minced**
- **1 can (8 oz.) tomato sauce**
- **½ cup reduced-sodium chicken broth**
- **½ cup minced fresh parsley**
- **1 jar (4 oz.) diced pimientos, drained**
- **1 to 2 Tbsp. Louisiana-style hot sauce**
- **¼ tsp. onion salt**
- **¼ tsp. pepper**
- **2 lbs. uncooked large shrimp, peeled and deveined**
- **5⅔ cups hot cooked rice**

1. In a large skillet, saute the onion and green pepper in oil until tender. Add garlic; cook 1 minute longer. Stir in the tomato sauce, broth, parsley, pimientos, hot sauce, onion salt and pepper.
2. Bring to a boil. Reduce heat; cover and simmer for 10 minutes, stirring occasionally. Stir in shrimp; cook 5-7 minutes longer or until shrimp turn pink. Serve with rice.
1 SERVING: 273 cal., 3g fat (1g sat. fat), 168mg chol., 425mg sod., 37g carb. (3g sugars, 2g fiber), 22g pro. **Diabetic exchanges:** 3 lean meat, 2 starch, 1 vegetable.

SPICY SHRIMP WITH RICE

EAT SMART

SWEET POTATO STEW

Beef broth and herbs pair nicely with the potatoes' subtle sweetness in this hearty stew that's perfect for cold weather months.
—Helen Vail, Glenside, PA

PREP: 5 MIN. • **COOK:** 35 MIN. • **MAKES:** 4 SERVINGS

- **2 cans (14½ oz. each) reduced-sodium beef broth**
- **¾ lb. lean ground beef (90% lean)**
- **2 medium sweet potatoes, peeled and cut into ½-in. cubes**
- **1 small onion, finely chopped**
- **½ cup V8 juice**
- **1 Tbsp. golden raisins**
- **1 garlic clove, minced**
- **½ tsp. dried thyme**
- **Dash cayenne pepper**

In a large saucepan, bring broth to a boil. Crumble beef into broth. Cook, covered, for 3 minutes, stirring occasionally. Add remaining ingredients; return to a boil. Reduce the heat; simmer, uncovered, until the meat is no longer pink and the sweet potatoes are tender, about 15 minutes.

1¼ CUPS: 265 cal., 7g fat (3g sat. fat), 58mg chol., 532mg sod., 29g carb. (13g sugars, 4g fiber), 20g pro. **Diabetic exchanges:** 2 starch, 2 lean meat.

GOES **GREAT** WITH

Yogurt Cornbread

1 cup yellow cornmeal • ¼ cup all-purpose flour • 2 tsp. baking powder • ½ tsp. salt • ¼ tsp. baking soda • 1 large egg, lightly beaten • 1 cup fat-free plain yogurt • ½ cup fat-free milk • ¼ cup canola oil • 1 Tbsp. honey • In a bowl, combine first five ingredients. In another bowl, combine egg, yogurt, milk, oil and honey. Stir into dry ingredients just until moistened. Pour into an 8-in. square baking dish coated with cooking spray. Bake at 425° for 16-20 minutes. **Makes 9 servings.**
—Amanda Andrews, Mansfield, TX

HONEY-GARLIC BRUSSELS SPROUTS

MEAT & POTATO PATTIES

EAT SMART

MEAT & POTATO PATTIES

During the food shortage of World War II, meat was rationed and had to be purchased with tokens. Cooks got creative and came up with clever ways to stretch ingredients. This economical meal went a long way in feeding a family. These days, I reach for it whenever I want a twist on regular hamburgers.
—Gladys Klein, Burlington, WI

PREP: 10 MIN. • **COOK:** 25 MIN.
MAKES: 4 SERVINGS

- ¾ **lb. lean ground beef (90% lean)**
- ¾ **cup finely shredded potatoes**
- ¼ **cup finely chopped onion**
- 2 **Tbsp. chopped green pepper**
- 1 **large egg, beaten**
- ¼ **tsp. salt**
- 1 **Tbsp. canola oil**
- 1 **cup tomato juice**
- 1 **Tbsp. all-purpose flour**
- ¼ **cup water**

1. Combine the first six ingredients. Shape into four patties; press to flatten slightly. In a large skillet, heat oil over medium-high heat. Brown patties on both sides; drain. Add tomato juice. Simmer, covered, until a thermometer inserted into meat reads 160°, 20-25 minutes. Remove patties to a serving platter; keep warm.
2. Whisk flour into water; gradually add to skillet. Reduce heat to medium-low; cook, stirring constantly, until thickened. Spoon over patties. Serve immediately.
1 PATTY: 237 cal., 12g fat (4g sat. fat), 99mg chol., 373mg sod., 12g carb. (2g sugars, 1g fiber), 20g pro.

GOES **GREAT** WITH

Honey-Garlic Brussels Sprouts

2 lbs. Brussels sprouts, trimmed and halved • 2 Tbsp. honey • 1 Tbsp. lemon juice • 1 Tbsp. olive oil • 2 tsp. garlic salt
Preheat oven to 425°. Toss all ingredients; spread in a foil-lined 15x10x1-in. baking pan. Bake, stirring halfway through cooking, until sprouts are tender and lightly browned, 15-20 minutes. **Makes 6 servings.**
—Robin Haas, Jamaica Plain, MA

TOMATO & PEPPER SIRLOIN STEAK

EAT SMART

TOMATO & PEPPER SIRLOIN STEAK

The beefy sauce and zippy peppers in this dish offer an amazing amount of flavor for under 300 calories.
—Gayle Tarkowski, Traverse City, MI

PREP: 15 MIN. • **COOK:** 35 MIN.
MAKES: 6 SERVINGS

- ½ **cup all-purpose flour**
- ¾ **tsp. salt**
- ½ **tsp. pepper**
- 1½ **lbs. beef top sirloin steak, thinly sliced**
- 3 **Tbsp. canola oil**
- 1 **small onion, chopped**
- 1 **garlic clove, minced**
- 1 **can (28 oz.) diced tomatoes, undrained**
- 2 **large green peppers, cut into strips**
- 2 **to 3 Tbsp. beef broth**
- 1½ **tsp. Worcestershire sauce**
- **Hot cooked rice**

1. In a large bowl or shallow dish, combine flour, salt and pepper. Add beef slices, a few pieces at a time. Toss gently to coat.
2. In a Dutch oven, heat oil over medium-high heat. Brown the beef in batches. Add the onion; cook and stir until tender, 3-4 minutes. Add garlic; cook 1 minute longer. Add tomatoes; bring to a boil. Reduce heat. Simmer, covered, stirring occasionally, until meat is tender, 10-15 minutes.
3. Stir in the green peppers, broth and Worcestershire sauce; simmer, covered, until peppers are tender, 10-15 minutes. Serve with rice.
1 CUP PEPPER STEAK MIXTURE: 284 cal., 12g fat (2g sat. fat), 46mg chol., 552mg sod., 17g carb. (6g sugars, 4g fiber), 27g pro. **Diabetic exchanges:** 3 lean meat, 2 starch, 1½ fat.

TEST KITCHEN TIP

Not a fan of green peppers? Feel free to use red, yellow, orange or a mix of all. Replace the sirloin with chicken or turkey for a leaner option that still packs tons of flavor.

ULTIMATE HARISSA SWEET POTATO FRITTERS
PAGE 140

SIDE DISHES & CONDIMENTS

Take meals from ordinary to extraordinary when you toss together these savory menu add-ons. From traditional veggie sides to change-of-pace dinner accompaniments, these recipes round out any entree with ease.

BAKED ACORN SQUASH WITH BLUEBERRY-WALNUT FILLING

BAKED ACORN SQUASH WITH BLUEBERRY-WALNUT FILLING

I absolutely love squash, and I've enjoyed it with a variety of fillings over the years. I have to say, however, that my favorite versions involve unexpected fruits. This sweet apple-blueberry filling is wonderful.
—Bruce Newcomer, Fredericksburg, VA

PREP: 15 MIN. • **BAKE:** 1 HOUR
MAKES: 4 SERVINGS

- 2 **medium acorn squash**
- 2 **Tbsp. butter, softened**
- ½ **tsp. salt**
- ¼ **tsp. pepper**
- 1 **medium apple, chopped**
- 1 **Tbsp. lime juice**
- 1 **cup fresh blueberries**
- ½ **cup chopped walnuts**
- ¼ **tsp. ground nutmeg**
- ¼ **cup maple syrup**

1. Preheat oven to 400°. Cut each squash lengthwise in half; remove and discard seeds. Using a sharp knife, cut a thin slice from bottom of each squash half to allow them to lie flat. Place in shallow roasting pan, cut side down. Add ½ in. of hot water. Bake, uncovered, until squash is tender, about 35 minutes. Drain water from pan; turn squash cut side up. Spread with butter; season with salt and pepper.
2. For filling, in a large bowl, toss apple pieces with lime juice; add blueberries, walnuts and nutmeg. Divide among squash halves; drizzle with maple syrup. Bake until heated through, about 30 minutes. Cover loosely with foil if filling browns too quickly.
1 FILLED SQUASH HALF: 378 cal., 16g fat (5g sat. fat), 15mg chol., 354mg sod., 62g carb. (28g sugars, 8g fiber), 5g pro.

TEST KITCHEN TIP

If blueberries aren't in season, you can substitute almost any kind of fresh berry.

VERY BERRY SPREAD

VERY BERRY SPREAD

Two kinds of berries make this jam deliciously different. I always keep some of this spread on hand to enjoy not only with breakfast, but also as a treat during the day.
—Irene Hagel, Choiceland, SK

PREP: 15 MIN. • **PROCESS:** 10 MIN.
MAKES: ABOUT 8 HALF-PINTS

- 5 **cups fresh or frozen raspberries**
- 3 **cups fresh or frozen blueberries**
- 1 **Tbsp. bottled lemon juice**
- 1 **Tbsp. grated lemon zest**
- 1 **pkg. (1¾ oz.) powdered fruit pectin**
- 6 **cups sugar**

1. In a Dutch oven, combine the berries, lemon juice, lemon zest and pectin. Bring to a full rolling boil over high heat, stirring constantly. Stir in sugar; return to a full rolling boil. Boil for 1 minute, stirring constantly.
2. Remove from the heat; skim off any foam. Carefully ladle hot mixture into hot half-pint jars, leaving ¼-in. headspace. Remove air bubbles; wipe rims and adjust lids. Process for 10 minutes in a boiling-water canner.
NOTE: The processing time listed is for altitudes of 1,000 feet or less. Add 1 minute to the processing time for each 1,000 feet of additional altitude.
2 TBSP.: 86 cal., 0 fat (0 sat. fat), 0 chol., 0 sod., 22g carb. (20g sugars, 1g fiber), 0 pro.

LEMON-GARLIC LIMA BEANS

EAT SMART

LEMON-GARLIC LIMA BEANS

When I was growing up on Cyprus, my mother would often make this side dish to serve alongside lamb. Although I hated lima beans when I was a kid (who didn't?), I love them now. They always remind me of home. —*Paris Paraskeva, San Francisco, CA*

PREP: 15 MIN. + SOAKING • **COOK:** 1¼ HOURS
MAKES: 6 SERVINGS

- **1 lb. dried lima beans**
- **2 bay leaves**
- **3 Tbsp. extra virgin olive oil, divided**
- **1 medium onion, chopped**
- **4 garlic cloves, thinly sliced**
- **¼ cup chopped fresh parsley**
- **2 Tbsp. lemon juice**
- **1 Tbsp. chopped fresh oregano**
- **2 tsp. grated lemon zest**
- **½ tsp. salt**
- **¼ tsp. pepper**
- **Additional chopped fresh parsley**

1. Rinse and sort beans; soak according to package directions. Drain and rinse beans, discarding liquid.
2. Place beans in a large saucepan; add bay leaves and water to cover by 2 in. Bring to a boil. Reduce heat; simmer, covered, until beans are tender, 1¼-1½ hours. Drain.
3. In a large skillet, heat 1 Tbsp. oil over medium heat. Add onion; cook and stir until tender, 3-4 minutes. Add garlic; cook 1 minute longer. Add next six ingredients. Stir in drained beans and remaining oil; toss. Sprinkle with additional parsley.
½ CUP: 326 cal., 8g fat (1g sat. fat), 0 chol., 209mg sod., 51g carb. (7g sugars, 16g fiber), 16g pro.

FAST FIX

CALICO CORN CAKES

Served with salsa, these fluffy corn cakes make a fantastic side for nearly any main dish, especially those with southwestern flair. Check out the spicy version, too. It's a fast and easy way to add a little heat to dinner. —Taste of Home *Test Kitchen*

TAKES: 25 MIN. • **MAKES:** 3 SERVINGS

- **¼ cup chopped onion**
- **¼ cup chopped green pepper**
- **1 tsp. canola oil**
- **¼ cup all-purpose flour**
- **2 Tbsp. yellow cornmeal**
- **½ tsp. sugar**
- **¼ tsp. salt**
- **¼ tsp. dried oregano**
- **⅛ tsp. baking powder**
- **⅛ tsp. ground cumin**
- **1 eggs, lightly beaten**
- **¼ cup 2% milk**
- **1 cup frozen corn, thawed**
- **1 Tbsp. diced pimientos**
- **½ cup salsa**

1. In a small skillet, saute onion and green pepper in oil until tender; set aside. In a large bowl, whisk the flour, cornmeal, sugar, salt, oregano, baking powder, cumin, egg and milk just until combined. Fold in the corn, pimientos and onion mixture.
2. Heat a large skillet coated with cooking spray; drop batter by ¼ cupfuls into skillet. Cook for 3 minutes on each side or until golden brown. Serve with salsa.
2 CORN CAKES: 135 cal., 3g fat (1g sat. fat), 54mg chol., 308mg sod., 23g carb. (4g sugars, 2g fiber), 5g pro.
CALICO CORN CAKES WITH A KICK: Omit oregano and cumin. Along with the corn, fold in 1 minced, seeded jalapeno pepper.

(5) INGREDIENTS SLOW COOKER

CREAMY HASH BROWN POTATOES

I like to fix a batch of these cheesy slow-cooker potatoes for potlucks and other big gatherings. Frozen hash browns, canned soup and flavored cream cheese make this wildly popular dish quick to put together.
—Julianne Henson, Streamwood, IL

PREP: 5 MIN. • **COOK:** 3½ HOURS
MAKES: 14 SERVINGS

- **1 pkg. (32 oz.) frozen cubed hash brown potatoes**
- **1 can (10¾ oz.) condensed cream of potato soup, undiluted**
- **2 cups shredded Colby-Monterey Jack cheese**
- **1 cup sour cream**
- **¼ tsp. pepper**
- **⅛ tsp. salt**
- **1 carton (8 oz.) spreadable chive and onion cream cheese**

1. Place potatoes in a lightly greased 4-qt. slow cooker. In a large bowl, combine the soup, cheese, sour cream, pepper and salt. Pour over potatoes and mix well.
2. Cover and cook on low for 3½-4 hours or until potatoes are tender. Stir in the cream cheese.
¾ CUP: 214 cal., 13g fat (9g sat. fat), 42mg chol., 387mg sod., 17g carb. (2g sugars, 2g fiber), 6g pro.

SPICY POTATOES WITH GARLIC AIOLI

SPICY POTATOES WITH GARLIC AIOLI

This is my take on Spanish patatas bravas. *The potatoes are tossed in a flavorful spice mix and then finished to a crispy golden brown. The garlic aioli takes it over the top for an unconventional potato salad that'll be a hit at any party.*
—John Stiver, Bowen Island, BC

PREP: 35 MIN. • **BAKE:** 25 MIN.
MAKES: 10 SERVINGS (8 CUPS)

- **3 lbs. medium Yukon Gold potatoes, cut into 1½-in. cubes (about 8 potatoes)**
- **2 Tbsp. olive oil**
- **2 garlic cloves, minced**
- **2 Tbsp. smoked paprika**
- **2 tsp. garlic powder**
- **1½ tsp. chili powder**
- **1½ tsp. ground cumin**
- **¼ tsp. salt**
- **¼ tsp. crushed red pepper flakes**
- **⅛ tsp. pepper**

AIOLI

- **1½ cups mayonnaise**
- **3 Tbsp. lemon juice**
- **3 garlic cloves, minced**
- **1 Tbsp. minced fresh chives plus additional for topping**
- **1 tsp. red wine vinegar**
- **¼ tsp. salt**
- **¼ tsp. pepper**

1. Preheat oven to 375°. Place potatoes in a Dutch oven; add water to cover. Bring to a boil. Reduce heat; cook, uncovered, 8-10 minutes or until just tender. Drain; pat dry with paper towels. Transfer potatoes to a mixing bowl. Toss potatoes in oil and minced garlic to coat evenly.
2. Combine the paprika, garlic powder, chili powder, cumin, salt, pepper flakes and pepper; sprinkle over potatoes. Gently toss to coat. Transfer potatoes to two greased 15x10x1-in. baking pans, spreading into a single layer. Bake until crispy, about 25 minutes, stirring potatoes and rotating pans halfway through cooking.
3. For aioli, combine ingredients until blended. Transfer potatoes to a serving platter; sprinkle with chives. Serve warm with aioli.
¾ CUP: 469 cal., 34g fat (5g sat. fat), 3mg chol., 396mg sod., 37g carb. (3g sugars, 4g fiber), 5g pro.

TEST KITCHEN TIP

The seasoning blend gives these potatoes a nice kick; smoked paprika makes them taste as if they were cooked over an open fire. Remember this spice mix the next time you're prepping Tater Tots, and sprinkle some on for an upgrade.

CORN OKRA CREOLE

EAT SMART FAST FIX

CORN OKRA CREOLE

This veggie-loaded side is a delicious representation of my region of the country, particularly the Texas-Louisiana border. The okra, corn and Creole seasonings are all cooking staples here.
—Ruth Aubey, San Antonio, TX

TAKES: 30 MIN. • **MAKES:** 6 SERVINGS

- **1 cup chopped green pepper**
- **½ cup chopped onion**
- **3 Tbsp. canola oil**
- **2 cups fresh or frozen corn or 1 can (15¼ oz.) whole-kernel corn**
- **1½ cups fresh sliced okra or 1 pkg. (16 oz.) frozen okra**
- **3 medium tomatoes, peeled and chopped (1½ cups)**
- **1 Tbsp. tomato paste**
- **¼ tsp. dried thyme**
- **Salt to taste**
- **¼ tsp. coarsely ground pepper**
- **½ tsp. hot pepper sauce, optional**

1. In a large skillet, saute green pepper and onion in oil until tender. Add corn and okra; cook over medium heat for 10 minutes, stirring occasionally.
2. Stir in the tomatoes, tomato paste, thyme, salt, pepper and, if desired, pepper sauce. Cover and simmer for 3-5 minutes, stirring occasionally.
⅔ CUP: 147 cal., 8g fat (1g sat. fat), 0 chol., 19mg sod., 20g carb. (8g sugars, 4g fiber), 4g pro. **Diabetic exchanges:** 1½ fat, 1 starch.

BACON & BLUE STUFFED SWEET POTATOES

Here's a tasty take on an all-time classic side. I give sweet potatoes a makeover with pear, bacon, honey and fresh tarragon. If Gorgonzola isn't your thing, swap in plain or smoked Gouda.
—Jeanne Holt, Mendota Heights, MN

PREP: 20 MIN. • **BAKE:** 65 MIN. • **MAKES:** 4 SERVINGS

- **4 medium sweet potatoes (about 10 oz. each)**
- **3 Tbsp. butter, softened**
- **2 tsp. honey**
- **½ tsp. salt**
- **⅛ tsp. cayenne pepper**
- **⅛ tsp. pepper**
- **1 small ripe pear, peeled and chopped**
- **4 bacon strips, cooked and chopped, divided**
- **¼ cup plus 3 Tbsp. crumbled Gorgonzola cheese, divided**
- **2 green onions, thinly sliced**
- **2 tsp. minced fresh tarragon or ¼ tsp. dried tarragon**

1. Preheat oven to 375°. Scrub sweet potatoes; pierce several times with a fork. Bake on a foil-lined baking sheet until tender, 45-60 minutes. Cool slightly.
2. Cut a thin slice from top of each potato. Scoop out pulp, leaving ¼-in.-thick shells. Mash pulp with butter, honey and seasonings. Stir in pear, ⅓ cup chopped bacon, ¼ cup cheese, green onions and tarragon. Spoon into shells; return to the baking sheet. Top with the remaining cheese.
3. Bake until heated through, 20-25 minutes. Sprinkle with the remaining bacon.
1 STUFFED POTATO: 388 cal., 16g fat (9g sat. fat), 42mg chol., 696mg sod., 55g carb. (25g sugars, 7g fiber), 9g pro.

BACON & BLUE STUFFED SWEET POTATOES

FAST FIX

FRESH THAI ASPARAGUS, KALE & GARLICKY MUSHROOMS

Hit the local farmers market and stock up! This quick, simple side is a perfect complement to any meal. The fish sauce gives it a wonderful depth of flavor without much effort.
—Julie Peterson, Crofton, MD

TAKES: 30 MIN. • **MAKES:** 4 SERVINGS

- **3 Tbsp. coconut oil**
- **10 oz. medium fresh mushrooms, quartered (about 4 cups)**
- **1 lb. fresh asparagus, trimmed and cut into 1½-in. pieces**
- **2 garlic cloves, thinly sliced**
- **½ tsp. dried oregano**
- **¼ tsp. salt**
- **¼ tsp. pepper**
- **2 cups chopped fresh kale**
- **2 tsp. fish sauce or soy sauce**
- **1 tsp. balsamic vinegar**
- **Toasted sesame seeds, optional**

In a large skillet, heat oil over medium-high heat. Add mushrooms; cook, stirring occasionally, 4-6 minutes or until lightly browned. Add asparagus, garlic, oregano, salt and pepper; cook and stir until crisp-tender, 2-4 minutes. Stir in kale; cook and stir until wilted, 2-4 minutes. Remove from heat; stir in fish sauce and vinegar. If desired, top with sesame seeds.

¾ CUP: 129 cal., 11g fat (9g sat. fat), 0 chol., 383mg sod., 7g carb. (1g sugars, 1g fiber), 4g pro.

FAST FIX

PRESSURE-COOKER CRANBERRY APPLE RED CABBAGE

When I was looking for something new, I started playing with flavors and came up with this very tasty dish. I truly think my German grandmother would be impressed. The colorful dish is just right with pork entrees, and it comes together fast in my multi cooker.
—Ann Sheehy, Lawrence, MA

TAKES: 20 MIN. • **MAKES:** 9 SERVINGS

- **1 medium head red cabbage, coarsely chopped**
- **1 can (14 oz.) whole-berry cranberry sauce**
- **2 medium Granny Smith apples, peeled and coarsely chopped**
- **1 medium onion, chopped**
- **½ cup cider vinegar**
- **¼ cup sweet vermouth, white wine or unsweetened apple juice, optional**
- **1 tsp. kosher salt**
- **¾ tsp. caraway seeds**
- **½ tsp. coarsely ground pepper**

Combine all ingredients; transfer to a 8.5-qt. electric pressure cooker. Lock lid; make sure vent is closed. Select manual setting; adjust pressure to high, and set time for 3 minutes. When finished cooking, allow pressure to naturally release for 5 minutes, then quick-release any remaining pressure according to manufacturer's directions. Serve with a slotted spoon.

¾ CUP: 144 cal., 0 fat (0 sat. fat), 0 chol., 296mg sod., 34g carb. (21g sugars, 4g fiber), 2g pro.

ULTIMATE HARISSA SWEET POTATO FRITTERS

ULTIMATE HARISSA SWEET POTATO FRITTERS

I had leftover sweet potatoes and had to think up a new way to use them. We love spice, so I flavored these fun fritters with harissa, just enough for flavor but not too spicy. If you want more heat, you can always adjust the spice to please your taste buds.
—Teri Rasey, Cadillac, MI

PREP: 20 MIN. + STANDING
COOK: 5 MIN./BATCH • **MAKES:** 6 SERVINGS

- **6 cups boiling water**
- **3 cups shredded and peeled sweet potatoes, slightly packed (about 2 medium)**
- **2 large eggs**
- **¼ cup all-purpose flour**
- **1 tsp. baking powder**
- **1 tsp. cornstarch**
- **1 tsp. seasoned salt**
- **2 to 3 tsp. harissa**
- **1 small onion, grated**
- **¼ cup coconut oil**
- **½ cup crumbled queso fresco**
- **Sliced avocado, sliced tomato and minced fresh cilantro, optional**

1. Pour boiling water over sweet potatoes in a large bowl; let stand 20 minutes. Drain, squeezing to remove excess liquid. Pat dry.
2. In a large bowl, whisk the eggs, flour, baking powder, cornstarch, seasoned salt and harissa. Add the sweet potatoes and onion; toss to coat.
3. In a large nonstick skillet, heat 2 Tbsp. coconut oil over medium heat. Working in batches, drop sweet potato mixture by ¼ cupfuls into oil; press slightly to flatten. Fry 1-2 minutes on each side until golden brown, using remaining oil as needed. Drain on paper towels. Serve with queso fresco, and optional ingredients as desired.

2 FRITTERS: 217 cal., 13g fat (10g sat. fat), 69mg chol., 421mg sod., 20g carb. (3g sugars, 2g fiber), 6g pro.

JALAPENO & COTIJA CHEESE POTATO STACK PIE

Pie isn't just for dessert anymore. Stacking thinly sliced potatoes with layers of minced jalapenos and crumbled cotija cheese helps turn ordinary potatoes into something truly spectacular—especially when served with salsa and sour cream.
—Colleen Delawder, Herndon, VA

PREP: 20 MIN. • **BAKE:** 50 MIN.
MAKES: 8 SERVINGS

- **2½ lbs. red potatoes, peeled and thinly sliced**
- **¼ cup butter, melted**
- **½ tsp. salt**
- **¼ tsp. pepper**
- **2 jalapeno peppers, seeded and minced**
- **1¼ cups crumbled cotija cheese or crumbled feta cheese**
- **Salsa and sour cream, optional**

1. Preheat oven to 375°. Line a 15x10x1-in. pan with parchment paper. Remove the bottom of a 9-in. springform pan and place the round outer edge in the middle of the parchment paper.
2. Place the potatoes, butter, salt and pepper in a large bowl; toss to coat. Layer a third of the potatoes evenly within the springform ring. Sprinkle with a third of the jalapenos and a third of the cheese. Repeat layers. Top with the remaining potatoes and jalapenos.
3. Bake for 35 minutes. Top with remaining cheese. Bake 15-20 minutes longer or until potatoes are tender. Let stand 5 minutes before removing ring. If desired, serve with salsa and sour cream.

1 SERVING: 223 cal., 12g fat (7g sat. fat), 34mg chol., 477mg sod., 23g carb. (2g sugars, 3g fiber), 7g pro.

TEST KITCHEN TIP

If jalapenos are spicier than you'd like, toss them with a little vodka and let them sit for 15 minutes. Then drain and rinse them, and proceed with the recipe.

JALAPENO & COTIJA CHEESE
POTATO STACK PIE

POTATO LATKES

POTATO LATKES

These potato and onion pancakes are tasty at any meal. For the ultimate crispiness, squeeze out all the liquid from the grated veggies before you fry them up.
—Taste of Home *Test Kitchen*

PREP: 20 MIN. • **COOK:** 20 MIN. • **MAKES:** 2 DOZEN

- **2 lbs. russet potatoes, peeled**
- **1 medium onion**
- **½ cup chopped green onions**
- **1 large egg, lightly beaten**
- **1 tsp. salt**
- **¼ tsp. pepper**
- **Oil for frying**
- **Applesauce**

1. Coarsely grate potatoes and onion; drain any liquid. Place in a bowl; add green onions, egg, salt and pepper.
2. In an electric skillet, heat ⅛ in. of oil to 375°. Drop batter by heaping tablespoonfuls into hot oil. Flatten to form patties. Fry until golden brown; turn and cook the other side. Drain on paper towels. Serve with applesauce.
2 PANCAKES: 115 cal., 7g fat (1g sat. fat), 16mg chol., 205mg sod., 11g carb. (1g sugars, 1g fiber), 2g pro.

FAST FIX

LEMONY ALMOND-FETA GREEN BEANS

When you find a vegetable recipe that demands second helpings, it's definitely worth sharing. I made these green beans for a dinner party, and that's exactly what happened! I like to use haricot verts, the skinny type of green bean.
—Samantha Bowman, Houston, TX

TAKES: 30 MIN. • **MAKES:** 6 SERVINGS

- **1 lb. fresh green beans, trimmed**
- **2 Tbsp. butter**
- **1 small onion, halved and sliced**
- **3 garlic cloves, sliced**
- **½ cup sliced almonds**
- **1 tsp. grated lemon zest**
- **3 Tbsp. lemon juice**
- **¼ tsp. salt**
- **⅛ tsp. pepper**
- **½ cup crumbled feta cheese**

1. In a large saucepan, bring 4 cups water to a boil. Add green beans; cook, uncovered, 4-5 minutes or until beans turn bright green. Remove beans and immediately drop into ice water. Drain and pat dry.
2. In a large skillet, heat butter over medium heat. Add the onion; cook and stir until tender, 6-8 minutes. Add the garlic; cook 1 minute longer.
3. Add green beans and almonds; cook and stir until beans are crisp-tender, 3-4 minutes. Sprinkle with lemon zest, lemon juice, salt and pepper; toss to combine. Top with cheese.
¾ CUP: 134 cal., 9g fat (4g sat. fat), 15mg chol., 224mg sod., 10g carb. (3g sugars, 4g fiber), 5g pro.

LEMONY ALMOND-FETA GREEN BEANS

GINGER APPLESAUCE

EAT SMART (5)INGREDIENTS SLOW COOKER

GINGER APPLESAUCE

I love making applesauce, and this easy slow-cooker version is my favorite way to prepare it. The ginger adds a whole new flavor profile to the cinnamon-spiced sauce.
—Renee Pajestka, Brunswick, OH

PREP: 25 MIN. • **COOK:** 4 HOURS
MAKES: ABOUT 5 CUPS (8 SERVINGS)

- **4 lbs. apples (about 12 medium), peeled and cubed**
- **¼ cup water**
- **2 Tbsp. brown sugar**
- **2 tsp. ground cinnamon**
- **2 tsp. minced fresh gingerroot**
- **2 tsp. vanilla extract**

In a 4-qt. slow cooker, combine all ingredients. Cook, covered, on low until the apples are tender, 4-5 hours. Mash if desired. Refrigerate leftovers.
⅔ CUP: 128 cal., 1g fat (0 sat. fat), 0 chol., 2mg sod., 33g carb. (27g sugars, 4g fiber), 0 pro.

CAULIFLOWER-BROCCOLI CHEESE BAKE

One of the first recipes my mom taught me how to make is a tasty pairing of broccoli and cauliflower in a thick, comforting cheese sauce. It's absolutely my best side dish.
—Devin Mulertt, Cedarburg, WI

PREP: 15 MIN. • **BAKE:** 50 MIN. + STANDING • **MAKES:** 9 SERVINGS

- **2 Tbsp. butter**
- **1 small onion, chopped**
- **2 Tbsp. all-purpose flour**
- **½ cup 2% milk**
- **1 pkg. (8 oz.) process cheese (Velveeta), cubed**
- **¼ tsp. salt**
- **3 large eggs, lightly beaten**
- **2 pkg. (12 oz. each) frozen broccoli-cauliflower blend, thawed**

1. Preheat oven to 325°. In a Dutch oven, heat butter over medium-high heat. Add onion; cook and stir until tender, 2-3 minutes. Stir in flour until blended; gradually whisk in milk. Bring to a boil, stirring constantly; cook and stir until thickened, 1-2 minutes. Stir in cheese and salt until cheese is melted.
2. Remove from heat. Gradually whisk in eggs. Stir in vegetable blend. Transfer to a greased 8-in. square baking dish. Bake, uncovered, until set, 50-60 minutes. Let stand for 10 minutes before serving.
1 PIECE: 170 cal., 11g fat (6g sat. fat), 95mg chol., 461mg sod., 8g carb. (2g sugars, 1g fiber), 8g pro.

CAULIFLOWER-BROCCOLI CHEESE BAKE

SAUSAGE-HERB DRESSING

SLOW COOKER

SAUSAGE-HERB DRESSING

To make time for last-minute Thanksgiving essentials, I prep the sausage part of this recipe a day or two ahead of time, then finish the dressing in my slow cooker on the big day. It has stood the test two years running!
—Judy Batson, Tampa, FL

PREP: 20 MIN. • **COOK:** 2 HOURS
MAKES: 10 SERVINGS

- **1 lb. bulk sage pork sausage**
- **1 medium sweet onion, chopped (about 2 cups)**
- **2 celery ribs, chopped**
- **¼ cup brewed coffee**
- **½ tsp. poultry seasoning**
- **½ tsp. dried oregano**
- **½ tsp. rubbed sage**
- **½ tsp. dried thyme**
- **½ tsp. pepper**
- **1½ cups chicken or turkey broth**
- **1 pkg. (12 oz.) seasoned stuffing cubes (8 cups)**
- **Chopped fresh parsley**

1. In a 6-qt. stockpot, cook and crumble sausage with onion and celery over medium heat until no longer pink, 5-7 minutes; drain. Stir in coffee and seasonings; cook 3 minutes, stirring occasionally.
2. Add broth; bring to a boil. Remove from heat; stir in stuffing cubes. Transfer to a greased 4- or 5-qt. slow cooker.
3. Cook, covered, on low until heated through and edges are lightly browned, 2-2½ hours, stirring once. Sprinkle with the parsley.
¾ CUP: 254 cal., 11g fat (3g sat. fat), 25mg chol., 919mg sod., 29g carb. (4g sugars, 2g fiber), 9g pro.

TEST KITCHEN TIP

Don't be tempted to add more broth. The dressing will moisten as it cooks. Stir once during cooking so the mixture heats evenly.

5 INGREDIENTS

LEMON-ROSEMARY MARMALADE

I love bringing lemon and rosemary together. This unique marmalade goes beautifully with roast chicken, herbed pork roast and lamb chops. It's also superb on a biscuit or dinner roll.
—Birdie Shannon, Arlington, VA

PREP: 2¼ HOURS • **PROCESS:** 10 MIN.
MAKES: 5 HALF-PINTS

- **7 medium lemons (about 2 lbs.)**
- **½ tsp. baking soda, divided**
- **7 cups water**
- **4 cups sugar**
- **4 tsp. minced fresh rosemary**
- **2 drops yellow food coloring, optional**

1. Using a vegetable peeler, peel lemons into wide strips. With a sharp knife, carefully remove white pith from peels. Cut peels into ⅛-in. strips. Set fruit aside.
2. Place lemon strips in a small saucepan; add water to cover and ¼ tsp. baking soda. Bring to a boil. Reduce heat to medium. Cook, covered, 10 minutes; drain. Repeat with remaining baking soda.
3. Cut a thin slice from the top and bottom of lemons; stand lemons upright on a cutting board. With a knife, cut outer membrane from lemons. Working over a bowl to catch juices, cut along the membrane of each segment to remove fruit. Squeeze membrane to reserve additional juice.
4. Place lemon sections and reserved juices in a Dutch oven. Stir in 7 cups water and lemon peel. Bring to a boil. Reduce heat; simmer, uncovered, 25 minutes. Add sugar. Bring to a boil. Reduce heat; simmer, uncovered, 40-50 minutes or until slightly thickened, stirring occasionally. Remove from heat; immediately stir in rosemary and, if desired, food coloring.
5. Ladle hot mixture into five hot half-pint jars, leaving ¼-in. headspace. Wipe rims. Center lids on jars; screw on bands until fingertip tight.
6. Place jars into canner with simmering water, ensuring that they are completely covered with water. Bring to a boil; process for 10 minutes. Remove jars and cool.
2 TBSP.: 81 cal., 0 fat (0 sat. fat), 0 chol., 16mg sod., 21g carb. (20g sugars, 0 fiber), 0 pro.

FAVORITE BREAD & BUTTER PICKLES

I made these pickles while growing up and love them because you can eat them with just about anything. Now, both of my children adore the pickles, too. I think you'll enjoy them as much as we do.
—Linda Weger, Robinson, IL

PREP: 45 MIN. + STANDING
PROCESS: 10 MIN./BATCH • **MAKES:** 11 PINTS

- **20 cups sliced cucumbers (about 12 medium)**
- **3 cups sliced onions (about 4 medium)**
- **1 medium sweet red pepper, sliced**
- **1 medium green pepper, sliced**
- **3 qt. ice water**
- **½ cup canning salt**
- **6 cups sugar**
- **6 cups white vinegar**
- **3 Tbsp. mustard seed**
- **3 tsp. celery seed**
- **1½ tsp. ground turmeric**
- **¼ tsp. plus ⅛ tsp. ground cloves**

1. Place cucumbers, onions and peppers in a large bowl. In another large bowl, mix ice water and salt; pour over vegetables. Let stand 3 hours.
2. Rinse vegetables and drain well. Pack vegetables into eleven hot 1-pint jars to within ½ in. of the top.
3. In a Dutch oven, bring sugar, vinegar, mustard seed, celery seed, turmeric and cloves to a boil. Carefully ladle hot liquid over vegetable mixture, leaving ½-in. headspace. Remove air bubbles and adjust headspace, if necessary, by adding hot liquid. Wipe rims. Center lids on jars; screw on bands until fingertip tight.
4. Place jars into canner, ensuring that they are completely covered with water. Bring to a boil; process for 10 minutes. Remove jars and cool.
NOTE: The processing time listed is for altitudes of 1,000 feet or less. For altitudes up to 3,000 feet, add 5 minutes; 6,000 feet, add 10 minutes; 8,000 feet, add 15 minutes; 10,000 feet, add 20 minutes.
¼ CUP: 60 cal., 0 fat (0 sat. fat), 0 chol., 645mg sod., 15g carb. (14g sugars, 0 fiber), 0 pro.

MUSHROOMS MARSALA WITH BARLEY
ARLENE ERLBACH
Morton Grove, IL

EAT SMART SLOW COOKER

MUSHROOMS MARSALA WITH BARLEY

This recipe makes a hearty side to any meal. You can even enjoy it as a meatless entree if you'd like. Best of all, it's a healthy dish that simmers on its own in the slow cooker!
—Arlene Erlbach, Morton Grove, IL

PREP: 20 MIN. • **COOK:** 4 HOURS
MAKES: 6 SERVINGS

- **1½ lbs. baby portobello mushrooms, cut into ¾-in. chunks**
- **1 cup thinly sliced shallots**
- **3 Tbsp. olive oil**
- **½ tsp. minced fresh thyme**
- **¾ cup Marsala wine, divided**
- **3 Tbsp. reduced-fat sour cream**
- **2 Tbsp. all-purpose flour**
- **1½ tsp. grated lemon zest**
- **¼ tsp. salt**
- **¼ cup crumbled goat cheese**
- **¼ cup minced fresh parsley**
- **2½ cups cooked barley**

1. In a 4- or 5-qt. slow cooker, combine mushrooms, shallots, olive oil and thyme. Add ¼ cup Marsala wine. Cook, covered, on low until vegetables are tender, 4 hours.
2. Stir in sour cream, flour, lemon zest, salt and remaining Marsala. Cook, covered, on low 15 minutes longer. Sprinkle with goat cheese and parsley. Serve with hot cooked barley.
¾ CUP MUSHROOMS WITH ABOUT ⅓ CUP BARLEY: 235 cal., 9g fat (2g sat. fat), 7mg chol., 139mg sod., 31g carb. (6g sugars, 5g fiber), 7g pro. **Diabetic exchanges:** 2 starch, 2 fat, 1 vegetable.

HOW TO MAKE

MASHED POTATOES

Show off your spud savvy with a few pounds of potatoes and a happy dollop of butter. Total comfort is just 30 minutes away.

TRADITIONAL MASHED POTATOES

Smash Smarts

You may be tempted to spare your arm muscles by dumping the cooked spuds into a blender or food processor, but the potatoes will become gooey and gluey. Instead, use a potato masher or ricer. And, hey, a few lumps merely prove the potatoes didn't come from a box.

Layers of Flavor

Go green—mix in a few tablespoons of thinly sliced green onion, snipped chives or chopped parsley. Or roast a head of garlic, then stir the paste into the potatoes for extra richness.

Finishing Touch

Spread mashed potatoes into a baking dish. Then sprinkle with a combo of bread crumbs and grated Parmesan. Broil until the topping is golden brown, 1-2 minutes.

5 INGREDIENTS **FAST FIX**

TRADITIONAL MASHED POTATOES

Mashed potatoes go with just about any meal, and this classic recipe is one you might want to keep at the ready.
—Taste of Home *Test Kitchen*

TAKES: 30 MIN.
MAKES: 6 SERVINGS (ABOUT 4½ CUPS)

- 6 **medium russet potatoes (about 2 lbs.), peeled and cubed**
- ½ **cup warm whole milk or heavy whipping cream**
- ¼ **cup butter, cubed**
- ¾ **tsp. salt**
- **Dash pepper**

Place potatoes in a large saucepan; add water to cover. Bring to a boil. Reduce heat to medium; cook, uncovered, until very tender (easily pierced with a fork), 20-25 minutes. Drain. Add remaining ingredients; mash until light and fluffy.

¾ CUP: 168 cal., 8g fat (5g sat. fat), 22mg chol., 367mg sod., 22g carb. (3g sugars, 1g fiber), 3g pro.

Picking Potatoes

Whether mashed, baked or fried, the type of potato you use affects the outcome of a side dish. Potatoes fall into three categories: starchy, waxy and all-purpose. For the best results, choose the type that best fits your cooking method.

Russet: **High starch, low moisture**
- Thicker skin and fluffy flesh
- Good for baking, boiling, mashing and frying
- Flesh breaks down when cooked, so best used for recipes with a smooth texture

Red/New: **Low starch, high moisture**
- Thinner skin and creamy, waxy flesh
- Good for roasting and boiling
- Firm flesh holds up well, so best used in dishes where the potato needs to maintain its shape, such as salads, soups and casseroles

Yukon Gold: **Medium starch, high moisture**
- Thinner skin and firm, waxy flesh
- Good for boiling, baking, mashing, frying, roasting and grilling
- Stands up well to most cooking applications, so a versatile choice for many dishes

HOW-TO

To-Do's (and Ta-Da's)

- Cut all the potatoes to roughly the same size to allow for even cooking.
- Cover the cubed potatoes completely with water to keep them from drying out. Boil gently.
- While most cooks mash potatoes with milk, some choose to use cream. Do whatever you prefer! Warm the milk and add the cubed butter, allowing it to melt. Then add the milk mixture to the potatoes.
- Cooking for someone who's dairy-free? Mash the potatoes with warmed chicken broth or even some of the starchy cooking water.

CHOCOLATE BOURBON PECAN MONKEY BREAD,
PAGE 153

BREADS, ROLLS & MUFFINS

Nothing warms the heart like the aroma of fresh-baked bread—and this chapter is bursting with sweet and savory choices to make any meal more special. Just add butter!

FRUITY PULL-APART BREAD

FRUITY PULL-APART BREAD

Who wouldn't love to start the day with monkey bread? My skillet version is packed with bright berries and topped off with irresistibly rich cream cheese. A sprinkle of fresh basil brings it all together.
—Darla Andrews, Schertz, TX

PREP: 15 MIN. • **BAKE:** 35 MIN.
MAKES: 8 SERVINGS

- **1 tube (16.3 oz.) large refrigerated flaky honey butter biscuits**
- **½ cup packed dark brown sugar**
- **½ cup sugar**
- **⅓ cup butter, melted**
- **1 cup fresh blueberries**
- **1 cup chopped fresh strawberries**
- **4 oz. cream cheese, softened**
- **1 Tbsp. minced fresh basil**

1. Preheat oven to 350°. Separate dough into eight biscuits; cut biscuits into fourths.
2. In a shallow bowl, combine sugars. Dip biscuits in melted butter, then in sugar mixture. Place biscuits in a greased 10¼-in. cast-iron skillet. Top with fresh berries; dollop with cream cheese. Bake until biscuits are golden brown and cooked through, 35-40 minutes. Sprinkle with basil.

1 SERVING: 383 cal., 20g fat (9g sat. fat), 30mg chol., 641mg sod., 49g carb. (28g sugars, 2g fiber), 5g pro.

EAT SMART

BLACKBERRY MUFFINS

Take advantage of blackberry season by adding the delicious berries to muffins. These are easy to prepare and disappear as soon as they're served.
—Candy Woelk, Lexington, MO

PREP: 15 MIN. • **BAKE:** 20 MIN.
MAKES: 1 DOZEN

- **¼ cup butter, softened**
- **½ cup sugar**
- **1 large egg, lightly beaten**
- **¾ cup 2% milk**
- **¼ tsp. vanilla extract**
- **1¾ cups plus 1 Tbsp. all-purpose flour, divided**
- **2½ tsp. baking powder**
- **¼ tsp. salt**
- **1 cup fresh blackberries**
- **Honey, optional**

In a bowl, cream butter and sugar. Add egg and mix well. Beat in milk and vanilla until almost smooth, about 1 minute. Combine 1¾ cups flour, baking powder and salt; stir into creamed mixture just until combined (batter will be thick). Toss blackberries with the remaining flour until coated; fold into batter. Fill greased or paper-lined muffin cups half full. Bake at 400° for 20-25 minutes or until muffins are golden and test done. Serve muffins warm with honey if desired.

1 MUFFIN: 156 cal., 5g fat (3g sat. fat), 30mg chol., 184mg sod., 25g carb. (10g sugars, 1g fiber), 3g pro. **Diabetic exchanges:** 1½ starch, 1 fat.

BLACKBERRY MUFFINS

SWISS MUSHROOM LOAF

SWISS MUSHROOM LOAF

I get tons of recipe requests when I serve this savory loaf stuffed with Swiss cheese and mushrooms. It's excellent as an appetizer or served with pasta, chili or spaghetti.
—Heidi Mellon, Waukesha, WI

PREP: 15 MIN. • **BAKE:** 40 MIN.
MAKES: 12 SERVINGS

- **1 loaf (1 lb.) Italian bread, unsliced**
- **1 block (8 oz.) Swiss cheese, cut into cubes**
- **1 cup sliced fresh mushrooms**
- **¼ cup softened butter, cubed**
- **1 small onion, finely chopped**
- **1½ tsp. poppy seeds**
- **2 garlic cloves, minced**
- **½ tsp. seasoned salt**
- **½ tsp. ground mustard**
- **½ tsp. lemon juice**

1. Preheat oven to 350°, Cut bread diagonally into 1-in. slices to within 1 in. of bottom of loaf. Repeat cuts in opposite direction. Place cheese cubes and mushrooms in cuts.
2. In a microwave-safe bowl, combine the remaining ingredients; microwave, covered, on high until butter is melted, 30-60 seconds. Stir until blended. Spoon over bread.
3. Wrap loaf in foil and place on a baking sheet. Bake until cheese is melted, about 40 minutes.
1 SERVING: 214 cal., 11g fat (6g sat. fat), 28mg chol., 372mg sod., 21g carb. (2g sugars, 1g fiber), 9g pro.

BUTTERMILK CRANBERRY MUFFINS

I've been making these muffins for years, and have never met anyone who didn't like them. I buy bags of fresh cranberries when they're available and freeze them to use throughout the year, because even when the holidays pass, my family can't get enough.
—Jane Yunker, Rochester, NY

PREP: 15 MIN. • **BAKE:** 25 MIN. • **MAKES:** 1½ DOZEN

- **1 heaping cup cranberries, coarsely chopped**
- **¾ cup sugar, divided**
- **3 cups all-purpose flour**
- **3½ tsp. baking powder**
- **½ tsp. salt**
- **¼ tsp. baking soda**
- **½ cup butter**
- **1 large egg**
- **1½ cups buttermilk, room temperature**
- **2 Tbsp. thawed orange juice concentrate**

CRANBERRY BUTTER

- **1 cup dried cranberries**
- **1 cup confectioners' sugar**
- **½ cup butter**
- **1 Tbsp. lemon juice**

1. Preheat oven to 375°. Combine cranberries with ¼ cup sugar; set aside. Sift together flour, remaining sugar, baking powder, salt and baking soda. Cut in butter until mixture resembles coarse meal.
2. Lightly beat together the egg, buttermilk and orange juice concentrate. Add egg mixture and sweetened cranberries to dry ingredients, stirring just until well-combined. Spoon batter into buttered muffin cups, filling two-thirds full. Bake until a toothpick inserted in muffins comes out clean, about 25 minutes.
3. For cranberry butter, puree dried cranberries in food processor or blender. Add sugar, butter and lemon juice; process mixture until smooth. Refrigerate until serving.
1 MUFFIN: 270 cal., 11g fat (7g sat. fat), 38mg chol., 284mg sod., 41g carb. (23g sugars, 1g fiber), 3g pro.

BUTTERMILK CRANBERRY MUFFINS

CHOCOLATE BOURBON PECAN MONKEY BREAD

It's time to give rum cake a little bit of competition! And this chocolate-stuffed treat certainly does.
—James Schend, Pleasant Prairie, WI

PREP: 1½ HOURS + CHILLING
BAKE: 50 MIN. + COOLING
MAKES: 18 SERVINGS

- ¾ cup butter, divided
- 1 pkg. (¼ oz.) active dry yeast
- ½ cup warm water (110° to 115°)
- ½ cup warm 2% milk (110° to 115°)
- 2 large eggs, room temperature
- 3 Tbsp. bourbon or whiskey
- 4½ to 5 cups all-purpose flour
- 1¼ cups granulated sugar, divided
- ¾ tsp. salt
- 2 semisweet baking chocolate bars (4 oz. each) plus 1 oz., broken into ¼-oz. pieces (36 pieces total)

BOURBON CARAMEL

- ⅔ cup packed brown sugar
- ¼ cup butter, cubed
- ¼ cup bourbon or whiskey
- 1 cup chopped pecans

BOURBON CHOCOLATE GLAZE

- 1 semisweet baking chocolate bar (4 oz.), chopped
- ¼ cup bourbon or whiskey

1. Microwave ¼ cup butter until melted. Dissolve yeast in warm water and milk; let stand until foamy, about 10 minutes. In another bowl, combine eggs, bourbon and melted butter; stir in 2 cups flour, ¼ cup sugar, salt and yeast mixture. Beat on medium speed 3 minutes. Stir in enough remaining flour to form a soft dough.

2. Turn dough onto a floured surface; knead until smooth and elastic, 6-8 minutes. Place in a greased bowl, turning once to grease the top. Cover; refrigerate overnight.

3. Punch down dough. Turn onto a lightly floured surface; divide and shape into 36 rolls. Flatten rolls into circles; place 1 chocolate piece in center of each. Fold dough over filling; pinch edges well to seal. Melt remaining butter; pour into a shallow bowl. Place the remaining sugar in another shallow bowl. Dip the balls of dough in butter, allowing excess to drip off, then roll in sugar.

4. For bourbon caramel, bring brown sugar, butter and bourbon to a boil in a small saucepan over medium heat. Cook and stir 3 minutes. Pour half of the caramel into a greased 10-in. fluted tube pan; layer with half the pecans and half the dough balls; repeat. Cover pan with a kitchen towel; let rise in a warm place until doubled, about 45 minutes.

5. Preheat oven to 350°. Place a sheet of foil on bottom oven rack. Bake on the middle oven rack until golden brown, 50-55 minutes. (Cover loosely with foil for last 10-15 minutes if top browns too quickly.) Cool in pan 10 minutes before inverting onto a serving plate. Meanwhile, for the bourbon chocolate glaze, melt chocolate in a small heavy saucepan over medium-low heat. Remove from heat; stir in bourbon until smooth. Drizzle glaze over warm bread.

2 PIECES: 445 cal., 20g fat (10g sat. fat), 42mg chol., 174mg sod., 52g carb. (26g sugars, 2g fiber), 6g pro.

TEST KITCHEN TIP

You can make this treat in a greased 13x9-in. baking dish if you don't have the right size tube pan. Its bourbon flavor is very pronounced. Feel free to substitute milk for some or all of the bourbon. Rye whiskey, brandy or spiced rum may also be used instead of bourbon.

CHOCOLATE & CHERRY STROMBOLI

CHOCOLATE & CHERRY STROMBOLI

This melty, chocolaty spin on stromboli is delicious for both breakfast and dessert, or anytime at all. Serve it with a cup of coffee, and even the coldest winter day instantly feels more snug.
—Lorraine Caland, Shuniah, ON

PREP: 40 MIN. + RISING
BAKE: 20 MIN. + COOLING
MAKES: 1 LOAF (12 SERVINGS)

- 4 **cups all-purpose flour**
- 1 **pkg. (¼ oz.) quick-rise yeast**
- 1 **tsp. salt**
- 1 **cup warm water (120° to 130°)**
- 3 **Tbsp. canola oil**
- 2 **Tbsp. honey**
- 1 **large egg, room temperature, lightly beaten**
- 1 **tsp. lemon juice**
- 8 **oz. finely chopped bittersweet chocolate, divided**
- ½ **cup dried cherries, chopped**
- 2 **Tbsp. coarse sugar**

1. Whisk 3 cups flour, yeast and salt. In another bowl, mix water, oil and honey. Add to dry ingredients; beat on medium speed 2 minutes. Stir in enough remaining flour to form a soft dough (dough will be sticky).
2. Turn dough onto a floured surface; knead dough until smooth and elastic, 3-5 minutes. Place in a greased bowl, turning once to grease top. Cover; let dough rise in a warm place until doubled, about 30 minutes.
3. Preheat oven to 400°. Press dough into a greased 15x10x1-in. baking pan. Whisk egg with lemon juice; brush dough with half of egg wash. Sprinkle half of chocolate evenly over dough; top with cherries. Fold long sides of dough over chocolate and cherries, overlapping edges, and leaving ends open. Brush with remaining egg wash. Sprinkle with coarse sugar. Bake on lowest oven rack until bread sounds hollow when tapped, about 20 minutes. Cool on wire rack.
4. Meanwhile, in a microwave oven, melt the remaining chocolate. Drizzle over cooled bread.
1 SLICE: 248 cal., 8g fat (2g sat. fat), 16mg chol., 205mg sod., 36g carb. (10g sugars, 2g fiber), 5g pro.

EAT SMART (5) INGREDIENTS

ONE-DISH NO-KNEAD BREAD

Here's a very easy way to have homemade bread for dinner tonight. Don't worry if you're new to baking. Anyone who can stir can make this a success!
—Heather Chambers, Largo, FL

PREP: 15 MIN. + RISING • **BAKE:** 40 MIN.
MAKES: 1 LOAF (12 SLICES)

- 1 **tsp. active dry yeast**
- 1½ **cups warm water (110° to 115°)**
- 2¾ **cups all-purpose flour**
- 2 **Tbsp. sugar**
- 2 **Tbsp. olive oil**
- 1½ **tsp. salt**

1. In a large bowl, dissolve yeast in warm water. Stir in remaining ingredients to form a wet dough; transfer to a greased 2½-qt. baking dish. Cover; let stand in a warm place 1 hour.
2. Stir down dough. Cover; let stand 1 hour. Preheat oven to 425°.
3. Bake 20 minutes. Reduce the oven setting to 350°. Bake until top is golden brown and a thermometer reads 210°, about 20 minutes.
4. Remove bread from baking dish to a wire rack to cool. Serve warm.
1 SLICE: 133 cal., 3g fat (0 sat. fat), 0 chol., 296mg sod., 24g carb. (2g sugars, 1g fiber), 3g pro. **Diabetic exchanges:** 1½ starch, ½ fat.

PARMESAN-BACON BUBBLE BREAD

When I needed to put some leftover bread dough to good use, I started with a recipe I often use for bubble bread and substituted savory ingredients for the sweet.
—Lori McLain, Denton, TX

PREP: 20 MIN. + RISING • **BAKE:** 20 MIN.
MAKES: 16 SERVINGS

- 1 **loaf frozen bread dough, thawed (16 oz.)**
- ¼ **cup butter, melted**
- ¾ **cup shredded Parmesan cheese**
- 6 **bacon strips, cooked and finely crumbled**
- ⅓ **cup finely chopped green onions**
- 2 **Tbsp. grated Parmesan cheese**
- 2 **Tbsp. salt-free herb seasoning blend**
- 1½ **tsp. sugar**
- **Alfredo sauce, optional**

1. Turn dough onto a lightly floured surface; divide and shape into 16 rolls. Place butter in a shallow bowl. In a large bowl, combine the next six ingredients. Dip dough pieces in melted butter, then toss with cheese mixture to coat. Stack pieces in a greased 9-in. cast-iron skillet.
2. Cover with a kitchen towel; let rise in a warm place until almost doubled, about 45 minutes. Preheat oven to 350°. Bake until golden brown, 20-25 minutes. Serve warm and, if desired, with Alfredo sauce.
1 PIECE: 140 cal., 6g fat (3g sat. fat), 14mg chol., 311mg sod., 14g carb. (2g sugars, 1g fiber), 6g pro.

TEST KITCHEN TIP

Serve the bubble bread with pesto, marinara or Alfredo dipping sauces, or set out all three and let guests choose their favorite! You can also bake the dough in a greased 9x5-in. loaf pan.

5 INGREDIENTS FAST FIX

SOUTHERN BUTTERMILK BISCUITS

The recipe for these four-ingredient biscuits has been handed down for many generations. It's a classic.
—Fran Thompson, Tarboro, NC

TAKES: 30 MIN. • **MAKES:** 8 BISCUITS

- ½ **cup cold butter, cubed**
- 2 **cups self-rising flour**
- ¾ **cup buttermilk**
- **Melted butter**

1. In a large bowl, cut butter into flour until mixture resembles coarse crumbs. Stir in buttermilk just until moistened. Turn onto a lightly floured surface; knead 3-4 times. Pat or lightly roll to ¾-in. thickness. Cut with a floured 2½-in. biscuit cutter.
2. Place on a greased baking sheet. Bake at 425° until golden brown, 11-13 minutes. Brush tops with butter. Serve warm.
NOTE: As a substitute for each cup of self-rising flour, place 1½ tsp. baking powder and ½ tsp. salt in a measuring cup. Add all-purpose flour to measure 1 cup.
1 BISCUIT: 197 cal., 11 g fat (7 g sat. fat), 28 mg chol., 451 mg sod., 22 g carb., 1 g fiber, 4 g pro.

SOUTHERN BUTTERMILK BISCUITS

CARROT HONEY LOAF

CARROT HONEY LOAF

As a health-care professional and busy mom, I believe my time and skills in the kitchen are among the most meaningful gifts I can give. This loaf is one I love to share for events like a housewarming or welcoming a new baby. It is especially good toasted with butter.
—Krystal Horudko, Charlottetown, PE

PREP: 20 MIN. • **BAKE:** 1 HOUR • **MAKES:** 1 LOAF (16 SLICES)

- **2 large eggs, room temperature**
- **¾ cup canola oil**
- **¾ cup honey**
- **2 tsp. vanilla extract**
- **1 cup all-purpose flour**
- **1 cup whole wheat flour**
- **2 tsp. baking powder**
- **2 tsp. ground cinnamon**
- **1 tsp. ground nutmeg**
- **½ tsp. salt**
- **¼ tsp. baking soda**
- **2 cups grated carrots (about 3 large carrots)**

1. Preheat oven to 350°. Combine eggs, oil, honey and vanilla; beat until smooth. In another bowl, whisk next seven ingredients for 30 seconds. Stir flour mixture into egg mixture just until combined. Add carrots; mix well.
2. Pour batter into a lightly greased 9x5-in. loaf pan; bake until a toothpick inserted in center of loaf comes out clean, about 1 hour. Cool 10 minutes before removing to a wire rack.
1 SLICE: 212 cal., 11g fat (1g sat. fat), 23mg chol., 173mg sod., 26g carb. (14g sugars, 2g fiber), 3g pro.

PESTO PULL-APART BREAD

I combined some of my favorite flavors in an easy bread that complements many Italian meals. I make the pesto, oven-dried tomatoes and roasted red peppers, but store-bought versions will work just as well.
—Sue Gronholz, Beaver Dam, WI

PREP: 10 MIN. • **BAKE:** 30 MIN. • **MAKES:** 1 LOAF (16 SERVINGS)

- **1 tube (16.3 oz.) large refrigerated buttermilk biscuits**
- **¼ cup olive oil**
- **2 Tbsp. prepared pesto**
- **¼ cup sun-dried tomatoes (not packed in oil)**
- **¼ cup roasted sweet red peppers, drained and diced**
- **¼ cup sliced ripe olives**
- **1 cup shredded mozzarella and provolone cheese blend**
- **Additional prepared pesto, optional**

1. Preheat oven to 350°. Cut each biscuit into four pieces. Combine olive oil and pesto. Dip biscuit pieces into pesto mixture until coated; place in an 8-in. round baking pan. Top with sun-dried tomatoes, roasted red peppers and ripe olives.
2. Bake until golden brown, about 25 minutes. Sprinkle with cheese; return to oven, and bake until melted, 5 minutes longer. Cut into wedges or pull apart; serve warm with additional pesto if desired.
1 SERVING: 152 cal., 9g fat (3g sat. fat), 5mg chol., 410mg sod., 13g carb. (2g sugars, 1g fiber), 3g pro.

PESTO PULL-APART BREAD

HAWAIIAN DINNER ROLLS

Pineapple and coconut give subtle sweetness to these golden homemade rolls. If there are any leftovers, they're great for sandwiches.
—Kathy Kurtz, Glendora, CA

PREP: 35 MIN. + RISING • **BAKE:** 15 MIN.
MAKES: 15 ROLLS

- **1 can (8 oz.) crushed pineapple, undrained**
- **¼ cup warm pineapple juice (70° to 80°)**
- **¼ cup water (70° to 80°)**
- **1 large egg**
- **¼ cup butter, cubed**
- **¼ cup nonfat dry milk powder**
- **1 Tbsp. sugar**
- **1½ tsp. salt**
- **3¼ cups bread flour**
- **2¼ tsp. active dry yeast**
- **¾ cup sweetened shredded coconut**

1. In bread machine pan, place the first 10 ingredients in the order suggested by manufacturer. Select dough setting (check the dough after 5 minutes of mixing; add 1-2 Tbsp. of water or flour if needed). Just before final kneading (your machine may audibly signal this), add coconut.
2. When cycle is complete, turn dough onto a lightly floured surface. Cover and let rest for 10 minutes. Divide into 15 portions; roll each into a ball. Place in a greased 13x9-in. baking pan.
3. Cover and let rise in a warm place for 45 minutes or until doubled. Bake at 375° for 15-20 minutes or until golden brown.
NOTE: We recommend you do not use a bread machine's time-delay feature for this recipe.
1 SERVING: 165 cal., 5g fat (3g sat. fat), 23mg chol., 294mg sod., 26g carb. (6g sugars, 1g fiber), 5g pro.

JALAPENO CORNBREAD FILLED WITH BLUEBERRY QUICK JAM

JALAPENO CORNBREAD FILLED WITH BLUEBERRY QUICK JAM

Fresh jalapenos and blueberry quick jam make the perfect blend of sweet and spicy in this special cornbread. Once you eat one piece, you won't be able to resist going back for another one. You'll love the unexpected combination of flavors.
—Colleen Delawder, Herndon, VA

PREP: 20 MIN. + CHILLING
BAKE: 30 MIN. + COOLING
MAKES: 12 SERVINGS

- **2 cups fresh blueberries**
- **1 cup sugar**
- **1 Tbsp. cider vinegar**
- **¼ tsp. kosher salt**

CORNBREAD

- **½ cup whole milk**
- **1 Tbsp. lemon juice**
- **1½ cups all-purpose flour**
- **½ cup yellow cornmeal**
- **½ cup sugar**
- **3 tsp. baking powder**
- **½ tsp. kosher salt**
- **2 Tbsp. unsalted butter**
- **1 Tbsp. honey**
- **2 large eggs**
- **⅓ cup canola oil**
- **2 jalapeno peppers, seeded and minced**

1. In a large heavy saucepan, combine blueberries, sugar, vinegar and kosher salt. Bring to a boil over high heat. Cook, stirring constantly, 5 minutes. Cool completely. Refrigerate, covered, overnight.
2. For cornbread, preheat oven to 350°. Combine milk and lemon juice; let stand briefly. In another bowl, whisk next five ingredients. In a small bowl, microwave butter and honey on high for 30 seconds; cool slightly. Whisk eggs and oil into milk mixture (mixture may appear curdled). Add butter mixture; whisk until well combined. Add flour mixture; whisk just until combined. Fold in jalapenos.
3. Pour 2 cups batter into a well-buttered 10-in. fluted tube pan. Spoon half to three-fourths of blueberry quick jam over batter. Cover with remaining batter. Bake until a toothpick inserted in center comes out clean, 30-35 minutes. Cool 10 minutes; invert onto a cake plate or serving platter. Drizzle with remaining blueberry quick jam.
1 SLICE: 289 cal., 10g fat (2g sat. fat), 37mg chol., 258mg sod., 48g carb. (30g sugars, 1g fiber), 4g pro.

DENVER OMELET SALAD, PAGE 169

BREAKFAST & BRUNCH

Everyone will want to rise and shine when these beautiful specialties are on the menu. Here you'll find the fixings for lazy weekends, holidays, and power-packed mornings.

BAKED FRENCH TOAST

BAKED FRENCH TOAST

Any day is special when Mom makes one of her French toast recipes, like this do-ahead baked version.
—Jill Baughman, New York, NY

PREP: 20 MIN. + CHILLING
BAKE: 40 MIN. + STANDING
MAKES: 8 SERVINGS

- **8 oz. day-old French bread, unsliced**
- **4 large eggs**
- **2 Tbsp. sugar**
- **1 Tbsp. brown sugar**
- **2 tsp. vanilla extract**
- **1 tsp. maple extract**
- **¼ tsp. kosher salt**
- **2 cups whole milk**
- **½ cup heavy whipping cream**

TOPPING
- **¼ cup all-purpose flour**
- **3 Tbsp. brown sugar**
- **3 Tbsp. unsalted butter, cut into ¼-in. cubes**
- **1 tsp. ground cinnamon**
- **Freshly grated nutmeg, optional**
- **Fresh blueberries or raspberries**
- **Confectioners' sugar**

1. Cut bread into 1-in.-thick slices. Arrange in a single layer in a greased 13x9-in. baking dish. Lightly beat next six ingredients; stir in milk and cream. Pour egg mixture over bread, turning once to coat. Refrigerate, covered, overnight.
2. Preheat oven to 375°. Turn bread again to coat. For topping, combine flour, brown sugar, butter, cinnamon and, if desired, nutmeg. Sprinkle flour mixture over bread.
3. Bake, uncovered, until a knife inserted in center comes out clean and topping is golden brown, 40-45 minutes. Let stand 10 minutes before cutting. Top with blueberries or raspberries; sprinkle with confectioners' sugar.
1 SERVING: 297 cal., 15g fat (8g sat. fat), 128mg chol., 299mg sod., 32g carb. (15g sugars, 1g fiber), 9g pro.

PEAR & APPLE COFFEE CAKE

The mix of apples, pears and sour cream in this tender coffee cake gives it an incredibly moist and appealing texture.
—Debbie Vanni, Libertyville, IL

PREP: 25 MIN. • **BAKE:** 30 MIN.
MAKES: 12 SERVINGS

- **½ cup plus 2 Tbsp. unsalted butter, softened, divided**
- **1 cup sugar**
- **2 large eggs**
- **1 tsp. vanilla extract**
- **2 cups all-purpose flour**
- **1 tsp. baking soda**
- **1 tsp. baking powder**
- **½ tsp. salt**
- **1 cup sour cream**
- **1 medium apple, peeled and finely chopped**
- **1 medium pear, peeled and finely chopped**
- **1 cup packed brown sugar**
- **1 tsp. ground cinnamon**
- **½ cup chopped walnuts or pecans**

1. Preheat oven to 350°. Grease a 13x9-in. baking pan. In a large bowl, cream ½ cup butter and sugar until light and fluffy. Add eggs, one at a time, beating well after each addition. Beat in vanilla. In another bowl, whisk flour, baking soda, baking powder and salt; add to creamed mixture alternately with sour cream, beating well after each addition. Fold in apples and pears. Transfer to prepared pan.
2. For topping, combine brown sugar, remaining 2 Tbsp. of butter and cinnamon in a small bowl; mix with a fork until crumbly. Stir in nuts. Sprinkle over batter. Bake until a toothpick inserted in center comes out clean, 30-35 minutes. Cool slightly in pan on a wire rack.
1 PIECE: 395 cal., 18g fat (9g sat. fat), 61mg chol., 269mg sod., 56g carb. (38g sugars, 2g fiber), 5g pro.

REUBEN EGGS BENEDICT

EAT SMART FAST FIX

BAKED BLUEBERRY GINGER PANCAKE

My kids love pancakes, so I came up with this baked version that saves a lot of time in the morning. My kids always gobble these ginger-kissed breakfast squares right up!
—Erin Wright, Wallace, KS

TAKES: 30 MIN. • **MAKES:** 9 SERVINGS

2 large eggs
1½ cups 2% milk
¼ cup butter, melted
2 cups all-purpose flour
2 Tbsp. sugar
3 tsp. baking powder
1½ tsp. ground ginger
½ tsp. salt
2 cups fresh or frozen unsweetened blueberries
Maple syrup

1. Preheat oven to 350°. Combine eggs, milk and butter. Whisk the next five ingredients; add to egg mixture. Spoon batter into a 9-in. square baking pan coated with cooking spray. Sprinkle blueberries over top.
2. Bake until a toothpick inserted in the center comes out clean, 20-25 minutes. Cut into squares; serve with warm maple syrup.
1 PIECE: 213 cal., 7g fat (4g sat. fat), 58mg chol., 368mg sod., 31g carb. (8g sugars, 2g fiber), 6g pro. **Diabetic exchanges:** 2 starch, 1½ fat.

REUBEN EGGS BENEDICT

When it comes to food, two of my all-time favorites are Reuben sandwiches and eggs Benedict. So naturally I combined them into this incredible breakfast dish. I serve mine with bacon on the side, but hash browns and fresh fruit go great, too!
—Jessica Rehs, Akron, OH

PREP: 20 MIN. • **COOK:** 15 MIN. • **MAKES:** 4 SERVINGS

4 large eggs
Coarsely ground pepper
⅛ tsp. salt
2 pretzel hamburger buns, split
4 slices Swiss cheese (¾ oz. each)
⅓ cup sauerkraut, rinsed, drained well and chopped
¼ lb. sliced deli corned beef
Prepared Thousand Island salad dressing

1. Preheat oven to 350°. Heat a large skillet coated with cooking spray over medium-high heat. Break eggs, one at a time, into pan; sprinkle with coarsely ground pepper. Reduce heat to low. Cook to desired doneness, turning after whites are set, about 2-3 minutes. Sprinkle with salt; keep warm.
2. While eggs are cooking, hollow out split pretzel buns. Toast buns on a baking sheet or oven rack, 3-4 minutes. Top with cheese; return to oven until cheese is melted.
3. To assemble, layer a fourth of the sauerkraut, a fourth of the corned beef and one egg on each bun half. Drizzle with salad dressing.
1 OPEN-FACED SANDWICH: 317 cal., 15g fat (6g sat. fat), 222mg chol., 784mg sod., 25g carb. (2g sugars, 1g fiber), 21g pro.

BAKED BLUEBERRY GINGER PANCAKE

HOME-FOR-CHRISTMAS FRUIT BAKE

HOME-FOR-CHRISTMAS FRUIT BAKE

Pop this special dish in the oven and mouths will water in anticipation— the cinnamony aroma is tantalizing! The fruit comes out tender and slightly tart, while the pecan halves add a rich and buttery crunch.
—Bonnie Baumgardner, Sylva, NC

PREP: 15 MIN. • **BAKE:** 45 MIN. • **MAKES:** 12 SERVINGS

- **1 medium apple, peeled and thinly sliced**
- **1 tsp. lemon juice**
- **1 can (20 oz.) pineapple chunks**
- **1 can (29 oz.) peach halves, drained**
- **1 can (29 oz.) pear halves, drained**
- **1 jar (6 to 8 oz.) maraschino cherries**
- **½ cup pecan halves**
- **⅓ cup packed brown sugar**
- **1 Tbsp. butter, melted**
- **1 tsp. ground cinnamon**

1. Preheat oven to 325°. Toss apple slices with lemon juice. Arrange in a greased 2½-qt. baking dish. Drain pineapple, reserving ¼ cup juice. Combine pineapple, peaches and pears; spoon over apples. Top with cherries and pecans; set aside.
2. In a small saucepan, combine brown sugar, butter, cinnamon and reserved pineapple juice. Cook and stir over low heat until sugar is dissolved and butter is melted. Pour over fruit. Bake, uncovered, until apples are tender, about 45 minutes. Serve warm.
¾ CUP: 220 cal., 4g fat (1g sat. fat), 3mg chol., 21mg sod., 49g carb. (44g sugars, 3g fiber), 1g pro.

(5) INGREDIENTS FAST FIX

TOAD IN THE HOLE BACON & CHEESE SANDWICH

Switch up the cheese—pepper jack gives a nice kick—or use sliced kielbasa, ham or sausage in place of the bacon in this versatile grilled cheese sandwich.
—Kallee Krong-McCreery, Escondido, CA

TAKES: 15 MIN. • **MAKES:** 1 SERVING

- **2 slices sourdough bread**
- **1 Tbsp. mayonnaise**
- **1 large egg**
- **1 slice cheddar cheese**
- **2 cooked bacon strips**

1. Using a biscuit cutter or round cookie cutter, cut out center of one slice of bread (discard center or save for another use). Spread mayonnaise on one side of bread slices. In a large skillet coated with cooking spray, lightly toast cutout slice, mayonnaise side down, over medium-low heat. Flip slice; crack an egg into center. Add remaining bread slice mayonnaise side down, to skillet; layer with cheese and bacon.
2. Cook, covered, until egg white is set, yolk is soft-set and cheese begins to melt. If needed, flip slice with egg to finish cooking. To assemble sandwich, use solid slice as the bottom and cutout slice as the top.
1 SANDWICH: 610 cal., 34g fat (11g sat. fat), 240mg chol., 1220mg sod., 46g carb. (4g sugars, 2g fiber), 30g pro.

TOAD IN THE HOLE BACON & CHEESE SANDWICH

EAT SMART

BLT GRAIN BOWLS

I absolutely love a BLT with sliced avocado and an egg. Recently, I've been trying out grain bowls, and I thought the flavors of my favorite sandwich would work really well in one. My family agreed!
—Elisabeth Larsen, Pleasant Grove, UT

PREP: 15 MIN. • **COOK:** 20 MIN.
MAKES: 4 SERVINGS

- **1 cup quinoa, rinsed**
- **¼ cup olive oil, divided**
- **2 Tbsp. minced fresh basil**
- **2 Tbsp. white wine vinegar, divided**
- **1 Tbsp. lemon juice**
- **4 large eggs**
- **8 oz. cherry tomatoes**
- **3 cups fresh arugula**
- **1 small ripe avocado, peeled and sliced**
- **4 bacon strips, cooked and crumbled**

1. Prepare quinoa according to package directions. Combine 3 Tbsp. olive oil, basil, 1 Tbsp. vinegar and lemon juice. Add to cooked quinoa; stir to combine.
2. Place 2-3 in. of water in a large skillet with high sides; add remaining vinegar. Bring to a boil; adjust heat to maintain a gentle simmer. Break cold eggs, one at a time, into a small cup; holding cup close to surface of water, slip egg into water. Cook, uncovered, until whites are completely set and yolks begin to thicken but are not hard, 3-5 minutes. Using a slotted spoon, lift eggs out of water. Keep warm.
3. In a large skillet, heat remaining oil over medium heat. Cook tomatoes until they begin to release their juices, 8-10 minutes. Add arugula; cook and stir just until arugula is wilted, 1-2 minutes.
4. To serve, divide quinoa evenly among four bowls. Add cherry tomatoes, arugula, avocado slices and crumbled bacon. Top each with a poached egg.
NOTE: Look for quinoa in the cereal, rice or organic food aisle.
1 SERVING: 446 cal., 28g fat (5g sat. fat), 194mg chol., 228mg sod., 33g carb. (2g sugars, 6g fiber), 17g pro.

MEXICAN RICE WITH POACHED EGGS

MEXICAN RICE WITH POACHED EGGS

This Mexican rice recipe topped with soft poached eggs works for breakfast or dinner. I like to serve this dish with hot tortillas and a side of refried beans for a complete meal.
—Jean Lewis, Adrian, MI

PREP: 20 MIN. • **COOK:** 30 MIN.
MAKES: 6 SERVINGS

- **1 lb. bulk spicy pork sausage**
- **1 medium onion, diced**
- **1 medium sweet red pepper, diced**
- **1 to 2 seeded jalapeno peppers, minced**
- **2 garlic cloves, minced**
- **1 Tbsp. beef base**
- **2 tsp. ground cumin**
- **1 tsp. pepper**
- **1 cup uncooked long grain rice**
- **2 cups water**
- **6 large eggs**
- **1 cup shredded sharp cheddar cheese**
- **Warm corn or flour tortillas (6 in.)**

1. In a Dutch oven over medium heat, cook sausage, crumbling meat, with onion and peppers until meat is no longer pink; drain. Add garlic; cook 1 minute longer. Stir in beef base, cumin and black pepper.
2. Add rice; brown lightly. Pour in water. Bring to a boil. Reduce heat; simmer, covered, until liquid is absorbed and rice is tender, 18-20 minutes. Fluff with a fork. Transfer to a platter; keep warm.
3. Meanwhile, poach eggs by bringing 2-3 in. water to a boil in a large saucepan or skillet with high sides; adjust heat to maintain a gentle simmer. Break cold eggs, one at a time, into a small bowl; holding bowl close to water surface, slip egg into water. Cook, uncovered, until whites are completely set and yolks begin to thicken but are not hard, 3-5 minutes. Using a slotted spoon, lift eggs out of water. Place on rice; sprinkle with cheese. Serve with warm tortillas.
1 SERVING: 482 cal., 28g fat (10g sat. fat), 246mg chol., 998mg sod., 34g carb. (3g sugars, 1g fiber), 22g pro.

COLLEN DELAWDER
HERNDON, VA

HEARTY SLOW-COOKER BREAKFAST HASH

SLOW COOKER

HEARTY SLOW-COOKER BREAKFAST HASH

This sweet and savory hash certainly won't leave you hungry. The sausage, veggies and eggs fill you up, and the hint of maple syrup makes it all feel extra cozy.
—Colleen Delawder, Herndon, VA

PREP: 25 MIN. • **COOK:** 5 HOURS • **MAKES:** 4 SERVINGS

- **8 to 10 frozen fully cooked breakfast sausage links**
- **4 cups diced red potatoes (about 1½ lbs.)**
- **4 medium carrots, diced**
- **2 green onions, thinly sliced (white and pale green parts only)**
- **2 Tbsp. extra virgin olive oil**
- **1 Tbsp. red wine vinegar**
- **1 Tbsp. plus 2 tsp. snipped fresh dill, divided**
- **1 tsp. kosher salt**
- **½ tsp. coarsely ground pepper, divided**
- **¼ tsp. crushed red pepper flakes**
- **2 Tbsp. crumbled feta cheese**
- **1 Tbsp. butter**
- **4 large eggs**
- **2 Tbsp. maple syrup**

1. In a large skillet over medium heat, cook sausages, turning occasionally, until heated through, 8-9 minutes. Combine next five ingredients in a 3-qt. slow cooker. Add 1 Tbsp. dill, kosher salt, ¼ tsp. pepper and red pepper flakes. Arrange sausages on top of vegetable mixture. Cook, covered, on low until vegetables are tender, 5-6 hours. Transfer vegetables to a serving platter; sprinkle with feta cheese. Top with sausages.
2. Meanwhile, in a large skillet, heat butter over medium heat. Break eggs, one at a time, into a small bowl; slip into skillet. Reduce heat to low; cook slowly until the whites are completely set. For sunny-side up eggs, cover pan and cook until yolks thicken, but are not hard. Arrange eggs over vegetables. Sprinkle with remaining dill and pepper; drizzle with maple syrup.
1 SERVING: 446 cal., 25g fat (8g sat. fat), 212mg chol., 911mg sod., 42g carb. (12g sugars, 5g fiber), 14g pro.

TEST KITCHEN TIP

Drop everything into the slow cooker insert and pop it in the fridge before bedtime for a smooth-sailing breakfast in the morning. Or mix up this hash before heading to work so it's ready when you get home. While there are many versions of hash across the globe, its origins can be traced back to 17th-century France. Since then, many countries have put their own spin on it. For a flavor twist, substitute any fully cooked sausage.

SALMON & ARTICHOKE QUICHE

Salmon, goat cheese and artichoke hearts make this quiche feel a little fancy and taste extra delicious. Baked in an 11x7-inch dish, it comes together in a snap with flaky crescent dough.
—Jeanne Holt, Mendota Heights, MN

PREP: 15 MIN. • **BAKE:** 40 MIN. + COOLING • **MAKES:** 8 SERVINGS

- **1 tube (8 oz.) refrigerated crescent rolls**
- **⅔ cup shredded Parmesan cheese, divided**
- **½ cup crumbled goat cheese**
- **1 cup thinly sliced smoked salmon fillets**
- **1 cup water-packed artichoke hearts, drained**
- **¼ cup chopped green onion (green portion only)**
- **2 Tbsp. finely chopped fresh dill**
- **¼ tsp. pepper**
- **5 large eggs**
- **1 cup heavy whipping cream**

1. Preheat oven to 350°. Unroll dough into one long rectangle; place in ungreased 11x7-in. baking dish. Press dough over bottom and up sides of dish, pressing perforations to seal.
2. Sprinkle with ⅓ cup Parmesan cheese. Top with goat cheese, salmon and artichoke hearts. Sprinkle with onion, chopped dill and pepper. Whisk eggs and cream; pour over salmon mixture. Sprinkle with remaining Parmesan cheese.
3. Bake until a knife inserted in the center comes out clean, 40-45 minutes (loosely cover with foil if edges are getting too dark). Cool 20 minutes. Cut into squares.
1 SERVING: 336 cal., 24g fat (13g sat. fat),167mg chol., 619mg sod., 15g carb. (4g sugars, 0 fiber), 15g pro.

SALMON & ARTICHOKE QUICHE

OAXACA TWIST BUTTER

(5) INGREDIENTS

OAXACA TWIST BUTTER

This Mexican-inspired butter elevates fresh-baked bread, croissants or muffins to new heights. The combination of raspberries with dark chocolate, toasted pecans and just a touch of hot chili makes your tastebuds dance every time.
—Nicole Filizetti, Stevens Point, WI

PREP: 10 MIN. + CHILLING
MAKES: 1 CUP

- **⅓ cup fresh raspberries**
- **½ cup unsalted butter, softened**
- **¼ cup finely grated dark chocolate candy bar**
- **⅛ tsp. ground ancho chili pepper**
- **⅓ cup ground pecans, toasted**

Crush raspberries and drain; combine berries with butter, grated chocolate and ancho chili, mixing well. Place butter in a small serving bowl; sprinkle with nuts. Wrap tightly with plastic wrap; refrigerate 5 hours or overnight.

1 TBSP.: 80 cal., 8g fat (4g sat. fat), 16mg chol., 1mg sod., 2g carb. (2g sugars, 1g fiber), 0 pro.

TEST KITCHEN TIP

For a breakfast like no other, serve this butter on pancakes or French toast in place of syrup, or on fresh-baked muffins. Spread on graham crackers for a salty-sweet breakfast treat. This butter will keep in the fridge for up to a week — if it lasts that long.

EAT SMART FAST FIX

BERRY PUFF PANCAKE

Breakfast is my husband's favorite meal of the day. I use our homegrown blueberries in this sweet morning treat.
—Cecilia Morgan, Milwaukie, OR

TAKES: 25 MIN. • **MAKES:** 6 SERVINGS

- **1 Tbsp. butter**
- **3 large eggs**
- **¾ cup 2% milk**
- **¾ cup all-purpose flour**
- **½ tsp. salt**

BERRY TOPPING

- **1 cup each fresh raspberries, blueberries and sliced strawberries**
- **⅓ cup orange marmalade**
- **2 Tbsp. confectioners' sugar**
- **Whipped cream, optional**

1. Place the butter in a 9-in. pie plate; place in a 400° oven for 4-5 minutes or until melted. Tilt pie plate to evenly coat bottom and sides with butter.
2. In a small bowl, whisk the eggs and milk. In another small bowl, combine the flour and salt; whisk in egg mixture until smooth. Pour batter into prepared pie plate. Bake until sides are crisp and golden brown, 15-20 minutes.
3. Meanwhile, in a large bowl, gently combine the berries and marmalade. Sprinkle pancake with confectioners' sugar; fill with berry mixture. Serve immediately. If desired, serve with whipped cream.

1 PIECE: 215 cal., 6g fat (3g sat. fat), 116mg chol., 273mg sod., 36g carb. (21g sugars, 3g fiber), 6g pro.

BERRY PUFF PANCAKE

CHEESY BACON BREAKFAST LASAGNA

I came up with this unique breakfast dish after looking for a way to use up a few extra no-boil lasagna noodles. Try switching up the different cheeses—Swiss, pepper jack and mozzarella taste delicious in this breakfast lasagna, too!
—Susan Kieboam, Streetsboro, OH

PREP: 30 MIN. + SOAKING • **BAKE:** 10 MIN. + COOLING
MAKES: 4 SERVINGS

- **3 no-cook lasagna noodles**
- **3 bacon strips, diced**
- **2 Tbsp. diced sweet or green onion**
- **2 Tbsp. diced sweet red pepper**
- **4 large eggs**

CHEESE SAUCE
- **2 Tbsp. butter**
- **2 Tbsp. all-purpose flour**
- **1 cup 2% milk**
- **1 tsp. grated Parmesan cheese**
- **¼ tsp. salt**
- **1 cup shredded sharp cheddar cheese**
- **3 Tbsp. whole-milk ricotta cheese**

1. Soak lasagna noodles in warm water for 20 minutes. In a small skillet, cook bacon, onion and red pepper over medium heat until bacon is crisp, 8-10 minutes. Remove 2 Tbsp. bacon mixture and drain on paper towels; reserve. Whisk eggs into skillet; cook and stir until cooked through.
2. Preheat oven to 350°. For cheese sauce, melt butter in a small saucepan over medium heat; whisk in flour until smooth. Add milk, Parmesan cheese and salt; cook and stir until thickened, 2-3 minutes. Remove from heat; stir cheddar cheese into hot mixture until smooth.
3. Drain noodles on paper towels. To assemble lasagna, spread 3 Tbsp. cheese sauce over bottom of a greased 8x4-in. loaf pan. Layer with one lasagna noodle, 3 Tbsp. cheese sauce, half the egg mixture and another lasagna noodle. Layer with 3 Tbsp. cheese sauce, ricotta cheese and remaining egg mixture. Top with the third noodle, remaining cheese sauce and reserved bacon mixture.
4. Bake until bubbly, 10-15 minutes. Cool 5 minutes before cutting.
1 SERVING: 443 cal., 31g fat (15g sat. fat), 253mg chol., 638mg sod., 19g carb. (5g sugars, 1g fiber), 21g pro.

CREAMY EGGS & MUSHROOMS AU GRATIN

When I want a brunch recipe that has the crowd appeal of scrambled eggs but is a little more special, I turn to this dish. The Parmesan sauce is simple, yet rich and delicious.
—Deborah Williams, Peoria, AZ

PREP: 15 MIN. • **COOK:** 25 MIN. • **MAKES:** 8 SERVINGS

- **2 Tbsp. butter**
- **1 lb. sliced fresh mushrooms**
- **1 green onion, chopped**

SAUCE
- **2 Tbsp. butter, melted**
- **3 Tbsp. all-purpose flour**
- **½ tsp. salt**
- **⅛ tsp. pepper**
- **1 cup 2% milk**
- **½ cup heavy whipping cream**
- **2 Tbsp. grated Parmesan cheese**

EGGS
- **16 large eggs**
- **¼ tsp. salt**
- **⅛ tsp. pepper**
- **¼ cup butter, cubed**
- **½ cup grated Parmesan cheese**
- **1 green onion, finely chopped**

1. In a large broiler-safe skillet, heat butter over medium-high heat. Add mushrooms; cook and stir until browned, 4-6 minutes. Add green onion; cook 1 minute longer. Remove from pan with a slotted spoon. Wipe skillet clean.
2. For sauce, in a small saucepan, melt butter over medium heat. Stir in flour, salt and pepper until smooth; gradually whisk in milk and cream. Bring to a boil, stirring constantly; cook and stir until thickened, 2-4 minutes. Remove from heat; stir in cheese.
3. Preheat broiler. For eggs, in a large bowl, whisk eggs, salt and pepper until blended. In same skillet, heat butter over medium heat. Pour in egg mixture; cook and stir just until eggs are thickened and no liquid egg remains. Remove from heat.
4. Spoon half of the sauce over the eggs; top with mushrooms. Add remaining sauce; sprinkle with cheese. Broil 4-5 in. from heat until top is lightly browned, 4-6 minutes. Sprinkle with onion.
1 SERVING: 363 cal., 29g fat (15g sat. fat), 431mg chol., 591mg sod., 8g carb. (3g sugars, 1g fiber), 18g pro.

CREAMY EGGS & MUSHROOMS AU GRATIN

CARROT CAKE PANCAKES

FAST FIX
CARROT CAKE PANCAKES

Here's a way for fans of carrot cake to have their favorite dessert for breakfast. These delicate, decadent pancakes are drizzled with sweet and spicy syrup that complements the creamy, nutty toppings.
—Leane Goering, Salem, IN

TAKES: 30 MIN. • **MAKES:** 1 DOZEN (½ CUP SYRUP)

- **2 cups pancake mix**
- **1 tsp. ground cinnamon**
- **¼ tsp. ground nutmeg**
- **⅛ tsp. ground cloves**
- **2 large eggs**
- **1 cup whole milk**
- **1 cup finely shredded carrots**

TOPPINGS
- **½ cup maple syrup**
- **⅛ tsp. ground cinnamon**
- **⅔ cup whipped cream cheese**
- **1 Tbsp. whole milk**
- **½ cup chopped walnuts or pecans, toasted**
- **Finely shredded carrots, optional**

1. In a large bowl, combine the pancake mix, cinnamon, nutmeg and cloves. In a small bowl, beat eggs and milk; stir into the dry ingredients just until moistened. Stir in carrots.
2. Pour batter by ¼ cupfuls onto a greased hot griddle. Turn pancakes when bubbles form on top; cook until second side is golden brown.
3. For syrup, in a small saucepan, combine the maple syrup and cinnamon. Bring to a boil. Reduce heat; simmer for 2 minutes. In a small bowl, combine cream cheese and milk. Serve pancakes with cream cheese mixture and half the syrup (save remaining syrup for another use). Sprinkle with nuts and, if desired, carrots.
2 PANCAKES WITH TOPPINGS: 388 cal., 16g fat (6g sat. fat), 84mg chol., 673mg sod., 52g carb. (21g sugars, 4g fiber), 10g pro.

FAST FIX
SHIITAKE & MANCHEGO SCRAMBLE

This savory breakfast dish takes everyday scrambled eggs up a few notches. The rich flavor is so satisfying in the morning, and it's even better served with buttery toasted Italian bread.
—Thomas Faglon, Somerset, NJ

TAKES: 25 MIN. • **MAKES:** 8 SERVINGS

- **2 Tbsp. extra virgin olive oil, divided**
- **½ cup diced onion**
- **½ cup diced sweet red pepper**
- **2 cups thinly sliced fresh shiitake mushrooms (about 4 oz.)**
- **1 tsp. prepared horseradish**
- **8 large eggs, beaten**
- **1 cup heavy whipping cream**
- **1 cup shredded Manchego cheese**
- **1 tsp. kosher salt**
- **1 tsp. coarsely ground pepper**

1. In a large nonstick skillet, heat 1 Tbsp. olive oil over medium heat. Add onion and red pepper; cook and stir until crisp-tender, 2-3 minutes. Add the mushrooms; cook and stir until tender, 3-4 minutes. Stir in horseradish; cook 2 minutes more.
2. In a small bowl, whisk together remaining ingredients and remaining olive oil. Pour into skillet; cook and stir until eggs are thickened and no liquid egg remains.
1 SERVING: 274 cal., 24g fat (12g sat. fat), 234mg chol., 405mg sod., 4g carb. (2g sugars, 1g fiber), 11g pro.

SHIITAKE & MANCHEGO SCRAMBLE

EAT SMART FAST FIX

DENVER OMELET SALAD

(SHOWN ON PAGE 158)

I love this recipe—it's not your typical breakfast, but it has all the right elements: easy, healthy and fast. Turn your favorite omelet ingredients into a morning salad!
—Pauline Custer, Duluth, MN

TAKES: 25 MIN. • **MAKES:** 4 SERVINGS

- **8 cups fresh baby spinach**
- **1 cup chopped tomatoes**
- **2 Tbsp. olive oil, divided**
- **1½ cups chopped fully cooked ham**
- **1 small onion, chopped**
- **1 small green pepper, chopped**
- **4 large eggs**
- **Salt and pepper to taste**

1. Arrange spinach and tomatoes on a platter; set aside. In a large skillet, heat 1 Tbsp. olive oil over medium-high heat. Add ham, onion and green pepper; saute until ham is heated through and vegetables are tender, 5-7 minutes. Spoon over spinach and tomatoes.
2. In same skillet, heat remaining olive oil over medium heat. Break eggs, one at a time, into a small cup, then gently slide into skillet. Immediately reduce heat to low; season with salt and pepper. To prepare sunny-side up eggs, cover pan and cook until whites are completely set and yolks thicken but are not hard. Top salad with the fried eggs.
1 SERVING: 229 cal., 14g fat (3g sat. fat), 217mg chol., 756mg sod., 7g carb. (3g sugars, 2g fiber), 20g pro. **Diabetic exchanges:** 3 lean meat, 2 fat, 1 vegetable.

EAT SMART

LOADED QUINOA BREAKFAST BOWL

After I was diagnosed with multiple sclerosis in 2001, I embarked on a journey to improve my diet and live a healthier lifestyle. I began developing recipes that were deliciously satisfying, but also anti-inflammatory and highly nutritious.
—Chantale Michaud, Guelph, ON

PREP: 15 MIN. + SOAKING • **COOK:** 15 MIN.
MAKES: 1 SERVING

- **¾ cup water, divided**
- **¼ cup tri-colored quinoa, rinsed**
- **2 Tbsp. dried goji berries or dried cranberries**
- **1 small banana**
- **¼ cup unsweetened almond milk**
- **1 Tbsp. maple syrup**
- **⅛ tsp. ground cinnamon**
- **⅛ tsp. vanilla extract**
- **¼ cup fresh or frozen unsweetened blueberries**
- **1 Tbsp. chopped walnuts**
- **1 Tbsp. slivered almonds**
- **1 Tbsp. fresh pumpkin seeds**
- **Additional unsweetened almond milk and maple syrup, optional**

1. In a small saucepan, bring ½ cup water to a boil. Add the quinoa. Reduce heat; simmer, covered, until liquid is absorbed, 12-15 minutes. Meanwhile, soak berries in remaining water for 10 minutes; drain. Halve banana crosswise. Slice one half; mash the other.
2. Remove quinoa from heat; fluff with a fork. Mix in the mashed banana, almond milk, maple syrup, cinnamon and vanilla. Transfer mixture to an individual bowl; add blueberries, walnuts, almonds, pumpkin seeds, banana slices and goji berries. If desired, serve with additional almond milk.
1 SERVING: 475 cal., 13g fat (1g sat. fat), 0 chol., 85mg sod., 83g carb. (35g sugars, 10g fiber), 13g pro.

LOADED QUINOA BREAKFAST BOWL

EAT SMART

APPLE CINNAMON OVERNIGHT OATS

Many folks love this oatmeal cold, but I like to heat it up a little since I'm not a big fan of it right out of the fridge. Toss in a handful of nuts for crunch, flavor and additional health benefits.
—Sarah Farmer, Waukesha, WI

PREP: 5 MIN. + CHILLING • **MAKES:** 1½ CUPS

- **½ cup old-fashioned oats**
- **½ medium Gala or Honeycrisp apple, chopped**
- **1 Tbsp. raisins**
- **1 cup 2% milk**
- **¼ tsp. ground cinnamon**
- **Dash salt**
- **Toasted, chopped nuts, optional**

In a small container or mason jar, combine all ingredients. Seal; refrigerate overnight.
1½ CUPS: 349 cal., 8g fat (4g sat. fat), 20mg chol., 263mg sod., 59g carb. (28g sugars, 7g fiber), 14g pro.

TEX-MEX BREAKFAST HAYSTACKS

TEX-MEX BREAKFAST HAYSTACKS

I love haystacks and wanted to make my own Tex-Mex version. Adding panko and cheese to the hash browns before cooking gives them a wonderful golden color and crisp texture.
—Donna Ryan, Topsfield, MA

PREP: 25 MIN. • **COOK:** 15 MIN.
MAKES: 6 SERVINGS

- **⅔ cup sour cream**
- **3 thinly sliced green onions**
- **2 Tbsp. oil-packed sun-dried tomatoes, chopped**
- **2 Tbsp. minced fresh cilantro**
- **2½ tsp. Tex-Mex seasoning, divided**
- **1 pkg. (3½ cups) refrigerated shredded hash brown potatoes**
- **½ cup panko (Japanese) bread crumbs**
- **⅓ cup shredded Mexican cheese blend**
- **¼ tsp. salt**
- **5 Tbsp. canola oil, divided**
- **6 large eggs**
- **½ cup salsa**
- **4 cooked bacon strips, coarsely chopped**
- **Finely chopped green onions, optional**

1. Combine sour cream, green onions, sun-dried tomatoes, cilantro, and ½ tsp. Tex-Mex seasoning; set aside.
2. Squeeze hash brown potatoes dry with paper towel to remove excess liquid. In a large bowl, combine potatoes, bread crumbs, cheese, salt and remaining Tex-Mex seasoning.
3. On an electric griddle, heat 3 Tbsp. oil over medium-high heat. Drop potato mixture by ⅔ cupfuls into oil; press to flatten slightly. Fry, adding oil as needed, until crisp and golden brown on each side, 5-7 minutes. Drain haystacks on paper towels; keep warm.
4. On same griddle, heat remaining oil over medium heat. Break eggs, one at a time, onto griddle. Reduce heat; cook until whites are set and yolks have begun to thicken. Flip the eggs if desired and continue cooking to desired doneness.
5. To assemble, top each potato patty with an egg, salsa, bacon and sour cream mixture. If desired, sprinkle with onions.

1 SERVING: 399 cal., 27g fat (8g sat. fat), 205mg chol., 688mg sod., 25g carb. (3g sugars, 2g fiber), 14g pro.

FAST FIX

BLINTZ PANCAKES

Blending sour cream and cottage cheese—ingredients traditionally associated with blintzes—into the batter of these pancakes provides them with their old-fashioned flavor. Top these family favorites with berry syrup to turn an ordinary morning into an extraordinary day.
—Dianna Digoy, San Diego, CA

TAKES: 30 MIN. • **MAKES:** 12 PANCAKES

- **1 cup all-purpose flour**
- **1 Tbsp. sugar**
- **½ tsp. salt**
- **1 cup sour cream**
- **1 cup 4% cottage cheese**
- **4 large eggs, lightly beaten**
- **Strawberry or blueberry syrup**
- **Sliced fresh strawberries, optional**

1. In a large bowl, combine the flour, sugar and salt. Stir in the sour cream, cottage cheese and eggs until blended.
2. Pour batter by ¼ cupfuls onto a greased hot griddle in batches; turn when bubbles form on top. Cook until the second side is golden brown. Serve with syrup and, if desired, strawberries.

2 PANCAKES: 248 cal., 13g fat (7g sat. fat), 136mg chol., 371mg sod., 21g carb. (5g sugars, 1g fiber), 11g pro.

BLINTZ PANCAKES

BLUE-RIBBON DOUGHNUTS

I received this recipe from my sister about 30 years ago. Our eight children are grown and no longer live at home, but I'm still making these doughnuts—they've become a favorite with my 16 grandchildren! They can't seem to get enough of these tasty treats, and they love to cut them out for me to fry.
—Kay McEwen, Sussex, NB

PREP: 30 MIN. + CHILLING
COOK: 5 MIN./BATCH • **MAKES:** 3 DOZEN

- **3 large eggs**
- **2 cups sugar**
- **1 cup heavy whipping cream**
- **1 cup whole milk**
- **1 tsp. vanilla extract**
- **6 to 7 cups all-purpose flour**
- **4 tsp. cream of tartar**
- **2 tsp. baking soda**
- **1 tsp. salt**
- **1 tsp. ground nutmeg**
- **Oil for deep-fat frying**

1. In a large bowl, beat eggs for 5 minutes. Gradually add sugar; beat 1-2 minutes longer (mixture will be thick and light in color). Add cream, milk, vanilla, 2 cups flour, cream of tartar, baking soda, salt and nutmeg; beat until smooth. Add enough remaining flour to form a soft dough.
2. Turn onto a floured surface; knead until smooth, 8-10 minutes. Place in a greased bowl, turning once to grease top. Cover and refrigerate for 2-3 hours.
3. On a floured surface, roll dough to ½-in. thickness. Cut with a lightly floured 2½-in. doughnut cutter.
4. In an electric skillet or deep-fat fryer, heat oil to 375°. Fry doughnuts, a few at a time, or until browned, about 2 minutes on each side. Drain on paper towels.

1 DOUGHNUT: 197 cal., 8g fat (2g sat. fat), 27mg chol., 147mg sod., 28g carb. (12g sugars, 1g fiber), 3g pro.

SUGARED DOUGHNUTS: Roll warm doughnuts in sugar or cinnamon sugar.

BLUE-RIBBON DOUGHNUTS

5 INGREDIENTS FAST FIX

MAPLE GLAZE FOR DOUGHNUTS

Perfect to usher in the cozy feeling of fall, my glaze of choice features a delicious kiss of sweet maple syrup.
—Barbara Elliott, Tyler, TX

TAKES: 5 MIN. • **MAKES:** 1 CUP

- **2 cups confectioners' sugar**
- **3 Tbsp. 2% milk**
- **2 Tbsp. maple syrup**
- **½ tsp. maple flavoring**

In a small bowl, whisk all ingredients until smooth.

4 TSP.: 89 cal., 0 fat (0 sat. fat), 0 chol., 3mg sod., 22g carb. (22g sugars, 0 fiber), 0 pro.

RHUBARB SOUR CREAM COFFEE CAKE

RHUBARB SOUR CREAM COFFEE CAKE

With a tart kick from fresh spring rhubarb, this coffee cake is an irresistible way to start the day—or end it!
—Roberta Schauer, Williamsport, PA

PREP: 20 MIN. • **BAKE:** 45 MIN. + COOLING • **MAKES:** 15 SERVINGS

- **¾ cup butter, softened**
- **1½ cups sugar**
- **3 large eggs**
- **1½ tsp. vanilla extract**
- **3 cups all-purpose flour**
- **2 tsp. baking powder**
- **1 tsp. baking soda**
- **¾ tsp. salt**
- **1 cup sour cream**
- **3 cups chopped fresh or frozen rhubarb**

TOPPING

- **½ cup packed brown sugar**
- **¼ cup all-purpose flour**
- **1 tsp. ground cinnamon**
- **¼ cup cold butter**

1. In a large mixing bowl, cream butter and sugar until light and fluffy. Add eggs, one at a time, beating well after each addition. Add vanilla; mix well.
2. In a bowl, combine the flour, baking powder, baking soda and salt. Add to the creamed mixture alternately with the sour cream. Fold in rhubarb. Spread into a greased 13x9-in. baking dish.
3. For topping, in a small bowl, combine the brown sugar, flour and cinnamon. Cut in butter until mixture resembles coarse crumbs; sprinkle over the top.
4. Bake at 350° until a toothpick inserted in center comes out clean, 45-50 minutes. Cool on a wire rack.
1 PIECE: 366 cal., 17g fat (10g sat. fat), 74mg chol., 387mg sod., 50g carb. (28g sugars, 1g fiber), 5g pro.

BACON & ASPARAGUS FRITTATA

Especially during the summertime, this makes a nice light meal. When I prepare it for guests, I'll also serve rice or bread—it's quick and easy, but it always wins me many compliments!
—Gwen Clemon, Soldier, IA

PREP: 10 MIN. • **COOK:** 25 MIN. • **MAKES:** 6 SERVINGS

- **12 oz. bacon**
- **2 cups sliced fresh asparagus (cut in ½-in. pieces)**
- **1 cup chopped onion**
- **2 garlic cloves, minced**
- **10 large eggs, beaten**
- **¼ cup minced parsley**
- **½ tsp. seasoned salt**
- **¼ tsp. pepper**
- **1 large tomato, thinly sliced**
- **1 cup shredded cheddar cheese**

1. In a 9- or 10-in. ovenproof skillet, cook bacon until crisp. Drain, reserving 1 Tbsp. drippings. Heat reserved drippings on medium-high. Add asparagus, onion and garlic; saute until onion is tender. Crumble bacon; set aside a third. In a large bowl, combine the remaining bacon, eggs, parsley, salt and pepper.
2. Pour egg mixture into skillet; stir. Top with tomato, cheese and reserved bacon. Cover and cook over medium-low until eggs are nearly set, 10-15 minutes. Preheat the broiler; place skillet 6 in. from heat. Broil frittata until lightly browned, about 2 minutes. Serve immediately.
1 PIECE: 344 cal., 24g fat (10g sat. fat), 351mg chol., 738mg sod., 7g carb. (3g sugars, 2g fiber), 23g pro.

BACON & ASPARAGUS FRITTATA

BIRTHDAY CAKE WAFFLES

These super fun waffles—soft on the inside, crisp on the outside—taste just like cake batter! They are quick to whip up anytime but would make birthday mornings feel even more special.
—Andrea Fetting, Franklin, WI

PREP: 20 MIN. • **COOK:** 25 MIN.
MAKES: 6 WAFFLES

- **1 cup all-purpose flour**
- **1 cup (about 5 oz.) confetti cake mix or flavor of choice**
- **2 Tbsp. cornstarch**
- **3 tsp. baking powder**
- **¼ tsp. salt**
- **2 Tbsp. rainbow sprinkles, optional**
- **2 large eggs**
- **1¾ cups 2% milk**
- **¾ to 1 cup plain Greek yogurt**
- **½ tsp. vanilla extract**
- **½ tsp. almond extract**

CREAM CHEESE FROSTING

- **4 oz. softened cream cheese or reduced-fat cream cheese**
- **¼ cup butter, softened**
- **1½ to 2 cups confectioners' sugar**
- **½ tsp. vanilla extract**
- **1 to 3 Tbsp. 2% milk**

1. Preheat oven to 300°. Combine the first five ingredients and, if desired, rainbow sprinkles. In another bowl, whisk eggs, milk, yogurt and extracts. Add yogurt mixture to flour mixture; mix until smooth.
2. Preheat waffle maker coated with cooking spray. Bake waffles according to manufacturer's directions until golden brown. Transfer cooked waffles to oven until ready to serve.
3. For frosting, beat cream cheese and butter on high until light and fluffy, 2-3 minutes. Gradually beat in confectioners' sugar, ½ cup at a time, until smooth. Beat in vanilla. Add enough milk to reach desired consistency. Spread over warm waffles. For a cakelike look, cut waffles into fourths and stack them; decorate with birthday candles.
1 WAFFLE: 528 cal., 22g fat (13g sat. fat), 115mg chol., 695mg sod., 72g carb. (45g sugars, 1g fiber), 10g pro.

BREAKFAST RELLENO

BREAKFAST RELLENO

My family loves anything with a southwestern flavor, so I turned classic chiles relleno into a breakfast casserole and they became fans in an instant.
—Joan Hallford, North Richland Hills, TX

PREP: 10 MIN. • **BAKE:** 35 MIN. + STANDING
MAKES: 15 SERVINGS

- **1 pkg. (20 oz.) refrigerated shredded hash brown potatoes**
- **1 can (27 to 28 oz.) whole green chilies**
- **1 cup chunky salsa**
- **1 lb. bulk pork sausage or fresh chorizo, cooked, drained and crumbled**
- **2 cups shredded Mexican cheese blend**
- **6 large eggs**
- **½ cup 2% milk**
- **¼ tsp. ground cumin**
- **Salt and pepper to taste**
- **Optional ingredients: warm flour tortillas (8 in.), sour cream and salsa**

1. Preheat oven to 350°. In a greased 13x9-in. baking dish, layer half the potatoes; all the chilies, opened flat; all the salsa; half the sausage; and half the cheese. Cover with the remaining potatoes, sausage and cheese.
2. Beat eggs and milk; add cumin, salt and pepper. Pour over potato mixture.
3. Bake, uncovered, until eggs are set in center, 35-40 minutes. Let stand for 15 minutes. If desired, serve with warm tortillas, sour cream and additional salsa.
1 PIECE: 210 cal., 13g fat (5g sat. fat), 105mg chol., 440mg sod., 11g carb. (3g sugars, 1g fiber), 10g pro.

HERBED SAUSAGE GRAVY OVER CHEESE BISCUITS

HERBED SAUSAGE GRAVY OVER CHEESE BISCUITS

The crowd at my house loves anything with biscuits, and this rich sausage gravy is the best we've ever tasted! It's a real favorite of my husband and two toddlers.
—Lynn Crosby, Homerville, OH

PREP: 20 MIN. • **BAKE:** 15 MIN.
MAKES: 4 SERVINGS

- **2¼ cups all-purpose flour**
- **3 tsp. baking powder**
- **½ tsp. salt**
- **½ cup 2% milk**
- **¼ cup canola oil**
- **½ tsp. dried oregano**
- **1 oz. part-skim mozzarella cheese, cut into 8 cubes (about ½-in.)**

GRAVY
- **½ lb. bulk pork sausage**
- **¾ cup 2% milk**
- **1 tsp. dried oregano**
- **¼ cup all-purpose flour**
- **1 cup cold water**

1. Preheat oven to 450°. Whisk flour, baking powder and salt. Stir in milk and oil just until moistened. Turn onto a lightly floured surface; knead gently 8-10 times. Roll to ½-in. thickness; cut with a floured 2½-in. biscuit cutter. Place a pinch of oregano in the center of each biscuit and top with a cheese cube.
2. Moisten edge of dough with water and pull up over cheese, forming a pouch; pinch tightly to seal. Place seam side down on a lightly greased baking sheet, pressing down lightly. Bake until biscuits are golden brown, 12-15 minutes.
3. Meanwhile, in a large skillet, cook the sausage over medium heat until no longer pink; drain. Stir in milk and oregano. Mix flour and water until smooth; add to the sausage mixture. Bring to a boil; cook and stir until thickened, about 2 minutes. Spoon gravy over biscuits.

2 BISCUITS WITH ½ CUP GRAVY: 626 cal., 31g fat (8g sat. fat), 46mg chol., 1132mg sod., 65g carb. (4g sugars, 2g fiber), 20g pro.

FAST FIX
ORANGE HAM STEAK

I turn orange marmalade, mustard and just a hint of ginger into a glaze for ham that comes together super quick, but feels extra special. And that makes it perfect for when I'm entertaining brunch guests!
—Connie Moore, Medway, OH

TAKES: 15 MIN. • **MAKES:** 4 SERVINGS

- **1 bone-in fully cooked ham steak (about 1 lb.)**
- **¼ cup orange marmalade**
- **2 Tbsp. water**
- **1 Tbsp. butter**
- **1 Tbsp. prepared mustard**
- **1 tsp. corn syrup**
- **⅛ to ¼ tsp. ground ginger**

1. In a large skillet coated with cooking spray, brown ham 3-4 minutes on each side; drain. Return to skillet.
2. Meanwhile, in a small saucepan, combine remaining ingredients; bring to a boil. Spoon over ham. Cook, covered, until heated through, 1-2 minutes.

1 SERVING: 188 cal., 8g fat (4g sat. fat), 51mg chol., 885mg sod., 16g carb. (14g sugars, 0 fiber), 14g pro.

ORANGE HAM STEAK

CREAMY LEMON ALMOND PASTRIES

CREAMY LEMON ALMOND PASTRIES

I love lemon-filled doughnuts when I can find them. This recipe brings the concept to a new level by placing the filling into a baked beignet and enhancing it with a bit of almond flavoring and toasted almonds. The result? Sunshine in a bite.
—Arlene Erlbach, Morton Grove, IL

PREP: 30 MIN. + CHILLING • **BAKE:** 15 MIN. • **MAKES:** 9 SERVINGS

- **½ cup plus 1 Tbsp. cream cheese, softened (4½ oz.)**
- **⅔ cup confectioners' sugar, divided**
- **2 Tbsp. lemon curd**
- **2 tsp. grated lemon zest**
- **¼ tsp. almond extract**
- **1 sheet frozen puff pastry, thawed**
- **1 large egg, beaten**
- **2 Tbsp. water**
- **2 tsp. lemon juice**
- **2 tsp. 2% milk**
- **3 Tbsp. sliced almonds, toasted**

1. Beat cream cheese, 3 Tbsp. confectioners' sugar, lemon curd, lemon zest and almond extract on medium until combined. Refrigerate, covered, for 30 minutes.
2. Preheat oven to 400°. On a lightly floured surface, unfold puff pastry. Roll into a 12x9-in. rectangle. Using a pastry cutter or sharp knife, cut into nine rectangles. Spoon rounded tablespoon of cream cheese mixture in center of each rectangle. In a small bowl, whisk egg with water. Brush edges with egg mixture.
3. Wrap puff pastry around filling to cover completely. Pinch edges together to form a ball. Place seam side down, 2 in. apart, on a parchment paper-lined baking sheet. Brush pastries with remaining egg mixture. Pierce each once with a fork. Bake until golden brown, 15-18 minutes. Cool on wire rack for 5 minutes. Loosen pastries from parchment paper.
4. Meanwhile, combine lemon juice, milk and the remaining confectioners' sugar. Brush each pastry with lemon glaze. Top with almonds. When glaze is set, in 1-2 minutes, peel off paper. Serve warm.
NOTE: To toast nuts, bake in a shallow pan in a 350° oven for 5-10 minutes or cook in a skillet over low heat until lightly browned, stirring occasionally.
1 PASTRY: 255 cal., 14g fat (5g sat. fat), 39mg chol., 148mg sod., 29g carb. (12g sugars, 2g fiber), 4g pro.

BOURBON-SOAKED BACON & GINGER CINNAMON ROLLS

This recipe is the perfect combination of savory and sweet. The bourbon-soaked bacon adds a smoky, savory, bold taste to cinnamon rolls. The ginger and pecan topping makes for a spicy finish.
—Shannen Casey, Berkeley, CA

PREP: 25 MIN. + MARINATING • **BAKE:** 10 MIN. • **MAKES:** 8 ROLLS

- **8 bacon strips**
- **¾ cup bourbon**
- **1 tube (12.4 oz.) refrigerated cinnamon rolls with icing**
- **½ cup chopped pecans**
- **2 Tbsp. maple syrup**
- **1 tsp. minced fresh gingerroot**

1. Place bacon in a shallow dish; add bourbon. Seal and refrigerate overnight. Remove bacon and pat dry; discard bourbon.
2. In a large skillet, cook bacon in batches over medium heat until nearly crisp but still pliable. Remove to paper towels to drain. Discard all but 1 tsp. drippings.
3. Preheat oven to 375°. Separate dough into eight rolls, reserving icing packet. Unroll spiral rolls into long strips; pat dough to form 6x1-in. strips. Place one bacon strip on each strip of dough, trimming bacon as needed, then reroll forming a spiral. Pinch ends to seal. Repeat with remaining dough. Transfer to a parchment paper-lined baking sheet; bake until golden brown, 9-11 minutes.
4. Meanwhile, combine pecans and maple syrup. In another bowl, stir together ginger with contents of icing packet. In same skillet, heat remaining bacon drippings over medium heat. Add pecans; cook, stirring frequently, until lightly toasted, 2-3 minutes.
5. Drizzle icing over warm cinnamon rolls; top with pecans.
1 ROLL: 267 cal., 14g fat (3g sat. fat), 9mg chol., 490mg sod., 28g carb. (13g sugars, 1g fiber), 5g pro.

BOURBON-SOAKED BACON & GINGER CINNAMON ROLLS

BRUNCH EGG CASSEROLE

BRUNCH EGG CASSEROLE

This hearty egg bake has become a favorite in our family. It's cheesy, crispy and loaded up with smoky bacon. What's not to love?
—Lelia Brown, Annandale, VA

PREP: 10 MIN. • **BAKE:** 1 HOUR • **MAKES:** 6 SERVINGS

- **2 cups unseasoned stuffing cubes or croutons**
- **1 cup shredded cheddar cheese**
- **4 large eggs, lightly beaten**
- **2 cups whole milk**
- **½ tsp. salt**
- **½ tsp. ground mustard**
- **⅛ tsp. onion powder**
- **Dash pepper**
- **4 bacon strips, chopped and partly cooked**

Preheat oven to 325°. Place croutons in a greased 11x7-in. baking dish; sprinkle with cheese. Combine eggs, milk and seasonings; pour into baking dish. Top with partly cooked bacon. Bake until bacon is crisp and a knife inserted in center comes out clean, 45-55 minutes.

1 PIECE: 254 cal., 14g fat (7g sat. fat), 176mg chol., 597mg sod., 18g carb. (5g sugars, 1g fiber), 14g pro.

CREAMY, CHEESY GRITS WITH CURRIED POACHED EGGS

I first tried curried poached eggs when I lived in Germany. They were delicious with that rich, runny yolk, and serving them over cheesy grits seemed like the next best move to try. I'm happy to say that my instincts were right.
—Shannon Copley, Upper Arlington, OH

PREP: 20 MIN. • **COOK:** 15 MIN. • **MAKES:** 4 SERVINGS

- **2 bacon strips, coarsely chopped**
- **2 cups vegetable broth**
- **½ cup quick-cooking corn grits**
- **1 cup shredded sharp cheddar cheese**
- **2 oz. reduced-fat cream cheese**
- **¼ tsp. salt**
- **¼ tsp. pepper**
- **2 to 3 cups water**
- **2 tsp. white vinegar**
- **2 tsp. curry powder**
- **4 large eggs**
- **Additional shredded cheddar cheese, optional**
- **1 to 2 Tbsp. minced chives or parsley**

1. In a large saucepan, cook bacon over medium heat until crisp, stirring occasionally. Remove with a slotted spoon; drain on paper towels. Discard drippings.
2. In same saucepan over medium heat, bring vegetable broth to a boil. Slowly stir in grits. Reduce heat to low; simmer, covered, stirring occasionally, until thickened, about 7 minutes. Add cheeses, salt and pepper; stir well. Cover and remove from heat.
3. In a small saucepan, bring 2 cups water, vinegar and curry powder to a boil; adjust heat to maintain a gentle simmer. Break one egg into a small bowl; with a spoon, swirl cooking water in a circle around edge of saucepan. Holding bowl close to surface, slip egg into center of swirling water. Repeat with remaining eggs, adding water if necessary.
4. Poach, uncovered, until whites are completely set and yolks begin to thicken but are not hard, 3-5 minutes. Meanwhile, divide grits evenly among four bowls. Using a slotted spoon, remove eggs from water. Place one on top of each serving of grits; top with chopped bacon and, if desired, additional shredded cheese. Sprinkle with chives or parsley. Serve immediately.

1 EGG AND ¾ CUP GRITS: 316 cal., 19g fat (9g sat. fat), 228mg chol., 870mg sod., 18g carb. (2g sugars, 1g fiber), 18g pro.

THE TASTY 10

MORNING SCRAMBLE

SLATHER EGGS WITH SYRUP OR SPIKE 'EM WITH WASABI. OUR FACEBOOK FANS SCRAMBLE UP BREAKFASTS THAT ARE ANYTHING BUT A SNOOZE.

1 I top my scrambled eggs with pickled ginger, soy sauce and wasabi.
—Angela Ragen Stewart, Cape Coral, FL

2 My favorite: Add a heaping tablespoon of cottage cheese per egg, beat, add grated cheese, and pour into a buttered skillet to cook until done.
—Sandra McFadin, Lubbock, TX

3 Scramble eggs first, then stir in some sauteed mushrooms, onions, spinach, chickpeas and cooked quinoa.
—Linda Dorrough Bagby, Van Buren, AR

4 Turn scrambled eggs into an egg burrito—a whole wheat tortilla, eggs, black beans, salsa, taco cheese, cilantro and a few dashes of hot sauce to finish it off.
—LeeAnn Brewer, Valparaiso, IN

5 I put two eggs in a mug, add a splash of milk, salt and pepper, then scramble with a fork and microwave in 30-second increments until they're no longer gooey. Stir in a bit of cheese and you've got breakfast-to-go on the way to work!
—Kristyn Mayo, Bakersfield, CA

6 Cook scrambled eggs in a skillet, add green asparagus and artichoke, then season with salt and lots of black pepper.
—Jeanine Vander-straeten, Belgium

7 I can't eat scrambled eggs without pouring maple syrup on top!
—Bonnie Kisiel, Laval, QC

8 Scramble two eggs with onion, a splash of milk, ham, mushrooms, garlic salt and pepper. Then fry a third egg over easy and put it on top.
—Nick Verzino, St. Louis, MO

9 I season eggs with spicy chili powder, garlic salt and black pepper. Then I heat up canola oil, toss in the eggs, and add some scallions, tomato and bell pepper. Add Crystal hot sauce once plated.
—Kam Prakash, San Francisco, CA

10 My favorite way to dress up scrambled eggs is to add cream cheese and some chopped chives. I always take the eggs off the heat while a little "wet" and never overstir them.
—Susan Haley, Naruna, TX

GRANOLA SNACK BARS, PAGE 184

COOKIES, BARS & CANDIES

When it's time for a sweet snack, let these popular recipes lend a hand. With the 23 specialties that follow, you'll always have a terrific treat at your fingertips.

CHILI-CHIPOTLE BROWNIE BARS

CHILI-CHIPOTLE BROWNIE BARS

What fun I had creating these sweet and spiced-up brownies—and those who helped me taste test each version had a great time, too! It took a few tweaks to reach perfection, but after one bite, I knew I'd nailed the recipe.
—Sheri Dunlap, Shawnee, OK

PREP: 20 MIN. • **BAKE:** 25 MIN. + COOLING
MAKES: 2 DOZEN

- **1¾ cups sugar**
- **¾ cup all-purpose flour**
- **¾ tsp. ground chipotle pepper**
- **¼ tsp. salt**
- **1 cup butter**
- **4 oz. unsweetened chocolate**
- **1 chili dark chocolate candy bar (3½ oz.)**
- **4 large eggs, lightly beaten**
- **1 tsp. vanilla extract**

ICING
- **12 oz. cream cheese, softened**
- **2 cups confectioners' sugar**
- **1½ tsp. vanilla extract**
- **¼ tsp. ground chipotle pepper**

1. Preheat oven to 350°. Sift together sugar, flour, ground chipotle pepper and salt. Set mixture aside.
2. In top of a double boiler or a metal bowl over simmering water, melt butter and both types of chocolate; stir until smooth. Cool slightly. Stir chocolate mixture into dry ingredients. Beat in eggs and vanilla.
3. Spread batter into a 13x9-in. baking pan coated with cooking spray. Bake until center is set, about 25 minutes (do not overbake). Cool completely.
4. For icing, beat together cream cheese, confectioners' sugar, vanilla and chipotle pepper. Spread over the brownies. Cut into 24 bars.
1 BROWNIE: 281 cal., 17g fat (10g sat. fat), 66mg chol., 147mg sod., 30g carb. (25g sugars, 1g fiber), 3g pro.

NEAPOLITAN FUDGE

I love experimenting with different flavors of fudge and creating unique combinations. My Neapolitan fudge tastes just like vanilla, strawberry and chocolate ice cream.
—Faith Leonard, Delbarton, WV

PREP: 35 MIN. + CHILLING
MAKES: ABOUT 6½ LBS. (117 PIECES)

- **1½ tsp. butter**
- **1 pkg. (8 oz.) cream cheese, softened**
- **3 cups confectioners' sugar**
- **16 oz. milk chocolate, melted and cooled**

VANILLA LAYER
- **1 pkg. (8 oz.) cream cheese, softened**
- **3 cups confectioners' sugar**
- **16 oz. white baking chocolate, melted and cooled**
- **1 Tbsp. vanilla extract**

RASPBERRY LAYER
- **1 pkg. (8 oz.) cream cheese, softened**
- **3 cups confectioners' sugar**
- **16 oz. white baking chocolate, melted and cooled**
- **1 Tbsp. raspberry extract**
- **8 to 10 drops red food coloring, optional**

1. Line a 13x9-in. pan with foil and grease foil with butter. In a large bowl, beat cream cheese until fluffy. Gradually beat in confectioners' sugar. Beat in melted milk chocolate. Spread into prepared pan. Refrigerate 10 minutes.
2. For vanilla layer, in a large bowl, beat cream cheese until fluffy. Gradually beat in confectioners' sugar. Beat in melted white chocolate and vanilla. Spread over the chocolate layer. Refrigerate 10 minutes.
3. For the raspberry layer, in a large bowl, beat cream cheese until fluffy. Gradually beat in confectioners' sugar. Beat in melted white chocolate and raspberry extract. If desired, tint with food coloring. Spread over the top. Refrigerate, covered, at least 8 hours or overnight.
4. Using foil, lift fudge out of pan. Remove foil; cut fudge into 1-in. squares. Store between layers of waxed paper in an airtight container in the refrigerator.
1 PIECE: 114 cal., 5g fat (3g sat. fat), 7mg chol., 20mg sod., 16g carb. (15g sugars, 0 fiber), 1g pro.

PUMPKIN BARS

PUMPKIN BARS

What could be a more appropriate fall treat than a pan of pumpkin-flavored bars? Actually, my family loves these any time of year.
—Brenda Keller, Andalusia, AL

PREP: 20 MIN. • **BAKE:** 25 MIN. + COOLING • **MAKES:** 2 DOZEN

- 4 **large eggs**
- 1⅔ **cups sugar**
- 1 **cup canola oil**
- 1 **can (15 oz.) solid-pack pumpkin**
- 2 **cups all-purpose flour**
- 2 **tsp. ground cinnamon**
- 2 **tsp. baking powder**
- 1 **tsp. baking soda**
- 1 **tsp. salt**

ICING

- 6 **oz. cream cheese, softened**
- 2 **cups confectioners' sugar**
- ¼ **cup butter, softened**
- 1 **tsp. vanilla extract**
- 1 **to 2 Tbsp. whole milk**

1. In a bowl, beat the eggs, sugar, oil and pumpkin until well blended. Combine the flour, cinnamon, baking powder, baking soda and salt; gradually add to pumpkin mixture and mix well. Pour into an ungreased 15x10x1-in. baking pan. Bake at 350° for 25-30 minutes or until set. Cool completely.
2. For icing, beat the cream cheese, confectioners' sugar, butter and vanilla in a small bowl. Add enough milk to achieve spreading consistency. Spread over bars. Store in the refrigerator.
1 BAR: 260 cal., 13g fat (3g sat. fat), 45mg chol., 226mg sod., 34g carb. (24g sugars, 1g fiber), 3g pro.

FAST FIX

DEEP-FRIED COOKIES

My kids love this delicious, indulgent treat. I like to give the batter a kick by adding a pinch of cinnamon and a teaspoon of vanilla extract.
—Margarita Torres, Bayamon, PR

TAKES: 25 MIN. • **MAKES:** 1½ DOZEN

- 18 **Oreo cookies**
- **Oil for deep-fat frying**
- 1 **cup biscuit/baking mix**
- 1 **large egg**
- ½ **cup 2% milk**
- **Confectioners' sugar**

1. On each of eighteen 4-in. wooden skewers, thread one cookie, inserting pointed end of skewer into filling. Freeze until firm, about 1 hour.
2. In an electric skillet or deep fryer, heat oil to 375°. Place biscuit mix in a shallow bowl. In another bowl, combine egg and milk; whisk into biscuit mix just until moistened.
3. Holding skewer, dip cookie into biscuit mixture to coat both sides; shake off excess.
4. Fry cookies, a few at a time, 1-2 minutes on each side until golden brown. Drain on paper towels. Dust with confectioners' sugar before serving.
1 COOKIE: 100 cal., 5g fat (1g sat. fat), 11mg chol., 123mg sod., 13g carb. (5g sugars, 1g fiber), 1g pro.

DEEP-FRIED COOKIES

BOMB POP COOKIES

BOMB POP COOKIES

The sound of an ice cream truck has even my husband running out to the curb with money in hand. So when our neighborhood was planning big potluck on the Fourth of July, I decided to make cookies that resemble Bomb Pops. They were a big hit with everyone!
—Darlene Brenden, Salem, OR

PREP: 30 MIN. + CHILLING • **BAKE:** 10 MIN./BATCH + COOLING
MAKES: 40 COOKIES

- **½ cup butter, softened**
- **½ cup confectioners' sugar**
- **½ cup granulated sugar**
- **1 large egg**
- **⅓ cup canola oil**
- **2¾ to 3 cups all-purpose flour**
- **½ tsp. baking soda**
- **½ tsp. cream of tartar**
- **¼ tsp. salt**
- **Red and blue paste food coloring**
- **½ tsp. each cherry, raspberry and lemon extract**

1. Cream butter and sugars until light and fluffy. Add egg and oil, beating well. In another bowl, whisk 2¾ cups flour, baking soda, cream of tartar and salt. Gradually beat into creamed mixture, adding flour if needed, until dough forms a ball.
2. Divide dough into three portions. Add red food coloring and cherry extract to one portion. Add blue food coloring and raspberry extract to second portion. Add lemon extract to untinted portion.
3. Shape each portion into a 10-in.-long block. Place red, white and blue logs side by side. Lightly press blocks together. Wrap and refrigerate 30 minutes or until firm.
4. Preheat oven to 350°. Unwrap and cut dough crosswise into ¼-in. slices. Place 1 in. apart on parchment paper-lined baking sheets. To create ridges, lightly press cookies with a fork. Bake 10-12 minutes or until set. Cool on pans 2 minutes; remove to wire racks to cool completely.
1 COOKIE: 86 cal., 4g fat (2g sat. fat), 11mg chol., 51mg sod., 11g carb. (4g sugars, 0 fiber), 1g pro.

(5) INGREDIENTS

GIANDUJA

Friends can't believe these sophisticated layered squares start with four ingredients. I think the candies are popular because so many love the pairing of chocolate and hazelnuts.
—Virginia Sauer, Wantagh, NY

PREP: 20 MIN. + CHILLING • **MAKES:** ABOUT 3 LBS. (64 SERVINGS)

- **1½ lbs. shelled hazelnuts, skins removed**
- **¾ cup canola oil**
- **1½ lbs. bittersweet chocolate, chopped**
- **3 milk chocolate Toblerone candy bars (3.52 oz. each), chopped**

1. Line an 8-in. square dish with foil. Place hazelnuts and oil in a food processor; cover and process until mixture forms a paste.
2. In a large saucepan, melt bittersweet chocolate. Stir in 2¼ cups of the hazelnut mixture. Pour half of mixture into prepared dish. Refrigerate until firm.
3. Melt candy bars; stir in remaining hazelnut mixture. Pour over bittersweet layer. Refrigerate until firm.
4. Reheat remaining bittersweet mixture if necessary; pour over candy bar layer. Refrigerate until firm. Cut into 1-in. squares. Store in an airtight container in the refrigerator.
1 PIECE: 168 cal., 15g fat (4g sat. fat), 1mg chol., 2mg sod., 10g carb. (7g sugars, 2g fiber), 2g pro.

(5) INGREDIENTS FAST FIX

GUMDROP CEREAL BARS

I was planning to make traditional marshmallow treats but didn't have enough Rice Krispies on hand, so I used Corn Pops instead. I added gumdrops for color, and the result was spectacular.
—Laura Tryssenaar, Listowel, ON

TAKES: 30 MIN. • **MAKES:** 16 BARS

- **5 cups Corn Pops cereal**
- **1 cup gumdrops**
- **4 cups miniature marshmallows**
- **¼ cup butter, cubed**
- **1 tsp. vanilla extract**

1. Place cereal and gumdrops in a large bowl; set aside. In a microwave-safe bowl, place marshmallows and butter. Microwave, uncovered for 45 seconds to 1½ minutes or until melted; stir until smooth. Stir in vanilla.
2. Pour over cereal mixture; toss to coat. Spread into a greased 9-in. square pan. Cool on a wire rack. Cut with a buttered knife.
1 PIECE: 146 cal., 3g fat (2g sat. fat), 8mg chol., 77mg sod., 30g carb. (21g sugars, 0 fiber), 1g pro.

CHOCOLATE CHIP-CHERRY CHUNK COOKIES

My grandmas and mom created this recipe. It's a special mix of chocolate chips, cherries and spices, and a combo of their favorite flavors of different cookies. Dad turned them into ice cream sandwiches that we'd enjoy each summer to beat the heat.
—Wade Rouse, Fennville, MI

PREP: 30 MIN. • **BAKE:** 10 MIN./BATCH + COOLING • **MAKES:** ABOUT 4 DOZEN

- **½ cup plus 1 Tbsp. butter, softened**
- **½ cup sugar**
- **¼ cup packed dark brown sugar**
- **1 large egg, room temperature**
- **1 tsp. vanilla extract**
- **1 tsp. maple flavoring**
- **1½ cups all-purpose flour**
- **5 tsp. baking cocoa**
- **½ tsp. baking soda**
- **¼ tsp. salt**
- **1 cup semisweet chocolate chips**
- **1 cup white baking chips**
- **½ cup dried cherries or dried cranberries**
- **¼ cup sweetened shredded coconut**

1. Preheat oven to 350°. Cream butter, gradually adding sugars, until light and fluffy. Slowly beat in egg, vanilla and maple flavoring.

2. In another bowl, sift together flour, baking cocoa, baking soda and salt. Gradually beat into creamed mixture just until moistened (do not overbeat). Stir in semisweet chocolate and white baking chips, dried cherries and coconut.

3. Drop dough by tablespoonfuls 2 in. apart onto ungreased baking sheets. Flatten slightly. Bake until golden brown, 10-12 minutes. Cool on pans 5 minutes. Remove to wire racks to cool completely.

1 COOKIE: 92 cal., 5g fat (3g sat. fat), 10mg chol., 49mg sod., 12g carb. (9g sugars, 0 fiber), 1g pro.

CHOCOLATE CHIP-CHERRY CHUNK COOKIES

ROSEMARY-LEMON SLICE & BAKE COOKIES

The tastes of tart lemon and fresh rosemary make these luscious treats a sweet surprise.
—Malorie Harris, Wildomar, CA

PREP: 25 MIN. + FREEZING
BAKE: 10 MIN./BATCH • **MAKES:** 8 DOZEN

- **1 cup butter, softened**
- **½ cup sugar**
- **3 Tbsp. lemon juice**
- **1 tsp. grated lemon peel**
- **½ tsp. vanilla extract**
- **2 cups all-purpose flour**
- **4½ tsp. minced fresh rosemary**
- **¼ tsp. salt**

1. In a large bowl, cream butter and sugar until light and fluffy. Beat in lemon juice, peel and vanilla. Combine flour, rosemary and salt; gradually add to creamed mixture and mix well.

2. Shape into two 12-in. rolls; wrap each in plastic. Freeze for 30 minutes or until firm. Cut into ¼-in. slices. Place 2 in. apart on ungreased baking sheets. Bake at 350° for 8-10 minutes or until edges begin to brown. Cool cookies for 2 minutes before removing them from pans to wire racks. Store in an airtight container.

1 COOKIE: 31 cal., 2g fat (1g sat. fat), 5mg chol., 20mg sod., 3g carb. (1g sugars, 0 fiber), 0 pro.

CHOCOLATE CHEESECAKE BARS

CHOCOLATE CHEESECAKE BARS

An almond-flavored dough serves as both crust and topping for a soft chocolaty filling in these rich treats.
—Louise Good, Flemington, NJ

PREP: 15 MIN. • **BAKE:** 35 MIN. + COOLING • **MAKES:** 4 DOZEN

- **1 cup butter, softened**
- **1½ cups sugar**
- **2 large eggs**
- **½ tsp. almond extract**
- **3 cups all-purpose flour**
- **1 tsp. baking powder**
- **½ tsp. salt**

FILLING

- **2 cups (12 oz.) semisweet chocolate chips**
- **1 pkg. (8 oz.) cream cheese**
- **1 can (5 oz.) evaporated milk**
- **1 cup chopped walnuts**
- **½ tsp. almond extract**

1. In a large bowl, cream butter and sugar until light and fluffy. Beat in eggs, one at a time, beating well after each addition. Beat in extract. Combine the flour, baking powder and salt; gradually add to the creamed mixture and mix well. Press half of the dough onto the bottom of a greased 13x9-in. baking pan. Set aside remaining dough for topping.
2. In a large saucepan, combine the chocolate chips, cream cheese and milk; cook and stir over low heat until smooth. Remove from the heat; stir in walnuts and extract. Spread over dough.
3. Break off small pieces of remaining dough and drop over filling. Bake at 375° for 35-40 minutes or until topping is golden brown. Cool completely on a wire rack. Cut into bars. Refrigerate leftovers.
1 BAR: 160 cal., 9g fat (5g sat. fat), 25mg chol., 92mg sod., 17g carb. (11g sugars, 1g fiber), 3g pro.

NUT BUTTER CUPS

My indulgent, nutty candies are simple to make and look great. At our house, we make them with all-natural ingredients.
—Courtney Stultz, Weir, KS

PREP: 20 MIN. + CHILLING • **MAKES:** 1 DOZEN

- **1 cup unblanched almonds**
- **1 cup pitted dates**
- **1 cup creamy cashew butter or peanut butter**
- **½ cup baking cocoa**
- **¼ cup coconut oil, melted**
- **2 tsp. honey**
- **Chopped almonds, optional**

Pulse almonds and dates in a food processor until mixture starts to hold together when pressed. Spoon nut mixture into paper-lined muffin cups; press into bottom. Gently spread cashew butter over nut mixture. In a small bowl, whisk together cocoa, coconut oil and honey; pour over nut butter. If desired, top with chopped almonds. Refrigerate, covered, until chocolate is set, about 1 hour.
1 NUT BUTTER CUP: 293 cal., 23g fat (7g sat. fat), 0 chol., 73mg sod., 21g carb. (11g sugars, 4g fiber), 6g pro.

GRANOLA SNACK BARS

(SHOWN ON PAGE 178)
These sweet peanut butter bars are perfect for quick snacks, casual desserts or even grab-and-go breakfasts.
—Helen Velichko, Kansas City, MO

PREP: 15 MIN. + COOLING • **MAKES:** 1 DOZEN

- **½ cup packed brown sugar**
- **½ cup creamy peanut butter**
- **¼ cup light corn syrup**
- **1 tsp. vanilla extract**
- **2 cups old-fashioned oats**
- **1½ cups crisp rice cereal**
- **¼ cup miniature chocolate chips**

In a microwave-safe bowl, combine the brown sugar, peanut butter and corn syrup; cover and microwave on high for 2 minutes or until mixture comes to a boil, stirring once. Stir in the vanilla; add oats and cereal. Fold in chocolate chips. Press into a 9-in. square pan coated with cooking spray. Cool and cut into bars.
1 BAR: 199 cal., 7g fat (2g sat. fat), 0 chol., 88mg sod., 31g carb. (0 sugars, 2g fiber), 5g pro.

COURTNEY STULTZ
Weir, KS

NUT BUTTER CUPS

CHERRY BARS

EAT SMART

BANANA CHOCOLATE CHIP COOKIES

If you like soft cookies with a cakelike texture and lots flavor, here's a treat for you!
—Vicki Raatz, Waterloo, WI

PREP: 20 MIN. • **BAKE:** 15 MIN./BATCH
MAKES: 3 DOZEN

- **⅓ cup butter, softened**
- **½ cup sugar**
- **1 large egg**
- **½ cup mashed ripe banana**
- **½ tsp. vanilla extract**
- **1¼ cups all-purpose flour**
- **1 tsp. baking powder**
- **¼ tsp. salt**
- **⅛ tsp. baking soda**
- **1 cup (6 oz.) semisweet chocolate chips**

1. In a small bowl, cream butter and sugar until light and fluffy. Beat in the egg, banana and vanilla. Combine the flour, baking powder, salt and baking soda; gradually add to creamed mixture and mix well. Stir in chocolate chips.
2. Drop by tablespoonfuls 2 in. apart onto baking sheets coated with cooking spray. Bake at 350° for 13-16 minutes or until edges are lightly browned. Remove to wire racks to cool.
1 COOKIE: 69 cal., 3g fat (2g sat. fat), 10mg chol., 50mg sod., 10g carb. (6g sugars, 0 fiber), 1g pro. **Diabetic exchanges:** ½ starch, ½ fat.

CHERRY BARS

Whip up a pan of these festive bars with canned pie filling and a few baking staples. Between the easy prep and pretty color, they're destined to become a favorite in your home all year long.
—Jane Kamp, Grand Rapids, MI

PREP: 20 MIN. • **BAKE:** 35 MIN. + COOLING
MAKES: 5 DOZEN

- **1 cup butter, softened**
- **2 cups sugar**
- **1 tsp. salt**
- **4 large eggs**
- **1 tsp. vanilla extract**
- **¼ tsp. almond extract**
- **3 cups all-purpose flour**
- **2 cans (21 oz. each) cherry pie filling**

GLAZE

- **1 cup confectioners' sugar**
- **½ tsp. vanilla extract**
- **½ tsp. almond extract**
- **2 to 3 Tbsp. whole milk**

1. Preheat oven to 350°. In a large bowl, cream butter, sugar and salt until light and fluffy. Add the eggs, one at a time, beating well after each addition. Beat in extracts. Gradually add flour.
2. Spread 3 cups dough into a greased 15x10x1-in. baking pan. Spread with pie filling. Drop the remaining dough by teaspoonfuls over filling. Bake until golden brown, 35-40 minutes. Cool completely in pan on a wire rack.
3. In a small bowl, mix confectioners' sugar, extracts and enough milk to reach desired consistency; drizzle over top.
1 BAR: 112 cal., 3g fat (2g sat. fat), 21mg chol., 72mg sod., 19g carb. (9g sugars, 0 fiber), 1g pro.

BANANA CHOCOLATE CHIP COOKIES

(5) INGREDIENTS **FAST FIX**

PEANUT BUTTER COOKIES

It is amazing how much flavor these flourless cookies have. I make them often because I always have the ingredients on hand. It's nice that the recipe makes a tiny batch.
—Maggie Schimmel, Wauwatosa, WI

TAKES: 30 MIN. • **MAKES:** 2 DOZEN

- 1 **large egg, beaten**
- 1 **cup sugar**
- 1 **cup creamy peanut butter**

1. In a large bowl, mix all ingredients. Scoop level tablespoonfuls and roll into balls. Place on ungreased baking sheets and flatten with a fork.
2. Bake at 350° for about 18 minutes or until set. Remove to wire racks to cool.
1 COOKIE: 99 cal., 6g fat (1g sat. fat), 8mg chol., 48mg sod., 11g carb. (10g sugars, 1g fiber), 3g pro.

(5) INGREDIENTS

CHOCOLATE MINT WAFERS

I created these melt-in-your-mouth treats for a cookie exchange, and everyone raved about them. To switch things up, try using different extracts instead of peppermint.
—Michelle Kester, Cleveland, OH

PREP: 20 MIN. + STANDING • **MAKES:** 2 DOZEN

- 4 **oz. dark chocolate candy coating**
- ⅛ **to ¼ tsp. peppermint extract**
- 24 **vanilla wafers**

1. Place candy coating and extract in a microwave-safe bowl. Microwave, uncovered, on high for 30-60 seconds or until smooth, stirring every 15 seconds.
2. Dip vanilla wafers in coating; allow excess to drip off. Place on waxed paper; let stand until set. Store in an airtight container.
1 COOKIE: 38 cal., 2g fat (1g sat. fat), 0 chol., 9mg sod., 5g carb. (4g sugars, 0 fiber), 0 pro.

MEXICAN CHOCOLATE OATMEAL COOKIES

These chewy chocolate cookies get a cozy kick from cinnamon and nutmeg. Oh, and the touch of rum in the batter adds some serious fun factor, too.
—Colleen Delawder, Herndon, VA

PREP: 25 MIN. • **BAKE:** 15 MIN. + COOLING • **MAKES:** 14 COOKIES

- ¾ **cup unsalted butter, cubed**
- 1½ **cups packed light brown sugar**
- 1 **large egg**
- 1 **large egg yolk**
- 2 **Tbsp. vanilla extract**
- 1 **Tbsp. dark rum**
- 2 **cups quick-cooking oats**
- 1¼ **cups all-purpose flour**
- 1 **tsp. ground cinnamon**
- ½ **tsp. kosher salt**
- ½ **tsp. baking soda**
- ⅛ **tsp. freshly ground nutmeg**
- 4 **oz. Mexican chocolate, finely chopped**

1. Preheat oven to 350°. In a small saucepan, melt butter over medium heat. Heat, stirring constantly, until golden brown, 8-10 minutes. Transfer to a large bowl. Add sugar; beat on medium speed 2 minutes. Add eggs, vanilla and rum; beat 2 minutes longer.
2. In another bowl, whisk together next six ingredients. Add to butter mixture; beat until combined. Fold in chocolate.
3. Drop dough by ¼ cupfuls 2 in. apart onto parchment paper-lined baking sheets. Bake until set, 12-15 minutes. Remove from pans to a wire rack to cool.
1 COOKIE: 310 cal., 13g fat (7g sat. fat), 53mg chol., 128mg sod., 46g carb. (29g sugars, 2g fiber), 4g pro

MEXICAN CHOCOLATE OATMEAL COOKIES

TEST KITCHEN TIP

No Mexican chocolate? No problem! Simply substitute an equal amount of semisweet or bittersweet chocolate, and get that special spicy kick by increasing the cinnamon to 1½-2 tsp. And while you can use jarred nutmeg in this recipe, the freshly ground variety takes the flavor to a whole new level.

MULLED WINE JELLY CANDIES

MULLED WINE JELLY CANDIES

These unique jelly candies make a nice hostess gift. I make the mulled red wine version for winter holidays, and a white wine variation in spring and summer. For white wine candy, I use a sweet wine like Moscato and 1 tsp. lemon juice. Omit the orange ingredients, spices and the simmering step—just combine wine and juice and proceed.
—Jennifer Mack, Pensacola, FL

PREP: 10 MIN. • **COOK:** 25 MIN. + STANDING
MAKES: 1¾ LBS. (3 DOZEN)

- **1 cup dry red wine**
- **4 orange peel strips (3x1 in. each)**
- **1 Tbsp. orange juice**
- **1 cinnamon stick (3 in.)**
- **3 whole cloves**
- **½ cup powdered fruit pectin**
- **¾ tsp. baking soda**
- **1⅓ cups sugar**
- **1⅓ cups light corn syrup**

COATING
- **¼ cup sugar**

1. In a small saucepan, combine the wine, orange peel, juice, cinnamon stick and cloves; bring just to a simmer (do not boil) over medium-low heat. Reduce heat; simmer gently, uncovered, 10 minutes to allow flavors to blend. Let stand 1 hour.
2. Line a 9x5-in. loaf pan with foil; coat foil with cooking spray. Strain wine mixture, discarding orange peel and spices. Return mulled wine to saucepan; stir in pectin and baking soda. Heat over medium-high heat.
3. Meanwhile, in a large saucepan, combine sugar and corn syrup; bring to a full rolling boil over high heat, stirring constantly. Stir in the wine mixture. Continue to boil 1 minute, stirring constantly. Remove from heat; skim off foam, if necessary. Immediately pour into prepared pan. Let stand until set, about 5 hours or overnight.
4. For coating, sprinkle 2 Tbsp. sugar over a 14x12-in. sheet of parchment paper. Invert candy onto sugar. With a knife dipped in warm water, cut candy into 1-in. squares; coat with the remaining sugar.
5. Transfer candies to a wire rack. Let stand, uncovered, at room temperature overnight. Store in airtight containers up to 1 week.
1 PIECE: 77 cal., 0 fat (0 sat. fat), 0 chol., 35mg sod., 19g carb. (19g sugars, 0 fiber), 0 pro.

COPYCAT BERGER COOKIES

Give these Baltimore classics a try, and create a new cookie-jar favorite in your home today.
—Marina Castle Kelley, Canyon Country, CA

PREP: 15 MIN. • **BAKE:** 10 MIN./BATCH + COOLING
MAKES: 35 COOKIES

- **1 cup unsalted butter, room temperature**
- **1 Tbsp. baking powder**
- **1½ tsp. salt**
- **2 tsp. vanilla extract**
- **1½ cups sugar**
- **3 large eggs**
- **4½ cups all-purpose flour**
- **1 cup sour cream**

CHOCOLATE ICING
- **4 Tbsp. unsalted butter**
- **3½ cups semisweet chocolate chips**
- **4 oz. unsweetened chocolate, chopped**
- **2 Tbsp. light corn syrup**
- **1½ cups sour cream**

1. Preheat oven to 400°. Beat butter, baking powder, salt and vanilla until combined. Add sugar; beat until light and fluffy. Add eggs, one at a time, beating well after each addition. Add flour alternately with sour cream, beginning and ending with flour; do not overmix.
2. Drop by 3 tablespoonfuls onto greased baking sheets. With wet fingers, flatten each into a 3-in. circle.
3. Bake 10 minutes or until edges start to brown. Cool on pan 5 minutes; remove to wire racks to cool completely.
4. In a small saucepan, stir chocolate icing ingredients over low heat just until chocolate melts and mixture is smooth. Remove from heat; cool to room temperature. Using a hand mixer, beat on high until mixture thickens and becomes slightly lighter in color, 6-7 minutes.
5. Spread 2 Tbsp. icing over flat side of cookies; let stand until set. Store in an airtight container in the refrigerator.
1 COOKIE: 296 cal., 17g fat (10g sat. fat), 37mg chol., 159mg sod., 34g carb. (19g sugars, 2g fiber), 4g pro.

COPYCAT BERGER COOKIES

FROSTY POLAR BEARS

VERMONT MAPLE COOKIES

Once I tasted maple cookies topped with a maple glaze at a bakery here in Vermont, I knew I had to re-create them at home. I get many requests to bring these to bake sales, parties and even vacations.
—Delores Day, Wolcott, VT

PREP: 20 MIN. • **BAKE:** 10 MIN./BATCH + COOLING • **MAKES:** 5 DOZEN

- 1 **cup butter, softened**
- ¾ **cup sugar**
- ¾ **cup packed brown sugar**
- 2 **large eggs**
- 1 **tsp. maple flavoring**
- 2½ **cups all-purpose flour**
- 1 **tsp. baking soda**
- 1 **tsp. salt**
- 2 **cups white baking chips**
- 1 **cup chopped pecans**

MAPLE GLAZE

- ⅓ **cup butter, cubed**
- 1¾ **cups confectioners' sugar**
- ⅓ **cup maple syrup**
- ¼ **tsp. maple flavoring**

1. Preheat oven to 350°. In a large bowl, cream butter and sugars until light and fluffy. Beat in eggs and maple flavoring. In another bowl, whisk flour, baking soda and salt; gradually beat into the creamed mixture. Stir in baking chips and pecans.
2. Drop dough by rounded tablespoonfuls 2 in. apart onto ungreased baking sheets. Bake 10-12 minutes or until golden brown. Cool on pans for 2 minutes. Remove to wire racks to
cool completely.
3. For glaze, in a saucepan, melt butter over medium heat. Remove from heat. Gradually beat in confectioners' sugar, syrup and maple flavoring until smooth.
4. Drizzle over cookies; let dry completely. Store between pieces of waxed paper in airtight containers.
1 COOKIE: 139 cal., 7g fat (4g sat. fat), 18mg chol., 101mg sod., 18g carb. (13g sugars, 0 fiber), 1g pro.0 fiber), 1g pro.

FROSTY POLAR BEARS

This is the perfect recipe to make with the little ones. Dang cute, easy and portable!
—Emily Tyra, Traverse City, MI

PREP: 25 MIN. + CHILLING
MAKES: 2½ DOZEN

- ¾ **cup creamy peanut butter**
- 60 **round butter-flavored crackers**
- 24 **oz. white candy coating, melted**
- 60 **miniature marshmallows**
- 30 **mini butter-flavored crackers**
- **Blue chocolate M&M's**
- **Black sugar pearls**
- **Black decorating icing, optional**

1. Spread peanut butter on half of the crackers; top with remaining crackers to make sandwiches. Refrigerate until firm.
2. Dip sandwiches in melted candy coating; allow excess to drip off. Place on waxed paper. Dip marshmallows in coating; allow excess to drip off. Place two marshmallows on top of each cookie for ears.
3. Dip mini crackers in melted candy coating; allow excess to drip off. Place on top of sandwiches for snouts. Top each snout with a blue M&M. Decorate with black sugar pearls for eyes and, if desired, use black decorating icing for mouths. Let stand until set. Refrigerate cookies in an airtight container.
1 SANDWICH COOKIE: 201 cal., 12g fat (7g sat. fat), 0 chol., 112mg sod., 23g carb. (16g sugars, 0 fiber), 2g pro.

ALMOND BARS

ALMOND BARS

This fast, delicious dessert always makes an appearance during our Christmas celebrations. Everyone likes the rich almond flavor.
—Cheryl Newendorp, Pella, IA

PREP: 15 MIN. • **BAKE:** 30 MIN. + COOLING • **MAKES:** 4½ DOZEN

- 1 **cup butter, softened**
- 1 **cup almond paste**
- 2¼ **cups sugar, divided**
- 2 **eggs**
- 1 **tsp. almond extract**
- 2 **cups all-purpose flour**
- ½ **cup slivered almonds**

1. In a large bowl, cream the butter, almond paste and 2 cups sugar until light and fluffy. Beat in eggs and extract. Gradually add flour just until moistened.
2. Spread into a greased 13x9-in. baking dish. Sprinkle with remaining sugar; top with almonds.
3. Bake at 350° for 30-35 minutes or until a toothpick inserted in the center comes out clean. Cool on a wire rack. Cut into squares. Store in the refrigerator.
1 SERVING: 107 cal., 5g fat (2g sat. fat), 17mg chol., 27mg sod., 14g carb. (10g sugars, 0 fiber), 1g pro. **Diabetic exchanges:** 1 starch, 1 fat.

SLEEPING BAG BLONDIES

This is the only golden brownie recipe you'll ever need! These tasty pecan bars can be dressed up for slumber parties, camping trips and Girl Scout events. We used mini vanilla wafers and marshmallows to make these adorable overnighters.
—Sharon Bickett, Chester, SC

PREP: 20 MIN. • **BAKE:** 35 MIN. + COOLING • **MAKES:** 16 BLONDIES

- 1 **cup butter, softened**
- 1 **cup sugar**
- 1 **cup packed brown sugar**
- 2 **large eggs**
- 2 **tsp. vanilla extract**
- 2 **cups self-rising flour**
- 2 **cups chopped pecans, optional**
- 1½ **cups white frosting**
  Brown, yellow, green, orange, pink and blue gel food coloring
- 8 **large marshmallows**
- 16 **miniature vanilla wafers**
  Assorted sprinkles and mini honey bear-shaped crackers, optional

1. Preheat oven to 325°. Line a 13x9-in. baking pan with foil, letting ends extend up sides; grease foil. In a large bowl, cream butter and sugars until light and fluffy. Beat in eggs and vanilla. Gradually beat in flour. If desired, stir in pecans.
2. Spread mixture into prepared pan. Bake for 35-40 minutes or until a toothpick inserted in center comes out clean. Cool on a wire rack.
3. Lifting with foil, remove brownie from pan. Trim ½ in. off edges. Cut remaining brownie lengthwise in half; cut each half crosswise into eight bars to make 16 sleeping bags.
4. Tint ¼ cup frosting brown and 2 Tbsp. yellow; transfer to two resealable plastic bags. Cut a small hole in a corner of each bag and set aside. Divide remaining frosting among four bowls; tint green, orange, pink and blue. Spread each of the four frostings over four brownies, reserving a small amount of each frosting to attach vanilla wafers.
5. For pillows, cut marshmallows vertically in half; place on one end of brownies, cut side down. Attach vanilla wafers to pillows. Pipe faces and hair on wafers using brown and yellow frostings. If desired, decorate with sprinkles and teddy bear crackers.
1 BLONDIE: 392 cal., 16g fat (9g sat. fat), 54mg chol., 352mg sod., 59g carb. (43g sugars, 0 fiber), 3g pro.

SLEEPING BAG BLONDIES

RUSTIC CARAMEL APPLE TART
PAGE 204

CAKES & PIES

Pretty pies and playful cupcakes, luscious layer cakes and nutty caramel tarts are just some of the treats you'll find here. These beauties make the celebration pop.

ARNOLD PALMER CUPCAKES

These fun cupcakes take a favorite sunny-day refresher and turn it into dessert. Add a slice of lemon on top for a puckery finish.
—Jesse Arriaga, Reno, NV

PREP: 20 MIN. • **BAKE:** 25 MIN. + COOLING
MAKES: 2½ DOZEN

- 1 **cup butter, softened**
- 2 **cups sugar**
- 3 **large eggs, room temperature**
- 1 **Tbsp. grated lemon zest**
- 2 **tsp. lemon juice**
- 3½ **cups all-purpose flour**
- 1 **tsp. baking soda**
- ½ **tsp. baking powder**
- ½ **tsp. salt**
- 2 **cups sour cream**

ICED TEA FROSTING

- 9 **Tbsp. butter, softened**
- 6¾ **cups confectioners' sugar**
- ¾ **cup 2% milk**
- ¾ **cup iced tea mix with lemon and sugar**

1. In a large bowl, cream butter and sugar until light and fluffy. Add eggs, one at a time, beating well after each addition. Beat in lemon zest and lemon juice. Combine the flour, baking soda, baking powder and salt; add to creamed mixture alternately with sour cream, beating well after each addition (batter will be thick).

2. Fill 30 lined muffin cups with ¼ cup batter. Bake at 350° until a toothpick inserted in the center comes out clean, 25-30 minutes. Cool 10 minutes before removing from pans to wire racks to cool completely.

3. For frosting, combine the butter and confectioners' sugar in a small bowl until light and fluffy. In another small bowl, stir together milk and tea mix until dissolved. Add to butter mixture; beat until smooth. Frost cupcakes.

1 CUPCAKE: 355 cal., 14g fat (8g sat. fat), 48mg chol., 182mg sod., 57g carb. (45g sugars, 0 fiber), 3g pro.

ARNOLD PALMER CUPCAKES

BUTTER PECAN PUMPKIN PIE

Whenever I serve this pie, everyone thinks I worked all day to make it, but it's actually easy to assemble. It's handy to have in the freezer when unexpected company stops in for coffee and dessert.
—Arletta Slocum, Venice, FL

PREP: 20 MIN. + FREEZING
MAKES: 8 SERVINGS

- 1 **qt. butter pecan ice cream, softened**
- 1 **pie shell (9 in.), baked**
- 1 **cup canned pumpkin**
- ½ **cup sugar**
- ¼ **tsp. each ground cinnamon, ginger and nutmeg**
- 1 **cup heavy whipping cream, whipped**
- ½ **cup caramel ice cream topping**
- ½ **cup chocolate ice cream topping, optional**
- **Additional whipped cream**

1. Spread ice cream into the crust; freeze for 2 hours or until firm.

2. In a small bowl, combine the pumpkin, sugar, cinnamon, ginger and nutmeg; fold in whipped cream. Spread over ice cream. Cover and freeze for 2 hours or until firm. May be frozen for up to 2 months.

3. Remove from the freezer 15 minutes before slicing. Drizzle with caramel ice cream topping. If desired, drizzle with chocolate ice cream topping. Dollop with whipped cream.

1 SLICE: 452 cal., 25g fat (11g sat. fat), 51mg chol., 289mg sod., 56g carb. (41g sugars, 1g fiber), 5g pro.

★★★★★ **READER REVIEW**

"Yummy and pleasing for the whole family. My husband enjoyed the pie and now requests it every year! I add a teaspoon of almond flavor."
CHANNIBEAR
TASTEOFHOME.COM

EAT SMART FREEZE IT

GRAPEFRUIT YOGURT CAKE

We eat grapefruit for breakfast and in salads—so why not for dessert? Here's a sweet-tart cake that's easy, delicious and one of a kind. Oh, and healthy, too!
—Maiah Miller, Montclair, VA

PREP: 10 MIN. • **BAKE:** 25 MIN. + COOLING
MAKES: 12 SERVINGS

- **1½ cups all-purpose flour**
- **2 tsp. baking powder**
- **¼ tsp. salt**
- **3 large eggs**
- **1 cup fat-free plain yogurt**
- **⅓ cup sugar**
- **5 Tbsp. grated grapefruit zest**
- **¼ cup agave nectar or honey**
- **½ tsp. vanilla extract**
- **¼ cup canola oil**

GLAZE

- **½ cup confectioners' sugar**
- **2 to 3 tsp. grapefruit juice**
- **Grapefruit wheels and fresh mint leaves, optional**

1. Preheat oven to 350°. Whisk together flour, baking powder and salt. Combine next seven ingredients. Gradually stir flour mixture into yogurt mixture, then pour into a 9-in. round baking pan coated with cooking spray. Bake until a toothpick inserted in center of cake comes out clean, 25-30 minutes. Cool.

2. For glaze, mix confectioners' sugar with enough grapefruit juice to reach desired consistency; drizzle glaze over top, allowing some to flow over sides. Top the cake with grapefruit and mint if desired.

FREEZE OPTION: Omit glaze. Securely wrap cooled cake in plastic and foil; freeze. To use, thaw at room temperature. Prepare glaze; top as directed.

1 SLICE: 187 cal., 6g fat (1g sat. fat), 47mg chol., 159mg sod., 30g carb. (17g sugars, 1g fiber), 4g pro. **Diabetic exchanges:** 2 starch, 1 fat.

GRAPEFRUIT YOGURT CAKE

EAT SMART

MAKEOVER ORANGE CUPCAKES

The classic pairing of vanilla and orange comes through in these cute cupcakes. We lightened up the batter and swapped out buttercream icing to save big on fat and calories. And here's a bonus: Now they're lactose-free!
—Taste of Home Test Kitchen

PREP: 30 MIN. • **BAKE:** 20 MIN. + COOLING
MAKES: 2 DOZEN

- **6 large egg whites**
- **3 large eggs**
- **1 cup sugar**
- **¾ cup vanilla soy milk**
- **⅓ cup canola oil**
- **⅓ cup unsweetened applesauce**
- **⅓ cup plus ¼ cup thawed orange juice concentrate, divided**
- **3 cups all-purpose flour**
- **1 Tbsp. plus 1½ tsp. baking powder**
- **1½ tsp. salt**
- **1½ cups confectioners' sugar**
- **Assorted sprinkles, optional**

1. Preheat oven to 350°. Line 24 muffin cups with paper liners.

2. In a large bowl, beat egg whites, eggs, sugar, soy milk, oil, applesauce and ⅓ cup orange juice concentrate until well blended. In a small bowl, whisk flour, baking powder and salt; gradually beat into egg mixture.

3. Fill prepared cups two-thirds full. Bake 18-22 minutes or until a toothpick inserted in center comes out clean. Cool in pans 10 minutes before removing to wire racks to cool completely.

4. In a small bowl, mix confectioners' sugar and remaining orange juice concentrate until smooth. Dip cupcakes into glaze. If desired, decorate with sprinkles. Let stand until set.

1 CUPCAKE: 164 cal., 4g fat (0 sat. fat), 26mg chol., 249mg sod., 29g carb. (16g sugars, 0 fiber), 4g pro. **Diabetic exchanges:** 2 starch, 1 fat.

EASY FRESH STRAWBERRY PIE

EAT SMART

RIBBON PUDDING PIE

Cool, smooth and creamy, this pretty pie is a slice of heaven for anyone who enjoys a little dessert. The lovely pudding layers feature a yummy combination of vanilla, chocolate and butterscotch.
—Doris Morgan, Verona, MS

PREP: 20 MIN. + CHILLING • **MAKES:** 8 SERVINGS

- **4 cups cold fat-free milk, divided**
- **1 pkg. (1 oz.) sugar-free instant vanilla pudding mix**
- **1 reduced-fat graham cracker crust (6 oz.)**
- **1 pkg. (1 oz.) sugar-free instant butterscotch pudding mix**
- **1 pkg. (1.4 oz.) sugar-free instant chocolate pudding mix**
- **Whipped topping and finely chopped pecans, optional**

1. Whisk 1⅓ cups milk and vanilla pudding mix 2 minutes. Spread into crust.
2. In another bowl, whisk 1⅓ cups milk and butterscotch pudding mix 2 minutes. Carefully spoon over vanilla layer, spreading evenly.
3. In a third bowl, whisk remaining 1⅓ cups milk and chocolate pudding mix 2 minutes. Carefully spread over top. Refrigerate until set, at least 30 minutes. If desired, serve with topping and pecans.
1 PIECE: 184 cal., 3g fat (1g sat. fat), 2mg chol., 427mg sod., 32g carb. (13g sugars, 1g fiber), 6g pro. **Diabetic exchanges:** 2 starch, 1 fat.

RIBBON PUDDING PIE

EASY FRESH STRAWBERRY PIE

For my mother's 70th birthday and Mother's Day, I made two of these strawberry pies instead of a cake. Since it was mid-May in Texas, the berries were absolutely perfect. It was a memorable occasion for the whole family.
—Josh Carter, Birmingham, AL

PREP: 20 MIN. + COOLING • **BAKE:** 15 MIN. + CHILLING
MAKES: 8 SERVINGS

- **1 unbaked pie crust (9 in.)**
- **¾ cup sugar**
- **2 Tbsp. cornstarch**
- **1 cup water**
- **1 pkg. (3 oz.) strawberry gelatin**
- **4 cups sliced fresh strawberries**
- **Whipped cream, optional**

1. Line unpricked pie crust with a double thickness of heavy-duty foil. Bake at 450° for 8 minutes. Remove foil; bake 5 minutes longer. Cool on a wire rack.
2. In a small saucepan, combine the sugar, cornstarch and water until smooth. Bring to a boil; cook and stir for 2 minutes or until thickened. Remove from the heat; stir in gelatin until dissolved. Refrigerate for 15-20 minutes or until slightly cooled.
3. Meanwhile, arrange strawberries in the crust. Pour gelatin mixture over berries. Refrigerate until set. Serve with whipped cream if desired.
1 SLICE: 264 cal., 7g fat (3g sat. fat), 5mg chol., 125mg sod., 49g carb. (32g sugars, 2g fiber), 2g pro.

SALTED CARAMEL WALNUT TART

It took me a while to figure out how to convert one of my favorite ice cream flavors into a pie—one of my favorite desserts. The result took quite a few tries, but in the end, it was so worth it.
—Ruth Ealy, Plain City, OH

RUTH EALY
Plain City, OH

PREP: 20 MIN. + CHILLING
BAKE: 20 MIN. + COOLING
MAKES: 12 SERVINGS

- **2 large eggs, lightly beaten**
- **¼ cup plus 2 Tbsp. heavy whipping cream**
- **¾ cup packed light brown sugar**
- **¼ cup plus 2 Tbsp. golden syrup or light corn syrup**
- **3 Tbsp. unsalted butter, cubed**
- **1½ tsp. vanilla extract**
- **¾ tsp. sea salt**
- **1 sheet refrigerated pie crust**
- **1 cup chopped walnuts, toasted**

1. Let eggs stand at room temperature 30 minutes. In a microwave, heat whipping cream on high for 20 seconds. Keep warm. Meanwhile, in a large, heavy saucepan over medium heat, combine sugar and syrup, stirring frequently. Bring to a boil; cook, stirring constantly, for 1 minute. Remove from heat. Slowly pour cream into pan; continue stirring constantly (cream may spatter) until well blended. Gradually add butter, stirring until melted. Add vanilla and sea salt; stir until smooth. Cool.

2. Unroll crust into a 9-in. tart pan; trim edges. Refrigerate 30 minutes. Preheat oven to 400°. Line unpricked crust with a double thickness of foil. Fill with pie weights, dried beans or uncooked rice. Bake on a lower oven rack until edges are golden brown, 10-12 minutes. Remove the foil and weights; bake until the bottom is golden brown, 3-5 minutes longer. Cool on a wire rack.

3. Reduce oven setting to 350°. Whisk eggs into caramel mixture; stir in walnuts. Add filling to crust. Bake until center is just set (mixture will jiggle), 20-25 minutes. Cool completely. Refrigerate leftovers.

1 SLICE: 293 cal., 17g fat (6g sat. fat), 50mg chol., 238mg sod., 32g carb. (23g sugars, 1g fiber), 3g pro.

SALTED CARAMEL WALNUT TART

WHIPPED CHOCOLATE & CHERRY PIE

We have a large family, and they like trying all the cakes and pies I make. This wonderful pie is one of their favorites, so I make it about six times a year.
—Bonnie Phillips, Cedar Hill, MO

PREP: 20 MIN. + CHILLING
MAKES: 8 SERVINGS

- **11 large marshmallows**
- **⅓ cup whole milk**
- **1 piece (3 oz.) milk chocolate candy bar, chopped**
- **1 container (8 oz.) frozen whipped topping, thawed and divided**
- **1 graham cracker crust (10 in.)**
- **1 can (21 oz.) cherry pie filling**

1. In a large saucepan, combine the marshmallows, milk and chocolate. Cook and stir over medium-low heat until smooth. Cool completely.

2. Fold ¾ cup whipped topping into chocolate mixture. Pour into prepared crust. Cover and refrigerate for at least 30 minutes.

3. Top with pie filling and remaining whipped topping. Cover and refrigerate for 8 hours or overnight.

NOTE: This recipe uses half of a 6-oz. milk chocolate candy bar.

1 PIECE: 416 cal., 16g fat (8g sat. fat), 3mg chol., 213mg sod., 63g carb. (48g sugars, 1g fiber), 3g pro.

SAUERKRAUT CHOCOLATE CAKE

SAUERKRAUT CHOCOLATE CAKE

For an adventurous cake, try this recipe. People might need a little coaxing to try it but once they do, they will love it.
—Taste of Home *Test Kitchen*

PREP: 20 MIN. • **BAKE:** 35 MIN. + COOLING
MAKES: 16 SERVINGS

- ½ **cup butter, softened**
- 1½ **cups sugar**
- 3 **large eggs**
- 1 **tsp. vanilla extract**
- 2 **cups all-purpose flour**
- ½ **cup baking cocoa**
- 1 **tsp. baking powder**
- 1 **tsp. baking soda**
- ½ **tsp. salt**
- 1 **cup water**
- ¾ **cup sauerkraut, drained, squeezed dry and chopped**

SILK CHOCOLATE FROSTING

- 1⅓ **cups butter, softened**
- 4 **oz. unsweetened chocolate, melted**
- 1½ **tsp. vanilla extract**
- 4 **cups confectioners' sugar**
- ¼ **cup whole milk**

1. In a bowl, cream the butter and sugar. Add eggs, one at a time, beating well after each addition. Add vanilla. Combine flour, cocoa, baking powder, baking soda and salt; add to the creamed mixture alternately with water. Stir in sauerkraut. Pour into two greased and floured 8-in. round baking pans.
2. Bake at 350° for 35-40 minutes or until a toothpick inserted in the center comes out clean. Cool in pans for 10 minutes before removing to wire racks to cool completely.
3. For frosting, beat butter, chocolate and vanilla in a bowl; add sugar and beat well. Add milk; beat until smooth and fluffy. Spread between layers and over top and sides of cake.
1 PIECE: 505 cal., 26g fat (16g sat. fat), 91mg chol., 412mg sod., 65g carb. (49g sugars, 2g fiber), 5g pro.

HUMMINGBIRD CUPCAKES

Turn the traditional hummingbird cake—flavored with pineapple, bananas and walnuts—into a bite-sized treat.
—Jessie Oleson, Santa Fe, NM

PREP: 40 MIN. • **BAKE:** 20 MIN. + COOLING
MAKES: 2 DOZEN

- 1 **cup butter, softened**
- 2 **cups sugar**
- 3 **large eggs**
- 2 **tsp. vanilla extract**
- 2 **cups mashed ripe bananas**
- ½ **cup drained canned crushed pineapple**
- 3 **cups all-purpose flour**
- 1 **tsp. baking soda**
- 1 **tsp. ground cinnamon**
- ½ **tsp. salt**
- 1 **cup sweetened shredded coconut**
- 1 **cup chopped walnuts**

CREAM CHEESE FROSTING

- 1 **pkg. (8 oz.) cream cheese, softened**
- ½ **cup butter, softened**
- 3¾ **cups confectioners' sugar**
- 1 **tsp. vanilla extract**

1. In a large bowl, cream butter and sugar until light and fluffy. Add eggs, one at a time, beating well after each addition. Beat in vanilla. In a small bowl, combine bananas and pineapple.
2. Combine the flour, baking soda, cinnamon and salt; add to the creamed mixture alternately with banana mixture, beating well after each addition. Fold in coconut and walnuts.
3. Fill paper-lined muffin cups two-thirds full. Bake at 350° for 20-25 minutes or until a toothpick inserted in the center comes out clean. Cool for 10 minutes before removing from pans to wire racks to cool completely.
4. In a small bowl, beat cream cheese and butter until fluffy. Add the confectioners' sugar and vanilla; beat until smooth. Frost the cupcakes.
1 CUPCAKE: 410 cal., 20g fat (11g sat. fat), 67mg chol., 230mg sod., 56g carb. (39g sugars, 2g fiber), 4g pro.

PINEAPPLE COCONUT CAKE

This pretty layer cake is a guaranteed showstopper at any holiday meal. The flakes of coconut are reminiscent of snow. But one taste of the sunny pineapple will transport you to the tropics.
—Monica Kennedy, Johnson City, TN

PREP: 45 MIN. + CHILLING • **BAKE:** 20 MIN. + COOLING
MAKES: 12 SERVINGS

- **5 large eggs, separated**
- **1 can (20 oz.) crushed pineapple**
- **1½ cups all-purpose flour**
- **2½ tsp. baking powder**
- **1¼ cups sugar, divided**
- **¼ cup butter, melted**
- **2 tsp. coconut extract**
- **1 tsp. vanilla extract**

MOUSSE

- **4 cups heavy whipping cream**
- **1½ cups confectioners' sugar, divided**
- **2 pkg. (8 oz. each) cream cheese, softened**
- **5 cups sweetened shredded coconut, divided**

1. Place egg whites in a large bowl; let stand at room temperature for 30 minutes. Drain pineapple, reserving 1 cup juice; set aside.
2. Preheat oven to 350°. In a small bowl, combine flour and baking powder. In another bowl, beat egg yolks until slightly thickened. Gradually add 1 cup sugar, beating on high speed until thick and lemon-colored. Beat in butter, extracts and ½ cup reserved juice. Add dry ingredients; beat until well blended.
3. Beat egg whites with clean beaters on medium speed until soft peaks form. Gradually add remaining sugar, 1 Tbsp. at a time, beating on high until stiff peaks form. Fold into batter.
4. Transfer to two greased and floured 9-in. round baking pans. Bake 18-22 minutes or until cake springs back when lightly touched. Cool 10 minutes before removing from pans to wire racks to cool completely.
5. In a large bowl, beat cream until it begins to thicken. Add 1 cup confectioners' sugar; beat until stiff peaks form. In another bowl, beat cream cheese, pineapple and remaining confectioners' sugar until blended; stir in 2 cups coconut. Fold in whipped cream. Cover and refrigerate at least 1 hour.
6. Cut each cake horizontally into two layers. Place bottom layer on a serving plate; drizzle with 2 Tbsp. reserved juice. Spread with 2 cups mousse. Repeat layers twice. Top with remaining cake layer and drizzle with remaining juice. Spread remaining mousse over top and sides of cake. Press remaining coconut onto top and sides. Refrigerate at least 1 hour before serving.
1 PIECE: 899 cal., 62g fat (42g sat. fat), 248mg chol., 388mg sod., 78g carb. (56g sugars, 3g fiber), 10g pro.

CITRUS-RASPBERRY COFFEE CAKE

Orange and lemon beautifully complement the raspberry flavor in this dense cake. Add a dusting of confectioners' sugar for a pretty finishing touch.
—Pat Harlow, Cataldo, ID

PREP: 20 MIN. • **BAKE:** 55 MIN. + COOLING • **MAKES:** 16 SERVINGS

- **3 cups all-purpose flour**
- **2 cups sugar**
- **3 tsp. baking powder**
- **1 tsp. salt**
- **4 large eggs**
- **1 cup canola oil**
- **½ cup orange juice**
- **1 tsp. lemon extract**
- **2 cups fresh or frozen unsweetened raspberries**
- **Confectioners' sugar**

1. In a large bowl, combine the flour, sugar, baking powder and salt. In another bowl, combine the eggs, oil, orange juice and extract. Stir into dry ingredients just until moistened.
2. Pour half of the batter into a greased and floured 10-in. fluted tube pan. Sprinkle with raspberries. Top with remaining batter. Bake at 350° for 55-65 minutes or until a toothpick inserted in the center comes out clean.
3. Cool in pan for 10 minutes before removing from pan to a wire rack to cool completely. Dust with confectioners' sugar.
NOTE: If using frozen raspberries, use without thawing to avoid discoloring the batter.
1 SLICE: 337 cal., 15g fat (1g sat. fat), 53mg chol., 241mg sod., 46g carb. (27g sugars, 1g fiber), 4g pro.

CITRUS-RASPBERRY COFFEE CAKE

GOLDEN PEACH PIE

GOLDEN PEACH PIE

Years ago, I entered this pie in the Park County Fair in Livingston. It won a first-place blue ribbon plus a purple ribbon for best all around! Family and friends agree with the judges—it's a perfectly peachy pie. —Shirley Olson, Polson, MT

PREP: 20 MIN. • **BAKE:** 50 MIN. + COOLING **MAKES:** 8 SERVINGS

- 2 **sheets refrigerated pie crust**
- 5 **cups sliced peeled fresh peaches (about 5 medium)**
- 2 **tsp. lemon juice**
- ½ **tsp. grated orange zest**
- ⅛ **tsp. almond extract**
- 1 **cup sugar**
- ¼ **cup cornstarch**
- ¼ **tsp. ground nutmeg**
- ⅛ **tsp. salt**
- 2 **Tbsp. butter**

1. Line a 9-in. pie plate with one crust; trim, leaving a 1-in. overhang around edge. Set aside. In a large bowl, combine peaches, lemon juice, orange zest and extract. Combine sugar, cornstarch, nutmeg and salt. Add to peach mixture; toss gently to coat. Pour into crust; dot with butter.
2. Roll out remaining crust to a ⅛-in.-thick circle; cut into strips of various widths. Arrange over filling in a lattice pattern. Trim and seal strips to bottom crust; fold overhang over. Lightly press or flute edge. Cover the edges loosely with foil.
3. Bake at 400° for 40 minutes. Remove foil; bake 10-15 minutes longer or until crust is golden brown and filling is bubbly. Cool on a wire rack. Store in the refrigerator.
1 PIECE: 425 cal., 17g fat (8g sat. fat), 18mg chol., 267mg sod., 67g carb. (36g sugars, 2g fiber), 3g pro.

RHUBARB TARTS

The rhubarb flavor in this tart balances nicely with the honey and amaretto. The mascarpone cheese makes it rich and creamy. Sometimes I'll even double the rhubarb for really sumptuous tarts. —Ellen Riley, Murfreesboro, TN

PREP: 35 MIN. • **BAKE:** 15 MIN. + COOLING
MAKES: 2 TARTS (8 SERVINGS EACH)

- 1 **pkg. frozen puff pastry (17.30 oz.), thawed**
- 1 **large egg**
- 1 **Tbsp. water**

RHUBARB TOPPING

- 12 **rhubarb ribs (½ in. x 7 in.)**
- 1 **cup orange juice**
- ½ **cup honey**
- 2 **Tbsp. amaretto**

FILLING

- 1 **pkg. (8 oz.) mascarpone cheese**
- 2 **Tbsp. amaretto**
- 1 **Tbsp. honey**

RHUBARB TART

1. Preheat oven to 400°. Unfold one pastry sheet and place on a parchment paper-lined baking sheet; repeat with remaining pastry sheet. Whisk egg and water; brush over pastries. Using a sharp knife, score a 1-in. border around edges of pastry sheets (do not cut through). With a fork, prick center of pastries. Bake until golden brown, about 15 minutes. With a spatula, press down center portion of pastries, leaving outer edges intact. Remove to wire racks to cool.
2. Meanwhile, for topping, arrange rhubarb in a single layer in a 13x9-in. baking dish. Combine orange juice, honey and amaretto; pour over rhubarb. Bake at 400° until rhubarb is just tender but still holds its shape, about 10 minutes. Remove with a slotted spoon, reserving cooking liquid; let rhubarb cool. Transfer reserved cooking liquid to a small saucepan; bring to a boil over medium-high heat. Reduce heat; simmer until reduced to ½ cup, about 20 minutes. Cool.
3. For filling, stir together mascarpone cheese, amaretto and honey until smooth. Spread mascarpone mixture over center of each pastry. Top with rhubarb ribs. Brush rhubarb with cooled cooking liquid. Refrigerate leftovers.
1 PIECE: 259 cal., 15g fat (6g sat. fat), 29mg chol., 115mg sod., 26g carb. (8g sugars, 3g fiber), 4g pro.

TEST KITCHEN TIP

Normally we'd say you could use frozen rhubarb with equally good results, but in this case you definitely need the fresh, long stalks to achieve this spectacular look. Scoring around the edge of the pastry before baking creates a border in the finished tarts.

CARAMEL PEANUT FANTASY

CARAMEL PEANUT FANTASY

Packed with peanuts and gooey with caramel, this do-ahead treat is one sweet dream of a dessert to serve company. With an easy cookie crust and scrumptious candy bar layers, it goes together quickly and will disappear just as fast!
—Taste of Home *Test Kitchen*

PREP: 30 MIN. + CHILLING • **MAKES:** 12 SERVINGS

- **2 cups crushed vanilla wafers (about 60 wafers)**
- **⅓ cup butter, melted**
- **20 caramels**
- **15 miniature Snickers candy bars**
- **½ cup caramel ice cream topping**
- **½ cup heavy whipping cream, divided**
- **2 cups salted peanuts, chopped**
- **¾ cup semisweet chocolate chips**
- **Additional chopped salted peanuts, optional**

1. In a small bowl, combine wafer crumbs and butter. Press onto the bottom of a greased 9-in. springform pan. Place on a baking sheet. Bake at 350° for 8-10 minutes. Cool on a wire rack.
2. In a heavy saucepan, combine the caramels, candy bars, caramel topping and ¼ cup cream; cook and stir over low heat until smooth and blended. Remove from the heat; stir in peanuts. Spread over crust. Cover and refrigerate for 1 hour.
3. In a microwave, melt chocolate chips and remaining cream; stir until smooth. Spread over caramel layer. If desired, sprinkle with additional peanuts. Refrigerate for 1 hour or until serving.
1 SLICE: 504 cal., 30g fat (11g sat. fat), 32mg chol., 335mg sod., 55g carb. (40g sugars, 4g fiber), 10g pro.

WALNUT HONEY CAKE

Here's a fluffy old-fashioned cake that all but melts in your mouth. Back in the day, it took effort for my grandmother's kitchen helper to make it, but it's a breeze now that we have stand mixers.
—Lily Julow, Lawrenceville, GA

PREP: 25 MIN. • **BAKE:** 30 MIN. + COOLING • **MAKES:** 15 SERVINGS

- **1 cup sugar**
- **4 large eggs, room temperature**
- **½ cup canola oil**
- **1 cup honey**
- **2 tsp. grated orange zest**
- **1 cup orange juice (with pulp)**
- **3 cups all-purpose flour**
- **3 tsp. baking powder**
- **½ tsp. salt**
- **½ tsp. baking soda**
- **½ tsp. ground ginger**
- **½ tsp. ground cinnamon**
- **¾ cup chopped walnuts, divided**
- **Confectioners' sugar, optional**

1. Preheat oven to 350°. Line the bottom of a 13x9-in. baking pan with parchment paper; grease paper.
2. Beat sugar and eggs for 10 minutes. Gradually add oil; beat 1 minute. Gradually add honey, and beat 1 minute longer. Add orange zest and orange juice; beat 1 minute more.
3. In another bowl, sift flour with next five ingredients. On low speed, beat dry ingredients with egg mixture until combined. Increase speed to medium; beat until well mixed. Fold in half of the walnuts.
4. Pour batter into prepared pan; sprinkle with remaining walnuts. Bake until a toothpick inserted in center comes out clean, 30-35 minutes. Cool; if desired, lightly dust with confectioners' sugar. Cut into squares.
1 PIECE: 342 cal., 13g fat (1g sat. fat), 50mg chol., 237mg sod., 54g carb. (34g sugars, 1g fiber), 5g pro.

WALNUT HONEY CAKE

APPLE FRITTER CAKE

I was experimenting with a beer bread to make it into a dessert and came up with this delectable cake that tastes just like our favorite apple fritters.
—Ann Marie Eberhart, Gig Harbor, WA

PREP: 10 MIN. • **BAKE:** 40 MIN. + COOLING
MAKES: 12 SERVINGS

- **3 cups all-purpose flour, sifted**
- **¼ cup sugar**
- **2 Tbsp. ground cinnamon**
- **3 tsp. baking powder**
- **1 tsp. salt**
- **2 medium apples, peeled and chopped (about 2 cups)**
- **1 bottle (12 oz.) beer or unsweetened apple juice, room temperature**
- **¼ cup butter, melted**

ICING

- **2 cups confectioners' sugar**
- **3 to 5 Tbsp. 2% milk**
- **½ tsp. vanilla extract**

1. Preheat oven to 350°. Line an 8-in. square baking pan with parchment paper, letting ends extend up sides.
2. Whisk together the first five ingredients. Add apples and beer; mix just until blended (do not overmix; batter will be thick). Transfer to prepared pan. Bake until a toothpick inserted in center comes out clean, 40-45 minutes. Lifting with the parchment paper, immediately remove cake from pan. Brush all sides with melted butter. Cool. Meanwhile, combine the icing ingredients. Spread or drizzle over the cooled cake.
1 PIECE: 261 cal., 4g fat (3g sat. fat), 10mg chol., 350mg sod., 52g carb. (27g sugars, 2g fiber), 4g pro.

CHERRY-ALMOND STREUSEL TART

CHERRY-ALMOND STREUSEL TART

Brimming with fresh cherries and topped with crunchy streusel, this tempting tart will end dinner on a sweet note. It is fast to fix, looks elegant and tastes delicious.
—Marion Lee, Mount Hope, ON

PREP: 20 MIN. • **BAKE:** 30 MIN. + COOLING
MAKES: 8 SERVINGS

- **Pastry for single-crust pie (9 in.)**
- **⅔ cup sugar**
- **3 Tbsp. cornstarch**
- **Dash salt**
- **4 cups fresh or frozen pitted tart cherries, thawed**
- **⅛ tsp. almond extract**

TOPPING

- **¼ cup quick-cooking oats**
- **3 Tbsp. all-purpose flour**
- **2 Tbsp. brown sugar**
- **1 Tbsp. slivered almonds**
- **2 Tbsp. cold butter**

1. Press pastry onto the bottom and up the sides of an ungreased 9-in. fluted tart pan with removable bottom; trim edges.
2. In a large saucepan, combine the sugar, cornstarch and salt. Stir in cherries; bring to a boil over medium heat, stirring mixture constantly. Cook and stir for 1-2 minutes or until thickened. Remove from the heat; stir in extract. Pour into crust.
3. For streusel topping, combine the oats, flour, brown sugar and almonds. Cut in butter until the mixture resembles coarse crumbs. Sprinkle over filling. Bake at 350° for 30-35 minutes or until topping is golden brown. Cool on a wire rack.
1 PIECE: 298 cal., 11g fat (5g sat. fat), 13mg chol., 143mg sod., 49g carb. (27g sugars, 2g fiber), 3g pro.

BERRIES & CREAM TORTE

RUSTIC CARAMEL APPLE TART

(SHOWN ON PAGE 192)

Like an apple pie without the pan, this most scrumptious tart has a crispy crust that cuts nicely and a yummy caramel topping.
—Betty Fulks, Onia, AR

PREP: 20 MIN. + CHILLING
BAKE: 25 MIN. • **MAKES:** 4 SERVINGS

- **⅔ cup all-purpose flour**
- **1 Tbsp. sugar**
- **⅛ tsp. salt**
- **¼ cup cold butter, cubed**
- **6½ tsp. cold water**
- **⅛ tsp. vanilla extract**

FILLING
- **1½ cups chopped peeled tart apples**
- **3 Tbsp. sugar**
- **1 Tbsp. all-purpose flour**

TOPPING
- **1 tsp. sugar**
- **¼ tsp. ground cinnamon**
- **1 large egg**
- **1 Tbsp. water**
- **2 Tbsp. caramel ice cream topping, warmed**

1. In a large bowl, combine flour, sugar and salt; cut in butter until crumbly. Gradually add water and vanilla, tossing with a fork until dough forms a ball. Refrigerate for 30 minutes or until easy to handle.
2. Preheat oven to 400°. On a lightly floured surface, roll the dough into a 10-in. circle. Transfer to a parchment paper-lined baking sheet. Combine filling ingredients; spoon over crust to within 2 in. of edges. Fold up edges of crust over filling, leaving center uncovered. Combine sugar and cinnamon; sprinkle over filling. Whisk egg and water; brush over crust.
3. Bake 25-30 minutes or until the crust is golden and filling is bubbly. Use parchment paper to slide tart onto a wire rack. Drizzle with caramel topping. Serve warm.
1 SLICE: 298 cal., 13g fat (8g sat. fat), 77mg chol., 218mg sod., 42g carb. (24g sugars, 1g fiber), 4g pro.

BERRIES & CREAM TORTE

It's so easy to see why this fruity dessert always impresses dinner guests. I sometimes substitute sliced bananas for the berries.
—Tina Sawchuk, Ardmore, AB

PREP: 40 MIN.
BAKE: 10 MIN./BATCH + CHILLING
MAKES: 12 SERVINGS

- **1 cup butter, softened**
- **1 cup sugar**
- **2 large eggs**
- **2 cups all-purpose flour**
- **2 tsp. baking powder**
- **½ tsp. salt**

FILLING
- **½ cup sugar**
- **4½ tsp. confectioners' sugar**
- **4½ tsp. cornstarch**
- **3 cups heavy whipping cream**
- **4 cups sliced fresh strawberries**
- **2 cups fresh blueberries**
- **2 cups fresh raspberries**

1. In a large bowl, cream butter and sugar. Add eggs, one at a time, beating well after each addition. Combine the flour, baking powder and salt; gradually add to the creamed mixture.
2. Line two baking sheets with parchment paper or greased aluminum foil; draw a 9¾-in. circle on each. Spoon a fourth of the batter onto each circle; spread evenly with a spoon to within ¼ in. of edge. Bake at 350° for 8-10 minutes or until edges are golden brown. Remove to wire racks to cool completely. Repeat with the remaining batter.
3. Combine the sugar, confectioner's sugar and cornstarch. In a large bowl, beat cream and sugar mixture until stiff peaks form. To assemble, place one cookie layer on a large serving plate. Top with 1½ cups whipped cream mixture and 2 cups of mixed berries. Repeat layers twice. Top with remaining cookie layer and whipped cream mixture. Arrange remaining berries on top. Cover and refrigerate for 4 hours.
1 PIECE: 572 cal., 39g fat (23g sat. fat), 158mg chol., 354mg sod., 54g carb. (33g sugars, 4g fiber), 5g pro.

CONTEST-WINNING GINGERBREAD WITH LEMON SAUCE

I asked my mother-in-law for this recipe once I learned it's my husband's favorite. Now I bake it whenever he needs an extra-special treat. Spice cake topped with lemony sauce makes us both smile.
—Kristen Oak, Pocatello, ID

PREP: 15 MIN. • **BAKE:** 35 MIN. + COOLING • **MAKES:** 20 SERVINGS

- **1 cup shortening**
- **1 cup sugar**
- **1 cup molasses**
- **2 large eggs**
- **3 cups all-purpose flour**
- **1½ tsp. baking soda**
- **1½ tsp. salt**
- **1 tsp. ground ginger**
- **1 tsp. ground cinnamon**
- **1 cup hot water**

LEMON SAUCE

- **½ cup sugar**
- **2 tsp. cornstarch**
- **Dash salt**
- **Dash nutmeg**
- **1 cup half-and-half cream**
- **2 large egg yolks, beaten**
- **2 Tbsp. butter**
- **3 to 4 Tbsp. lemon juice**
- **1 tsp. grated lemon zest**

1. Preheat oven to 350°. Beat shortening, sugar, molasses and eggs until well blended. Combine next five ingredients; add to molasses mixture alternately with hot water.
2. Pour into a greased 13x9-in. baking pan. Bake until a toothpick inserted in the center comes out clean, 35-40 minutes. Cool on a wire rack.
3. Meanwhile, for lemon sauce, combine first five ingredients in a small saucepan until smooth. Cook and stir over medium-high heat until thickened and bubbly. Reduce heat; cook and stir 2 minutes longer. Remove from heat.
4. Stir a small amount of hot filling into egg yolks; return all to pan, stirring constantly. Bring to a gentle boil; cook and stir 2 minutes longer. Remove from heat. Gently stir in butter, lemon juice and zest, increasing juice if needed to thin sauce. Serve with warm cake. Refrigerate leftover sauce.
1 PIECE WITH ABOUT 1 TBSP. SAUCE: 283 cal., 12g fat (3g sat. fat), 46mg chol., 304mg sod., 41g carb. (25g sugars, 1g fiber), 3g pro.

COOKIE CUPCAKES

These cupcakes taste a lot like chocolate chip cookies, and they were the signature dish of my husband's Aunt Lois. He just loves them.
—Sue Smith, Joaquin, TX

PREP: 20 MIN. • **BAKE:** 25 MIN. + COOLING • **MAKES:** 1 DOZEN

- **½ cup butter, softened**
- **6 Tbsp. sugar**
- **6 Tbsp. packed brown sugar**
- **1 large egg**
- **½ tsp. vanilla extract**
- **1 cup plus 2 Tbsp. all-purpose flour**
- **½ tsp. baking soda**
- **½ tsp. salt**

FILLING

- **½ cup packed brown sugar**
- **1 large egg**
- **⅛ tsp. salt**
- **1 cup (6 oz.) semisweet chocolate chips**
- **½ cup chopped walnuts**

1. In a large bowl, cream the butter and sugars until light and fluffy. Beat in egg and vanilla. Combine the flour, baking soda and salt; gradually add to creamed mixture and mix well.
2. Spoon about 2 Tbsp. dough into each of 12 paper-lined muffin cups, filling each halfway. Bake at 375° for 10 minutes or until edges are light brown.
3. Meanwhile, in a small bowl, beat the brown sugar, egg and salt for 5 minutes or until lighter in color. Stir in the chocolate chips and walnuts.
4. Remove partially-baked cupcakes from oven. Spoon rounded tablespoonfuls of filling into the center of each cupcake. Bake 12-14 minutes longer or until deep golden brown. Cool about 10 minutes before removing from pan to a wire rack to cool.
1 CUPCAKE: 305 cal., 16g fat (8g sat. fat), 55mg chol., 249mg sod., 40g carb. (30g sugars, 1g fiber), 4g pro.

COOKIE CUPCAKES

SOUR CREAM-LEMON PIE

SOUR CREAM-LEMON PIE

I first tasted this pie at a local restaurant and hunted around until I found a similar recipe. After adding my own personal touch, it's now my husband's favorite.
—Martha Sorensen, Fallon, NV

PREP: 20 MIN. + CHILLING
MAKES: 8 SERVINGS

- **Pastry for single-crust pie (9 in.)**
- **1 cup sugar**
- **3 Tbsp. plus 1½ tsp. cornstarch**
- **1 cup whole milk**
- **½ cup lemon juice**
- **3 large egg yolks, lightly beaten**
- **¼ cup butter, cubed**
- **1 Tbsp. grated lemon zest**
- **1 cup sour cream**
- **1 cup heavy whipping cream, whipped**

1. Preheat oven to 450°. On a lightly floured surface, roll dough to a ⅛-in.-thick circle; transfer to a 9-in. pie plate. Trim pastry to ½ in. beyond rim of plate; flute edge.
2. Line unpricked pastry with a double thickness of foil. Fill with pie weights, dried beans or uncooked rice. Bake 8 minutes or until bottom is lightly browned. Remove foil and weights; bake 5-7 minutes longer or until golden brown. Cool on a wire rack.
3. In a large heavy saucepan, mix sugar and cornstarch. Whisk in milk and lemon juice until smooth. Cook and stir over medium-high heat until thickened and bubbly. Reduce heat to low; cook and stir about 2 minutes longer. Remove from heat.
4. In a small bowl, whisk a small amount of hot mixture into egg yolks; return all to the pan, whisking constantly. Bring to a gentle boil; cook and stir 2 minutes. Remove from heat. Stir in butter and lemon zest. Cool without stirring.
5. Stir in the sour cream. Add filling to crust. Top with whipped cream. Store in the refrigerator.
1 PIECE: 437 cal., 26g fat (15g sat. fat), 145mg chol., 197mg sod., 46g carb. (29g sugars, 0 fiber), 4g pro.

BLACK BOTTOM CUPCAKES

Our family has been enjoying these cupcakes for years, and I've learned that it just makes sense to double or triple the recipe. You'll see what I mean if you make them at your place because people will be asking for seconds.
—Julie Briceland, Windsor, PA

PREP: 20 MIN. • **BAKE:** 20 MIN. + COOLING
MAKES: 2 DOZEN

FILLING
- **1 pkg. (8 oz.) cream cheese, softened**
- **⅓ cup sugar**
- **1 large egg**
- **⅛ tsp. salt**
- **1 cup (6 oz.) semisweet chocolate chips**

CUPCAKES
- **1 cup sugar**
- **1 cup water**
- **⅓ cup vegetable oil**
- **1 large egg**
- **1 Tbsp. white vinegar**
- **1 tsp. vanilla extract**
- **1½ cups all-purpose flour**
- **¼ cup baking cocoa**
- **1 tsp. baking soda**
- **½ tsp. salt**

TOPPING
- **Sugar**
- **Chopped almonds, optional**

1. In a small bowl, beat the cream cheese, sugar, egg and salt until smooth. Stir in chips; set aside.
2. For cupcakes, in a large bowl, beat the sugar, water, oil, egg, vinegar and vanilla until well blended. Combine flour, cocoa, baking soda and salt; gradually beat into egg mixture until blended.
3. Fill 24 paper-lined muffin cups half full with chocolate batter. Drop a heaping tablespoonful of cheese mixture in center of batter of each cupcake. Sprinkle with sugar and chopped almonds if desired.
4. Bake at 350° for 18-20 minutes or until a toothpick inserted in the cake portion comes out clean. Cool cupcakes in pans for 10 minutes before removing to racks to cool completely. Refrigerate leftovers.
1 SERVING: 174 cal., 9g fat (4g sat. fat), 28mg chol., 148mg sod., 22g carb. (15g sugars, 1g fiber), 3g pro.

MINI KEY LIME & COCONUT PIES

Savor the flavor of Key Lime Pie with these individual muffin-size treats. Expecting a big crowd? These little pies are ready to party.
—Lisa Speer, Palm Beach, FL

PREP: 25 MIN. • **BAKE:** 10 MIN. + COOLING • **MAKES:** 1½ DOZEN

- **1 tube (16½ oz.) refrigerated sugar cookie dough**
- **1 can (14 oz.) sweetened condensed milk**
- **½ cup Key lime juice**
- **3 large egg yolks**
- **2 tsp. grated lime zest**
- **½ cup heavy whipping cream**
- **¼ cup confectioners' sugar**
- **¼ tsp. vanilla extract**
- **⅛ tsp. coconut extract**
- **¼ cup sweetened shredded coconut, toasted**

1. Slice cookie dough into 18 pieces. With floured fingers, press onto the bottom and ½-in. up the sides of 18 greased muffin cups. Bake at 350° for 8-10 minutes or until edges are lightly browned.
2. Meanwhile, in a small bowl, combine the milk, lime juice, egg yolks and lime zest. Spoon into hot crusts. Bake 7-9 minutes longer or until filling is set. Cool completely in pans on wire racks. Cover and refrigerate until serving.
3. Just before serving, in a small bowl, beat cream until it begins to thicken. Add the confectioners' sugar and extracts; beat until soft peaks form. Remove pies from muffin cups. Top with whipped cream and sprinkle with coconut.
1 PIE: 231 cal., 11g fat (5g sat. fat), 49mg chol., 120mg sod., 31g carb. (24g sugars, 0 fiber), 3g pro.

CONTEST-WINNING GERMAN CHOCOLATE PIE

Thanksgiving dinner at our house averages 25 guests and a dozen different pies. This particular pie resembles a luscious German chocolate cake.
—Debbie Clay, Farmington, NM

PREP: 40 MIN. + CHILLING • **BAKE:** 30 MIN. + COOLING
MAKES: 8 SERVINGS

Pastry for single-crust pie (9 in.)

FILLING
- **4 oz. German sweet chocolate, chopped**
- **1 Tbsp. butter**
- **1 tsp. vanilla extract**
- **⅓ cup sugar**
- **3 Tbsp. cornstarch**
- **1½ cups whole milk**
- **2 large egg yolks**

TOPPING
- **⅔ cup evaporated milk**
- **½ cup sugar**
- **¼ cup butter, cubed**
- **1 large egg, lightly beaten**
- **1⅓ cups sweetened shredded coconut, toasted**
- **½ cup chopped pecans, toasted**

1. Preheat oven to 400°. On a lightly floured surface, roll pastry dough to a ⅛-in.-thick circle; transfer to a 9-in. pie plate. Trim pastry to ½ in. beyond rim of plate; flute edge.
2. Line unpricked pastry with a double thickness of foil. Fill with pie weights, dried beans or uncooked rice. Bake 25 minutes. Remove foil and weights; bake 4-6 minutes longer or until golden brown. Cool on a wire rack.
3. For filling, in a microwave, melt chocolate and butter; stir until smooth. Stir in vanilla. In a small heavy saucepan, mix sugar and cornstarch. Whisk in whole milk. Cook and stir over medium heat until thickened and bubbly. Reduce heat to low; cook and stir 2 minutes longer. Remove from heat.
4. In a small bowl, whisk a small amount of hot mixture into egg yolks; return all to pan, whisking constantly. Bring to a gentle boil; cook and stir 2 minutes. Remove from heat. Stir in chocolate mixture. Pour into crust.
5. For topping, in a small saucepan, combine evaporated milk, sugar and butter. Cook and stir until butter is melted and mixture just comes to a boil. Remove from heat.
6. In a small bowl, whisk a small amount of hot mixture into egg; return all to pan, whisking constantly. Bring to a gentle boil; cook and stir 2 minutes. Remove from heat. Stir in coconut and pecans. Pour over filling.
7. Cool pie 30 minutes on a wire rack. Refrigerate, covered, until cold, at least 3 hours.
1 SLICE: 549 cal., 34g fat (17g sat. fat), 117mg chol., 265mg sod., 58g carb. (40g sugars, 1g fiber), 8g pro.
PASTRY FOR SINGLE-CRUST PIE (9 IN.): Combine 1¼ cups all-purpose flour and ¼ tsp. salt; cut in ½ cup cold butter until crumbly. Gradually add 3-5 Tbsp. ice water, tossing with a fork until dough holds together when pressed. Wrap and refrigerate 1 hour.

CONTEST-WINNING GERMAN CHOCOLATE PIE

PEANUT BUTTER ROCKY ROAD CHEESECAKE, PAGE 210

JUST DESSERTS

Life is short...eat dessert first! From effortless snacks to impressive finales that cap off special meals, it's nearly impossible to resist these sensational treats. With 25+ tempting delights to choose from, you'll always find room for dessert.

BERRY BLISS COBBLER

PEANUT BUTTER ROCKY ROAD CHEESECAKE

(SHOWN ON PAGE 208)

The classic pairing of chocolate and peanut butter updates my tried-and-true cheesecake filling with an unbeatable rich flavor that everyone enjoys.
—Jacyn Siebert, San Francisco, CA

PREP: 30 MIN. • **BAKE:** 55 MIN. + CHILLING
MAKES: 16 SERVINGS

- **2 cups graham cracker crumbs**
- **½ cup butter, melted**
- **¼ cup sugar**

FILLING

- **4 pkg. (8 oz. each) cream cheese, softened**
- **1½ cups sugar**
- **3 Tbsp. vanilla extract**
- **⅛ tsp. salt**
- **4 large eggs, lightly beaten**

TOPPING

- **2 Tbsp. creamy peanut butter**
- **2 Tbsp. honey**
- **1 jar (7 oz.) marshmallow creme**
- **½ cup hot fudge ice cream topping, warmed slightly**
- **½ cup chopped salted peanuts**

1. Preheat oven to 325°. Mix cracker crumbs, butter and sugar; press onto bottom and 1 in. up sides of a greased 9-in. springform pan.
2. In a large bowl, beat cream cheese and sugar until smooth. Beat in vanilla and salt. Add eggs; beat on low speed just until blended. Pour into crust. Place pan on a baking sheet.
3. Bake until center is almost set, 55-60 minutes. Cool on a wire rack 10 minutes. Loosen sides from pan with a knife. Cool 1 hour longer. Refrigerate overnight, covering when completely cooled.
4. Remove rim from pan. In a microwave, warm peanut butter and honey; mix until smooth. Drop spoonfuls of marshmallow creme, fudge topping and peanut butter mixture alternately over top of cheesecake. Swirl together using a toothpick or skewer. Sprinkle with peanuts.

1 SLICE: 533 cal., 32g fat (17g sat. fat), 119mg chol., 363mg sod., 52g carb. (42g sugars, 1g fiber), 8g pro.

BERRY BLISS COBBLER

A little bit sweet, a little bit tart and topped with golden, sugar-kissed biscuits, this easy cobbler is summer perfection.
—Taste of Home *Test Kitchen*

PREP: 10 MIN. + STANDING • **BAKE:** 20 MIN.
MAKES: 6 SERVINGS

- **3 cups fresh strawberries, halved**
- **1½ cups fresh raspberries**
- **1½ cups fresh blueberries**
- **⅔ cup sugar**
- **3 Tbsp. quick-cooking tapioca**
- **1 cup all-purpose flour**
- **1 Tbsp. sugar**
- **1½ tsp. baking powder**
- **¼ tsp. salt**
- **¼ cup cold butter, cubed**
- **1 large egg**
- **¼ cup 2% milk**
- **Coarse sugar**

1. Preheat oven to 400°. Toss strawberries, raspberries and blueberries with the sugar and tapioca. Transfer to a greased 10-in. ovenproof skillet; let stand 20 minutes.
2. Meanwhile, whisk flour, sugar, baking powder and salt. Cut in butter until mixture resembles coarse crumbs. In another bowl, whisk together the egg and milk; stir into crumb mixture just until moistened. Drop by tablespoonfuls onto fruit. Sprinkle with coarse sugar.
3. Bake cobbler, uncovered, until filling is bubbly and the topping is golden brown, 20-25 minutes. Serve warm.

1 SERVING: 335 cal., 9g fat (5g sat. fat), 52mg chol., 298mg sod., 60g carb. (34g sugars, 5g fiber), 5g pro.

EAT SMART (5)INGREDIENTS

PATRIOTIC POPS

My kids love homemade ice pops, and I love knowing the ones we make are good for them. We whip up a big batch with multiple flavors so they have many choices, but these patriotic red, white and blue ones are always a favorite!
—Shannon Carino, Frisco, TX

PREP: 15 MIN. + FREEZING • **MAKES:** 1 DOZEN

- **1¾ cups (about 14 oz.) vanilla yogurt, divided**
- **2 Tbsp. honey, divided**
- **1¼ cups sliced fresh strawberries, divided**
- **1¼ cups fresh or frozen blueberries, thawed, divided**
- **12 freezer pop molds or 12 paper cups (3 oz. each) and wooden pop sticks**

1. Place 2 Tbsp. yogurt, 1 Tbsp. honey and 1 cup strawberries in a blender; cover and process until blended. Remove to a small bowl. Chop remaining strawberries; stir into strawberry mixture.
2. In blender, process 2 Tbsp. yogurt, remaining honey and 1 cup blueberries until blended; remove mixture to another bowl. Stir in remaining blueberries.
3. In each mold, layer 1 Tbsp. strawberry mixture, 2 Tbsp. yogurt and 1 Tbsp. blueberry mixture. Top with holders. (If using paper cups, top with foil and carefully insert sticks through the foil.) Freeze until firm.
1 POP: 55 cal., 1g fat (0 sat. fat), 2mg chol., 24mg sod., 11g carb. (10g sugars, 1g fiber), 2g pro. **Diabetic exchanges:** 1 starch.

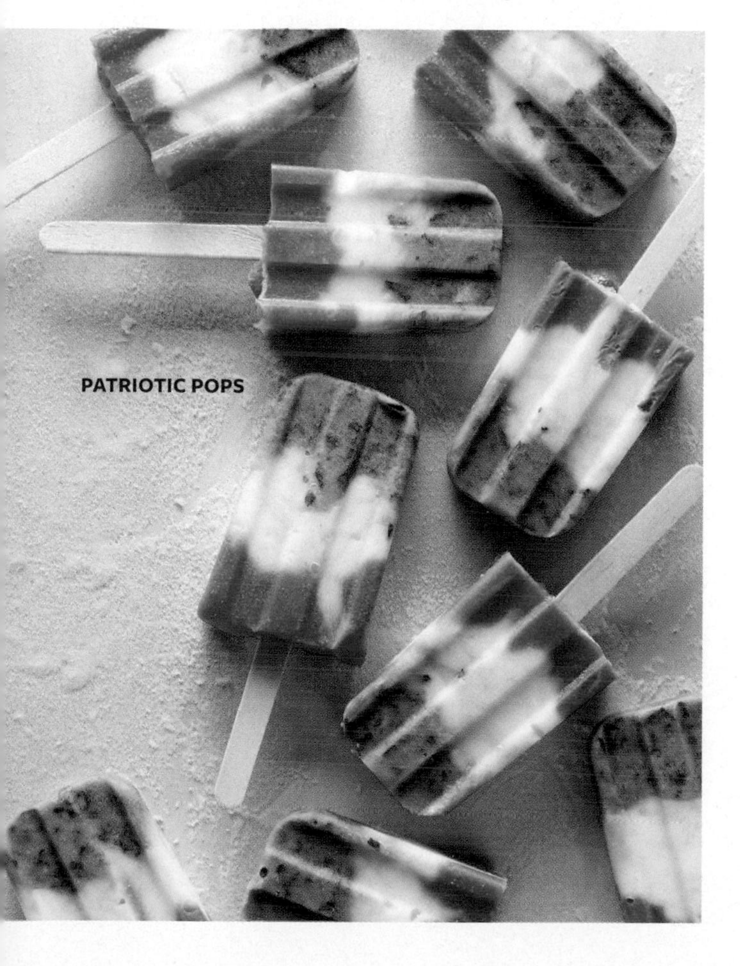

PATRIOTIC POPS

GRILLED BANANA BROWNIE SUNDAES

GRILLED BANANA BROWNIE SUNDAES

My niece Amanda Jean and I have a lot of fun in the kitchen creating different dishes. One of us will start with recipe idea and it just grows from there—and so does the mess. We always have a blast. That's exactly what happened when we topped prepared brownies with ice cream, grilled bananas and a quick peanut butter cream.
—Carol Farnsworth, Greenwood, IN

PREP: 10 MIN. • **GRILL:** 5 MIN. + COOLING • **MAKES:** 8 SERVINGS

- **2 medium bananas, unpeeled**
- **4 oz. cream cheese, softened**
- **¼ cup packed brown sugar**
- **3 Tbsp. creamy peanut butter**
- **8 prepared brownies (2-in. squares)**
- **4 cups vanilla ice cream**
- **½ cup hot fudge ice cream topping, warmed**
- **½ cup chopped salted peanuts**

1. Cut unpeeled bananas crosswise in half, then lengthwise in half. Place quartered bananas on an oiled grill rack, cut side down. Grill, covered, over medium-high heat 2-3 minutes on each side or until lightly browned. Cool slightly.
2. In a small bowl, beat cream cheese, brown sugar and peanut butter until smooth.
3. To serve, remove bananas from peel; place over brownies. Top with cream cheese mixture, ice cream, fudge topping and peanuts.
1 SERVING: 505 cal., 28g fat (11g sat. fat), 62mg chol., 277mg sod., 57g carb. (33g sugars, 3g fiber), 10g pro.

STRAWBERRY-CITRUS FREEZER POPS

EAT SMART 5 INGREDIENTS

STRAWBERRY-CITRUS FREEZER POPS

I knew clementines and strawberries would create a luscious combination in a fruit pop, and I have to say these are delicious!
—Colleen Ludovice, Wauwatosa, WI

PREP: 20 MIN. + FREEZING • **MAKES:** 10 POPS

- **2 cups fresh strawberries, sliced**
- **6 Tbsp. water**
- **1 Tbsp. sugar**
- **10 freezer pop molds or paper cups (3 oz. each)**
- **10 wooden pop sticks**
- **2 cups clementine segments (about 10), seeded if necessary**
- **6 Tbsp. orange juice**

1. Place strawberries, water and sugar in a food processor; pulse until combined. Divide among molds or cups. Top with foil and insert sticks through foil. Freeze until firm, about 2 hours.
2. Wipe food processor clean. Add clementines and orange juice; pulse until combined. Spoon over strawberry layer. Freeze, covered, until firm.
1 POP: 82 cal., 0 fat (0 sat. fat), 0 chol., 3mg sod., 20g carb. (16g sugars, 3g fiber), 1g pro. **Diabetic exchanges:** 1 fruit.

SPICED PEACH PUFFS

Growing up, we always made cream puffs for special occasions. My favorite version, then and now, features a nutmeg-spiced puff with peaches in vanilla-flavored whipped cream.
—Agnes Ward, Stratford, ON

PREP: 70 MIN. • **BAKE:** 25 MIN. + COOLING • **MAKES:** 3 DOZEN

- **1 cup water**
- **½ cup butter, cubed**
- **1 tsp. ground nutmeg**
- **⅛ tsp. salt**
- **1 cup all-purpose flour**
- **4 large eggs**
- **2 cups heavy whipping cream**
- **½ cup confectioners' sugar**
- **1 tsp. vanilla extract**
- **2 cups coarsely chopped fresh or frozen peaches, thawed**
- **Additional confectioners' sugar**

1. In a large saucepan, bring the water, butter, nutmeg and salt to a boil. Add flour all at once and stir until a smooth ball forms. Remove from the heat; let stand for 5 minutes. Add eggs, one at a time, beating well after each addition. Continue beating until mixture is smooth and shiny.
2. Drop by tablespoonfuls 2 in. apart onto greased baking sheets. Bake at 400° for 25-30 minutes or until golden brown. Remove to a wire rack. Immediately split puffs open; remove tops and set aside. Discard soft dough from inside. Cool puffs.
3. For filling, in a large bowl, beat cream until it begins to thicken. Add confectioners' sugar and vanilla; beat until stiff peaks form.
4. Just before serving, fill puffs with whipped cream and peaches. Dust with additional confectioners' sugar.
1 CREAM PUFF: 99 cal., 8g fat (5g sat. fat), 48mg chol., 39mg sod., 6g carb. (2g sugars, 0 fiber), 1g pro.

SPICED PEACH PUFFS

HONEYED PEARS IN PUFF PASTRY

A honey of a salute to late-summer pear season, this cozy dessert looks both elegant and decadent. Wrapped in puff pastry, the pears resemble little beehives.
—Heather Baird, Knoxville, TN

PREP: 25 MIN. • **BAKE:** 25 MIN.
MAKES: 4 SERVINGS

- 4 **small pears**
- 4 **cups water**
- 2 **cups sugar**
- 1 **cup honey**
- 1 **small lemon, halved**
- 3 **cinnamon sticks (3 in.)**
- 6 **to 8 whole cloves**
- 1 **vanilla bean**
- 1 **sheet frozen puff pastry, thawed**
- 1 **large egg, lightly beaten**

1. Core pears from bottom, leaving stems intact. Peel pears; cut ¼ in. from the bottom of each to level if necessary.
2. In a large saucepan, combine the water, sugar, honey, lemon halves, cinnamon and cloves. Split vanilla bean and scrape seeds; add bean and seeds to sugar mixture. Bring to a boil. Reduce heat; place pears on their sides in saucepan and poach, uncovered, until the pears are almost tender, basting them occasionally with poaching liquid, 16-20 minutes.
3. Remove pears with a slotted spoon; cool slightly. Strain and reserve 1½ cups of the poaching liquid; set aside.
4. Unfold puff pastry on a lightly floured surface. Cut into ½-in.-wide strips. Brush lightly with beaten egg. Starting at the bottom of a pear, wrap a pastry strip around fruit, adding additional strips until the pear is completely wrapped in pastry. Repeat with the remaining pears and puff pastry strips.
5. Transfer to a parchment paper-lined 15x10x1-in. baking pan. Bake pears on a lower oven rack at 400° until golden brown, 25-30 minutes.
6. Meanwhile, bring reserved poaching liquid to a boil; cook until liquid is thick and syrupy, about 10 minutes. Place pears on dessert plates and drizzle with syrup. Serve warm.
1 PEAR WITH 3 TBSP. SYRUP: 518 cal., 17g fat (4g sat. fat), 0 chol., 205mg sod., 92g carb. (49g sugars, 9g fiber), 5g pro.

CHOCOLATE PEANUT BUTTER PIZZA

FAST FIX

CHOCOLATE PEANUT BUTTER PIZZA

Kids go crazy for this gooey dessert pizza, although adults snap it up, too. Everyone loves the chewy homemade crust and the amazingly delicious combination of chocolate and peanut butter.
—Bernice Arnett, Marshfield, MO

TAKES: 30 MIN. • **MAKES:** 16 SLICES

- ½ **cup shortening**
- ½ **cup peanut butter**
- ½ **cup granulated sugar**
- ½ **cup packed brown sugar**
- 2 **large eggs**
- ½ **tsp. vanilla extract**
- 1½ **cups plus 5 Tbsp. all-purpose flour**
- 2 **cups miniature marshmallows**
- 1 **cup (6 oz.) semisweet chocolate chips**

Preheat oven to 375°. Cream shortening, peanut butter and sugars until light and fluffy. Beat in eggs and vanilla. Add flour and mix well. Pat the crust into a greased 12-in. pizza pan. Bake 16 minutes. Sprinkle with the marshmallows and chocolate chips; bake until pizza is lightly browned, 3-5 minutes longer.
1 SLICE: 220 cal., 11g fat (4g sat. fat), 21mg chol., 42mg sod., 28g carb. (19g sugars, 1g fiber), 4g pro.

MOM'S HAZELNUT & CHOCOLATE BREAD PUDDING

SLOW COOKER

MOM'S HAZELNUT & CHOCOLATE BREAD PUDDING

Mom combined her love of hazelnut spread and bread pudding into one delicious recipe. I adapted it for my slow cooker to save time in the kitchen. It's a great make-ahead dessert.
—Jo Hahn, Newport News, VA

PREP: 10 MIN. • **COOK:** 4 HOURS • **MAKES:** 12 SERVINGS

- **¼ cup unsalted butter**
- **2 Tbsp. semisweet chocolate chips**
- **8 cups cubed challah or brioche**
- **½ cup chopped hazelnuts**
- **4 large eggs**
- **1½ cups fat-free milk**
- **½ cup fat-free half-and-half**
- **½ cup hazelnut spread**
- **¼ cup sugar**
- **½ tsp. vanilla extract**
- **¼ tsp. salt**
- **Heavy whipping cream, whipped**

1. Microwave the butter and chips until melted, 30-45 seconds; stir until smooth. Cool. In a 3- or 4-qt. slow cooker coated with cooking spray, combine bread cubes and hazelnuts. In a large bowl, combine next seven ingredients, mixing well. Add chocolate mixture to bowl; whisk until smooth.
2. Pour egg mixture over bread and hazelnuts, gently pressing bread cubes to help them absorb liquid. Cook, covered, on low until a knife inserted in center comes out clean, 4-5 hours. Serve warm, dolloped with whipped cream.
½ CUP: 259 cal., 14g fat (4g sat. fat), 85mg chol., 190mg sod., 28g carb. (15g sugars, 1g fiber), 7g pro.

EAT SMART SLOW COOKER

SLOW-COOKER TEQUILA POACHED PEARS

Bring out this change-of-pace sweet when you want to impress dinner guests. It's an unusual dessert to make with tequila, but it is deliciously refreshing with fresh pears and mint.
—Nancy Heishman, Las Vegas, NV

PREP: 20 MIN. • **COOK:** 4 HOURS • **MAKES:** 8 SERVINGS

- **2 cups water**
- **1 can (11.3 oz.) pear nectar**
- **1 cup tequila**
- **½ cup sugar**
- **2 Tbsp. lime juice**
- **2 tsp. grated lime zest**
- **1 cinnamon stick (3 in.)**
- **¼ tsp. ground nutmeg**
- **8 whole Anjou pears, peeled**
- **Sweetened whipped cream**
- **Fresh mint leaves**

1. In a large saucepan, combine the first eight ingredients. Bring to a boil over medium-high heat; boil 2 minutes, stirring constantly.
2. Place pears in a 4- or 5-qt. slow cooker; add liquid. Cook, covered, on low until tender, 4-5 hours. Remove cinnamon stick and discard. Pour 3 cups cooking liquid in a small saucepan. Bring to a boil; cook, uncovered, until liquid is reduced to 1 cup, about 20 minutes.
3. Halve pears lengthwise and core them. Serve with sauce, whipped cream and mint leaves.
1 PEAR WITH 2 TBSP. SAUCE: 155 cal., 0 fat (0 sat. fat), 0 chol., 3mg sod., 40g carb. (30g sugars, 6g fiber), 1g pro.

SLOW-COOKER TEQUILA POACHED PEARS

BREAD PUDDING BLISS

Turning day-old bread into a pan of custardy amazingness is smart. Doing so with leftover dinner rolls? Sweet genius!

BEST EVER BREAD PUDDING

BEST EVER BREAD PUDDING

Leftover dinner rolls are the secret to incredible bread pudding with a soft inside and crispy edges. A generous drizzle of the rich brown sugar sauce puts this dessert over the top.
—Taste of Home *Test Kitchen*

PREP: 20 MIN. + STANDING • **BAKE:** 40 MIN.
MAKES: 15 SERVINGS

- 2 **large eggs**
- 2 **large egg yolks**
- 2¼ **cups half-and-half cream**
- 2 **cups whole milk**
- ½ **cup butter, melted**
- ¼ **cup granulated sugar**
- 1 **Tbsp. vanilla extract**
- 1½ **tsp. ground cinnamon**
- ½ **tsp. ground nutmeg**
- ¼ **tsp. sea salt**
- 20 **dinner rolls (1¼ lbs.), cut into 1-in. cubes (18 cups)**
- 3 **Tbsp. brown sugar**

SAUCE
- 1 **cup butter, cubed**
- 1 **cup packed brown sugar**
- 1 **cup half-and-half cream**
- 2 **tsp. vanilla extract**
- ¼ **tsp. sea salt**
- ⅛ **tsp. baking soda**

1. Preheat oven to 350°. Whisk together the first 10 ingredients until blended. Gently stir in the cubed dinner rolls. Transfer to a greased 3-qt. or 13x9-in. baking dish. Sprinkle with the brown sugar; let stand until the rolls are softened, about 15 minutes. Bake until puffed and a knife inserted in the center comes out clean, 40-45 minutes.

2. Meanwhile, for sauce, melt butter in a large heavy saucepan over medium heat. Add brown sugar; stir until dissolved. Gradually stir in cream. Bring to a boil. Reduce heat; simmer until thickened, 15-20 minutes, stirring constantly. Remove from heat; add vanilla, sea salt and baking soda, stirring well. Serve the sauce with warm bread pudding.

1 SERVING: 497 cal., 29g fat (17g sat. fat), 151mg chol., 540mg sod., 49g carb. (26g sugars, 2g fiber), 9g pro.

CHOCOLATE-CHERRY VARIATION: Stir in ¾ cup dried cherries and ¾ cup dark chocolate chips before baking.

APRICOT-ALMOND VARIATION: Stir in ¾ cup chopped dried apricots and ¾ cup toasted sliced almonds before baking.

CRANBERRY-WALNUT VARIATION: Stir in ¾ cup dried cranberries and ¾ cup toasted chopped walnuts before baking.

FIG-PISTACHIO VARIATION: Stir in ¾ cup chopped dried figs and ¾ cup toasted pistachios before baking.

SUCCESS TIPS

- Make sure you beat the eggs well; the bread will absorb them better that way. And that will reduce the chance that you'll wind up with a scrambled-egg texture in your custard.
- Most leftover breads work well in this recipe—if it'll make good French toast, it'll make good bread pudding.
- In general, soft and airy breads are best for absorbing the custard.
- To reheat, cut bread pudding into pieces and cook them in a little butter on the stovetop until crisp on each side. The texture is wonderful!

CARAMEL APPLE CHEESECAKE

CARAMEL APPLE CHEESECAKE

This cheesecake won the grand prize in an apple recipe contest. With caramel both on the bottom and over the top, every bite is sinfully delicious. See for yourself!
—Lisa Morman, Minot, ND

PREP: 45 MIN. • **BAKE:** 50 MIN. + CHILLING • **MAKES:** 12 SERVINGS

- **1½ cups cinnamon graham cracker crumbs (about 8 whole crackers)**
- **¾ cup sugar, divided**
- **¼ cup butter, melted**
- **1 pkg. (14 oz.) caramels**
- **⅔ cup evaporated milk**
- **½ cup chopped pecans, divided**
- **2 pkg. (8 oz. each) cream cheese, softened**
- **2 Tbsp. all-purpose flour, divided**
- **2 large eggs, lightly beaten**
- **1½ cups chopped peeled apples**
- **½ tsp. ground cinnamon**

1. Place a greased 9-in. springform pan on a double thickness of heavy-duty foil (about 18 in. square). Securely wrap the foil around the pan.
2. In a small bowl, combine the cracker crumbs, ¼ cup sugar and butter. Press onto the bottom and 1 in. up the sides of prepared pan. Place on a baking sheet. Bake at 350° for 10 minutes or until lightly browned. Cool on a wire rack.
3. In a heavy saucepan over medium-low heat, cook and stir the caramels and milk until melted and smooth. Pour 1 cup over crust; sprinkle with ¼ cup pecans. Set remaining caramel mixture aside.
4. In a large bowl, beat the cream cheese, 1 Tbsp. flour and remaining sugar until smooth. Add eggs; beat on low speed just until combined. Combine the apples, cinnamon and remaining flour; fold into cream cheese mixture. Pour into crust.
5. Place springform pan in a large baking pan; add 1 in. of hot water to larger pan. Bake for 40 minutes. Reheat the reserved caramel mixture if necessary; gently spoon over cheesecake. Sprinkle with remaining pecans.
6. Bake 10-15 minutes longer or until center is just set. Remove pan from water bath. Cool on a wire rack for 10 minutes. Carefully run a knife around edge of pan to loosen; cool 1 hour longer. Refrigerate overnight. Remove sides of pan.

1 SLICE: 446 cal., 26g fat (13g sat. fat), 93mg chol., 313mg sod., 55g carb. (42g sugars, 1g fiber), 8g pro.

POACHED PEARS WITH ORANGE CREAM

End any meal with a flourish with this easy yet elegant dessert. A hint of orange lends just enough sweetness to temper the wine's bold flavor. It's hard to believe it comes together in only a few minutes.
—Julianne Schnuck, Milwaukee, WI

PREP: 10 MIN. • **COOK:** 45 MIN. + COOLING • **MAKES:** 2 SERVINGS

- **2 firm medium pears**
- **1½ cups water**
- **1 cup dry red wine or red grape juice**
- **½ cup sugar**
- **2 tsp. vanilla extract**
- **¼ cup reduced-fat sour cream**
- **2 tsp. confectioners' sugar**
- **½ tsp. grated orange zest**
- **⅛ tsp. orange extract**
- **Additional grated orange zest, optional**

1. Core pears from bottom, leaving stems intact. Peel pears; cut ¼ in. from bottom to level if necessary. Place pears on their sides in a large saucepan. Add water, wine, sugar and vanilla. Bring to a boil. Reduce heat; simmer, covered, turning once, until pears are almost tender, 35-40 minutes. (For more intense flavor and color, leave fruit in cooking liquid and refrigerate overnight.)
2. Meanwhile, combine sour cream, confectioners' sugar, orange zest and extract. Refrigerate until serving.
3. Remove pears with a slotted spoon; pat dry and, if warm, cool to room temperature. Discard cooking liquid. Place pears on dessert plates. Serve with orange cream; if desired, top with additional grated orange zest.

1 SERVING: 239 cal., 3g fat (2g sat. fat), 10mg chol., 23mg sod., 46g carb. (36g sugars, 5g fiber), 3g pro.

POACHED PEARS WITH ORANGE CREAM

FROZEN PEANUT BUTTER & CHOCOLATE TERRINE

FROZEN PEANUT BUTTER & CHOCOLATE TERRINE

This terrine can be made ahead of time and stored in the freezer. When served, it cuts easily, revealing the lovely layers of banana, peanut butter and chocolate.
—Jennifer Jackson, Keller, TX

PREP: 30 MIN. + FREEZING • **MAKES:** 12 SERVINGS

- **15 Nutter Butter cookies, crushed (about 2 cups)**
- **1 carton (16 oz.) mascarpone cheese**
- **1 cup sugar**
- **2 tsp. vanilla extract**
- **1 carton (8 oz.) frozen whipped topping, thawed**
- **1 medium banana, sliced**
- **1 cup semisweet chocolate chips, melted and cooled slightly**
- **1 Tbsp. baking cocoa**
- **1 cup chunky peanut butter**

1. Line a 9x5-in. loaf pan with plastic wrap, letting edges extend up and over all sides. Sprinkle with a third of the crushed cookies.
2. In a large bowl, mix mascarpone cheese, sugar and vanilla; fold in whipped topping. Divide mixture evenly among three bowls.
3. To one portion, fold in sliced banana; add to loaf pan, spreading evenly. Repeat cookie layer. To a second portion, stir in melted chocolate and cocoa; add to loaf pan. Sprinkle with remaining cookies. To third portion, stir in peanut butter. Spread over top.
4. Freeze, covered, until firm, at least 5 hours. To serve, invert terrine onto a platter; remove plastic wrap. Cut into slices.
1 SLICE: 568 cal., 39g fat (18g sat. fat), 47mg chol., 190mg sod., 49g carb. (38g sugars, 3g fiber), 10g pro.

SLOW COOKER

COCONUT MANGO DESSERT WITH SUGARED RUM SAUCE

All the fun flavors of Puerto Rico come together in this tropical treat. It's delightful served with a scoop of vanilla ice cream.
—Jennifer Jackson, Keller, TX

PREP: 30 MIN. • **COOK:** 3 HOURS • **MAKES:** 6 SERVINGS

- **4 large eggs, beaten**
- **1 can (13.66 oz.) coconut milk**
- **⅓ cup packed brown sugar**
- **1 tsp. rum extract**
- **½ tsp. vanilla extract**
- **½ tsp. ground cinnamon**
- **4 cups torn French bread**
- **⅓ cup chopped dried mangoes**
- **¼ cup unsweetened coconut flakes, toasted**

SAUCE

- **¼ cup butter**
- **½ cup packed brown sugar**
- **2 Tbsp. water**
- **1 large egg yolk, beaten**
- **½ tsp. rum extract**
- **Toasted unsweetened coconut flakes, optional**

1. In a large bowl, whisk the first six ingredients until blended. Gently stir in bread, mango and coconut flakes. Transfer to a greased 3-qt. slow cooker. Cook, covered, on low until puffed and edges are dark golden, about 3 hours.
2. In a small heavy saucepan, heat butter and brown sugar over medium-low heat until blended. Whisk in water and yolk. Cook and stir until mixture is slightly thickened and a thermometer reads 175°, about 10 minutes. Do not allow to boil. Immediately transfer to a bowl; stir in rum extract. Serve warm bread pudding with rum sauce. If desired, top with additional coconut.
¾ CUPS WITH 2 TBSP. SAUCE: 447 cal., 24g fat (18g sat. fat), 175mg chol., 285mg sod., 49g carb. (37g sugars, 1g fiber), 8g pro.

COCONUT MANGO DESSERT WITH SUGARED RUM SAUCE

CREAMY CARAMEL FLAN

A small slice of this impressively rich, creamy treat goes a long way. What a delightful finish for a special meal or holiday celebration.
—Pat Forete, Miami, FL

PREP: 25 MIN. + STANDING
BAKE: 50 MIN. + CHILLING
MAKES: 10 SERVINGS

- ¾ **cup sugar**
- 1 **pkg. (8 oz.) cream cheese, softened**
- 5 **large eggs**
- 1 **can (14 oz.) sweetened condensed milk**
- 1 **can (12 oz.) evaporated milk**
- 1 **tsp. vanilla extract**

1. In a heavy saucepan, cook and stir sugar over medium-low heat until melted and golden, about 15 minutes. Quickly pour into an ungreased 2-qt. round baking or souffle dish, tilting to coat the bottom; let stand for 10 minutes.
2. In a bowl, beat the cream cheese until smooth. Beat in eggs, one at a time, until thoroughly combined. Add the remaining ingredients; mix well. Pour over the caramelized sugar.
3. Place the dish in a larger baking pan. Pour boiling water into larger pan to a depth of 1 in. Bake at 350° for 50-60 minutes or until center is just set (mixture will jiggle).
4. Remove dish from a larger pan to a wire rack; cool for 1 hour. Refrigerate overnight.
5. To unmold, run a knife around edges and invert onto a large rimmed serving platter. Cut into wedges or spoon onto dessert plates; spoon sauce over each serving.
NOTE: Pay close attention when melting sugar as it changes quickly. Be sure to find a pan for the water bath before starting to prepare the recipe.
1 SLICE: 346 cal., 16g fat (10g sat. fat), 155mg chol., 182mg sod., 41g carb. (40g sugars, 0 fiber), 10g pro.

CREAMY CARAMEL FLAN

LAVENDER PEACH GELATO

This sophisticated herbal gelato can be served as an appetizer, a palate-pleaser between courses or a dessert that tastes like heaven on a spoon.
—Christine Wendland, Browns Mills, NJ

PREP: 40 MIN. + FREEZING • **MAKES:** 3 CUPS

- 2 **cups 2% milk**
- 2 **Tbsp. cardamom pods, crushed**
- 1 **Tbsp. dried lavender flowers**
- 1 **vanilla bean**
- ¾ **cup sugar**
- 5 **large egg yolks, beaten**
- 2 **medium peaches, peeled and finely chopped**

1. In a large heavy saucepan, combine the milk, cardamom pods and lavender. Split vanilla bean and scrape seeds; add bean and seeds to milk mixture. Heat until bubbles form around sides of pan. Remove from the heat; cover and let steep for 10 minutes. Strain, discarding flowers and spices.
2. Return milk to the heat; stir in sugar. Cook until bubbles form around sides of pan. Whisk a small amount of hot mixture into the egg yolks. Return all to the pan, whisking constantly.
3. Cook and stir over low heat until mixture is thickened and coats the back of a spoon. Quickly transfer to a bowl; place in ice water and stir for 2 minutes. Press waxed paper onto surface of custard. Refrigerate for several hours or overnight.
4. Fill the cylinder of an ice cream freezer two-thirds full; freeze according to the manufacturer's directions. When gelato is frozen, stir in the peaches. Transfer to a freezer container; freeze for 2-4 hours before serving.
NOTE: Look for dried lavender flowers in spice shops. If using lavender from the garden, make sure it hasn't been treated with chemicals.
½ CUP: 206 cal., 5g fat (2g sat. fat), 177mg chol., 47mg sod., 35g carb. (32g sugars, 1g fiber), 5g pro.

TERI RASEY
Cadillac, MI

INDULGENT COCONUT RICE PUDDING

SLOW COOKER

INDULGENT COCONUT RICE PUDDING

This classic slow-cooked comfort dessert is a healthier option for your family that doesn't sacrifice flavor. If you can't find turbinado or raw sugar, you can use brown sugar, adjusting to ¾ cup. This can also be made in the oven.
—Teri Rasey, Cadillac, MI

PREP: 10 MIN. • **COOK:** 4 HOURS
MAKES: 12 SERVINGS

- **1 cup uncooked long grain rice**
- **5 cups coconut milk, divided**
- **2 Tbsp. coconut oil**
- **1 cup turbinado (washed raw) sugar**
- **1 cup dried cranberries**
- **2 tsp. vanilla extract**
- **1 tsp. ground cinnamon**
- **Dash salt**
- **Toasted sweetened shredded coconut and additional coconut milk, optional**

Place the rice in a 3- or 4-qt. slow cooker coated with cooking spray; pour in 4 cups coconut milk. Add coconut oil; distribute evenly over top. Add next five ingredients. Cook, covered, on low until rice is tender, 4-5 hours, adding enough of the remaining coconut milk to reach desired consistency. Let stand, uncovered, 10 minutes. Serve warm, with toasted coconut and additional coconut milk if desired.

½ CUP: 340 cal., 18g fat (17g sat. fat), 0 chol., 39mg sod., 43g carb. (28g sugars, 1g fiber), 3g pro.

RICH & CREAMY TIRAMISU

My version of the classic Tuscan trifle has both coffee and espresso for layer after layer of java goodness.
—Lauren Knoelke, Milwaukee, WI

PREP: 15 MIN. + STANDING
COOK: 10 MIN. + CHILLING
MAKES: 16 SERVINGS

- **2 cartons (8 oz. each) mascarpone cheese**
- **5 large egg yolks**
- **½ cup plus 2 Tbsp. sugar, divided**
- **⅓ cup plus 2 Tbsp. Marsala wine or liqueur, divided**
- **½ tsp. salt**
- **1 cup heavy whipping cream**
- **¾ cup strong brewed coffee, room temperature**
- **2 tsp. instant espresso powder**
- **1 pkg. (7 oz.) crisp ladyfinger cookies**
- **1 Tbsp. Dutch-processed cocoa**

1. Stir mascarpone cheese; let stand at room temperature 30 minutes. Whisk yolks, ½ cup sugar, ⅓ cup Marsala and salt in top of a double boiler until the mixture is thickened (ribbon stage) and a thermometer reads 160°. Remove from heat; whisk in mascarpone cheese until almost smooth. Whip cream and remaining sugar until soft peaks form; fold into the mascarpone mixture.

2. Combine coffee, espresso powder and remaining Marsala. Briefly dip eight of the ladyfingers into coffee mixture and place in the bottom of a 9-in. springform pan. Top with 1½ cups mascarpone mixture. Repeat two more times. Refrigerate, covered, 6 hours or overnight. To serve, loosen and remove rim; sprinkle with cocoa powder.

1 SERVING: 280 cal., 21g fat (11g sat. fat), 123mg chol., 115mg sod., 19g carb. (14g sugars, 0 fiber), 5g pro.

RICH & CREAMY TIRAMISU

PRESSURE COOKER BLACK & BLUE COBBLER

PRESSURE-COOKER BLACK & BLUE COBBLER

It never occurred to me that I could bake a cobbler in my pressure cooker until I saw a few similar recipes. I decided to give it a try with my own favorite fruity dessert recipe. It took a bit of experimenting, but the tasty results were "berry" well worth it.
—Martha Creveling, Orlando, FL

PREP: 15 MIN. • **COOK:** 15 MIN. + STANDING • **MAKES:** 6 SERVINGS

- **1 cup all-purpose flour**
- **1½ cups sugar, divided**
- **1 tsp. baking powder**
- **¼ tsp. salt**
- **¼ tsp. ground cinnamon**
- **¼ tsp. ground nutmeg**
- **2 large eggs, lightly beaten**
- **2 Tbsp. whole milk**
- **2 Tbsp. canola oil**
- **2 cups fresh or frozen blackberries**
- **2 cups fresh or frozen blueberries**
- **¾ cup water**
- **1 tsp. grated orange zest**
- **Whipped cream or vanilla ice cream, optional**

1. In an 8-qt. electric pressure cooker, add 1 cup of water.
2. In a large bowl, combine the flour, ¾ cup sugar, baking powder, salt, cinnamon and nutmeg. Combine the eggs, milk and oil; stir into dry ingredients just until moistened. Spread the batter evenly onto the bottom of a greased 1½-qt. baking dish.
3. In a large saucepan, combine the berries, water, orange zest and remaining sugar; bring to a boil. Remove from the heat; immediately pour over batter. Place a piece of aluminum foil loosely on top of dish to prevent moisture from getting inside; place on a trivet with handles; lower into pressure cooker. Lock lid; make sure vent is closed. Select manual setting; adjust pressure to high and set time for 15 minutes. When finished cooking, allow pressure to naturally release for 10 minutes, then quick-release any remaining pressure according to manufacturer's directions.
4. Uncover and let stand for 30 minutes before serving. Serve with whipped cream or ice cream if desired.
1 SERVING: 391 cal., 7g fat (1g sat. fat), 72mg chol., 190mg sod., 80g carb. (58g sugars, 4g fiber), 5g pro.

EAT SMART

PEACH CRISP PARFAIT POPS

My little ones love fruit crisps and Popsicles, so I created a healthy but fun treat that combines the two. For a sweet addition, use cinnamon sticks in place of the pop sticks.
—Carmell Childs, Clawson, UT

PREP: 15 MIN. + FREEZING • **MAKES:** 8 SERVINGS

- **2 cartons (5.3 oz. each) fat-free vanilla Greek yogurt**
- **2 tsp. brown sugar**
- **¼ tsp. ground cinnamon**
- **Pinch ground nutmeg**
- **1 cup granola without raisins**
- **8 freezer pop molds or paper cups (3 oz. each) and wooden pop sticks**
- **1 can (15 oz.) sliced peaches in extra-light syrup or juice, drained and chopped**

In a small bowl, combine yogurt, brown sugar, cinnamon and nutmeg; fold in granola. Divide half of yogurt mixture among molds or paper cups. Top with with half of peaches; repeat layers. Top molds with holders. If using cups, top with foil and insert sticks through foil. Freeze until firm.
1 POP: 167 cal., 3g fat (0 sat. fat), 0 chol., 40mg sod., 28g carb. (15g sugars, 5g fiber), 10g pro. Diabetic exchanges: 1½ starch, ½ fat-free milk.

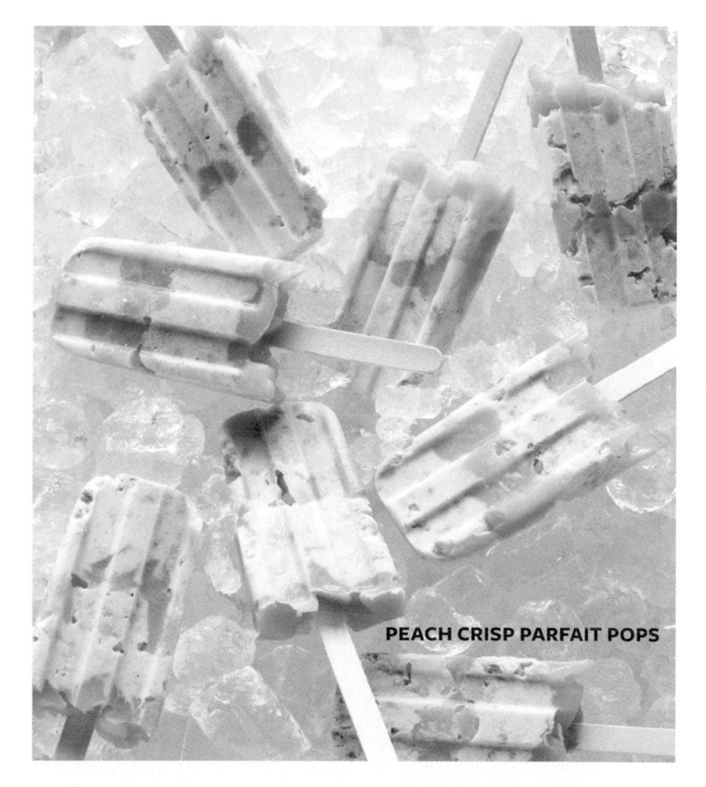
PEACH CRISP PARFAIT POPS

APPLE PANDOWDY

APPLE PANDOWDY

I adapted this fragrantly spiced pandowdy recipe from a very old cookbook. It's filled with fresh tart apples and topped with an irresistibly tender crust.
—Doreen Lindquist, Thompson, MB

PREP: 25 MIN. • **BAKE:** 55 MIN. • **MAKES:** 9 SERVINGS

- **1 cup packed brown sugar**
- **1¼ cups all-purpose flour, divided**
- **½ tsp. salt, divided**
- **1 cup water**
- **1 tsp. lemon juice**
- **2 tsp. baking powder**
- **5 Tbsp. butter, divided**
- **¾ cup whole milk**
- **5 cups sliced peeled apples**
- **½ tsp. plus ⅛ tsp. ground cinnamon, divided**
- **½ tsp. ground nutmeg**
- **1 tsp. vanilla extract**
- **1 Tbsp. coarse sugar**
- **Whipped cream, optional**

1. In a saucepan, combine brown sugar, ¼ cup flour and ¼ tsp. salt. Add water and lemon juice; cook and stir over medium heat until thick. Cover and set aside.
2. In a bowl, combine baking powder and remaining flour and salt. Cut in 3 Tbsp. butter. Add the milk and mix just until moistened (a few lumps will remain); set aside.
3. Arrange apples in a 1½-qt. baking dish; sprinkle with ½ tsp. cinnamon. Add nutmeg, vanilla and remaining butter to sauce; pour over apples. Drop dough by spoonfuls over sauce. Combine remaining cinnamon and coarse sugar; sprinkle over dough. Bake at 350° until top is brown and apples are tender, about 55 minutes. Serve warm, with whipped cream if desired.
1 SERVING: 260 cal., 7g fat (4g sat. fat), 20mg chol., 304mg sod., 47g carb. (33g sugars, 2g fiber), 3g pro.

FAST FIX

CANNOLI DIP

Ricotta is one of my family's favorite ingredients. I made up the cannoli filling, and I broke up some ice cream waffle shells to use as chips. It was an instant hit! It's also good served slightly warm.
—Ann Marie Eberhart, Gig Harbor, WA

TAKES: 10 MIN. • **MAKES:** 8 SERVINGS

- **1 carton (15 oz.) whole-milk ricotta cheese**
- **¾ cup confectioners' sugar**
- **1 Tbsp. finely chopped candied citron**
- **1 Tbsp. grated lime zest**
- **2 Tbsp. lime juice**
- **Mini ice cream sugar cones, optional**
- **Miniature semisweet chocolate chips, optional**

Beat together ricotta cheese, sugar, candied citron, lime zest and juice. If desired, scoop ricotta mixture into cones and sprinkle with chocolate chips.
NOTE: Do not use a food processor to chop the citron. Doing so could result in an ultra-fine texture, adversely affecting the overall flavor of this recipe.
¼ CUP: 128 cal., 5g fat (3g sat. fat), 21mg chol., 70mg sod., 16g carb. (15g sugars, 0 fiber), 6g pro.

CANNOLI DIP

CARAMEL CASHEW CHEESECAKE

A friend served this luscious cheesecake at a birthday party, and I made sure I left with the recipe. Every time I make it, rave reviews and recipe requests come my way, too.
—Pat Price, Bucyrus, OH

PREP: 30 MIN. • **BAKE:** 65 MIN. + CHILLING
MAKES: 16 SERVINGS

- **¼ cup cold butter**
- **½ cup all-purpose flour**
- **¾ cup chopped unsalted cashews, toasted**
- **2 Tbsp. confectioners' sugar**
- **⅛ tsp. salt**

FILLING

- **4 pkg. (8 oz. each) cream cheese, softened**
- **1¼ cups sugar**
- **1 Tbsp. vanilla extract**
- **5 large eggs**
- **2 Tbsp. heavy whipping cream**

TOPPING

- **1 cup sugar**
- **3 Tbsp. water**
- **¾ cup heavy whipping cream**
- **1 cup unsalted cashews, toasted**

CARAMEL CASHEW CHEESECAKE

1. Preheat oven to 350°. Place a greased 9-in. springform pan on a double thickness of heavy-duty foil (about 18 in. square). Wrap foil securely around pan. Place on a baking sheet.
2. In a small bowl, cut butter into flour until mixture resembles coarse crumbs. Stir in cashews, confectioners' sugar and salt. Press onto the bottom and ½ in. up the sides of prepared pan. Bake 15 minutes. Cool on a wire rack. Reduce heat to 325°.
3. In a large bowl, beat cream cheese, sugar and vanilla until smooth. Add eggs and cream; beat on low speed just until combined. Pour over crust. Place the springform pan in a larger baking pan; add 1 in. hot water to larger pan.
4. Bake until the center is just set and top appears dull, 65-75 minutes. Remove springform pan from water bath. Cool on a wire rack 10 minutes. Carefully run a knife around edge of pan to loosen. Cool 1 hour longer. Refrigerate overnight, covering when completely cooled.
5. Before serving cheesecake, combine sugar and water in saucepan. Cook over medium-low heat until sugar is dissolved. Bring to a boil over medium-high heat; cover and boil 2 minutes. Uncover; boil until mixture is golden brown and a candy thermometer reads 300° (hard-crack stage), about 8 minutes.
6. Remove from heat. Stir in cream until smooth, about 5 minutes (mixture will appear lumpy at first). Add cashews; cool to lukewarm.
7. Remove cheesecake to a serving platter. Spoon cooled caramel over cheesecake. Refrigerate leftovers.

1 SLICE: 507 cal., 36g fat (18g sat. fat), 138mg chol., 248mg sod., 41g carb. (33g sugars, 1g fiber), 9g pro.

SLOW COOKER

BUTTERSCOTCH-PECAN DELIGHT

Comfort-food fans will absolutely adore this treat. Topping it with a luscious drizzle of butterscotch makes it irresistible.
—Lisa Varner, El Paso, TX

PREP: 15 MIN. • **COOK:** 3 HOURS
MAKES: 8 SERVINGS

- **9 cups cubed day-old white bread (about 8 slices)**
- **½ cup chopped pecans**
- **½ cup butterscotch chips**
- **4 large eggs**
- **2 cups half-and-half cream**
- **½ cup packed brown sugar**
- **½ cup butter, melted**
- **1 tsp. vanilla extract**
- **Whipped cream and butterscotch ice cream topping**

1. Place bread, pecans and butterscotch chips in a greased 4-qt. slow cooker. In a large bowl, whisk eggs, cream, brown sugar, melted butter and vanilla until blended. Pour over bread mixture; stir mixture gently to combine.
2. Cook, covered, on low until a knife inserted in the center comes out clean, 3-4 hours. Serve warm with whipped cream and butterscotch topping.

1 SERVING: 502 cal., 30g fat (16g sat. fat), 154mg chol., 384mg sod., 47g carb. (26g sugars, 2g fiber), 10g pro.

HOW TO MAKE
LEMON CURD

Slathered on biscuits, drizzled over cake or dolloped onto yogurt, lemon curd makes every bite happier, brighter and better. This guide helps you get it right every time.

HOMEMADE LEMON CURD

Get Real

Always use fresh lemon juice for lemon curd, not the bottled kind. The results are much tastier.

Pick Your Citrus

You don't need to limit yourself to lemons! This curd recipe will work with limes, grapefruit, or even oranges (though you may need to add in a little lemon to brighten up and enhance the orange flavor). If you're feeling fancy, blood oranges create a lovely rose-colored curd.

Make It Last

Lemon curd can be made up to 7 days in advance. Cover the surface with plastic wrap so a skin does not form on top, and then store it in the refrigerator. To freeze curd, place it in a plastic zip-top bag and store in the freezer for up to 2 months. Thaw it in the fridge overnight, and use it within a week.

5 INGREDIENTS

HOMEMADE LEMON CURD

Lemon curd is a scrumptious spread for scones, biscuits or other baked goods. You can find it in larger grocery stores alongside the jams and jellies or with the baking supplies, but I like making it from scratch.
—Mark Hagen, Milwaukee, WI

PREP: 20 MIN. + CHILLING • **MAKES:** 1⅔ CUPS

- **3 large eggs**
- **1 cup sugar**
- **½ cup lemon juice (about 2 lemons)**
- **¼ cup butter, cubed**
- **1 Tbsp. grated lemon zest**

In a small heavy saucepan over medium heat, whisk eggs, sugar and lemon juice until blended. Add butter and lemon zest; cook, whisking constantly, until mixture is thickened and coats the back of a metal spoon. Transfer to a small bowl; cool 10 minutes. Refrigerate, covered, until cold.

2 TBSP.: 110 cal., 5g fat (3g sat. fat), 52mg chol., 45mg sod., 16g carb. (16g sugars, 0 fiber), 2g pro.

LIME CURD: Substitute lime juice and zest for lemon juice and zest. Proceed as directed.

SUCCESS TIPS

- Don't use aluminum or unlined copper pans or spoons when making curd. They could react with the acid in the lemons, discoloring the curd and leaving a metallic aftertaste.
- To know when the curd is ready, coat the back of a spoon and run your finger through it; if it leaves a path, the curd is ready. It will thicken slightly as it cools.

FILL pastry shells for tiny tarts and top with powdered sugar.

Ways to Love It

Refreshing lemon curd is delicious on its own, but that's not the only way to enjoy this tangy treat.

Add a dollop as filling for sandwich cookies.

Slather between layers of white or yellow cake rounds.

Swirl into cheesecake with a knife before baking.

Layer with ice cream for a sweet and tart parfait.

CHICKEN PAPRIKASH, PAGE 230

POTLUCK PLEASERS

Crowd-sized cooking just got simpler with these easy, impressive (and tasty!) recipes. Discover spatchcocked turkey, celebration tamales, make-and-take dishes that folks will love, and more in this unique chapter.

BBQ CHICKEN & APPLE BREAD PUDDING

FAST FIX

FRUIT CHARCUTERIE BOARD

Who says cheese and sausage get to have all the fun? Make this a party go-to.
—Taste of Home *Test Kitchen*

TAKES: 25 MIN.
MAKES: 14 SERVINGS

- 10 fresh strawberries, halved
- 8 fresh or dried figs, halved
- 2 small navel oranges, thinly sliced
- 12 oz. seedless red grapes, about 1½ cups
- 1 medium mango, halved and scored
- ½ cup fresh blueberries
- 1 cup fresh blackberries
- ½ cup dried banana chips
- 2 large kiwifruit, peeled, halved, and thinly sliced
- 12 oz. seedless watermelon, about six slices
- ½ cup unblanched almonds
- 8 oz. Brie cheese
- 8 oz. mascarpone cheese
- ½ cup honey

On a large platter or cutting board, arrange the fruit, almonds, cheeses and honey. If desired, drizzle some of the honey over the mascarpone for serving.

1 SERVING: 304 cal., 17g fat (8g sat. fat), 36mg chol., 116mg sod., 36g carb. (30g sugars, 4g fiber), 7g pro.

FRUIT CHARCUTERIE BOARD

BBQ CHICKEN & APPLE BREAD PUDDING

To me, bread pudding is the epitome of comfort food, and it's simply too good to reserve only for dessert. This sweet and savory twist on the classic is a delicious new way to enjoy an old favorite.
—Shauna Havey, Roy, UT

PREP: 45 MIN. + COOLING • **BAKE:** 35 MIN.
MAKES: 8 SERVINGS

- 1 pkg. (8½ oz.) cornbread/muffin mix
- 6 Tbsp. butter, divided
- 1 large sweet onion, thinly sliced
- ⅔ cup barbecue sauce, divided
- 2 cups diced cooked chicken
- 2 large eggs, beaten
- 1 cup half-and-half cream
- 1 tsp. salt
- ½ tsp. pepper
- 1¼ cups shredded Monterey Jack cheese
- 1 small green apple, peeled and diced
- Minced chives

1. Prepare cornbread according to package directions and bake using a greased and floured 8-in. square baking pan. Cool. Reduce oven setting to 375°. Meanwhile, in a small skillet, heat 2 Tbsp. butter over medium heat. Add onion; cook and stir until softened. Reduce heat to medium-low; cook until deep golden brown and caramelized, 30-40 minutes. Remove from heat and set aside.

2. Pour ¼ cup barbecue sauce over chicken; toss to coat.

3. Cube cornbread. Microwave remaining butter, covered, on high until melted, about 30 seconds. Whisk in eggs, cream, salt and pepper. Add caramelized onions. Pour egg mixture over cornbread cubes. Add chicken, cheese and apple. Toss gently to combine.

4. Pour mixture into a greased 8-in. square or 1½-qt. baking dish; bake until bubbly and top is golden brown, about 35 minutes. Drizzle remaining barbecue sauce over bread pudding. Sprinkle with chives.

1 SERVING: 465 cal., 25g fat (13g sat. fat), 156mg chol., 1028mg sod., 37g carb. (19g sugars, 3g fiber), 21g pro.

PICKLED PEPPERONCINI DEVILED EGGS

EAT SMART FAST FIX

PICKLED PEPPERONCINI DEVILED EGGS

It's hard to resist these adorable deviled trees on our buffet table. The avocado filling has pepperoncini and cilantro for extra zip.
—Carmell Childs, Clawson, UT

TAKES: 30 MIN. • **MAKES:** 1 DOZEN

- **6 hard-boiled large eggs**
- **1 jar (16 oz.) garlic and dill pepperoncini**
- **1 medium ripe avocado, peeled and pitted**
- **1 Tbsp. minced fresh cilantro, divided**
- **¼ tsp. salt**
- **⅛ tsp. pepper**
- **1 Tbsp. minced sweet red pepper**
- **¼ tsp. chili powder**

1. Cut eggs lengthwise in half. Remove yolks, reserving whites. Mash yolks. Stir in 1 tsp. minced garlic from the pepperoncini jar and 2 tsp. pepperoncini juice. Add 3 Tbsp. minced pepperoncini and the whole avocado; mash with a fork until smooth. Stir in 2 tsp. cilantro, salt and pepper.
2. Cut a small hole in the tip of a pastry bag; insert a medium star tip. Transfer avocado mixture to bag. Pipe into egg whites, swirling it upward to resemble Christmas trees. Sprinkle trees with minced red pepper, chili powder and remaining cilantro.
3. Cut open and seed one larger pepperoncini; slice into 12 small diamond shapes to top Christmas trees. Refrigerate, covered, until serving. Save remaining pepperoncini for another use.
1 STUFFED EGG HALF: 59 cal., 4g fat (1g sat. fat), 93mg chol., 125mg sod., 1g carb. (0 sugars, 1g fiber), 3g pro.

EAT SMART

APRICOT CRAB STUFFED ACORN SQUASH

This light squash recipe is quick, simple and bursting with rich flavors. It looks so elegant when served on a lovely platter.
—Judy Armstrong, Prairieville, LA

PREP: 20 MIN. • **BAKE:** 35 MIN. • **MAKES:** 8 SERVINGS

- **2 large acorn squash, quartered and seeds removed**
- **½ cup apricot nectar, divided**
- **1 tsp. salt, divided**
- **1 tsp. white pepper, divided**
- **1 tsp. butter**
- **1 tsp. olive oil**
- **4 green onions, thinly sliced, plus additional for garnish**
- **⅓ cup dried apricots, chopped**
- **1 garlic clove, minced**
- **½ cup half-and-half cream**
- **4 cans (6 oz. each) lump crabmeat, drained**

1. Preheat the oven to 375°. Place squash in a greased 13x9-in. baking pan; add ¼ cup apricot nectar. Sprinkle with ½ tsp. each salt and white pepper. Bake, covered, until fork-tender, 35-40 minutes.
2. Meanwhile, in a large skillet, heat butter and oil over medium-high heat. Add green onions; cook and stir 3-5 minutes or until tender. Add apricots and garlic; cook 1 minute longer. Stir in half-and-half and the remaining apricot nectar, salt and white pepper. Bring to a boil; reduce heat. Simmer for 5 minutes. Gently stir in crab; heat through.
3. Arrange squash on a serving dish; spoon crab mixture over top. Sprinkle with additional green onions.
1 SERVING: 217 cal., 3g fat (2g sat. fat), 91mg chol., 794mg sod., 31g carb. (11g sugars, 4g fiber), 18g pro. **Diabetic exchanges:** 2 starch, 2 lean meat, ½ fat.

JUDY ARMSTRONG
Prairieville, LA

APRICOT CRAB STUFFED ACORN SQUASH

GOLDEN BUTTERNUT SQUASH LASAGNA

GOLDEN BUTTERNUT SQUASH LASAGNA

My rich, saucy lasagna features winter squash at its finest. Whipped cream topping adds a unique twist to this meatless casserole packed with roasted butternut squash, two kinds of cheese and a host of seasonings. Allow the lasagna to stand 10 to 15 minutes before serving for ease in cutting.
—Lisa Sheets, Carmel, IN

PREP: 55 MIN. • **BAKE:** 40 MIN. + STANDING • **MAKES:** 12 SERVINGS

- **1 medium butternut squash (3 lbs.), peeled, seeded and cut into ½-in. cubes**
- **3 Tbsp. canola oil**
- **9 lasagna noodles**
- **3½ cups 2% milk**
- **¼ cup chopped fresh rosemary**
- **2 Tbsp. butter**
- **3 garlic cloves, minced**
- **2 Tbsp. all-purpose flour**
- **1 tsp. salt**
- **¼ tsp. pepper**
- **8 oz. fontina cheese, thinly sliced**
- **1½ cups grated Parmesan cheese, divided**
- **½ cup heavy whipping cream**

1. Preheat oven to 425°. Divide squash between two greased 15x10x1-in. baking pans. Drizzle with oil; toss to coat. Bake, uncovered, stirring occasionally, until tender, 20-25 minutes.
2. Meanwhile, cook noodles according to package directions. In a small saucepan, combine milk and rosemary. Bring to a boil. Reduce heat; simmer, uncovered, for 10 minutes. Strain, reserving milk, and set aside. Discard rosemary.
3. In a Dutch oven, heat butter over medium heat. Add garlic; saute 1 minute. Stir in flour, salt and pepper until blended. Gradually add milk. Bring to a boil. Cook and stir until slightly thickened, about 2 minutes. Reserve 1 cup sauce; stir squash into remaining sauce.
4. Reduce oven setting to 375°. Drain noodles. Spread reserved sauce into a greased 13x9-in. baking dish. Layer with three noodles, half of squash mixture, half of fontina cheese and ½ cup Parmesan cheese. Repeat layers. Top with remaining noodles. Beat cream until soft peaks form. Spread over top. Sprinkle with remaining Parmesan cheese.
5. Bake, covered, for 30 minutes. Uncover; bake until bubbly and golden brown, 10-15 minutes longer. Let stand for 15 minutes before cutting.

1 PIECE: 353 cal., 20g fat (10g sat. fat), 55mg chol., 559mg sod., 31g carb. (7g sugars, 4g fiber), 15g pro.

CHICKEN PAPRIKASH

(SHOWN ON PAGE 226)

Some recipes for chicken paprikash include vegetables like celery and bell peppers, but not my Grandmother Alta's. Hers was a simple combination of chicken, onions, garlic, paprika and sour cream.
—Lily Julow, Lawrenceville, GA

PREP: 20 MIN. • **COOK:** 45 MIN. • **MAKES:** 12 SERVINGS

- **2 broiler/fryer chickens (about 3½ to 4 lbs. each), cut into 8 pieces each**
- **2 tsp. kosher salt**
- **1 tsp. pepper**
- **2 Tbsp. peanut oil or canola oil**
- **2 medium onions, halved and sliced**
- **2 large garlic cloves, chopped**
- **3 Tbsp. all-purpose flour**
- **1 Tbsp. sweet Hungarian paprika**
- **2 cups hot chicken broth or water**
- **1 cup sour cream**
- **Minced fresh parsley and additional sweet Hungarian paprika, optional**
- **Hot cooked noodles or mashed potatoes, optional**

1. Season chicken with kosher salt and pepper. In a Dutch oven, heat peanut oil over medium-high heat. Brown chicken in batches. Remove with a slotted spoon; drain and keep warm.
2. Reduce heat to medium-low. Add onions; cook, stirring to loosen browned bits from pan, until onions begin to soften, 6-8 minutes. Add garlic; cook 1 minute longer.
3. Stir in flour and paprika; reduce heat to low. Cook until paprika is fragrant, 3-5 minutes. Add broth; cook, stirring constantly, until smooth, 6-8 minutes. Return chicken to pan; simmer, covered, until a thermometer inserted into deepest part of thigh reads 170°, about 30 minutes. Transfer chicken to a serving platter.
4. Skim fat. Stir in sour cream; heat just until warmed through, 3-5 minutes (do not allow to boil). If desired, sprinkle with parsley and additional paprika. Serve with hot cooked noodles or mashed potatoes if desired.

1 SERVING: 422 cal., 26g fat (8g sat. fat), 127mg chol., 596mg sod., 5g carb. (2g sugars, 1g fiber), 40g pro.

SLOW COOKER

MY BRAZILIAN FEIJOADA

A co-worker's mom used to make this dish for him, and it was his favorite. So I made him my own version. Instead of sausage you can use ham hocks, or substitute lean white meat for the red meat if you prefer.
—Christiane Counts, Webster, TX

PREP: 20 MIN. + SOAKING • **COOK:** 7 HOURS
MAKES: 10 SERVINGS

- **8 oz. dried black beans (about 1 cup)**
- **2 lbs. boneless pork shoulder butt roast, trimmed and cut into 1-in. cubes**
- **3 bone-in beef short ribs (about 1½ lbs.)**
- **4 bacon strips, cooked and crumbled**
- **1¼ cups diced onion**
- **3 garlic cloves, minced**
- **1 bay leaf**
- **¾ tsp. salt**
- **¾ tsp. pepper**
- **1½ cups chicken broth**
- **1 cup water**
- **½ cup beef broth**
- **8 oz. smoked sausage, cut into ½-in. slices**
- **Orange sections**
- **Hot cooked rice, optional**

1. Rinse and sort beans; soak according to package directions. Meanwhile, place pork roast, short ribs and bacon in a 6-qt. slow cooker. Add onion, garlic, bay leaf and seasonings; pour chicken broth, water and beef broth over meat. Cook, covered, on high 2 hours.
2. Stir in beans and sausage. Cook, covered, on low until meat and beans are tender, 5-6 hours. Discard bay leaf. Remove short ribs. When cool enough to handle, remove meat from bones and discard bones. Shred rib meat with two forks; return to slow cooker. Top servings with orange sections. If desired, serve with hot cooked rice.
1 SERVING: 481 cal., 27g fat (11g sat. fat), 123mg chol., 772mg sod., 17g carb. (2g sugars, 4g fiber), 41g pro.

MY BRAZILIAN FEIJOADA

EAT SMART

VIBRANT BLACK-EYED PEA SALAD

My black-eyed pea salad reminds me of a southern cooking class my husband and I took while visiting Savannah, Georgia. People go nuts for it at picnics and potlucks.
—Danielle Lee, Sewickley, PA

PREP: 25 MIN. + CHILLING
MAKES: 10 SERVINGS

- **2 cans (15½ oz. each) black-eyed peas, rinsed and drained**
- **2 cups grape tomatoes, halved**
- **1 each small green, yellow and red peppers, finely chopped**
- **1 small red onion, chopped**
- **1 celery rib, chopped**
- **2 Tbsp. minced fresh basil**

DRESSING

- **¼ cup red wine vinegar or balsamic vinegar**
- **1 Tbsp. stone-ground mustard**
- **1 tsp. minced fresh oregano or ¼ tsp. dried oregano**
- **¾ tsp. salt**
- **½ tsp. freshly ground pepper**
- **¼ cup olive oil**

1. In a large bowl, combine peas, tomatoes, peppers, onion, celery and basil.
2. For dressing, in a small bowl, whisk the vinegar, mustard, oregano, salt and pepper. Gradually whisk in the oil until blended. Drizzle over salad; toss to coat. Refrigerate, covered, at least 3 hours before serving.
¾ CUP: 130 cal., 6g fat (1g sat. fat), 0 chol., 319mg sod., 15g carb. (3g sugars, 3g fiber), 5g pro. **Diabetic exchanges:** 1 starch, 1 fat.

HAM IT UP

Sit down and give thanks for a heaping platter of this classic holiday favorite. Say a little prayer for leftovers and heavenly ham sandwiches.

BAKED HAM WITH CHERRY SAUCE

BAKED HAM WITH CHERRY SAUCE

There's nothing I'd rather serve for Easter dinner or another springtime occasion than succulent baked ham. My recipe features a rub that adds flavor to the meat plus a delicious cherry sauce with a hint of almond.
—Lavonn Bormuth, Westerville, OH

PREP: 10 MIN. • **BAKE:** 1¾ HOURS
MAKES: 12 SERVINGS

- 1 **fully cooked bone-in ham (6 to 8 lbs.)**
- 1 **cup packed brown sugar**
- 3 **Tbsp. maple syrup**
- 1 **tsp. ground mustard**
- 3 **Tbsp. cornstarch**
- ½ **cup sugar**
- 1 **cup cold water**
- 1 **can (15 oz.) pitted dark sweet cherries, undrained**
- 2 **Tbsp. lemon juice**
- 1 **tsp. almond extract**

1. Preheat oven to 325°. Place ham on a rack in a roasting pan. Using a sharp knife, score surface of ham with ¼-in.-deep cuts in a diamond pattern. Mix brown sugar, syrup and mustard; rub over ham and press into cuts. Bake, covered, until a thermometer reads 140°, 1¾-2 hours.

2. In a small saucepan, mix cornstarch, sugar and water until smooth. Add the cherries; bring to a boil. Cook and stir until thickened, 1-2 minutes. Remove from heat; stir in lemon juice and extract. Serve warm with ham.

1 SERVING: 339 cal., 6g fat (2g sat. fat), 100mg chol., 1198mg sod., 38g carb. (35g sugars, 1g fiber), 34g pro.

HOW-TO

Carve Perfect Ham Slices

Carving a ham is easy! You're just four steps away from beautiful slices that are worthy of your best Easter serving platter.

- Begin by cutting off the cushion (boneless) portion of the meat.
- Holding the cushion portion steady with a meat fork, cut it into even slices from the top down.
- Cut the remaining (bone-in) portion of the ham horizontally above the bone.
- Carve into even vertical slices. Save the remaining bone-in slab for soup.

SLOW-COOKER SHORT RIB RAGU OVER PAPPARDELLE

SLOW COOKER

SLOW-COOKER SHORT RIB RAGU OVER PAPPARDELLE

An irresistible sauce gives this beef another dimension of flavor. Nearly any starchy side, such as potatoes or polenta, will work in place of the pasta. Short ribs are my crowd-pleaser weekend meal for all occasions.
—Missy Raho, Morristown, NJ

PREP: 30 MIN. • **COOK:** 7 HOURS • **MAKES:** 12 SERVINGS

- **1 Tbsp. olive oil**
- **2 lbs. boneless beef short ribs, cut into 2-in. pieces**
- **8 oz. sliced mushrooms**
- **1 small onion, chopped**
- **2 small carrots, peeled and chopped**
- **2 bay leaves**
- **1 can (12 oz.) tomato paste**
- **½ cup dry red wine**
- **3 garlic cloves, minced**
- **1 Tbsp. Italian seasoning**
- **1 tsp. crushed red pepper flakes**
- **½ tsp. salt**
- **½ tsp. pepper**
- **1 can (28 oz.) diced tomatoes**
- **1 lb. pappardelle**
- **Parmesan cheese, grated or shaved, optional**

1. In a large skillet, heat oil over medium-high heat; brown meat in batches. Transfer meat to a 5- or 6-qt. slow cooker. Add the mushrooms, onion, carrots and bay leaves.
2. In the same skillet, add tomato paste, wine, garlic and the seasonings. Cook and stir over medium heat until fragrant and slightly darkened, 2-4 minutes. Stir in diced tomatoes until blended. Transfer mixture to slow cooker; cover. Cook on low until beef is tender, 7-9 hours. Discard bay leaves.
3. Cook pasta according to package directions for al dente. Serve ragu over pasta. If desired, serve with Parmesan cheese.
¾ CUP RAGU OVER ¾ CUP PASTA: 302 cal., 8g fat (3g sat. fat), 31mg chol., 328mg sod., 39g carb. (7g sugars, 4g fiber), 18g pro.

CHILI COTTAGE PIE

This satisfying cottage pie is super simple and loaded with flavor. The kids love to help layer it up.
—Jacob Miller, Ledyard, CT

PREP: 25 MIN. • **BAKE:** 15 MIN. • **MAKES:** 8 SERVINGS

- **1 lb. ground beef**
- **¼ tsp. salt**
- **¼ tsp. pepper**
- **1 Tbsp. olive oil**
- **1 medium red onion, diced**
- **6 garlic cloves, minced**
- **1 pkg. (16 oz.) frozen mixed vegetables**
- **1 can (16 oz.) kidney beans, rinsed and drained**
- **1 can (14½ oz.) diced tomatoes**
- **1 cup beef stock**
- **1 envelope chili seasoning mix**
- **1 pkg. (24 oz.) refrigerated mashed potatoes**
- **1 cup shredded cheddar-Monterey Jack cheese**
- **4 green onions, thinly sliced**
- **Grated Parmesan cheese**

1. Preheat oven to 350°. In a large skillet, cook and crumble the beef, salt and pepper until beef is no longer pink. Drain beef; remove from skillet.
2. In same skillet, heat oil over medium heat. Add onion; cook and stir until tender, 2-3 minutes. Add garlic; cook 1 minute longer.
3. Add beef, mixed vegetables, kidney beans, tomatoes, beef stock and chili seasoning; bring to a boil. Cook and stir until thickened, about 5 minutes. Transfer to a greased 13x9-in. baking dish. Heat mashed potatoes according to microwave package directions; spread over top of beef mixture.
4. Sprinkle with cheese; bake until bubbly and cheese is melted, 15-20 minutes. Cool for 5 minutes; sprinkle with green onions and Parmesan cheese.
1 SERVING: 390 cal., 16g fat (8g sat. fat), 58mg chol., 992mg sod., 33g carb. (7g sugars, 7g fiber), 21g pro.

CHILI COTTAGE PIE

SAUSAGE-RICE PHYLLO CASSEROLE

SAUSAGE-RICE PHYLLO CASSEROLE

I created this recipe to use ingredients I had stocked in my kitchen. You can mix up the herbs and spices to fit any taste. Add rosemary or cayenne to give it a little more kick.
—Jenn Tidwell, Fair Oaks, CA

PREP: 1 HOUR • **BAKE:** 35 MIN. • **MAKES:** 8 SERVINGS

- **1 lb. bulk Italian sausage**
- **2 garlic cloves, minced**
- **1 tsp. dried basil**
- **1 tsp. dried oregano**
- **⅓ cup chardonnay or chicken broth**
- **6 medium tomatoes, peeled and crushed**
- **1 medium carrot, peeled and grated**
- **4½ tsp. tomato paste**
- **1 bay leaf**
- **½ tsp. salt**
- **¼ tsp. garlic powder**
- **¼ tsp. paprika**
- **1½ cups frozen peas**
- **3 cups cooked rice**
- **2 green onions, sliced**
- **1 Tbsp. minced fresh parsley**
- **1½ cups grated Parmesan cheese**
- **¾ cup grated Romano cheese**
- **10 sheets phyllo dough (14x9-in. size)**
- **¼ cup olive oil**

1. In a 6-qt. stockpot, cook sausage over medium heat until no longer pink, 6-8 minutes, breaking into crumbles. Remove with a slotted spoon; drain on paper towels. Add the garlic, basil and oregano to skillet; cook and stir 30 seconds. Add chardonnay, stirring to loosen browned bits from pan. Cook until liquid is almost evaporated, 1-2 minutes.
2. Stir in tomatoes, carrot, tomato paste, bay leaf, salt, garlic powder, paprika and sausage. Bring to a boil. Reduce heat; simmer, covered, 20 minutes. Cool. Discard bay leaf.
3. Preheat oven to 350°. Stir peas into sausage mixture. In a small bowl, combine rice, green onions and parsley. In a greased 13x9-in. baking dish, layer half of the rice mixture, ½ cup Parmesan cheese, ¼ cup Romano cheese, sausage mixture, ½ cup Parmesan cheese and ¼ cup Romano cheese. Top with remaining rice and cheeses.
4. Unroll phyllo dough. Layer five sheets of phyllo on top of filling, brushing each with oil. Brush remaining five phyllo sheets with oil, crumple gently and place on top of casserole.
5. Bake until golden and crisp, 35-40 minutes. Let stand 5 minutes before serving.

1 PIECE: 451 cal., 21g fat (8g sat. fat), 46mg chol., 1085mg sod., 45g carb. (6g sugars, 4g fiber), 22g pro.

NOTE: Recipe may be made a day in advance. After assembling casserole, cover and refrigerate. Remove from the refrigerator 30 minutes before baking. Bake as directed.

EAT SMART SLOW COOKER

COUNTRY FRENCH PORK WITH DRIED PLUMS AND APPLES

The classic flavors of herbes de Provence, apples and dried plums make this easy slow-cooked pork taste like a hearty meal at a French country cafe. For a traditional pairing, serve the pork with braised lentils.
—Suzanne Banfield, Basking Ridge, NJ

PREP: 20 MIN. • **COOK:** 4 HOURS + STANDING • **MAKES:** 10 SERVINGS

- **2 Tbsp. all-purpose flour**
- **1 Tbsp. herbes de Provence**
- **1½ tsp. salt**
- **¾ tsp. pepper**
- **1 boneless pork loin roast (3 to 4 lbs.)**
- **2 Tbsp. olive oil**
- **2 medium onions, halved and thinly sliced**
- **1 cup apple cider or unsweetened apple juice**
- **1 cup beef stock**
- **2 bay leaves**
- **2 large tart apples, peeled, cored and chopped**
- **1 cup pitted dried plums**

1. Mix flour, herbes de Provence, salt and pepper; rub over pork. In a large skillet, heat oil over medium-high heat. Brown roast on all sides. Place roast in a 5- or 6-qt. slow cooker. Add onions, apple cider, beef stock and bay leaves.
2. Cook, covered, on low 3 hours. Add apples and dried plums. Cook, covered, on low 1-1½ hours longer or until apples and pork are tender. Remove roast, onions, apples and plums to a serving platter, discarding bay leaves; tent with foil. Let stand 15 minutes before slicing.

4 OZ. COOKED PORK WITH ¾ CUP FRUIT MIXTURE: 286 cal., 9g fat (3g sat. fat), 68mg chol., 449mg sod., 22g carb. (13g sugars, 2g fiber), 28g pro.

SUZANNE BANFIELD
Basking Ridge, NJ

COUNTRY FRENCH PORK WITH DRIED PLUMS AND APPLES

CHICKEN TAMALES

I love to make tamales. They're time-consuming but worth the effort. I usually make them for Christmas, but my family requests them more often, so I freeze a big batch.
—Cindy Pruitt, Grove, OK

PREP: 2½ HOURS + SOAKING • **COOK:** 50 MIN.
MAKES: 20 TAMALES

- **24 dried corn husks**
- **1 broiler/fryer chicken (3 to 4 lbs.), cut up**
- **1 medium onion, quartered**
- **2 tsp. salt**
- **1 garlic clove, crushed**
- **3 qt. water**

DOUGH

- **1 cup shortening**
- **3 cups masa harina**

FILLING

- **6 Tbsp. canola oil**
- **6 Tbsp. all-purpose flour**
- **¾ cup chili powder**
- **½ tsp. salt**
- **¼ tsp. garlic powder**
- **¼ tsp. pepper**
- **2 cans (2¼ oz. each) sliced ripe olives, drained**
- **Hot water**

1. Cover corn husks with cold water; soak until softened, at least 2 hours.

2. Place chicken, onion, salt and garlic in a 6-qt. stockpot. Pour in 3 qt. water; bring to a boil. Reduce heat; simmer, covered, until chicken is tender, 45-60 minutes. Remove chicken from broth. When cool enough to handle, remove bones and skin; discard. Shred chicken. Strain cooking juices; skim fat. Reserve 6 cups stock.

3. For dough, beat shortening until light and fluffy, about 1 minute. Beat in small amounts of masa harina alternately with small amounts of reserved stock, using no more than 2 cups stock. Drop a small amount of dough into a cup of cold water; dough should float. If it doesn't, continue beating, rechecking every 1-2 minutes.

4. For filling, heat oil in a Dutch oven; stir in flour until blended. Cook and stir over medium heat until lightly browned, 7-9 minutes. Stir in seasonings, chicken and remaining stock; bring to a boil. Reduce heat; simmer, uncovered, stirring occasionally, until thickened, about 45 minutes.

5. Drain corn husks and pat dry; tear four husks to make 20 strips for tying tamales. (To prevent husks from drying out, cover with a damp towel until ready to use.) On wide end of each remaining husk, spread 3 Tbsp. dough to within ½ in. of side edges; top each with 2 Tbsp. chicken filling and 2 tsp. olives. Fold long sides of husk over filling, overlapping slightly. Fold over narrow end of husk; tie with a strip of husk to secure.

6. Place a steamer basket in the stockpot over water; place tamales upright in steamer. Bring to a boil; steam, covered, adding water as needed, until dough peels away from husk, about 45 minutes.

NOTE: Look for dried corn husks and masa harina in the international foods aisle.

2 TAMALES: 564 cal., 35g fat (7g sat. fat), 44mg chol., 835mg sod., 43g carb. (2g sugars, 7g fiber), 20g pro.

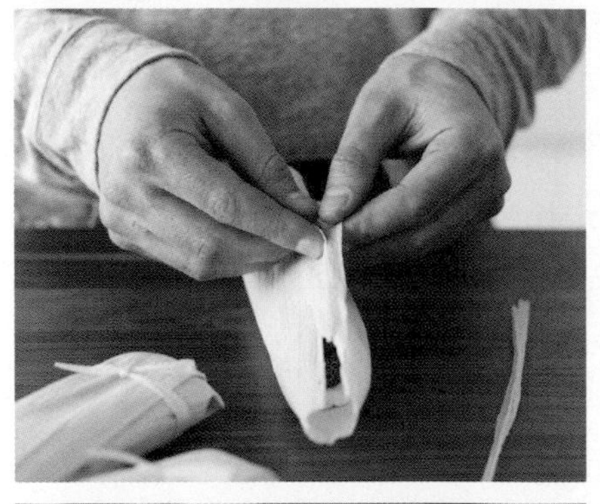

MORE FILLINGS TO CUSTOMIZE YOUR TAMALES

SLOW COOKER

BEEF BRISKET TAMALE FILLING

You'll get a hint of smoky flavor from the bit of bacon in this recipe.
—Ruth Weatherford, Huntington Beach, CA

MAKES: ABOUT 4 CUPS

- 2 **lbs. fresh beef brisket**
- 1 **cup chopped onion**
- 3 **bacon strips, diced**
- 1 **can (8 oz.) tomato sauce**
- ¾ **tsp. pepper**
- ¼ **tsp. salt**

Place brisket in a 5-qt. slow cooker; top with onion and bacon. Add the remaining ingredients. Cook, covered, on low for 4½-5 hours or until meat is tender. When cool enough to handle, shred meat with two forks.

MEXICAN TAMALE FILLING

Apple lends a hint of sweetness to this lightly spiced tamale filling.
—Marie Macy, Fort Collins, CO

MAKES: ABOUT 3 CUPS

- 1 **lb. ground pork or beef**
- ½ **cup chopped onion**
- 1 **garlic clove, minced**
- 1 **can (10¾ oz.) tomato puree**
- 1 **tart medium apple, peeled and chopped**
- ½ **cup chopped almonds, toasted**
- ¼ **cup minced fresh parsley**
- 1 **Tbsp. cider vinegar**
- 1 **tsp. sugar**
- ½ **tsp. ground coriander**
- ½ **tsp. coarsely ground pepper**
- ½ **tsp. chili powder**
- ¼ **tsp. ground cumin**

Cook pork and onion, crumbling meat, in a large skillet over medium heat until meat is no longer pink. Add garlic; cook 1 minute longer. Drain. Add remaining ingredients. Bring to a boil. Reduce the heat; simmer, covered, 25 minutes. Cool slightly.

FROSTED CHOCOLATE DELIGHTS

FROSTED CHOCOLATE DELIGHTS

These simple chocolate drop cookies are crowned with a creamy vanilla frosting.
—Patricia Ramczyk, Appleton, WI

PREP: 20 MIN.
BAKE: 15 MIN./BATCH + COOLING
MAKES: 5½ DOZEN

- ½ **cup shortening**
- 1 **cup packed brown sugar**
- 1 **large egg**
- ½ **cup milk**
- 1 **tsp. vanilla extract**
- 2 **oz. unsweetened chocolate, melted and cooled**
- 1¾ **cups all-purpose flour**
- 1 **tsp. baking powder**
- ½ **tsp. salt**
- ¼ **tsp. baking soda**
- ½ **cup chopped walnuts**

FROSTING
- 9 **Tbsp. butter, softened**
- 4½ **cups confectioners' sugar**
- 1½ **tsp. vanilla extract**
- 6 **to 8 Tbsp. milk**

1. In a large bowl, cream shortening and brown sugar. Beat in the egg, milk and vanilla. Beat in chocolate until blended. Combine the flour, baking powder, salt and baking soda; gradually add to the creamed mixture. Stir in walnuts.

2. Drop by tablespoonfuls 2 in. apart onto ungreased baking sheets. Bake at 350° for 11-13 minutes or until firm. Remove to wire racks to cool.

3. For frosting, in a bowl, cream butter and sugar. Beat in vanilla and enough milk to achieve spreading consistency. Frost the cooled cookies.

2 COOKIES: 190 cal., 8g fat (3g sat. fat), 16mg chol., 97mg sod., 29g carb. (22g sugars, 0 fiber), 2g pro.

SLOW-COOKER COUNTRY CAPTAIN CHICKEN

EAT SMART SLOW COOKER

SLOW-COOKER COUNTRY CAPTAIN CHICKEN

Legend has it that the recipe for country captain chicken was brought to Georgia in the early 1800s by a British sea captain. Although it's traditional to serve this over rice, it's also delicious with noodles or mashed potatoes.
—Suzanne Banfield, Basking Ridge, NJ

PREP: 20 MIN. • **COOK:** 3½ HOURS • **MAKES:** 8 SERVINGS

- **1 large onion, chopped**
- **1 medium sweet red pepper, chopped**
- **2 tsp. minced garlic**
- **3 lbs. boneless skinless chicken thighs**
- **1 Tbsp. curry powder**
- **1 tsp. ground cinnamon**
- **1 tsp. ground ginger**
- **1 tsp. dried thyme**
- **1 Tbsp. packed brown sugar**
- **½ cup chicken broth**
- **½ cup golden raisins or raisins**
- **1 can (14½ oz.) diced tomatoes, undrained**
- **Hot cooked rice**
- **Chopped fresh parsley, optional**

1. Place onion, pepper and garlic in a 6-qt. slow cooker. Arrange chicken pieces over vegetables.
2. Whisk the next five ingredients with the chicken broth. Pour over chicken. Cover and cook on high for 1 hour. Add raisins and tomatoes. Reduce heat to low and cook until chicken reaches 165°, 2½ hours. Serve over rice. Sprinkle with parsley if desired.
1 CUP: 298 cal., 13g fat (3g sat. fat), 114mg chol., 159mg sod., 13g carb. (9g sugars, 2g fiber), 32g pro. **Diabetic exchanges:** 4 lean meat, 1 vegetable, ½ starch.

FREEZE IT

GOLDEN CHICKEN POTPIE

The golden crust and creamy sauce make these veggie-packed pies a sure hit. This mild and comforting family favorite has convenient freezer instructions for a night when there's no time to prep.
—Taste of Home Test Kitchen

PREP: 20 MIN. • **BAKE:** 35 MIN. • **MAKES:** 2 POTPIES (6 SERVINGS EACH)

- **4 cups cubed cooked chicken**
- **4 cups frozen cubed hash brown potatoes, thawed**
- **1 pkg. (16 oz.) frozen mixed vegetables, thawed and drained**
- **1 can (10½ oz.) condensed cream of chicken soup, undiluted**
- **1 can (10½ oz.) condensed cream of onion soup, undiluted**
- **1 cup whole milk**
- **1 cup (8 oz.) sour cream**
- **2 Tbsp. all-purpose flour**
- **½ tsp. salt**
- **½ tsp. pepper**
- **¼ tsp. garlic powder**
- **2 sheets refrigerated pie crust**

1. Preheat oven to 400°. Combine the first 11 ingredients. Divide between two 9-in. deep-dish pie plates.
2. Roll out crusts to fit top of each pie. Place over filling; trim, seal and flute edges. Cut slits in top. Bake until golden brown, 35-40 minutes.
FREEZE OPTION: Cover and freeze unbaked pies up to 3 months. To use, remove from freezer 30 minutes before baking (do not thaw). Preheat oven to 425°. Place pie on a baking sheet; cover edges loosely with foil. Bake 30 minutes. Reduce heat to 350°. Remove foil and bake until golden brown or until heated through and a thermometer inserted in center reads 165°, 50-55 minutes longer.
1 SERVING: 415 cal., 19g fat (8g sat. fat), 69mg chol., 706mg sod., 39g carb. (5g sugars, 3g fiber), 20g pro.

GOLDEN CHICKEN POTPIE

SLOW-COOKER BACON MAC & CHEESE

SLOW COOKER

SLOW-COOKER BACON MAC & CHEESE

I'm all about easy slow-cooker meals. Using more cheese than ever, I've developed an addictive spin on this casserole favorite.
—Kristen Heigl, Staten Island, NY

PREP: 20 MIN. • **COOK:** 3 HOURS + STANDING
MAKES: 18 SERVINGS (½ CUP EACH)

- 2 **large eggs, lightly beaten**
- 4 **cups whole milk**
- 1 **can (12 oz.) evaporated milk**
- ¼ **cup butter, melted**
- 1 **Tbsp. all-purpose flour**
- 1 **tsp. salt**
- 1 **pkg. (16 oz.) small pasta shells**
- 1 **cup shredded provolone cheese**
- 1 **cup shredded Manchego or Monterey Jack cheese**
- 1 **cup shredded white cheddar cheese**
- 8 **bacon strips, cooked and crumbled**

1. In a large bowl, whisk the first six ingredients until blended. Stir in pasta shells and cheeses; transfer to a 4- or 5-qt. slow cooker.
2. Cook, covered, on low 3-3½ hours or until pasta is tender. Turn off slow cooker; remove insert. Let stand, uncovered, for 15 minutes before serving. Top with bacon.
½ CUP: 272 cal., 14g fat (8g sat. fat), 59mg chol., 400mg sod., 24g carb. (5g sugars, 1g fiber), 13g pro.

HOMEMADE CORNED BEEF

Here's a recipe you've gotta plan for, but you don't need to do much work to get this deli-quality corned beef.
—Nick Iverson, Denver, CO

PREP: 30 MIN. + CHILLING • **COOK:** 3 HOURS
MAKES: 12 SERVINGS

- 1 **gallon water**
- 1½ **cups kosher salt**
- ½ **cup packed brown sugar**
- ¼ **cup mixed pickling spices, divided**
- 4 **tsp. pink curing salt #1**
- 4 **garlic cloves, minced**
- 2 **oven roasting bags**
- 1 **fresh beef brisket (4 to 5 lbs.)**
- 2 **large carrots, chopped**
- 2 **medium onions, chopped**
- 2 **celery ribs, chopped**

1. In a large stockpot, combine water, kosher salt, brown sugar, 2 Tbsp. pickling spices, pink curing salt and garlic. Bring to a simmer, stirring until salt and sugar are dissolved. Remove from heat; cool to room temperature, then refrigerate until chilled.
2. Place one large oven roasting bag inside another. Place brisket inside inner bag; pour in cooled brine. Seal bags, pressing out as much air as possible; turn to coat meat. Refrigerate for 10 days, turning occasionally to keep meat coated. Remove brisket from brine; rinse thoroughly. Place in a Dutch oven with water to cover. Add carrots, onions, celery and remaining pickling spices. Bring to a boil over high heat. Reduce heat; simmer, covered, adding water if necessary to keep brisket covered, until meat is tender, about 3 hours.
3. Serve warm or cool. Slice brisket thinly and serve in a sandwich or with additional vegetables simmered until tender in cooking liquid.
NOTE: To make ahead, refrigerate cooked meat in cooking liquid several days; reheat in liquid.
4 OZ. COOKED CORNED BEEF: 277 cal., 21g fat (7g sat. fat), 108mg chol., 1252mg sod., 1g carb. (0 sugars, 0 fiber), 20g pro.

HOMEMADE CORNED BEEF

HOW TO MAKE

SPATCHCOCKED TURKEY

Finally! Roasting a juicy, perfectly cooked turkey is possible with this easy technique.

SPATCHCOCKED HERB-ROASTED TURKEY

SPATCHCOCKED HERB-ROASTED TURKEY

This moist and tender turkey cooks up with even browning and crispy skin in half the time of a whole turkey.
—Matthew Hass, Franklin, WI

PREP: 15 MIN. + CHILLING
BAKE: 1¼ HOURS + STANDING
MAKES: 16 SERVINGS

- **1 turkey (12 to 14 lbs.)**
- **3 Tbsp. kosher salt**
- **2 tsp. coarsely ground pepper**
- **1 Tbsp. minced fresh rosemary**
- **1 Tbsp. minced fresh thyme**
- **1 Tbsp. minced fresh sage**

1. Place turkey with its breast side down and tail end facing you on a work surface. Using kitchen shears, cut along each side of backbone; remove and save for making gravy. Turn over turkey so breast side is up; flatten by pressing down firmly on breastbone until it cracks. Twist and tuck wings under to secure in place.
2. Mix remaining ingredients; rub onto all sides of turkey. Transfer turkey to a rack in a foil-lined rimmed baking pan. Refrigerate, uncovered, overnight.
3. Preheat oven to 450°. Remove turkey from refrigerator while oven heats. Roast until a thermometer inserted in thickest part of a thigh reads 170°-175°, about 1¼-1½ hours. Remove turkey from oven; let stand 15 minutes before carving.
7 OZ. COOKED TURKEY: 399 cal., 18g fat (5g sat. fat), 184mg chol., 1210mg sod., 0 carb. (0 sugars, 0 fiber), 54g pro.

HOW-TO

To-Do's (and Ta-Da's)

- Pat bird dry with paper towels to remove any excess moisture. A dry bird makes for crispier skin.
- Use a sharp pair of kitchen shears to cut along both sides of the backbone. You may need to use both hands to press down on the shears.
- Remove backbone and, if desired, save for making gravy or homemade stock.
- Flip bird breast side up and unfold. Place both hands on the turkey breast and press down firmly to crack wishbone.
- Tuck wing tips under for even cooking and a tidy appearance.
- Season as directed and chill the bird, uncovered, overnight. Salt on the uncovered skin will draw up excess moisture and allow it to evaporate, creating a crispy finished bird.

EASY BOURBON PECAN PIE
PAGE 259

HOLIDAY & SEASONAL CELEBRATIONS

Every season brings reasons to celebrate. From springy sweets to spooky treats, Thanksgiving favorites and time-honored Christmas cookies, you'll find a lot to love here.

GAME ON

If you can't make it to the stadium, bring it home. Fill the stands with snacks to chow on as you cheer, and you'll be MVP in the homegating hall of fame.

ZESTY SNACK MIX

This crisp snack mix is a mouthwatering combination of sweet and spicy. I've taken it to numerous gatherings. Make a bowlful when the munchies hit.
—Jeanette Grantstein, Wichita, KS

PREP: 10 MIN. • **BAKE:** 20 MIN. + COOLING
MAKES: ABOUT 10 CUPS

- 4 **cups Corn Chex**
- 4 **cups corn chips**
- 1 **cup salted peanuts**
- 1 **cup quick-cooking oats**
- ⅓ **cup butter, melted**
- 3 **Tbsp. honey**
- 4 **tsp. chili powder**
- 1 **tsp. onion salt**
- 1 **tsp. dried oregano**

1. In a large bowl, combine the cereal, corn chips, peanuts and oats. Combine the melted butter and honey; drizzle over the cereal mixture. Sprinkle with the chili powder, onion salt and oregano; toss to coat.

2. Spread in a single layer in an ungreased 15x10x1-in. baking pan. Bake at 350° for 20-25 minutes, stirring once. Cool. Store in an airtight container.

¾ CUP: 258 cal., 16g fat (5g sat. fat), 13mg chol., 384mg sod., 25g carb. (6g sugars, 3g fiber), 6g pro.

EAT SMART

FRESH SALSA

No last-minute fuss is needed here—this salsa keeps well for several days in the refrigerator. The recipe uses a lot of ripe tomatoes and makes enough to feed a crowd.
—Myra Innes, Auburn, KS

PREP: 15 MIN. + STANDING
MAKES: 3½ CUPS

- **4 cups chopped peeled fresh tomatoes**
- **¼ cup finely chopped onion**
- **1 to 4 jalapeno peppers, seeded and finely chopped**
- **1 Tbsp. olive oil**
- **1 Tbsp. vinegar**
- **1 tsp. ground cumin**
- **1 tsp. salt, optional**
- **1 garlic clove, minced**

In a bowl, combine all ingredients; mix well. Let stand for about 1 hour. Serve at room temperature. Store in a covered container in the refrigerator.

NOTE: Wear disposable gloves when cutting hot peppers; the oils can burn skin. Avoid touching your face.

¼ CUP: 22 cal., 1g fat (0 sat. fat), 0 chol., 2mg sod., 3g carb. (0 sugars, 0 fiber), 1g pro. **Diabetic exchanges:** 1 vegetable.

★★★★★ **READER REVIEW**

"This was really easy and delicious! I added some black pepper and used extra garlic. Will make this again!"

DELICIOUSLYRESOURCEFUL_GINA
TASTEOFHOME.COM

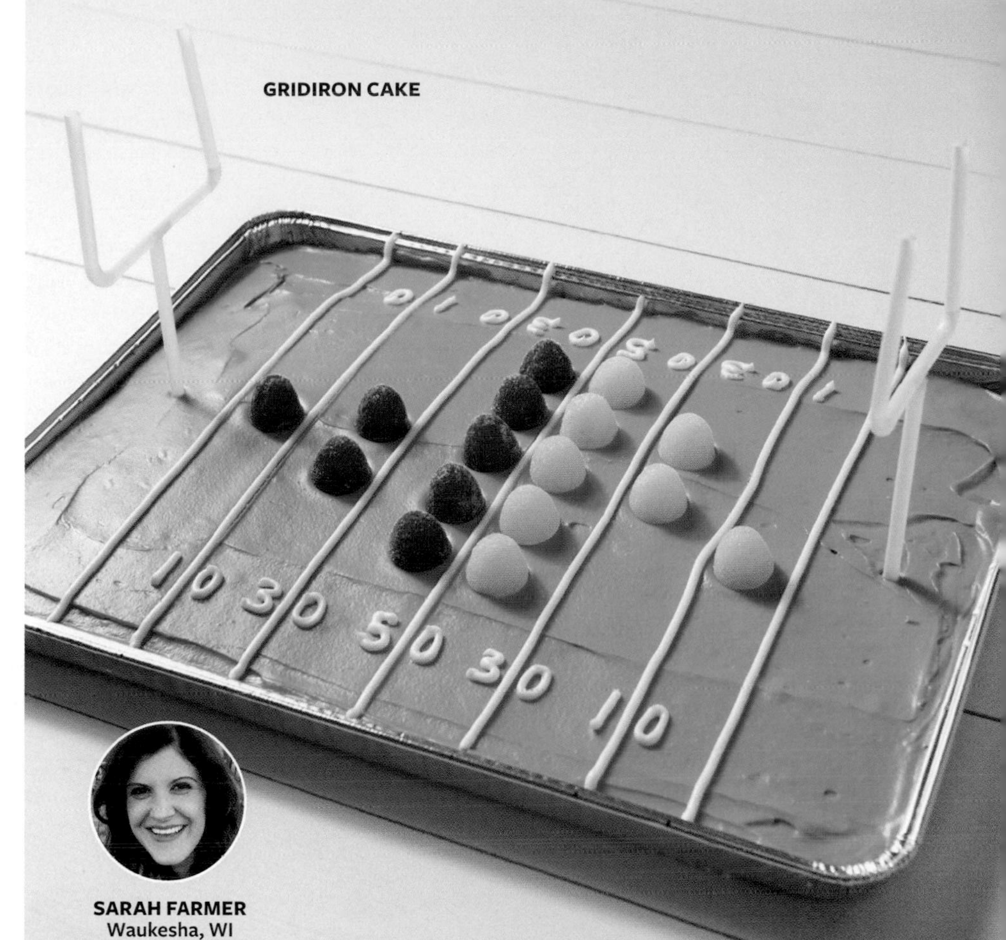

GRIDIRON CAKE

What better way to celebrate game day than with this easy-to-make snack cake with cream cheese frosting. If you're feeling ambitious, use it as the centerpiece of a snack stadium! (Use the photo at left as inspiration.)
—Sarah Farmer, Waukesha, WI

PREP: 45 MIN. • **BAKE:** 25 MIN. + COOLING
MAKES: 20 SERVINGS

CAKE

- **⅔ cup butter, softened**
- **1¾ cups sugar**
- **1 Tbsp. vanilla extract**
- **2 large eggs, room temperature**
- **2½ cups all-purpose flour**
- **2½ tsp. baking powder**
- **½ tsp. salt**
- **1¼ cups 2% milk**

FROSTING

- **1 pkg. (8 oz.) cream cheese, softened**
- **½ cup butter, softened**
- **3¾ cups confectioners' sugar**
- **1 Tbsp. 2% milk**
- **1 tsp. vanilla extract**
- **Green paste food coloring**

DECORATION

- **2 goals posts (made from yellow bendable straws)**
- **Large gumdrops**

1. Preheat oven to 350°. Grease a half sheet foil cake pan (measuring 17x12x1).

2. In a bowl, cream butter and sugar until light and fluffy. Add vanilla and eggs, one at at time, beating well. In another bowl, whisk together flour, baking powder and salt; beat into creamed mixture alternately with milk. Transfer to prepared pan.

3. Bake until a toothpick inserted in center comes out clean, 25-30 minutes. Place on a wire rack; cool completely.

4. For frosting, beat cream cheese and butter. Add the confectioners' sugar, milk and vanilla. Reserve ¼ cup of frosting for field markings. Tint the remaining frosting green; spread over top of the cake. Pipe white yard lines and numbers as desired. Decorate field with goal posts and gumdrops for football players.

1 PIECE: 365 cal., 16g fat (9g sat. fat), 60mg chol., 255mg sod., 54g carb. (41g sugars, 0 fiber), 4g pro.

SOFT BEER PRETZEL NUGGETS

FREEZE IT

SOFT BEER PRETZEL NUGGETS

What goes together better than beer and pretzels? Not much that I can think of. That's why I put them together into one recipe. I'm always looking for new ways to combine fun flavors, and these pretzel nuggets certainly fit the bill.
—Alyssa Wilhite, Whitehouse, TX

PREP: 1 HOUR + RISING • **BAKE:** 10 MIN./BATCH
MAKES: 8 DOZEN PRETZEL NUGGETS

- **1 bottle (12 oz.) amber beer or nonalcoholic beer**
- **1 pkg. (¼ oz.) active dry yeast**
- **2 Tbsp. unsalted butter, melted**
- **2 Tbsp. sugar**
- **1½ tsp. salt**
- **4 to 4½ cups all-purpose flour**
- **10 cups water**
- **⅔ cup baking soda**

TOPPING

- **1 large egg yolk**
- **1 Tbsp. water**
- **Coarse salt, optional**

1. In a small saucepan, heat beer to 110°-115°; remove from heat. Stir in yeast until dissolved. In a large bowl, combine butter, sugar, salt, yeast mixture and 3 cups flour; beat on medium speed until smooth. Stir in enough remaining flour to form a soft dough (dough will be sticky).
2. Turn dough onto a floured surface; knead until smooth and elastic, 6-8 minutes. Place in a greased bowl, turning once to grease the top. Cover and let rise in a warm place until doubled, about 1 hour.
3. Preheat oven to 425°. Punch dough down. Turn onto a lightly floured surface; divide and shape into eight balls. Roll each into a 12-in. rope; cut ropes into 1-in. pieces.
4. In a Dutch oven, bring 10 cups water and baking soda to a boil. Drop nuggets, 12 at a time, into boiling water. Cook 30 seconds. Remove with a slotted spoon; drain well on paper towels.
5. Place on greased baking sheets. In a small bowl, whisk egg yolk and 1 Tbsp. water; brush over pretzels. Sprinkle with coarse salt if desired. Bake 10-12 minutes or until golden brown. Remove from pans to a wire rack to cool.

FREEZE OPTION: Freeze cooled pretzel nuggets in airtight freezer containers. To use, thaw at room temperature or, if desired, microwave on high 20-30 seconds or until heated through.

6 PRETZEL NUGGETS: 144 cal., 2g fat (1g sat. fat), 8mg chol., 302mg sod., 26g carb. (2g sugars, 1g fiber), 4g pro.

(5) INGREDIENTS FAST FIX

SPINACH & TURKEY PINWHEELS

Need an awesome snack for football-watching? My kids love these easy turkey pinwheels. Go ahead and make them the day before—they don't get soggy. They're wonderful for lunch boxes, too.
—Amy Van Hemert, Ottumwa, IA

PREP: 15 MIN. • **MAKES:** 4 DOZEN

- **1 carton (8 oz.) spreadable garden vegetable cream cheese**
- **8 flour tortillas (8 in.)**
- **4 cups fresh baby spinach**
- **1 lb. sliced deli turkey**

Spread cream cheese over tortillas. Layer with spinach and turkey. Roll up tightly; if desired, wrap and refrigerate until serving. Cut rolls crosswise into 1-in. slices.

1 PINWHEEL: 51 cal., 2g fat (1g sat. fat), 9mg chol., 144mg sod., 5g carb. (0 sugars, 0 fiber), 3g pro.

SPINACH & TURKEY PINWHEELS

BEER DIP

(5) INGREDIENTS FAST FIX

BEER DIP

Ranch dressing mix amps up this simple dip. Packed with shredded cheese, it's absolutely perfect with pretzels. It's one of those snacks that when you start eating it, you can't stop! The dip can be made with any type of beer, including nonalcoholic. I've taken it to many parties, and I'm always asked for the recipe.
—Michelle Long, New Castle, CO

TAKES: 5 MIN. • **MAKES:** 3½ CUPS

- **2 pkg. (8 oz. each) cream cheese, softened**
- **⅓ cup beer or nonalcoholic beer**
- **1 envelope ranch salad dressing mix**
- **2 cups shredded cheddar cheese**
- **Pretzels**

In a large bowl, beat the cream cheese, beer and dressing mix until smooth. Stir in cheddar cheese. Serve with pretzels.
2 TBSP.: 89 cal., 8g fat (5g sat. fat), 26mg chol., 177mg sod., 1g carb. (0 sugars, 0 fiber), 3g pro.

VEGGIE DILL DIP

Served with a variety of cut-up veggies, this fat-free dip will satisfy snack cravings in a healthy way.
—Hazel Baber, Yuma, AZ

PREP: 10 MIN. + CHILLING • **MAKES:** 2½ CUPS

- **2 cups (16 oz.) 1% cottage cheese**
- **3 Tbsp. fat-free milk**
- **¾ cup fat-free mayonnaise**
- **1 Tbsp. dried minced onion**
- **1 Tbsp. dried parsley flakes**
- **1 tsp. dill weed**
- **1 tsp. seasoned salt**
- **¼ tsp. garlic powder**

In a blender, blend cottage cheese and milk until smooth. Stir in remaining ingredients and mix well. Chill overnight. Serve with raw vegetables.
2 TBSP.: 24 cal., 0 fat (0 sat. fat), 1mg chol., 233mg sod., 2g carb. (0 sugars, 0 fiber), 3g pro.

QUICK TORTILLA PINWHEELS

Prepare these tasty finger foods several days in advance if desired. Serve with your choice of mild or hot salsa or picante sauce.
—Barbara Keith, Faucett, MO

PREP: 15 MIN. + CHILLING • **MAKES:** ABOUT 5 DOZEN

- **1 cup (8 oz.) sour cream**
- **1 pkg. (8 oz.) cream cheese, softened**
- **¾ cup sliced green onions**
- **½ cup finely shredded cheddar cheese**
- **1 Tbsp. lime juice**
- **1 Tbsp. minced seeded jalapeno pepper**
- **8 to 10 flour tortillas (8 in.), room temperature**
- **Salsa or picante sauce**

Combine the first six ingredients in a bowl. Spread on one side of tortillas and roll up tightly. Wrap and refrigerate for at least 1 hour. Slice into 1-in. pieces. Serve with salsa or picante sauce.
NOTE: Wear disposable gloves when cutting hot peppers; the oils can burn skin. Avoid touching your face.
1 PINWHEEL: 47 cal., 3g fat (2g sat. fat), 6mg chol., 51mg sod., 4g carb. (0 sugars, 0 fiber), 1g pro.

QUICK TORTILLA PINWHEELS

TOUCHDOWN COOKIES

TOUCHDOWN COOKIES

With some simple sweet touches, you can transform regular sugar cookies into a special treat for football fans.
—Sister Judith LaBrozzi, Canton, OH

PREP: 25 MIN. + CHILLING
BAKE: 10 MIN./BATCH + COOLING
MAKES: 4½ DOZEN

- **1 cup butter, softened**
- **1 cup sugar**
- **2 large eggs, room temperature**
- **1 tsp. vanilla extract**
- **3 cups all-purpose flour**
- **2 tsp. cream of tartar**
- **1 tsp. baking soda**

GLAZE

- **4 cups confectioners' sugar**
- **8 to 10 Tbsp. hot water**
- **Black paste food coloring**
- **6 to 8 tsp. baking cocoa**

1. In a large bowl, cream butter and sugar until light and fluffy. Add eggs, one at a time, beating well after each addition. Beat in vanilla. Combine the flour, cream of tartar and baking soda; gradually add to creamed mixture and mix well. Cover and refrigerate for 3 hours or until easy to handle.
2. On a lightly floured surface, roll out dough to ⅛-in. thickness. Cut with a football-shaped and a small gingerbread man cookie cutter. Place 2 in. apart on ungreased baking sheets.
3. Bake at 350° until lightly browned, 8-10 minutes. Remove cookies to wire racks to cool.
4. In a large bowl, combine confectioners' sugar and enough hot water to achieve spreading consistency; beat until smooth. Divide glaze into thirds. Stir black food coloring into one third of the glaze; set aside. Add cocoa to another third; stir until smooth. Spread brown glaze over football cookies. Pipe white glaze for the football laces. Spread or pipe remaining white glaze over gingerbread men cookies to make shirts. Pipe black stripes over the white shirts to resemble referee stripes.
1 COOKIE: 108 cal., 4g fat (2g sat. fat), 16mg chol., 53mg sod., 18g carb. (12g sugars, 0 fiber), 1g pro.

CHIP CHAMPS

DELIGHT DIE-HARD SNACKERS WITH THESE CRAFTY TAKES ON NACHOS.

1 Our go-to nachos are Tex-Mex style: pulled pork BBQ, coleslaw, BBQ sauce, pickled red onions, nacho cheese and a sour cream drizzle! Boom!
—Dave Reed III, Charlotte, NC

2 I top my nachos with leftover chana masala (the Indian chickpea dish), then add onions, tomatoes and a squeeze of lime.
—Gwinn Jayne, Portland, ME

3 We go meatless with corn, black beans, onions and black olives.
—Becky Carver, North Royalton, OH

4 Put smoked pork loin or smoked pulled pork on tortilla chips or Fritos Scoops, top with grated cheddar cheese and melt. Then top it all off with BBQ sauce.
—Teresa Crawford, Lawton, OK

5 We love chorizo, queso and guacamole!
—Angela Lively, Conroe, TX

6 It's grinder nachos in our house, with Italian sausage, mushrooms, onions, pizza sauce (just a little), scamorza cheese and pickled pepper rings.
—Barbara Rankin, Des Moines, IA

7 I make what I call Italian Nachos using spicy Italian sausage, olives, tomatoes, onions, zucchini, white beans, mozzarella and (it sounds weird but it's delish) white country gravy...all on top of tortilla chips.
—Falon Marvin, Boise, ID

8 I love a dessert nacho: brownie brittle as the chips and marshmallow fluff for the nacho cheese. Then drizzle on chocolate sauce and top with grated white chocolate and chopped peanuts.
—Brigette Schroeder, Yorkville, IL

9 Chop up kalamata olives with all of the regular items—avocado, ground meat, cheese, peppers, onions, lettuce and pico de gallo. Then top with buttermilk ranch dressing and blue cheese.
—Bonnie Hawkins, Elkhorn, WI

10 I like to make Buffalo wing nachos using spicy Buffalo sauce, celery and shredded chicken, and finish it off with drizzles of both blue cheese and ranch dressing.
—Marina Castle Kelley, Canyon Country, CA

EASTER TREATS

Call off the hunt, peeps. These chocolaty treats, marshmallowy confections and more will satisfy your springtime sweet tooth.

MARSHMALLOW WANDS

5 INGREDIENTS FAST FIX

MARSHMALLOW WANDS

These marshmallow pops are a hit with the kids. Let them drizzle away with their favorite colors!
—James Schend, Pleasant Prairie, WI

TAKES: 10 MIN. • **MAKES:** 12 POPS

- **2 cups semisweet chocolate chips**
- **2 Tbsp. shortening**
- **36 large marshmallows**
- **12 lollipop sticks**
- **Assorted colored candy coating, melted**

In a microwave, melt chocolate and shortening; stir until smooth. Skewer three marshmallows on each stick. Spoon chocolate over marshmallows; set on waxed paper until firm. Drizzle with melted colored candy coating.

1 WAND: 74 cal., 3g fat (2g sat. fat), 0 chol., 7mg sod., 12g carb. (9g sugars, 1g fiber), 1g pro.

5 INGREDIENTS FAST FIX

WHITE CHOCOLATE CEREAL EGGS

A friend gave me this fresh take on traditional crispy treats. You can make these in bars, but they're really cute turned into egg shapes for Easter.
—Anne Powers, Munford, AL

TAKES: 15 MIN. • **MAKES:** ABOUT 3 DOZEN

- **4 cups miniature marshmallows**
- **8 oz. white baking chips (about 1⅓ cups)**
- **¼ cup butter, cubed**
- **6 cups crisp rice cereal**
- **½ cup sprinkles**

1. In a Dutch oven, combine marshmallows, baking chips and butter. Cook and stir over medium-low heat until melted. Remove from heat. Add cereal; stir to coat.
2. Form cereal mixture into egg shapes or pack into clean egg molds. Decorate as desired with sprinkles.

1 CEREAL EGG: 94 cal., 4g fat (2g sat. fat), 5mg chol., 46mg sod., 14g carb. (9g sugars, 0 fiber), 1g pro.

LEMON BARK

5 INGREDIENTS

LEMON BARK

I wasn't a fan of white chocolate until I made this candy. It's tangy, sweet and creamy all at the same time.
—Diana Wing, Bountiful, UT

PREP: 10 MIN. + CHILLING • **MAKES:** 1¾ LBS.

- **2 pkg. (10 to 12 oz. each) white baking chips**
- **1 cup crushed hard lemon candies, divided**

1. Line a 15x10x1-in. pan with foil; set aside. In top of a double boiler or a metal bowl over barely simmering water, melt baking chips; stir until smooth. Stir in ⅔ cup crushed candies; spread into prepared pan. Sprinkle with remaining candies. Cool. Refrigerate until set, about 1 hour.
2. Break into pieces. Store in an airtight container.

1 OZ.: 122 cal., 7g fat (4g sat. fat), 4mg chol., 20mg sod., 15g carb. (14g sugars, 0 fiber), 1g pro.

5 INGREDIENTS FAST FIX

BUNNY TAILS

My granddaughters and I came up with this clever and easy idea for Easter.
—Kelly Ciepluch, Kenosha, WI

TAKES: 20 MIN. • **MAKES:** ABOUT 4 DOZEN

- **1 cup white baking chocolate, melted**
- **1 cup sweetened shredded coconut**

Drop melted chocolate by teaspoonfuls onto waxed paper or parchment paper. Sprinkle each generously with sweetened flaked coconut and let stand until dry.

1 PIECE: 29 cal., 2g fat (1g sat. fat), 1mg chol., 8mg sod., 3g carb. (3g sugars, 0 fiber), 0 pro.

WHITE VELVET CUTOUTS

WHITE VELVET CUTOUTS

These rich cookies melt in your mouth, no matter what occasion they are made for. At Christmastime, we bake cutouts to give as gifts.
—*Kim Hinkle, Wauseon, OH*

PREP: 25 MIN. + CHILLING • **BAKE:** 10 MIN./BATCH + COOLING
MAKES: ABOUT 5½ DOZEN

- **2 cups butter, softened**
- **1 pkg. (8 oz.) cream cheese, softened**
- **2 cups granulated sugar**
- **2 large egg yolks**
- **1 tsp. vanilla extract**
- **4½ cups all-purpose flour**

FROSTING

- **3 Tbsp. butter, softened**
- **1 Tbsp. shortening**
- **½ tsp. vanilla extract**
- **3½ cups confectioners' sugar**
- **4 to 5 Tbsp. 2% milk**
- **Food coloring, optional**

1. In a large bowl, cream butter, cream cheese and sugar until light and fluffy. Beat in egg yolks and vanilla. Gradually beat flour into creamed mixture. Divide dough in half. Shape each into a disk; wrap and refrigerate for 2 hours or until firm enough to roll.
2. Preheat oven to 350°. On a lightly floured surface, roll each portion of dough to ¼-in. thickness. Cut with floured 3-in. cookie cutters. Place 1 in. apart on greased baking sheets. Bake for 10-12 minutes or until set (do not brown). Cool on pans 5 minutes. Remove to wire racks to cool completely.
3. For frosting, in a bowl, beat butter, shortening and vanilla until blended. Beat in confectioners' sugar and enough milk to reach spreading consistency; beat 3 minutes or until light and fluffy. If desired, beat in food coloring. Frost cookies. (Keep frosting covered with a damp towel to prevent it from drying out.)
1 COOKIE: 149 cal., 8g fat (5g sat. fat), 26mg chol., 62mg sod., 19g carb. (13g sugars, 0 fiber), 1g pro.

5 INGREDIENTS

WHITE CHOCOLATE EASTER EGG CANDIES

Candy making can be easy! Have kids help roll the candies in sprinkles, colored sugar or jimmies.
—Taste of Home *Test Kitchen*

PREP: 30 MIN. + CHILLING • **MAKES:** ABOUT 2 DOZEN (1½ LBS.)

- **1 pkg. (10 to 12 oz.) white baking chips**
- **3 oz. cream cheese, cubed**
- **1 tsp. water**
- **½ tsp. vanilla extract**
- **Colored sprinkles, colored sugar and/or jimmies**

In a microwave-safe bowl, melt the chips at 50% power. Add the cream cheese, water and vanilla; stir until blended. Chill until easy to handle, about 1 hour. Quickly shape into 1¼-in. eggs. Roll in sprinkles, colored sugar or jimmies. Store in an airtight container in the refrigerator.
1 PIECE: 76 cal., 5g fat (3g sat. fat), 6mg chol., 22mg sod., 7g carb. (7g sugars, 0 fiber), 1g pro.

WHITE CHOCOLATE EASTER EGG CANDIES

EASTER NESTS

5 INGREDIENTS

EASTER NESTS

With jelly bean eggs, these easy nests make fun treats for Easter.
—Taste of Home *Test Kitchen*

PREP: 30 MIN. + STANDING
MAKES: 15 NESTS

- 1 **pkg. (11 oz.) peanut butter and milk chocolate chips**
- 2 **cans (3 oz. each) crispy rice noodles**
- ⅓ **cup crisp rice cereal**
- ⅓ **cup chopped salted peanuts**
- 45 **jelly beans or peanut M&M's**

In a microwave, melt chips; stir until smooth. Stir in the rice noodles, cereal and peanuts. Divide into 15 mounds on waxed paper and shape into nests; press indentation in the center of each. Add three jelly beans to each nest. Let stand until set.

1 NEST: 217 cal., 12g fat (5g sat. fat), 0 chol., 110mg sod., 29g carb. (12g sugars, 1g fiber), 2g pro.

TEST KITCHEN TIP

We used Reese's chips in this recipe. If you can't find them, use 1 cup each of peanut butter and semisweet chocolate chips.

MARBLED ORANGE FUDGE

The Creamsicle flavor of this soft fudge brings on the smiles. Bright orange and marshmallow swirls make it perfect for get-togethers.
—Diane Wampler, Morristown, TN

PREP: 30 MIN. + CHILLING • **MAKES:** 4 DOZEN (2½ LBS.)

- 1½ **tsp. plus ¾ cup butter, divided**
- 3 **cups sugar**
- ¾ **cup heavy whipping cream**
- 1 **pkg. white baking chips (10 to 12 oz.)**
- 1 **jar (7 oz.) marshmallow creme**
- 3 **tsp. orange extract**
- 12 **drops yellow food coloring**
- 5 **drops red food coloring**
- **Green shoestring licorice, optional**

1. Grease a 13x9-in. pan with 1½ tsp. butter; set aside.
2. In a large heavy saucepan, combine the sugar, cream and remaining butter. Cook and stir over low heat until sugar is dissolved. Bring to a boil; cook and stir for 4 minutes. Remove from the heat; stir in chips and marshmallow creme until smooth.
3. Remove 1 cup and set aside. Add orange extract and food coloring to the remaining mixture; stir until blended. Pour into prepared pan. Drop reserved marshmallow mixture by tablespoonfuls over the top; cut through with a knife to swirl. Cover and refrigerate until set. Cut into 48 narrow triangles; decorate with licorice if desired.

1 PIECE: 109 cal., 3g fat (2g sat. fat), 7mg chol., 12mg sod., 20g carb. (15g sugars, 0 fiber), 0 pro.

MARBLED ORANGE FUDGE

BESTIES & BROOMSTICKS

It's no toil or trouble to gather your spooky sisters for a scary night in.

5 INGREDIENTS FAST FIX

WITCHES' BROOMS

Pair these edible mini brooms with Witches' Brew for a spellbinding treat. The only ingredients you need are pretzel rods and licorice!
—Taste of Home *Test Kitchen*

TAKES: 30 MIN. • **MAKES:** 6 BROOMS

- **6 pieces green shoestring licorice**
- **6 pretzel rods**
- **6 pieces black shoestring licorice**

Cut one green shoestring licorice into 1-in. lengths. Arrange around end of one pretzel rod to form broom bristles; tightly wrap bristles with one black shoestring licorice, tucking in end to secure. Repeat with remaining ingredients.
1 BROOM: 106 cal., 0 fat (0 sat. fat), 0 chol., 142mg sod., 24g carb. (10g sugars, 0 fiber), 1g pro.

5 INGREDIENTS FAST FIX

WITCHES' FINGERS

You don't need a cauldron to conjure these frightening fingers. They're a sweet-and-salty treat that's spooky easy to make.
—Beth Tomkiw, Milwaukee, WI

TAKES: 20 MIN. • **MAKES:** 1 DOZEN

- **1½ cups vibrant green candy coating disks**
- **6 pretzel rods, broken in half**
- **6 jelly beans, cut in half lengthwise**

In a microwave, melt candy coating; stir until smooth. Dip broken end of pretzel rods in coating; allow excess to drip off. Place on waxed paper; press a jelly bean half onto dipped end of each pretzel to resemble a fingernail. Let stand until almost set. Using a toothpick, make lines in each pretzel to resemble knuckles.
1 DIPPED PRETZEL HALF: 155 cal., 7g fat (7g sat. fat), 1mg chol., 131mg sod., 21g carb. (18g sugars, 0 fiber), 1g pro.

WITCHES' BREW

5 INGREDIENTS

WITCHES' BREW

Stir up some Halloween beverages that are as bewitching as the rest of your menu. For a nonalcoholic version, just omit the vodka. Then the kids can have some, too!
—Taste of Home *Test Kitchen*

PREP: 20 MIN. + CHILLING
MAKES: 6 SERVINGS

- **1 cup sugar**
- **1 cup water**
- **8 medium kiwifruit, peeled and quartered**
- **½ cup fresh mint leaves**
- **1 cup vodka, optional**
- **1 liter ginger ale, chilled**
- **Ice cubes**

1. In a small saucepan, bring sugar and water to a boil. Cook and stir until sugar is dissolved; set aside to cool.
2. Place the kiwi, mint and sugar syrup in a blender; cover and process until blended. Pour into a large pitcher; stir in vodka if desired. Refrigerate until chilled.
3. Just before serving, stir in ginger ale. Serve over ice.
1 CUP: 253 cal., 1g fat (0 sat. fat), 0 chol., 17mg sod., 64g carb. (57g sugars, 4g fiber), 1g pro.

WITCHES' CAVIAR

WITCHES' CAVIAR

I like to serve this dip with triangular tortilla chips because they look like pointy witch hats.
—Darlene Brenden, Salem, OR

PREP: 10 MIN. + CHILLING • **MAKES:** 4 CUPS

- **2 cans (4¼ oz. each) chopped ripe olives, undrained**
- **2 cans (4 oz. each) chopped green chilies, undrained**
- **2 medium tomatoes, seeded and chopped**
- **3 green onions, chopped**
- **2 garlic cloves, minced**
- **1 Tbsp. red wine vinegar**
- **1 Tbsp. olive oil**
- **½ tsp. pepper**
- **Dash seasoned salt**
- **Tortilla chips**

In a large bowl, combine the first nine ingredients. Cover and refrigerate overnight. Serve with tortilla chips.

2 TBSP.: 17 cal., 1g fat (0 sat. fat), 0 chol., 98mg sod., 1g carb. (1g sugars, 1g fiber), 0 pro.

GOURD-GEOUS HALLOWEEN NACHOS

My family loves nachos so much that I sometimes serve them for lunch. To get in the Halloween spirit, I used a pumpkin cookie cutter to cut out chips from pita bread.
—Kim Van Dunk, Caldwell, NJ

PREP: 40 MIN. • **BROIL:** 5 MIN. • **MAKES:** 10 SERVINGS

- **8 whole wheat pita breads (6 in.)**
- **¼ cup plus ½ tsp. olive oil, divided**
- **¼ tsp. garlic salt**
- **¼ tsp. pepper**
- **½ cup canned black beans, rinsed and drained**
- **⅛ tsp. salt**
- **2 cups finely shredded cheddar cheese**
- **½ cup crumbled cooked bacon**
- **4 green onions, thinly sliced**

1. Preheat oven to 350°. Cut pita breads with a 2½-in. pumpkin-shaped cookie cutter; brush both sides with ¼ cup oil. Place on two ungreased 15x10x1-in. baking pans; sprinkle with garlic salt and pepper. Bake 15-20 minutes or until toasted, stirring once halfway through baking.

2. Preheat broiler. In a small bowl, toss beans with salt and the remaining oil. Layer pita chips with cheese, bean mixture, bacon and onions. Broil 3-4 in. from heat 2-3 minutes or until cheese is melted. Serve immediately.

1 SERVING: 281 cal., 15g fat (6g sat. fat), 24mg chol., 604mg sod., 26g carb. (2g sugars, 3g fiber), 12g pro.

GOURD-GEOUS HALLOWEEN NACHOS

HOT DOG MUMMIES WITH HONEY MUSTARD DIP

HOT DOG MUMMIES WITH HONEY MUSTARD DIP

These flaky mummy sandwiches are instant party hits! The accompanying mustard dip adds just the right kick.
—Jessie Sarrazin, Livingston, MT

PREP: 25 MIN. • **BAKE:** 10 MIN.
MAKES: 20 APPETIZERS (ABOUT 1 CUP DIP)

- 1 **tube (8 oz.) refrigerated crescent rolls**
- 20 **miniature hot dogs**
- 1 **large egg**
- 2 **tsp. water**
- **Dijon mustard**

DIP
- ½ **cup mayonnaise**
- 3 **Tbsp. Dijon mustard**
- 3 **Tbsp. honey**
- 1 **Tbsp. cider vinegar**
- **Dash hot pepper sauce**

1. Separate crescent roll dough into two rectangles; seal seams and perforations. Cut each rectangle horizontally into 10 strips. Wrap one strip around each hot dog.
2. Place 1 in. apart on an ungreased baking sheet. In a small bowl, whisk egg and water; brush over tops. Bake at 375° until golden brown, 10-15 minutes. Using mustard, add eyes. In a small bowl, combine the dip ingredients; serve with mummies.
1 APPETIZER WITH 2 TSP. DIP: 128 cal., 10g fat (2g sat. fat), 18mg chol., 287mg sod., 8g carb. (4g sugars, 0 fiber), 2g pro.

FAST FIX

GRUESOME GREEK DIP

Guests will help themselves to seconds of this savory dip. The orange color makes it fitting for a Halloween party.
—Gina Wilson, Austin, TX

TAKES: 20 MIN. • **MAKES:** 2½ CUPS

- 1 **can (4 oz.) small shrimp, rinsed and drained**
- 3 **Tbsp. lemon juice, divided**
- 1 **tsp. Greek seasoning**
- 1 **pkg. (8 oz.) cream cheese, cubed**
- ¾ **cup crumbled feta cheese**
- ½ **cup chopped roasted sweet red peppers, drained**
- 1 **garlic clove, peeled**
- 1 **Tbsp. minced fresh parsley**
- **Baked pita chips**

1. In a small bowl, combine the shrimp, 1 Tbsp. lemon juice and the Greek seasoning; set aside.
2. In a food processor, combine the cheeses, red peppers, garlic and remaining lemon juice; cover and process until smooth. Stir into shrimp mixture.
3. Transfer to a serving bowl. Cover and refrigerate until serving. Just before serving, stir dip and garnish with parsley. Serve with pita chips.
¼ CUP: 113 cal., 9g fat (6g sat. fat), 53mg chol., 416mg sod., 2g carb. (1g sugars, 0 fiber), 5g pro.

GRUESOME GREEK DIP

TURKEY DAY HOTLINE

We're not here answering phones on Thanksgiving, we're home feasting just like you. But now, we're here to talk turkey—and unveil our most cherished family recipes.

MARINATED THANKSGIVING TURKEY

MARINATED THANKSGIVING TURKEY

My family enjoys this turkey because it cooks up tender, tasty and golden brown. Build up flavor by marinating the meat, then grill it to add a tempting barbecued taste.
—Ken Churches, Kailua-Kona, HI

PREP: 10 MIN. + MARINATING
GRILL: 2½ HOURS + STANDING
MAKES: 12 SERVINGS

- 2 **cups water**
- 1½ **cups chicken broth**
- 1 **cup reduced-sodium soy sauce**
- ⅔ **cup lemon juice**
- 2 **garlic cloves, minced**
- 1½ **tsp. ground ginger**
- 1 **tsp. pepper**
- 2 **large oven roasting bags**
- 1 **turkey (12 to 14 lbs.)**

1. Combine the first seven ingredients; set aside and refrigerate 1 cup for basting. Place one oven roasting bag inside the other. Place turkey inside the inner bag; pour in the remaining marinade. Seal bags, pressing out as much air as possible; turn to coat the turkey. Place in a shallow roasting pan. Refrigerate overnight, turning several times.

2. Remove turkey; drain and discard marinade.

3. Prepare grill for indirect medium heat. Tuck wings under turkey and arrange breast side down on grill rack. Grill, covered, for 1 hour.

4. If using a charcoal grill, add 10 briquettes to coals; turn the turkey. Baste with reserved marinade. Cook, covered, for 1½-2 hours, adding 10 briquettes to maintain heat and brushing with marinade every 30 minutes until a thermometer inserted in thigh reads 170°. Remove turkey from grill; tent with foil. Let stand for 20 minutes before carving.

9 OZ. COOKED TURKEY: 407 cal., 12g fat (4g sat. fat), 171mg chol., 383mg sod., 5g carb. (0 sugars, 1g fiber), 67g pro.

CONVENTIONAL ROASTING METHOD: Follow steps for marinating turkey overnight. Preheat the oven to 325°. Place turkey on a rack in a large roaster. Bake, uncovered, 3-3½ hours or until a thermometer inserted in a thigh reads 170°. Baste frequently with reserved marinade. When turkey begins to brown, cover lightly with a tent of aluminum foil. Remove turkey from oven; tent with foil. Let stand for 20 minutes before carving. If desired, skim fat and thicken pan drippings for gravy; serve with turkey.

EAT SMART (5) INGREDIENTS

CRUNCHY HONEY-GLAZED BUTTERNUT SQUASH

I'm now required to bring this to every family gathering during the holidays because it's so awesome! Why not start a new tradition for your family?
—Sarah Farmer, Waukesha, WI

PREP: 20 MIN. • **BAKE:** 45 MIN.
MAKES: 10 SERVINGS

- **½ cup honey**
- **1 tsp. dried thyme, divided**
- **1 large butternut squash (about 5 lbs.), peeled, halved, seeded and thinly sliced**
- **3 Tbsp. water**
- **¼ cup plus 2 Tbsp. olive oil, divided**
- **1½ tsp. salt, divided**
- **1½ tsp. pepper, divided**
- **½ cup panko (Japanese) bread crumbs**

1. Preheat the oven to 375°. In a large saucepan, heat honey and ½ tsp. thyme, stirring occasionally, over low heat until fragrant, 3-4 minutes.
2. Meanwhile, in a large microwave-safe dish, combine squash and the water; microwave, covered, on high until squash is tender, 6-8 minutes. Drain. Add ¼ cup olive oil, 1 tsp. salt and 1 tsp. pepper; toss to coat.
3. On a flat surface, stack squash slices. Arrange stacks on their sides in a greased 9-in. square baking dish. (To make stacking easier, set baking dish on end; fill with squash stacks. When dish is full, return to original position.) Drizzle 3 Tbsp. honey mixture over squash.
4. Bake until the squash is tender, 45-50 minutes. In a small skillet, heat remaining oil over medium heat. Add bread crumbs; toss with remaining thyme and remaining salt and pepper. Cook and stir until golden brown, about 5 minutes. Sprinkle over baked squash; if desired, drizzle with additional honey mixture.
1 SERVING: 237 cal., 8g fat (1g sat. fat), 0 chol., 373mg sod., 43g carb. (20g sugars, 8g fiber), 3g pro.

EASY BOURBON PECAN PIE

EASY BOURBON PECAN PIE

This pie has a mellow bourbon flavor—not too strong and not too sweet. It's easy, crunchy and chewy: just what you want in a pecan pie.
—Nick Iverson, Denver, CO

PREP: 10 MIN. + FREEZING
BAKE: 1¼ HOURS + COOLING
MAKES: 10 SERVINGS

- **12 oz. toasted pecan halves, divided**
- **4 large eggs**
- **½ cup packed dark brown sugar**
- **¼ cup granulated sugar**
- **1 cup dark corn syrup**
- **8 Tbsp. unsalted butter, melted**
- **¼ cup bourbon**
- **2 tsp. vanilla extract**
- **¼ tsp. salt**
- **1 sheet refrigerated pie crust**
- **Vanilla ice cream, optional**

1. In a food processor, pulse half the pecans until coarsely chopped; reserve remaining pecans. Combine eggs and sugars until well mixed. Add next five ingredients and the chopped pecans.
2. Unroll crust into a 9-in. metal pie plate; flute edge. Pour filling into crust. Arrange reserved pecan halves over filling. Place filled pie in freezer for 30 minutes.
3. Preheat oven to 425°. Bake until crust is set, about 15 minutes. Reduce oven setting to 350°; continue baking until pie is puffed and set in the middle, about 1 hour (tent pie loosely with foil if needed to prevent overbrowning). Cool. If desired, serve with vanilla ice cream.
NOTE: To toast nuts, bake in a shallow pan in a 350° oven for 5-10 minutes or cook in a skillet over low heat until lightly browned, stirring occasionally.
1 SLICE: 600 cal., 41g fat (11g sat. fat), 103mg chol., 221mg sod., 56g carb. (43g sugars, 3g fiber), 7g pro.

CRANBERRY BOURBON

SLOW COOKER

CELEBRATION BRUSSELS SPROUTS

This recipe hits all the flavor points and makes a fantastic Thanksgiving or Christmas side. The dish requires minimal effort and doesn't take up oven space—and you can omit the bacon for a vegetarian option.
—Lauren Knoelke, Milwaukee, WI

PREP: 20 MIN. • **COOK:** 2 HOURS
MAKES: 10 SERVINGS

- **2 lbs. fresh Brussels sprouts, halved and thinly sliced**
- **2 large apples (Fuji or Braeburn), chopped**
- **⅓ cup dried cranberries**
- **8 bacon strips, cooked and crumbled, divided**
- **⅓ cup cider vinegar**
- **¼ cup maple syrup**
- **2 Tbsp. olive oil**
- **1 tsp. salt**
- **½ tsp. fresh ground pepper**
- **¾ cup chopped hazelnuts or pecans, toasted**

Combine Brussels sprouts, apples, cranberries and ¼ cup bacon. In a small bowl, whisk vinegar, syrup, oil, salt and pepper; pour over Brussels sprouts mixture, tossing to coat. Transfer to a 5-qt. slow cooker. Cook, covered, on low, stirring once, until sprouts reach desired tenderness, 2-4 hours. To serve, sprinkle with hazelnuts and remaining bacon.

¾ CUP: 204 cal., 11g fat (2g sat. fat), 7mg chol., 375mg sod., 24g carb. (15g sugars, 5g fiber), 6g pro.

TEST KITCHEN TIP

To thinly slice Brussels sprouts, trim off the ends and put them in a food processor or slice with a mandoline; or trim, halve lengthwise, and slice using a very sharp knife. For the apples, we recommend Fuji or Braeburn because they have a crisp texture that will hold up to the heat.

CRANBERRY BOURBON

The subtle blend of cranberry, spices and orange makes this a delicious drink on its own, or you can use it as a base for an old-fashioned or a Manhattan. The longer you let it sit, the stronger the flavor gets.
—James Schend, Pleasant Prairie, WI

PREP: 10 MIN. + STANDING
MAKES: 20 SERVINGS

- **3 cups bourbon**
- **1 cup dried cranberries**
- **1 cinnamon stick (3 in.)**
- **4 orange peel strips (3 in.)**

ADDITIONAL INGREDIENTS FOR CRANBERRY MANHATTAN (EACH SERVING)

- **Ice cubes**
- **¾ oz. sweet vermouth**
- **Dash bitters**

ADDITIONAL INGREDIENTS FOR CRANBERRY OLD-FASHIONED (EACH SERVING)

- **1 orange slice**
- **4 dried cranberries**
- **2 dashes bitters**
- **Ice cubes**
- **3 oz. lemon-lime soda**
- **1 tsp. orange juice**

In an airtight glass container, combine bourbon, cranberries, cinnamon stick and orange peel. Store in a cool, dry place for 2-4 weeks. Strain, discarding cranberries, cinnamon and orange peel. Return bourbon to glass container. Store in a cool, dry place.

1 OZ. BOURBON: 64 cal., 0 fat (0 sat. fat), 0 chol., 0 sod., 0 carb. (0 sugars, 0 fiber), 0 pro.

TO PREPARE A CRANBERRY MANHATTAN: Fill a shaker three-fourths full with ice. Add 2 oz. Cranberry Bourbon, sweet vermouth and bitters; cover and shake until cold. Strain into a cocktail glass.

TO PREPARE A CRANBERRY OLD-FASHIONED: In a rocks glass, muddle orange, cranberries and bitters. Add ice. Pour in 1½ oz. of Cranberry Bourbon, soda and juice.

CELEBRATION BRUSSELS SPROUTS

SAUSAGE & MUSHROOM CORNBREAD DRESSING

SAUSAGE & MUSHROOM CORNBREAD DRESSING

I learned about cornbread dressing while living in the South for a few years. I decided to combine it with a few of my favorite stuffing ingredients to give it my own spin.
—James Schend, Pleasant Prairie, WI

PREP: 20 MIN. + CHILLING • **BAKE:** 55 MIN. • **MAKES:** 9 CUPS

- 1½ **cups yellow cornmeal**
- ½ **cup all-purpose flour**
- 1 **tsp. baking powder**
- ½ **tsp. baking soda**
- ½ **tsp. salt**
- 1½ **cups 2% milk**
- 2 **large eggs**
- ¼ **cup plus 1 Tbsp. olive oil, divided**
- 1 **Tbsp. honey**
- 1 **Tbsp. cider vinegar**

CORNBREAD DRESSING

- ½ **lb. bulk pork sausage**
- 8 **oz. sliced fresh mushrooms**
- 3 **celery ribs, chopped**
- 1 **large onion, chopped**
- 1½ **cups soft whole wheat bread crumbs (3-4 slices)**
- 3 **large eggs, beaten**
- 1 **carton (32 oz.) reduced-sodium chicken broth**
- 1 **Tbsp. minced fresh rosemary**
- 1 **tsp. pepper**

1. Place a 10-in. cast-iron skillet in the oven; preheat to 425°. Whisk together first five ingredients. In another bowl, whisk milk, eggs, ¼ cup olive oil, honey and vinegar; whisk into dry ingredients. Remove skillet from oven; lightly grease with remaining olive oil. Pour in batter. Bake until golden brown, about 15 minutes. Cool 10 minutes; remove from pan to a wire rack to cool completely.

2. Meanwhile, in a large skillet, cook sausage over medium-high heat, crumbling meat, until no longer pink. Remove and drain. In the same skillet, cook mushrooms, celery and onion until onion is tender, about 5 minutes. Crumble corn bread into a large bowl; stir in sausage, mushroom mixture and the remaining ingredients. Transfer to a greased 13x9-in. baking dish. Refrigerate, covered, at least 8 hours.

3. Remove from refrigerator 30 minutes before baking. Preheat oven to 375°. Bake, uncovered, until browned and mixture is set, 40-45 minutes.

¾ CUP: 276 cal., 13g fat (3g sat. fat), 90mg chol., 592mg sod., 29g carb. (5g sugars, 2g fiber), 11g pro.

(5) INGREDIENTS FAST FIX

PORT WINE CRANBERRY SAUCE

This crimson sauce has just the right amount of tartness to complement poultry, pork and game.
—Ellie Martin Cliffe, Milwaukee, WI

TAKES: 20 MIN. • **MAKES:** 2 CUPS

- 1 **pkg. (12 oz.) fresh or frozen cranberries**
- 1¼ **cups sugar**
- ¼ **cup port wine or grape juice**
- 2 **tsp. cornstarch**
- 2 **Tbsp. cold water**

In a small saucepan, cook cranberries, sugar and wine over medium heat just until berries begin to pop, 10-12 minutes. Combine cornstarch and water until smooth; stir into cranberry mixture. Bring to a boil; cook and stir until berries pop and sauce is thickened, about 2 minutes. Serve warm or cold. Refrigerate the leftovers.

¼ CUP: 146 cal., 0 fat (0 sat. fat), 0 chol., 1mg sod., 38g carb. (34g sugars, 2g fiber), 0 pro.

PORT WINE CRANBERRY SAUCE

SUGAR PLUM BREAD

EAT SMART

SUGAR PLUM BREAD

I grew up with my Grandma Mitchell's irresistible prune bread. We slathered it with butter and ate it with cottage cheese and fresh fruit for a simple breakfast. And it always makes an appearance at the holidays!
—Emily Tyra, Traverse City, MI

PREP: 15 MIN. + STANDING • **BAKE:** 40 MIN. + COOLING
MAKES: 1 LOAF (12 SLICES)

- **1 cup pitted dried plums, coarsely chopped**
- **¾ cup water**
- **2 Tbsp. plus ¾ cup granulated sugar, divided**
- **2 Tbsp. shortening**
- **1 large egg, room temperature**
- **2 cups all-purpose flour**
- **2 tsp. baking powder**
- **1 tsp. baking soda**
- **½ tsp. salt**
- **2 Tbsp. coarse sugar**

1. Preheat oven to 350°. In a small saucepan, combine dried plums, water and 2 Tbsp. granulated sugar. Bring to a simmer over medium heat for 1 minute. Remove from heat; let stand until plumped, about 10 minutes. Drain plums, reserving fruit and liquid. Measure liquid, adding enough water to yield ½ cup.
2. Cream shortening and remaining granulated sugar until light and fluffy, about 4 minutes. Beat in egg. In another bowl, whisk together flour, baking powder, baking soda and salt. Add to creamed mixture alternately with cooking liquid; fold in cooled dried plums (batter will be thick).
3. Transfer batter to a greased 8x4-in. loaf pan. Sprinkle with coarse sugar. Bake until a toothpick inserted in center comes out with moist crumbs, 40-45 minutes. Cool in pan 10 minutes before removing to a wire rack to cool completely.
1 SLICE: 202 cal., 3g fat (1g sat. fat), 16mg chol., 291mg sod., 41g carb. (21g sugars, 1g fiber), 3g pro.

SWEET POTATO-GINGERBREAD MERINGUE PIE

This delicious pie showcases gingerbread flavor in the meringue instead of the crust. Baking it on the bottom rack gets the crust nice and crisp without par-baking it.
—Shannon Roum, Cudahy, WI

PREP: 1 HOUR + CHILLING
BAKE: 40 MIN. + BROILING
MAKES: 10 SERVINGS

- **1¼ cups all-purpose flour**
- **4½ tsp. sugar**
- **Dash salt**
- **6 Tbsp. cold butter, cubed**
- **1 large egg yolk**
- **4 to 6 Tbsp. ice water**

FILLING
- **3 lbs. medium sweet potatoes**
- **1⅓ cups sugar**
- **⅔ cup butter, softened**
- **½ tsp. pumpkin pie spice**
- **Dash salt**
- **4 large eggs, lightly beaten**
- **2 tsp. vanilla extract**

MERINGUE
- **1 cup sugar**
- **⅓ cup water**
- **1 Tbsp. molasses**
- **Dash salt**
- **5 large egg whites, room temperature**
- **¾ tsp. cream of tartar**
- **¾ tsp. pumpkin pie spice**
- **½ tsp. ground ginger**

1. Pulse flour, sugar and salt in a food processor until blended. Add butter; pulse until butter is the size of peas. Combine egg yolk and 2 Tbsp. ice water; slowly add to processor until dough holds together, adding remaining ice water, if needed, 1 Tbsp. at a time. Shape dough into a disk; wrap and refrigerate 1 hour or overnight.
2. Preheat oven to 400°. Scrub sweet potatoes; pierce several times with a fork. Bake until tender, 45-50 minutes. Cool slightly; peel and mash to yield about 4 cups. Reduce oven setting to 350°.
3. On a lightly floured surface, roll dough to a ⅛-in.-thick circle; transfer to a 9-in. deep-dish pie plate. Trim crust to ½ in. beyond rim of plate; flute edge. Refrigerate 30 minutes.
4. For filling, beat sugar, butter, pie spice and salt until blended. Add eggs and vanilla; beat in cooled sweet potatoes until smooth. Add filling to chilled crust. Bake on bottom rack until a knife inserted in center comes out clean, 40-45 minutes. Keep warm.
5. Meanwhile, for meringue, combine sugar, water, molasses and salt in a small saucepan over medium-high heat; using a pastry brush dipped in water, wash down the sides of the pan to eliminate sugar crystals. When the mixture comes to a boil, stop brushing. Cook without stirring until a thermometer reads 240° (soft-ball stage).
6. As molasses mixture cooks, preheat broiler. Beat egg whites, cream of tartar and spices on medium speed until soft peaks form. While beating, gradually drizzle hot molasses mixture over egg whites; continue beating until stiff glossy peaks form. Spread meringue over hot filling; broil 4-6 in. from the heat until slightly browned, 1-2 minutes. Cool on a wire rack.

1 PIECE: 609 cal., 22g fat (13g sat. fat), 144mg chol., 663mg sod., 96g carb. (64g sugars, 5g fiber), 9g pro.

SWEET POTATO-GINGERBREAD MERINGUE PIE

NUTTY & NICE

Make a list and check it twice for all the crunchy nuts and goodies you need for these happy holiday sweets.

NUTTY STICKY BUN CANDIES

NUTTY STICKY BUN CANDIES

Save room on your holiday treat trays for these sweet and salty spirals. Oh, and hide some for yourself, too. They'll be in high demand!
—Josh Carter, Birmingham, AL

PREP: 20 MIN. • **COOK:** 15 MIN. + COOLING
MAKES: ABOUT 6 DOZEN (2¼ LBS.)

- **2 tsp. plus ½ cup softened butter, divided**
- **3¾ cups confectioners' sugar**
- **½ cup nonfat dry milk powder**
- **½ cup granulated sugar**
- **½ cup light corn syrup**
- **1 tsp. vanilla extract**

FILLING

- **¼ cup granulated sugar**
- **1 tsp. ground cinnamon**
- **2¼ cups deluxe mixed nuts, divided**
- **1 Tbsp. light corn syrup**

1. Butter an 8-in. square pan with 2 tsp. butter; set aside.
2. Combine confectioners' sugar and milk powder. In a large heavy saucepan, combine ½ cup granulated sugar, ½ cup corn syrup and remaining butter; cook and stir until sugar is dissolved and mixture comes to a boil. Stir in confectioners' sugar mixture, about a third at a time, until blended.
3. Remove from the heat; stir in vanilla. Continue stirring until mixture mounds slightly when dropped from a spoon and a thermometer reads 150°. Spread into prepared pan. Cool for 15 minutes.
4. For filling, combine ¼ cup granulated sugar and the cinnamon. Place ¾ cup nuts in a food processor; cover and pulse until ground.
5. Cut cooled candy into quarters. Roll each into a 9x5-in. rectangle. Sprinkle each rectangle with a fourth of the sugar mixture and a fourth of the ground nuts to within ½ in. of edges. Roll up tightly jelly-roll style, starting with a long side.
6. Chop remaining nuts. Brush each roll with corn syrup; roll in nuts. Using a serrated knife, cut into ½-in. slices. Store at room temperature in an airtight container.
1 PIECE: 71 cal., 3g fat (1g sat. fat), 4mg chol., 28mg sod., 11g carb. (10g sugars, 0 fiber), 1g pro.

HAZELNUT TOFFEE

The Willamette Valley produces a lot of hazelnuts, so this recipe is truly representative of our area. I always make plenty of this delicious toffee to serve at Christmas and to give as gifts.
—Earlene Ertelt, Woodburn, OR

PREP: 15 MIN. • **COOK:** 15 MIN. + STANDING
MAKES: 2 LBS.

- **1¾ cups finely chopped hazelnuts**
- **1½ cups sugar**
- **½ cup water**
- **⅓ cup light corn syrup**
- **1 cup butter**
- **¼ tsp. salt**
- **¼ tsp. baking soda**
- **¼ tsp. orange extract**
- **1 cup (6 oz.) semisweet chocolate chips**

1. Place hazelnuts in a greased 15x10x1-in. baking pan. Bake at 300° until toasted, about 15 minutes; set aside.
2. In a large heavy saucepan, combine sugar, water and corn syrup; bring to a boil over medium heat. Cover and boil for 2 minutes. Stir in butter; cook over medium heat, stirring occasionally, until a thermometer reads 300°-310° (hard-crack stage). Remove from heat; quickly stir in salt, baking soda, orange extract and 1¼ cups toasted hazelnuts.
3. Pour onto a greased baking sheet; spread to ¼-in. thickness. Sprinkle with chocolate chips. Let stand until chocolate is melted, about 5 minutes; spread chocolate over toffee. Sprinkle with remaining hazelnuts. Let stand 1 hour. Break into pieces.
1 OZ.: 163 cal., 11g fat (5g sat. fat), 15mg chol., 77mg sod., 17g carb. (15g sugars, 1g fiber), 1g pro.

GRANDMA'S PECAN RUM BARS

My grandmother handed down the recipe for these gooey bars, which we all love. The candied cherries are a must.
—Deborah Pennington, Decatur, AL

PREP: 20 MIN. • **BAKE:** 1 HOUR + COOLING
MAKES: 2 DOZEN

- 4 **large eggs**
- 4 **cups chopped pecans, divided**
- 1 **cup butter, softened**
- 2¼ **cups packed brown sugar**
- 2 **Tbsp. vanilla extract**
- 1 **cup all-purpose flour**
- 2¼ **cups red candied cherries**
- 1½ **cups chopped candied pineapple**
- ½ **cup chopped candied citron**
- ⅓ **cup rum**

1. Let eggs stand at room temperature 30 minutes. Sprinkle 3 cups pecans over a greased 15x10x1-in. baking pan.
2. Preheat oven to 350°. Cream butter and brown sugar until light and fluffy. Add the eggs, one at a time, beating well after each addition. Beat in vanilla. Gradually add flour to creamed mixture, beating well.
3. Spread batter into prepared pan. Combine candied fruit and remaining pecans. Spread fruit and pecans evenly over creamed mixture; press gently to help mixtures adhere. Bake until a toothpick inserted in center comes out clean, about 1 hour. Sprinkle rum over the top; cool completely in pan on a wire rack. Cut into bars. Store in an airtight container.
1 BAR: 401 cal., 22g fat (6g sat. fat), 51mg chol., 123mg sod., 49g carb. (40g sugars, 2g fiber), 4g pro.

TEST KITCHEN TIP

This holiday treat tastes like a cross between rum cake, fruitcake and pecan pie. For a decadent twist, serve these bars over a swirl of vanilla sauce.

PEANUT CARAMEL BROWNIE BITES

PEANUT CARAMEL BROWNIE BITES

With their three irresistible layers, these brownies are my family's absolute favorite.
—Ella Agans, Birch Tree, MO

PREP: 1 HOUR + CHILLING
BAKE: 20 MIN. + COOLING
MAKES: 4 DOZEN

- ¾ **cup butter, cubed and softened**
- ⅔ **cup sugar**
- 2 **Tbsp. water**
- 1 **cup (6 oz.) semisweet chocolate chips**
- 2 **large eggs**
- 1 **tsp. vanilla extract**
- 1 **cup all-purpose flour**
- ½ **tsp. baking powder**

CANDY BAR TOPPING

- 1 **cup sugar**
- ¼ **cup butter, cubed**
- ¼ **cup 2% milk**
- 1 **cup marshmallow creme**
- ½ **cup creamy peanut butter, divided**
- ½ **tsp. vanilla extract**
- 2½ **cups dry roasted peanuts, divided**
- 40 **caramels**
- 2 **Tbsp. water**
- 1¼ **cups (7½ oz.) semisweet chocolate chips**

1. Preheat oven to 350°. Line a 13x9-in. baking pan with foil, letting ends extend up sides; coat foil with cooking spray.
2. Microwave butter, sugar and water on high just until the mixture comes to a boil, 3-4 minutes; stir until blended. Stir in the chocolate chips until melted. Whisk in eggs, one at a time, and vanilla until blended. Stir in flour and baking powder.
3. Spread into prepared pan. Bake until a toothpick inserted in center comes out clean, 18-20 minutes. Cool 30 minutes.
4. For topping, combine sugar, butter and milk in a large saucepan; bring to a boil, stirring constantly, over medium heat. Boil 5 minutes, stirring frequently. Stir in marshmallow creme, ¼ cup peanut butter and vanilla; pour over brownies. Sprinkle with 2 cups peanuts.
5. In a small saucepan, combine caramels and water; cook, stirring, over medium-high heat until blended. Pour over peanuts.
6. Microwave chocolate chips on high until softened, about 1 minute. Stir in remaining peanut butter until smooth; pour over caramel layer. Chop remaining peanuts; sprinkle on top. Refrigerate at least 1 hour.
7. Lifting with foil, remove brownies from pan. Cut into bars. Store in an airtight container in the refrigerator.
1 BAR: 212 cal., 12g fat (5g sat. fat), 19mg chol., 135mg sod., 24g carb. (19g sugars, 1g fiber), 4g pro.

ORANGE-PISTACHIO DIVINITY

LORRI REINHARDT
Big Bend, WI

CINNAMON ALMOND BRITTLE

It simply wouldn't be Christmas at our house without this old-time favorite twist on peanut brittle. No one believes how easy it is!
—Lynette Kleinschmidt, Litchfield, MN

PREP: 15 MIN. • **COOK:** 20 MIN. + COOLING
MAKES: ABOUT 2 LBS.

- 1 tsp. plus 3 Tbsp. butter, cubed
- 2 cups sugar
- ¾ cup light corn syrup
- ¼ cup water
- 3 cups slivered almonds, toasted
- 2 tsp. ground cinnamon
- ½ tsp. salt
- 1½ tsp. baking soda
- 1 tsp. vanilla extract

1. Preheat oven to 200°. Grease two baking sheets with 1 tsp. butter; place in oven.
2. In a large heavy saucepan, combine sugar, corn syrup and water. Bring to a boil, stirring constantly to dissolve sugar. Using a pastry brush dipped in water, wash down the sides of the pan to eliminate sugar crystals. Cook, without stirring, over medium heat until a candy thermometer reads 240° (soft-ball stage). Stir in the almonds, cinnamon, salt and remaining butter; cook until thermometer reads 300° (hard-crack stage), stirring frequently and brushing sides of pan as needed.
3. Remove from heat; stir in the baking soda and vanilla. Immediately pour onto the prepared pans, spreading to ¼-in. thickness. Cool completely.
4. Break into pieces. Store between layers of waxed paper in an airtight container.
1 OZ.: 142 cal., 6g fat (1g sat. fat), 3mg chol., 111mg sod., 21g carb. (19g sugars, 1g fiber), 2g pro.

★★★★★ READER REVIEW

"My husband and I loved this brittle! It reminds us of the cinnamon almonds for sale at local fairs—delicious!"
GLD2BMOM
TASTEOFHOME.COM

ORANGE-PISTACHIO DIVINITY

Old-fashioned divinity candy is even yummier with a hint of refreshing orange zest and bits of crunchy pistachios. Store-bought versions just can't compare!
—Lorri Reinhardt, Big Bend, WI

PREP: 15 MIN. • **COOK:** 20 MIN. + STANDING
MAKES: ABOUT 4 DOZEN (1⅓ LBS.)

- 2 large egg whites
- 2⅔ cups sugar
- ⅔ cup light corn syrup
- ½ cup water
- 1 tsp. grated orange zest
- 1 tsp. vanilla extract
- ⅔ cup pistachios, coarsely chopped

1. Place egg whites in bowl of a stand mixer; let stand at room temperature 30 minutes. Meanwhile, line two 15x10x1-in. pans with waxed paper.
2. In a large heavy saucepan, combine sugar, corn syrup and water; cook and stir until sugar is dissolved and mixture comes to a boil. Cook, without stirring, over medium heat until a thermometer reads 252° (hard-ball stage). Just before that temperature is reached, beat egg whites on medium speed until stiff peaks form.
3. With mixer continuing to run on high speed, slowly add hot sugar mixture in a thin stream over egg whites, beating constantly and scraping sides of bowl occasionally. Add orange zest and vanilla. Beat until candy holds its shape and begins to lose its gloss, about 5-6 minutes. (Do not overbeat, or candy will stiffen and crumble.) Immediately fold in pistachios.
4. Quickly drop mixture by tablespoonfuls onto prepared pans. Let stand at room temperature until dry to the touch. Store between layers of waxed paper in an airtight container at room temperature.
1 PIECE: 68 cal., 1g fat (0 sat. fat), 0 chol., 13mg sod., 15g carb. (15g sugars, 0 fiber), 1g pro.

CINNAMON ALMOND BRITTLE

OLDIES BUT GOODIES

Introducing the cookie classics to know, love and make again and again. Once these evergreen wonders appear on the holiday tray, you can bet they'll be gone in a flurry.

GREAT-GRANDMA'S OATMEAL COOKIES

GREAT-GRANDMA'S OATMEAL COOKIES

This recipe—a favorite of my husband's—goes back to my great-grandmother. At Christmastime, we use colored sugar for a festive touch.
—Mary Ann Konechne, Kimball, SD

PREP: 35 MIN.
BAKE: 15 MIN./BATCH + COOLING
MAKES: ABOUT 12 DOZEN

- **1½ cups shortening**
- **2 cups sugar**
- **4 large eggs, room temperature**
- **4 tsp. water**
- **4 cups all-purpose flour**
- **2 tsp. baking soda**
- **2 tsp. ground cinnamon**
- **½ tsp. salt**
- **4 cups quick-cooking oats**
- **2 cups chopped raisins**
- **1 cup chopped walnuts**
- **Additional granulated sugar or colored sugar**

1. Preheat oven to 350°. Cream shortening and sugar until light and fluffy. Add eggs, one at a time, beating well after each addition. Beat in water. In another bowl, whisk the flour, baking soda, cinnamon and salt; add to creamed mixture, and mix well. Stir in oats, raisins and walnuts.

2. On a surface sprinkled with additional granulated or colored sugar, roll dough to ¼-in. thickness. Cut with floured 2½-in. cookie cutters in desired shapes. Place 2 in. apart on greased baking sheets. Bake until set, 12-15 minutes. Remove cookies to wire racks to cool.

1 COOKIE: 63 cal., 3g fat (1g sat. fat), 5mg chol., 28mg sod., 9g carb. (4g sugars, 0 fiber), 1g pro.

TEST KITCHEN TIP

If you want to add a finishing touch to these classic cookies, mix 1 cup confectioners' sugar with ¼ tsp. cinnamon and 5-6 tsp. water to make a quick glaze.

CRINKLE-TOP CHOCOLATE COOKIES

EAT SMART

CRINKLE-TOP CHOCOLATE COOKIES

When I baked these fudgy cookies for the first time, my three preschool children loved them! I like them because they're lower in fat and easy to mix and bake.
—Maria Groff, Ephrata, PA

PREP: 15 MIN. + CHILLING
BAKE: 10 MIN./BATCH + COOLING
MAKES: ABOUT 3½ DOZEN

- **2 cups (about 12 oz.) semisweet chocolate chips, divided**
- **2 Tbsp. butter, softened**
- **1 cup sugar**
- **2 large egg whites**
- **1½ tsp. vanilla extract**
- **1½ cups all-purpose flour**
- **1½ tsp. baking powder**
- **¼ tsp. salt**
- **¼ cup water**
- **½ cup confectioners' sugar**

1. In a microwave, melt 1 cup chocolate chips. Stir until smooth; set aside. Beat butter and sugar until crumbly, about 2 minutes. Add egg whites and vanilla; beat well. Stir in melted chocolate.

2. In another bowl, whisk together flour, baking powder and salt; gradually add to butter mixture alternately with water. Stir in remaining chocolate chips. Refrigerate, covered, until easy to handle, about 2 hours.

3. Preheat oven to 350°. Shape dough into 1-in. balls. Roll in confectioners' sugar. Place 2 in. apart on baking sheets coated with cooking spray. Bake until set, 10-12 minutes. Remove to wire racks to cool.

1 COOKIE: 85 cal., 3g fat (2g sat. fat), 1mg chol., 39mg sod., 15g carb. (11g sugars, 1g fiber), 1g pro. **Diabetic exchanges:** 1 starch, ½ fat.

GINGERSNAPS

GINGERSNAPS

My friends and neighbors look for these old-time cookies on the goodie trays that I give out every holiday. They're ideal for dunking in milk, and they bring back the spicy flavor of Christmases past.
—Elizabeth Flatt, Kelso, WA

PREP: 20 MIN. + CHILLING • **BAKE:** 10 MIN./BATCH + COOLING
MAKES: ABOUT 2 DOZEN

- **⅓ cup shortening**
- **½ cup sugar**
- **1 large egg, room temperature**
- **2 Tbsp. molasses**
- **1 cup all-purpose flour**
- **1 tsp. baking soda**
- **½ tsp. ground cinnamon**
- **½ tsp. ground cloves**
- **½ tsp. ground ginger**
- **⅛ tsp. salt**
- **Additional sugar**

1. Cream shortening and sugar until light and fluffy. Beat in egg and molasses. In another bowl, whisk together the next six ingredients; gradually beat into creamed mixture, and mix well. Refrigerate, covered, for at least 4 hours.
2. Preheat oven to 350°. Shape tablespoonfuls of cookie dough into balls; roll in additional sugar. Place 2 in. apart on lightly greased baking sheets.
3. Bake until edges are lightly browned and tops are set and starting to crack, 8-10 minutes. Cool 2 minutes before removing to wire racks.
FREEZE OPTION: Place balls of dough on waxed paper-lined baking sheets and freeze until firm. Remove from pan and place in freezer containers for up to 3 months. To bake, place frozen balls of dough 2 in. apart on lightly greased baking sheets. Bake until the edges are lightly browned and tops are set and starting to crack.
1 COOKIE: 68 cal., 3g fat (1g sat. fat), 8mg chol., 69mg sod., 10g carb. (5g sugars, 0 fiber), 1g pro.

(5) INGREDIENTS

SCOTTISH SHORTBREAD

My mother, who is of Scottish heritage, passed this recipe and many other favorites on to me. When I entered this shortbread at our local fair, it won a red ribbon.
—Rose Mabee, Selkirk, MB

PREP: 15 MIN. • **BAKE:** 20 MIN./BATCH + COOLING
MAKES: ABOUT 4 DOZEN

- **2 cups butter, softened**
- **1 cup packed brown sugar**
- **4 to 4½ cups all-purpose flour**

1. Preheat oven to 325°. Cream butter and brown sugar until light and fluffy. Add 3¾ cups flour; mix well. Turn dough onto a floured surface; knead for 5 minutes, adding enough remaining flour to form a soft dough.
2. Roll to ½-in. thickness. Cut into 3x1-in. strips. Place 1 in. apart on ungreased baking sheets. Prick with fork. Bake until cookies are lightly browned, 20-25 minutes. Cool.
1 COOKIE: 123 cal., 8g fat (5g sat. fat), 20mg chol., 62mg sod., 12g carb. (5g sugars, 0 fiber), 1g pro.

SCOTTISH SHORTBREAD

WHOLE WHEAT SNICKERDOODLES

WHOLE WHEAT SNICKERDOODLES

These soft, chewy cookies make a super snack. Their light cinnamon taste goes so well with a cold glass of milk.
—Jana Horsfall, Garden City, KS

PREP: 15 MIN. • **BAKE:** 10 MIN./BATCH + COOLING
MAKES: ABOUT 2½ DOZEN

- 1 **cup butter, softened**
- 1½ **cups sugar**
- 1 **large egg plus 1 large egg white, room temperature**
- 1½ **cups whole wheat flour**
- 1¼ **cups all-purpose flour**
- 1 **tsp. baking soda**
- ¼ **tsp. salt**

TOPPING
- 2 **Tbsp. sugar**
- 2 **tsp. ground cinnamon**

1. Preheat oven to 400°. Cream butter and sugar until light and fluffy. Beat in egg and egg white. In another bowl, whisk together flours, baking soda and salt; gradually beat into creamed mixture.
2. In a small bowl, combine topping ingredients. Shape dough into 1½-in. balls; roll in cinnamon sugar. Place 2 in. apart on ungreased baking sheets. Bake 8-10 minutes. As they bake, cookies will puff up, then flatten. Cool.
1 COOKIE: 139 cal., 7g fat (4g sat. fat), 22mg chol., 115mg sod., 19g carb. (11g sugars, 1g fiber), 2g pro.

PEANUT BUTTER BLOSSOM COOKIES

These are an easy family favorite that make my children smile.
—Tammie Merrill, Wake Forest, NC

PREP: 15 MIN. • **BAKE:** 10 MIN./BATCH + COOLING
MAKES: ABOUT 3 DOZEN

- ½ **cup butter, softened**
- ½ **cup creamy peanut butter**
- ½ **cup sugar**
- ½ **cup packed brown sugar**
- 1 **large egg**
- 1¼ **cups all-purpose flour**
- ¾ **tsp. baking soda**
- ½ **tsp. baking powder**
- ¼ **tsp. salt**
- 36 **milk chocolate kisses**

1. Preheat oven to 350°. Cream butter, peanut butter and sugars until light and fluffy. Beat in egg. In another bowl, sift together flour, baking soda, baking powder and salt; beat into the peanut butter mixture.
2. Drop by level tablespoonfuls 2 in. apart on ungreased baking sheets. Bake until light brown, 10-12 minutes. Remove from oven; immediately push a chocolate kiss into the top of each cookie. Cool on pans for 2 minutes; remove from pans to wire racks to cool completely.
1 COOKIE: 106 cal., 6g fat (3g sat. fat), 13mg chol., 92mg sod., 13g carb. (9g sugars, 0 fiber), 2g pro.

PEANUT BUTTER BLOSSOM COOKIES

HERMITS

HERMITS

Dress up a cookie plate with these old-fashioned spice bars full of raisins, molasses, cinnamon, ginger and nuts. The chewy treats are marvelous with coffee or hot cocoa on frosty days. The cookies are said to be called hermits because they keep well—and they're even better when hidden away like a hermit for several days!
—Jeri Tirmenstein, Apache Junction, AZ

PREP: 25 MIN. • **BAKE:** 10 MIN. + COOLING
MAKES: 14 COOKIES

- **⅓ cup raisins**
- **1 cup all-purpose flour**
- **⅓ cup packed brown sugar**
- **½ tsp. baking powder**
- **½ tsp. ground ginger**
- **½ tsp. ground cinnamon**
- **¼ tsp. salt**
- **¼ cup molasses**
- **3 Tbsp. butter, melted**
- **1 large egg white or 2 Tbsp. egg substitute**
- **1 tsp. vanilla extract**
- **⅓ cup chopped walnuts**

1. Preheat oven to 375°. Cover raisins with boiling water. Let stand for 5 minutes; drain and set aside.
2. Whisk together next six ingredients. In another bowl, combine molasses, butter, egg white and vanilla; stir into the dry ingredients just until moistened. Fold in walnuts and raisins (batter will be wet).
3. Divide batter in half; spread each half (wetting hands, if necessary) into a 12x2-in. rectangle 2 in. apart on a parchment paper-lined baking sheet. Bake until edges are lightly browned and set, 10-15 minutes.
4. Transfer rectangles to a cutting board; with a serrated knife, cut diagonally into 1½-in. bars. Remove to wire racks to cool. Store in an airtight container.
1 BAR: 122 cal., 4g fat (2g sat. fat), 7mg chol., 87mg sod., 20g carb. (12g sugars, 1g fiber), 2g pro.

ALMOND SANDIES

Buttery, rich and delicious, these sandies are my husband's favorite cookie and very popular wherever I take them.
—Joyce Pierce, Caledonia, MI

PREP: 20 MIN.
BAKE: 25 MIN./BATCH + COOLING
MAKES: ABOUT 4 DOZEN

- **1 cup butter, softened**
- **1 cup sugar**
- **1 tsp. almond extract**
- **1¾ cups all-purpose flour**
- **½ tsp. baking soda**
- **¼ tsp. baking powder**
- **¼ tsp. salt**
- **½ cup slivered almonds**

1. Preheat oven to 300°. Cream butter and sugar until light and fluffy. Beat in extract. In another bowl, whisk together flour, baking soda, baking powder and salt; gradually add to creamed mixture. Fold in almonds.
2. Drop by level tablespoonfuls onto ungreased baking sheets. Bake until edges are lightly browned, 22-24 minutes. Cool on pans for 1-2 minutes before removing to wire racks.
1 COOKIE: 74 cal., 4g fat (2g sat. fat), 10mg chol., 58mg sod., 8g carb. (4g sugars, 0 fiber), 1g pro.

ALMOND SANDIES

HARVEYS COCONUT MACAROONS

As the executive chef at Harveys, a resort hotel in Lake Tahoe, I modified this classic recipe, which originated a century ago at a renowned pastry shop in Vienna, Austria.
—Norbert Koblitz, Lake Tahoe, NV

PREP: 15 MIN.
BAKE: 15 MIN./BATCH + COOLING
MAKES: ABOUT 4 DOZEN

- **1 cup sweetened shredded coconut**
- **3½ cups almond paste**
- **1 cup all-purpose flour**
- **⅔ cup sugar**
- **5 large eggs**
- **½ cup chopped walnuts**
- **Red candied cherries, halved**

1. Preheat oven to 350°. In a food processor or blender, process coconut until finely chopped; set aside. Beat almond paste until crumbled. Gradually add flour, sugar and coconut; mix well. Add eggs, one at a time, beating well after each addition; beat until smooth. Stir in nuts.

2. Cut a small hole in the tip of a pastry bag or in a corner of a food-safe plastic bag; insert a large star tip. Transfer dough to bag. Pipe 1-in.-diameter cookies 2 in. apart onto parchment paper-lined baking sheets. Top with cherries. Bake until golden brown, 15-20 minutes. Cool 5 minutes before removing to wire racks.

1 COOKIE: 121 cal., 7g fat (1g sat. fat), 19mg chol., 14mg sod., 14g carb. (10g sugars, 1g fiber), 3g pro.

HOLIDAY TOAST

Be ready for drop-in guests with these chill-chasing classic drinks. They're guaranteed to warm hearts.

CHILLY SNOW DAY FLOATS

(5) INGREDIENTS

DULCE DE LECHE HOT CHOCOLATE PODS

Give your friends a little heaven in a cup with these divine hot chocolate pods and the perfect book to read while sipping the hot chocolate. Like Water for Chocolate, *penned by Laura Esquivel, introduces Tita, the extraordinary chef who puts herself and her emotions into every dish she creates.*
—Taste of Home *Test Kitchen*

PREP: 20 MIN. + CHILLING • **COOK:** 5 MIN.
MAKES: 14 PODS (2 SERVINGS PER POD)

- **24 oz. 53% cacao dark baking chocolate or semisweet chocolate, chopped**
- **1 can (13.4 oz.) dulce de leche**
- **½ cup heavy whipping cream**
- **Gold colored sugar and gold pearl dust, optional**

ADDITIONAL INGREDIENT (FOR EACH POD)

- **1½ cups whole milk**

1. Place chocolate in a large bowl. In a small saucepan, bring dulce de leche and cream just to a boil, stirring constantly. Pour over chocolate; whisk until smooth.
2. Spoon ¼ cup chocolate mixture into each of 14 paper-lined muffin cups; if desired, sprinkle with gold sugar. Refrigerate until firm, about 8 hours. If desired, brush with gold dust. Store in an airtight container in the refrigerator for up to 3 weeks.
3. To prepare hot chocolate: Bring 1½ cups milk just to a boil; add one pod. Whisk until dissolved.

NOTE: This recipe was tested with Nestle dulce de leche. Look for it in the international foods section. Pearl dust is available from Wilton Industries. Call 800-794-5866 or visit *wilton.com.*

¾ CUP: 289 cal., 17g fat (10g sat. fat), 28mg chol., 100mg sod., 30g carb. (26g sugars, 2g fiber), 8g pro.

(5) INGREDIENTS FAST FIX

CHILLY SNOW DAY FLOATS

On your next snow day, pass out these frothy floats and everybody will be glad they're cooped up with you. Cream soda works with the peppermint ice cream, too.
—Julianne Schnuck, Milwaukee, WI

TAKES: 10 MIN. • **MAKES:** 2 SERVINGS

- **½ cup lemon-lime soda**
- **1 cup peppermint ice cream**
- **½ cup whipped cream**
- **Peppermint candy, optional**

Pour lemon-lime soda into two glasses; add ice cream. Top with whipped cream. If desired, sprinkle with peppermint candy. Serve immediately with straws and spoons.

1 FLOAT: 248 cal., 15g fat (9g sat. fat), 44mg chol., 59mg sod., 27g carb. (19g sugars, 0 fiber), 3g pro.

HOMEMADE EGGNOG

After one sip, folks will know that this smooth and creamy holiday staple is homemade, not a store-bought variety. If desired, add a half cup rum or brandy.
—Pat Waymire, Yellow Springs, OH

PREP: 15 MIN. • **COOK:** 30 MIN. + CHILLING
MAKES: 12 SERVINGS (ABOUT 3 QT.)

- **12 large eggs**
- **1½ cups sugar**
- **½ tsp. salt**
- **8 cups whole milk, divided**
- **2 Tbsp. vanilla extract**
- **1 tsp. ground nutmeg**
- **2 cups heavy whipping cream**
- **Additional nutmeg, optional**

1. In a heavy saucepan, whisk together eggs, sugar and salt. Gradually add 4 cups milk; cook and stir over low heat until a thermometer reads 160°-170°, about 30-35 minutes. Do not allow to boil. Immediately transfer to a large bowl.
2. Stir in vanilla, nutmeg and remaining milk. Place bowl in an ice-water bath, stirring until milk mixture is cool. (If mixture separates, process in a blender until smooth.) Refrigerate, covered, until cold, at least 3 hours.
3. To serve, beat cream until soft peaks form. Whisk gently into milk mixture. If desired, sprinkle with additional nutmeg.
NOTE: Eggnog may be stored, covered, in the refrigerator for several days. Whisk before serving.
1 CUP: 411 cal., 25g fat (14g sat. fat), 247mg chol., 251mg sod., 35g carb. (35g sugars, 0 fiber), 13g pro.

★★★★★ **READER REVIEW**

"This was so AMAZING! My family loved it, and it tastes better than what we used to buy from the store. The only thing I would do different is add more nutmeg because I love that nutmeg flavor."
CARLYGILES
TASTEOFHOME.COM

DON'T FORGET FIDO

DOG BISCUITS

If members of your family are of the furry, four-legged kind, treat them to these homemade biscuits. They're a cinch to make, and your canine pals will go crazy for the peanut butter flavor.
—Shannon Roum, Cudahy, WI

PREP: 15 MIN.
BAKE: 30 MIN. + COOLING
MAKES: 31 DOG BISCUITS

- **2 cups whole wheat flour**
- **1 cup toasted wheat germ**
- **½ tsp. ground cinnamon**
- **¾ cup water**
- **¼ cup creamy peanut butter**
- **1 large egg**
- **2 Tbsp. canola oil**

1. Preheat oven to 350°. Combine flour, wheat germ and cinnamon. Stir in the remaining ingredients. On a floured surface, roll dough to ¼-in. thickness. Cut with a 3-in. bone-shaped cookie cutter.
2. Place 2 in. apart on ungreased baking sheets. Bake until bottoms are lightly browned (tops may crack), 30-35 minutes. Cool on a wire rack. Store in an airtight container.
NOTE: Reduced-fat peanut butter is not recommended for this recipe.
1 DOG BISCUIT: 61 cal., 3g fat (0 sat. fat), 7mg chol., 12mg sod., 8g carb. (0 sugars, 1g fiber), 3g pro.

TURKEY A LA KING
PAGE 280

CLASSIC COMEBACK

These tried-and-true dishes have been around for generations—for a good reason! They're comforting, delicious and the definition of heirloom recipes.

BACON CHICKEN CHOPPED SALAD

FAST FIX

BACON CHICKEN CHOPPED SALAD

Here's one of many reasons we love tomato season. Chopped salads are so simple and such a fantastic way to eat fresh.
—Donna Ryan, Topsfield, MA

TAKES: 20 MIN.
MAKES: 6 SERVINGS (1 CUP DRESSING)

- **1 pkg. (22 oz.) frozen grilled chicken breast strips**
- **1 cup crumbled blue cheese**
- **3 Tbsp. white wine vinegar**
- **1 Tbsp. water**
- **⅛ tsp. coarsely ground pepper**
- **¼ cup canola oil**
- **8 cups chopped romaine**
- **3 medium tomatoes, chopped**
- **6 bacon strips, cooked and crumbled**

1. Heat chicken according to package directions. Cool slightly; coarsely chop the chicken.
2. For the dressing, place cheese, vinegar, water and pepper in a small food processor; cover and process until smooth. While processing, gradually add the oil in a steady stream.
3. In a large bowl, combine romaine, chicken, tomatoes and bacon. Serve with the dressing.
2⅓ CUPS SALAD WITH ABOUT 2 TBSP. DRESSING: 348 cal., 22g fat (7g sat. fat), 87mg chol., 993mg sod., 6g carb. (2g sugars, 2g fiber), 35g pro.

FAST FIX

TURKEY A LA KING

(SHOWN ON PAGE 278)
This is a great way to use up leftover turkey. It's so good, you might want to make a double batch!
—Mary Gaylord, Balsam Lake, WI

TAKES: 25 MIN. • **MAKES:** 6 SERVINGS

- **1 medium onion, chopped**
- **¾ cup sliced celery**
- **¼ cup diced green pepper**
- **¼ cup butter, cubed**
- **¼ cup all-purpose flour**
- **1 tsp. sugar**
- **1½ cups chicken broth**
- **¼ cup half-and-half cream**
- **3 cups cubed cooked turkey or chicken**
- **1 can (4 oz.) sliced mushrooms, drained**
- **6 slices bread, toasted**

1. In a large skillet, saute onion, celery and green pepper in butter until tender. Stir in flour and sugar until a paste forms.
2. Gradually stir in broth. Bring to a boil; boil 1 minute or until thickened. Reduce heat. Add cream, turkey and mushrooms; heat through. Serve with toast.
1 SERVING: 297 cal., 13g fat (7g sat. fat), 98mg chol., 591mg sod., 21g carb. (4g sugars, 2g fiber), 24g pro.

FAST FIX

CRISPY SHRIMP CAESAR SALAD

My friend Jane and I have a favorite lunch spot that serves a fantastic salad that's only on the menu on Wednesdays. I made my own version at home so I can eat it whenever I want! To save prep time, buy peeled, deveined shrimp and prewashed lettuce.
—Marla Clark, Albuquerque, NM

TAKES: 30 MIN. • **MAKES:** 4 SERVINGS

- **2 romaine hearts, coarsely chopped**
- **1 cup cherry tomatoes, halved**
- **¼ cup shredded Parmesan cheese**
- **½ cup all-purpose flour**
- **¾ tsp. salt**
- **½ tsp. pepper**
- **1 lb. uncooked large shrimp, peeled and deveined**
- **Oil for frying**
- **½ cup creamy Caesar salad dressing**
- **Additional shredded Parmesan cheese and pepper, optional**

1. In a large bowl, combine romaine, tomatoes and cheese; refrigerate until serving. In another bowl, mix flour, salt and pepper. Add shrimp, a few pieces at a time, and toss to coat; shake off excess.
2. In a deep skillet, heat ¼ in. oil to 375°. Fry shrimp, a few at a time, 1-2 minutes on each side or until golden brown. Drain on paper towels.
3. Drizzle dressing over romaine mixture and toss to coat. Top with shrimp. If desired, sprinkle with additional cheese and pepper; serve immediately.
1 SERVING: 405 cal., 31g fat (5g sat. fat), 153mg chol., 680mg sod., 8g carb. (2g sugars, 2g fiber), 23g pro.

FAST FIX

MINI BLT APPETIZERS

Five simple ingredients are all you need to wow friends and family with a tasty appetizer. I love making these as much as sharing them.
—Nick Berg, Milwaukee, WI

TAKES: 30 MIN. • **MAKES:** 2½ DOZEN

- **30 cherry tomatoes**
- **¾ cup reduced-fat mayonnaise**
- **2 Bibb or Boston lettuce leaves, torn into 1-in. pieces**
- **¼ cup salad croutons, broken into pieces**
- **3 bacon strips, cooked and crumbled**
- **Coarsely ground pepper**

1. Cut a thin slice off the top of each tomato. Scoop out and discard pulp; invert tomatoes on paper towels to drain. Pipe mayonnaise into tomatoes.
2. Roll lettuce pieces and insert into tomatoes. Repeat with the croutons and bacon. Sprinkle with pepper. Cover and refrigerate up to 1 hour.
1 APPETIZER: 27 cal., 2g fat (0 sat. fat), 3mg chol., 55mg sod., 1g carb, (1g sugars, 0 fiber), 0 pro.

GRILLED PIZZA BURGERS

Pizza burgers are usually a kid's favorite, but adding spices and cheese and serving them on English muffins makes them a favorite for adults as well.
—Mitzi Sentiff, Annapolis, MD

PREP: 20 MIN. • **GRILL:** 15 MIN. • **MAKES:** 4 SERVINGS

- **1 large egg, lightly beaten**
- **¾ cup grated Parmesan cheese**
- **½ cup chopped onion**
- **¼ cup minced fresh parsley**
- **¾ tsp. dried basil**
- **¾ tsp. dried oregano**
- **¾ tsp. dried rosemary, crushed**
- **¾ tsp. pepper**
- **1 lb. ground beef**
- **4 slices provolone cheese**
- **4 English muffins, split and toasted**
- **½ cup pizza sauce**

1. In a large bowl, combine the first eight ingredients. Crumble beef over the mixture and mix well. Shape into four patties.
2. Grill burgers, covered, over medium heat for 5-7 minutes on each side or until a thermometer reads 160° and juices run clear. Top burgers with cheese; cover and grill 2-3 minutes longer or until cheese is melted. Serve on muffins with pizza sauce.
1 SERVING: 572 cal., 29g fat (14g sat. fat), 172mg chol., 902mg sod., 31g carb. (4g sugars, 3g fiber), 45g pro.

BARBECUED PICNIC CHICKEN

I like to serve this savory chicken at family picnics. Cooked on a covered grill, it stays so tender and juicy. Everyone loves the zesty, slightly sweet homemade barbecue sauce—and it's so easy to make.
—Priscilla Weaver, Hagerstown, MD

PREP: 15 MIN. • **GRILL:** 45 MIN. • **MAKES:** 8 SERVINGS

- **2 garlic cloves, minced**
- **2 tsp. butter**
- **1 cup ketchup**
- **¼ cup packed brown sugar**
- **¼ cup chili sauce**
- **2 Tbsp. Worcestershire sauce**
- **1 Tbsp. celery seed**
- **1 Tbsp. prepared mustard**
- **½ tsp. salt**
- **2 dashes hot pepper sauce**
- **2 broiler/fryer chickens (3½ to 4 lbs. each), cut up**

1. In a large saucepan, saute garlic in butter until tender. Add the next eight ingredients. Bring to a boil, stirring constantly. Remove from the heat; set aside.
2. On a lightly greased grill rack, grill chicken, covered, over medium heat for 30 minutes, turning occasionally. Baste with sauce. Grill 15 minutes longer or until a thermometer reaches 170°, basting and turning several times.
3 OZ. COOKED CHICKEN: 296 cal., 14g fat (4g sat. fat), 79mg chol., 761mg sod., 18g carb. (12g sugars, 1g fiber), 25g pro.

BARBECUED PICIC CHICKEN

SLOW COOKER CLAM SAUCE

EAT SMART SLOW COOKER

SLOW COOKER CLAM SAUCE

This delectable clam sauce does double-duty—as a bright and fresh pasta sauce, and as a hot dip for special get-togethers.
—Frances Pietsch, Flower Mound, TX

PREP: 10 MIN. • **COOK:** 3 HOURS • **MAKES:** 4 CUPS

- **4 Tbsp. butter**
- **2 Tbsp. olive oil**
- **½ cup finely chopped onion**
- **8 oz. fresh mushrooms, chopped**
- **2 garlic cloves, minced**
- **2 cans (10 oz. each) whole baby clams**
- **¾ tsp. dried oregano**
- **½ tsp. garlic salt**
- **¼ tsp. white pepper**
- **¼ tsp. black pepper**
- **¼ tsp. Italian seasoning**
- **1 bay leaf**
- **¼ cup sherry**
- **2 tsp. lemon juice**
- **½ cup water**
- **2 Tbsp. chopped fresh parsley**
- **Hot cooked pasta**
- **Grated Parmesan cheese, lemon juice and minced fresh parsley, optional**

1. Heat butter and oil in a skillet over medium-high heat. Add onion; cook and stir for 5 minutes. Add mushrooms and garlic; cook until the vegetables are tender, 5 minutes more.
2. Drain clams, reserving liquid; coarsely chop. Add clams, reserved clam juice, the mushroom mixture and the next nine ingredients in a 5-qt. slow cooker. Cook, covered, on low for 3 hours. Remove and discard bay leaf; stir in parsley. Serve with pasta. If desired, serve with optional ingredients.
½ CUP: 138 cal., 10g fat (4g sat. fat), 40mg chol., 580mg sod., 5g carb. (1g sugars, 0 fiber), 7g pro.0

FAST FIX

SENSATIONAL CRAB FONDUE

We entertain a lot, and this luxurious crab fondue makes our guests feel pampered!
—Debbie Obert, Middleburg, FL

TAKES: 30 MIN. • **MAKES:** 8 CUPS

- **½ cup butter, cubed**
- **3 green onions, finely chopped**
- **2 pkg. (8 oz. each) imitation crabmeat, coarsley chopped**
- **2 cups whole milk**
- **½ cup white wine or chicken broth**
- **¼ tsp. pepper**
- **2 cups shredded Monterey Jack cheese**
- **2 cups shredded Swiss cheese**
- **2 cups shredded Gruyere cheese or additional shredded Swiss cheese**
- **1 cup cubed process cheese (Velveeta)**
- **Cubed French bread**

1. In a 6-qt. stockpot, cook butter over medium-high heat. Add onions: cook and stir until tender. Add crab; cook 2-3 minutes longer or until heated through. Stir in milk, wine and pepper; heat until bubbles form around the sides of the pan.
2. Reduce heat to medium-low. Add ½ cup Monterey Jack cheese; stir constantly until almost completely melted. Continue adding the cheeses, ½ cup at a time, allowing cheese to almost melt completely between additions. Cook and stir until mixture is thickened and smooth.
3. Transfer to a heated fondue pot; keep fondue bubbling gently. Serve with bread cubes.
¼ CUP: 144 cal., 11g fat (6g sat. fat), 34mg chol., 257mg sod., 3g carb. (1g sugars, 0 fiber), 8g pro.

SENSATIONAL CRAB FONDUE

EAT SMART

LAUREN'S BOUILLABAISSE

This golden-colored soup is brimming with an assortment of seafood and is topped with savory and colorful sourdough croutons.
—Lauren Covas, New Brunswick, NJ

PREP: 30 MIN. • **COOK:** 20 MIN.
MAKES: 12 SERVINGS

- **⅔ cup chopped roasted sweet red pepper, drained**
- **¼ cup reduced-fat mayonnaise**

CROUTONS

- **6 slices sourdough bread**
- **1 garlic clove, halved**

BOUILLABAISSE

- **1 medium onion, chopped**
- **1 Tbsp. olive oil**
- **2 garlic cloves, minced**
- **2 plum tomatoes, chopped**
- **½ tsp. saffron threads or 2 tsp. ground turmeric**
- **3½ cups cubed red potatoes**
- **2½ cups thinly sliced fennel bulb**
- **1 carton (32 oz.) reduced-sodium chicken broth**
- **3 cups clam juice**
- **2 tsp. dried tarragon**
- **24 fresh littleneck clams**
- **24 fresh mussels, scrubbed and beards removed**
- **1 lb. red snapper fillet, cut into 2-in. pieces**
- **¾ lb. uncooked large shrimp, peeled and deveined**
- **¼ cup minced fresh parsley**

1. Place red pepper and mayonnaise in a food processor; cover and process until smooth. Refrigerate until serving.

2. For croutons, rub one side of each bread slice with garlic; discard garlic. Cut bread slices in half. Place on an ungreased baking sheet. Bake at 400° for 4-5 minutes on each side or until lightly browned.

3. In a stockpot, saute onion in oil until tender. Add garlic; cook 1 minute longer. Reduce heat; stir in tomatoes and saffron. Add the potatoes, fennel, broth, clam juice and tarragon. Bring to a boil. Reduce heat; simmer, uncovered, for 10-12 minutes or until potatoes are almost tender.

4. Add the clams, mussels, snapper and shrimp. Cook, stirring occasionally, for 10-15 minutes or until clams and mussels open and fish flakes easily with a fork. Discard any unopened clams or mussels. Spoon into bowls; sprinkle with parsley. Spread pepper mayo over croutons; serve with bouillabaisse.

1⅔ CUPS WITH 2 TSP. SPREAD ON ½ SLICE OF BREAD: 239 cal., 5g fat (1g sat. fat), 70mg chol., 684mg sod., 23g carb. (3g sugars, 2g fiber), 24g pro. **Diabetic exchanges:** 3 lean meat, 1½ starch, ½ fat.

SPUMONI BAKED ALASKA

SPUMONI BAKED ALASKA

For a refreshing end to a rich, special-occasion meal, try this freezer finale. It's an over-the-top dessert that won't overload your guests.
—Taste of Home *Test Kitchen*

PREP: 50 MIN. + FREEZING • **BAKE:** 5 MIN. • **MAKES:** 12 SERVINGS

- **½ cup butter, cubed**
- **2 oz. unsweetened chocolate, chopped**
- **1 cup sugar**
- **1 tsp. vanilla extract**
- **2 large eggs**
- **¾ cup all-purpose flour**
- **½ tsp. baking powder**
- **½ tsp. salt**
- **1 cup chopped hazelnuts**
- **2 qt. vanilla ice cream, softened, divided**
- **½ cup chopped pistachios**
- **½ tsp. almond extract**
- **6 drops green food coloring, optional**
- **⅓ cup chopped maraschino cherries**
- **1 Tbsp. maraschino cherry juice**
- **1 Tbsp. rum**

MERINGUE

- **8 large egg whites**
- **1 cup sugar**
- **1 tsp. cream of tartar**

1. Preheat oven to 350°. In a microwave-safe bowl, melt butter and chocolate; stir until smooth. Stir in sugar and vanilla. Add eggs, one at a time, beating well after each addition. Combine the flour, baking powder and salt; gradually stir into the chocolate mixture. Stir in hazelnuts.
2. Spread into a greased 8-in. round baking pan. Bake until a toothpick inserted in the center comes out with moist crumbs, 35-40 minutes (do not overbake). Cool 10 minutes before removing from pan to a wire rack to cool completely.
3. Meanwhile, line an 8-in. round bowl (1½ qt.) with foil. In another bowl, place 1 qt. ice cream; add the pistachios, almond extract and, if desired, food coloring. Quickly spread ice cream over bottom and up sides of foil-lined bowl, leaving the center hollow; cover and freeze for 30 minutes.
4. In a small bowl, combine cherries, cherry juice, rum and the remaining ice cream. Pack ice cream into hollow center of the first bowl; cover and freeze.
5. In a large heavy saucepan, combine egg whites, sugar and cream of tartar. With a hand mixer, beat on low speed 1 minute. Set over low heat and continue beating until the egg mixture reaches 160°, about 8 minutes. Transfer to a bowl; beat until stiff glossy peaks form and sugar is dissolved.
6. Place brownie on an ungreased foil-lined baking sheet; top with inverted ice cream mold. Remove foil. Immediately spread the meringue over the ice cream, sealing to the edges of the brownie. Freeze until ready to serve, up to 24 hours.
7. Preheat oven to 400°. Bake 2-5 minutes or until meringue is lightly browned. Transfer to a serving plate; serve immediately.
1 PIECE: 554 cal., 29g fat (13g sat. fat), 94mg chol., 314mg sod., 68g carb. (52g sugars, 3g fiber), 11g pro.

RAISIN BROCCOLI TOSS

This raisin salad is a lively addition to any country meal. It's easy to prepare and good for you, too. The walnuts and broccoli add lots of crunch.
—Bernice Morris, Marshfield, MO

PREP: 10 MIN. + CHILLING • **MAKES:** 8 SERVINGS

- **4 cups broccoli florets**
- **¾ cup coarsely chopped walnuts**
- **½ cup raisins**
- **½ cup golden raisins**
- **1 cup Miracle Whip**
- **¼ cup sugar**
- **2 Tbsp. lemon juice**
- **2 Tbsp. half-and-half cream**
- **1 Tbsp. vinegar**

In a large salad bowl, toss broccoli, walnuts and raisins. In a small bowl, combine the remaining ingredients. Pour over salad; toss to coat. Cover and refrigerate for 1 hour.
1 CUP: 366 cal., 29g fat (4g sat. fat), 12mg chol., 164mg sod., 24g carb. (19g sugars, 2g fiber), 5g pro.

5 INGREDIENTS FAST FIX

BEER CHEESE IN A BREAD BOWL

My entire family loves this cheese dip, and my friends always request I bring it to gatherings. It's also quite attractive thanks to the bread bowl. Chopped scallions make a pretty garnish.
—Julie Koch, Delaware, OH

TAKES: 15 MIN. • **MAKES:** 20 SERVINGS (2½ CUPS DIP)

- **1 round loaf (1 lb.) pumpernickel bread**
- **2 jars (5 oz. each) sharp American cheese spread**
- **1 pkg. (8 oz.) cream cheese, softened**
- **¼ cup beer or nonalcoholic beer**
- **½ cup bacon bits**

1. Cut the top fourth off loaf of bread; carefully hollow out the bottom portion, leaving a ½-in. shell. Cube the removed bread; set aside.
2. In a microwave-safe bowl, combine cheese spread and cream cheese. Microwave, uncovered, on high for 2 minutes, stirring every 30 seconds. Stir in beer. Microwave, uncovered, 20 seconds longer. Stir in bacon.
3. Fill the bread shell with cheese dip. Serve with the reserved bread cubes.
2 TBSP. DIP: 147 cal., 9g fat (5g sat. fat), 26mg chol., 506mg sod., 12g carb. (0 sugars, 1g fiber), 6g pro.

PASTEL GELATIN SALAD

I top my gelatin salad with pretty pastel mini marshmallows to add color. With its creamy lemon-lime base and tangy pineapple flavor, it's a tasty accompaniment to any meal.
—Teresa Ries, Santee, CA

PREP: 25 MIN. + CHILLING
MAKES: 15 SERVINGS

- **1 pkg. (3 oz.) lemon gelatin**
- **1 pkg. (3 oz.) lime gelatin**
- **2 cups boiling water**
- **1 pkg. (8 oz.) cream cheese, cubed**
- **½ cup evaporated milk**
- **½ cup mayonnaise**
- **1 can (8 oz.) unsweetened crushed pineapple, undrained**
- **½ cup chopped walnuts**
- **1 pkg. (10½ oz.) pastel miniature marshmallows**

1. In a large bowl, combine lemon and lime gelatin with boiling water; stir until dissolved. Add cream cheese; let stand for 10 minutes. Beat on high speed until smooth. Stir in milk and mayonnaise. Fold in pineapple.
2. Pour into an ungreased 13x9-in. dish. Sprinkle with nuts and marshmallows. Cover and refrigerate until set.
1 SERVING: 250 cal., 14g fat (5g sat. fat), 18mg chol., 135mg sod., 30g carb. (25g sugars, 0 fiber), 4g pro.

MINI CHERRY CHEESECAKES

These little cheesecakes make a fun dessert that's just right for cooks who don't have a lot of time for fussy recipes. Plus, you get to eat the whole thing yourself!
—Kay Keller, Morenci, MI

PREP: 20 MIN. + CHILLING
BAKE: 15 MIN. + COOLING
MAKES: 12 SERVINGS

- **1 cup crushed vanilla wafers (about 30 wafers)**
- **3 Tbsp. butter, melted**
- **1 pkg. (8 oz.) cream cheese, softened**
- **⅓ cup sugar**
- **2 tsp. lemon juice**
- **1½ tsp. vanilla extract**
- **1 large egg, lightly beaten**

TOPPING

- **1 lb. pitted canned or frozen tart red cherries**
- **½ cup sugar**
- **1 Tbsp. cornstarch**
- **Red food coloring, optional**

MINI CHERRY CHEESECAKES

1. Preheat oven to 350°. Combine crumbs and butter; press gently onto the bottoms of 12 foil-lined muffin cups. In another bowl, combine cream cheese, sugar, lemon juice and vanilla. Add egg; beat on low speed just until combined. Spoon filling over crusts.
2. Bake until the centers are almost set, 12-15 minutes. Let cool completely.
3. For topping, drain cherries, reserving ½ cup juice in a saucepan; discard the remaining juice. To reserved juice, add cherries, sugar, cornstarch and, if desired, food coloring. Bring to a boil; cook until thickened, about 1 minute. Cool; spoon over cheesecakes. Refrigerate, covered, at least 2 hours.
1 MINI CHEESECAKE: 213 cal., 12g fat (6g sat. fat), 44mg chol., 127mg sod., 26g carb. (21g sugars, 1g fiber), 2g pro.

TEST KITCHEN TIP

Give these a mini cheesecakes a sweet-salty spin by using crushed pretzels instead of vanilla wafers. You also can substitute strawberries for the cherries—an especially tasty option when they're in season and you can buy locally grown berries.

JELLIED CHAMPAGNE DESSERT

EAT SMART (5) INGREDIENTS

JELLIED CHAMPAGNE DESSERT

This refreshing and playful dessert looks just like a glass of bubbling champagne!
—Vickie McLaughlin, Kingsport, TN

PREP: 20 MIN. + CHILLING • **MAKES:** 8 SERVINGS

- **1 envelope unflavored gelatin**
- **2 cups cold white grape juice, divided**
- **2 Tbsp. sugar**
- **2 cups champagne or club soda**

1. In a small saucepan, sprinkle gelatin over 1 cup cold grape juice; let stand for 1 minute. Stir over low heat until gelatin is dissolved. Stir in sugar. Remove from heat; stir in remaining grape juice. Cool to room temperature.
2. Transfer to a large bowl. Slowly stir in champagne. Pour half of the mixture into eight champagne or parfait glasses. Refrigerate glasses and the remaining gelatin mixture until almost set, about 1 hour.
3. Place reserved gelatin mixture in a blender; cover and process until foamy. Pour into glasses. Chill until set, about 3 hours.
1 SERVING: 96 cal., 0 fat (0 sat. fat), 0 chol., 9mg sod., 13g carb. (12g sugars, 0 fiber), 1g pro.

BEEF WELLINGTON APPETIZERS

Flaky puff pastry, savory beef tenderloin and tangy horseradish cream easily come together for an hors d'oeuvre that's worthy of a holiday celebration—but so good you'll probably be getting requests for them year-round.
—Joan Cooper, Sussex, WI

PREP: 45 MIN. • **BAKE:** 15 MIN.
MAKES: 16 APPETIZERS (1½ CUPS SAUCE)

- **2 beef tenderloin steaks (8 oz. each), cut into ½-in. cubes**
- **2 Tbsp. olive oil, divided**
- **1¼ cups chopped fresh mushrooms**
- **2 shallots, chopped**
- **2 garlic cloves, minced**
- **⅓ cup sherry or chicken broth**
- **⅓ cup heavy whipping cream**
- **½ tsp. salt**
- **⅛ tsp. pepper**
- **1 Tbsp. minced fresh parsley**
- **1 pkg. (17.3 oz.) frozen puff pastry, thawed**
- **1 large egg, beaten**

HORSERADISH CREAM

- **1 cup sour cream**
- **½ cup mayonnaise**
- **2 Tbsp. prepared horseradish**
- **1 Tbsp. minced chives**
- **¼ tsp. pepper**
- **Additional minced chives, optional**

1. In a large skillet, brown cubed beef in 1 Tbsp. oil. Remove and keep warm.
2. In same skillet, saute mushrooms and shallots in remaining oil until tender. Add garlic; cook 1 minute longer. Add sherry, stirring to loosen browned bits from pan. Stir in cream, salt and pepper. Bring to a boil; cook until liquid is almost evaporated, about 7 minutes. Stir in beef and parsley; set aside and keep warm.
3. Preheat oven to 400°. On a lightly floured surface, unfold puff pastry sheets. Roll each sheet into a 12-in. square. Cut each into 16 squares.
4. Place 2 tablespoonfuls of beef mixture in center of half of squares. Top with remaining squares; press edges with a fork to seal. Place on parchment paper-lined baking sheets. Cut slits in top; brush with egg. Bake 14-16 minutes or until golden brown.
5. In a small bowl, combine horseradish cream ingredients; serve with appetizers. Garnish with additional chives if desired.
1 APPETIZER WITH ABOUT 4 TSP. SAUCE: 315 cal., 22g fat (6g sat. fat), 45mg chol., 231mg sod., 19g carb. (1g sugars, 2g fiber), 10g pro.

BEEF WELLINGTON APPETIZERS

SPICED PINEAPPLE UPSIDE-DOWN CAKE

SPICED PINEAPPLE UPSIDE-DOWN CAKE

Upside-down cakes, which have been around since the 1800s, were once called skillet cakes because they were cooked on the stovetop in cast-iron skillets.
—Jennifer Sergesketter, Newburgh, IN

PREP: 15 MIN. • **BAKE:** 40 MIN. • **MAKES:** 12 SERVINGS

- **1⅓ cups butter, softened, divided**
- **1 cup packed brown sugar**
- **1 can (20 oz.) pineapple slices, drained**
- **10 to 12 maraschino cherries**
- **½ cup chopped pecans**
- **1½ cups sugar**
- **2 large eggs**
- **1 tsp. vanilla extract**
- **2 cups all-purpose flour**
- **2 tsp. baking powder**
- **½ tsp. baking soda**
- **½ tsp. salt**
- **½ tsp. ground cinnamon**
- **½ tsp. ground nutmeg**
- **1 cup buttermilk**

1. Preheat oven to 350°. In a saucepan, melt ⅔ cup butter; stir in brown sugar. Spread in the bottom of an ungreased heavy 12-in. ovenproof skillet or a 13x9-in. baking pan. Arrange pineapple slices in a single layer over the sugar mixture; place a cherry in the center of each slice. Sprinkle with pecans and set aside.
2. In a large bowl, cream sugar and the remaining butter until light and fluffy. Add eggs, one at a time, beating well after each addition. Beat in vanilla. Combine flour, baking powder, baking soda, salt, cinnamon and nutmeg; add alternately to the batter with buttermilk, beating well after each addition.
3. Carefully pour over the pineapple. Bake until a toothpick inserted in the center comes out clean, about 40 minutes for skillet, 50-60 minutes for baking pan. Immediately invert onto a serving platter. Serve warm.
1 PIECE: 509 cal., 25g fat (13g sat. fat), 91mg chol., 467mg sod., 69g carb. (52g sugars, 2g fiber), 5g pro.

OYSTERS ROCKEFELLER

My husband and I delight guests with this classic dish that originated in New Orleans. It's deliciously simple!
—Beth Walton, Eastham, MA

PREP: 1¼ HOURS • **BAKE:** 10 MIN. • **MAKES:** 3 DOZEN

- **3 dozen fresh oysters in the shell, washed**
- **1 medium onion, finely chopped**
- **½ cup butter, cubed**
- **1 pkg. (9 oz.) fresh spinach, torn**
- **1 cup grated Romano cheese**
- **1 Tbsp. lemon juice**
- **⅛ tsp. pepper**
- **2 lbs. kosher salt**

1. Shuck oysters, reserving the bottom shells; set aside. In a large skillet, saute onion in butter until tender. Add spinach; cook and stir until wilted. Remove from the heat; stir in the cheese, lemon juice and pepper.
2. Spread kosher salt into two ungreased 15x10x1-in. baking pans. Lightly press the oyster shells down into the salt. Place one oyster in each shell; top each with 2½ tsp. of the spinach mixture.
3. Bake, uncovered, at 450° for 6-8 minutes or until the oysters are plump. Serve immediately.
1 OYSTER: 79 cal., 5g fat (3g sat. fat), 32mg chol., 133mg sod., 3g carb. (0 sugars, 0 fiber), 6g pro.

OYSTERS ROCKEFELLER

5 INGREDIENTS FAST FIX

CHICKEN WITH CHERRY WINE SAUCE

My dad's a chef, so I learned to cook at an early age. This saucy chicken was the first dish I made by myself.
—Ben Diaz, Azusa, CA

TAKES: 30 MIN. • **MAKES:** 4 SERVINGS

- **4 boneless skinless chicken breast halves (8 oz. each)**
- **¼ tsp. salt**
- **¼ tsp. pepper**
- **7 Tbsp. butter, divided**
- **⅔ cup dry red wine**
- **1 Tbsp. sugar**
- **½ cup fresh or frozen pitted dark sweet cherries, thawed**

1. Preheat oven to 350°. Sprinkle chicken with salt and pepper. In a large skillet, heat 2 Tbsp. butter over medium-high heat. Brown chicken on both sides. Transfer to a greased 15x10x1-in. baking pan. Bake until a thermometer reads 165°, 12-15 minutes.
2. Meanwhile, in a small saucepan, combine the wine and sugar. Bring to a boil; cook, uncovered, until liquid is reduced by half, 4-5 minutes. Reduce heat to low; whisk in the remaining butter, 1 Tbsp. at a time, until blended. Stir in cherries; serve with the chicken.

1 CHICKEN BREAST HALF WITH 3 TBSP. SAUCE: 480 cal., 25g fat (14g sat. fat), 179mg chol., 418mg sod., 8g carb. (5g sugars, 0 fiber), 46g pro.

PORK CHOPS WITH CHERRY WINE SAUCE: Substitute 6 bone-in pork loin chops (8 oz. each) for the chicken breasts. Proceed as directed, increasing bake time to 25-30 minutes or until a thermometer reads 145°. Let stand 5 minutes before serving.

BEN DIAZ
Azusa, CA

CHICKEN WITH CHERRY WINE SAUCE

GRANDMA PRUIT'S VINEGAR PIE

This historic pie has been in our family for many generations and is always at all of our family get-togethers.
—Suzette Pruit, Houston, TX

PREP: 40 MIN. • **BAKE:** 1 HOUR + COOLING
MAKES: 8 SERVINGS

- **2 cups sugar**
- **3 Tbsp. all-purpose flour**
- **¼ to ½ tsp. ground nutmeg**
- **Pastry for double-crust pie (9 in.)**
- **½ cup butter, cubed**
- **⅔ cup white vinegar**
- **1 qt. hot water**

1. Preheat oven to 450°. Whisk together sugar, flour and nutmeg; set aside. On a lightly floured surface, roll one-third of the pie dough to a ⅛-in.-thick circle; cut into 2x1-in. strips. Layer a deep 12-in. enamel-coated cast-iron skillet or ovenproof casserole with half the dough strips; sprinkle with half the sugar mixture. Dot with half the butter. Repeat the sugar and butter layers.
2. Roll the remaining two-thirds of pie dough to a ⅛-in.-thick circle. Place over the filling, pressing against sides of skillet or casserole to seal. Cut a slit in top.
3. Add vinegar to hot water; slowly pour the vinegar mixture through the top slit. Liquid may bubble up through crust; this is normal. To catch spills, line an oven rack with foil.
4. Bake until crust is golden brown, about 1 hour. Cover the edge loosely with foil during the last 15-20 minutes if needed to prevent overbrowning. Remove foil. Cool on a wire rack.

1 SLICE: 545 cal., 25g fat (13g sat. fat), 41mg chol., 316mg sod., 78g carb. (50g sugars, 0 fiber), 2g pro.

PASTRY FOR DOUBLE-CRUST PIE (9 IN.): Combine 2½ cups all-purpose flour and ½ tsp. salt; cut in 1 cup cold butter until crumbly. Gradually add ⅓-⅔ cup ice water, tossing with a fork until the dough holds together when pressed. Divide the dough into thirds. Shape each portion into a disk; wrap each disk in plastic. Refrigerate for at least 1 hour.

SPICY CAJUN POTATO SALAD
PAGE 295

FIELD EDITOR FAVORITES

Our volunteer Field Editors are the best cooks around—and they love sharing their recipes! Here's a roundup of their tropical treats, cookout staples and holiday sweets.

ALOHA, COCONUT

Invite your family to a taste of the island life. Make a toast with a tropical drink, and have a party for dinner.

ALOHA CUPCAKES

ALOHA CUPCAKES

A friend asked me to make a coconut and pineapple cupcake for a gathering she was hosting. Everyone agreed this beauty took them to the tropics. Because my friend is allergic, I didn't use macadamia nuts, but the cupcakes are fantastic with or without them.
—Shannon Dobos, Calgary, AB

PREP: 20 MIN. • **BAKE:** 15 MIN. + COOLING
MAKES: 1 DOZEN

- 1¼ **cups cake flour**
- 1¼ **tsp. baking powder**
- ½ **tsp. baking soda**
- ½ **tsp. salt**
- 2 **large eggs**
- ¾ **cup granulated sugar**
- ½ **cup canola oil**
- 1 **tsp. coconut extract**
- ½ **cup coconut milk**
- ½ **tsp. white vinegar**

PINEAPPLE FROSTING
- ½ **cup shortening**
- ½ **cup butter**
- 4 **cups confectioners' sugar**
- ½ **cup finely chopped fresh pineapple**
- 3 **Tbsp. unsweetened pineapple juice**

TOPPING
- ½ **cup sweetened shredded coconut, toasted**
- ½ **cup coarsely chopped macadamia nuts, optional**

1. Preheat oven to 350°. Line 12 muffin cups with paper or foil liners. Whisk first four ingredients; set aside. Beat eggs and sugar on medium speed for 1 minute. Add oil and coconut extract; beat 1 minute more. Add half the flour mixture; beat on low speed. Combine coconut milk and vinegar. Add half to batter; beat just until combined. Beat in remaining flour mixture, then remaining coconut milk mixture just until smooth.
2. Fill prepared cups two-thirds full. Bake until cupcakes are golden brown and spring back lightly when touched, 15-18 minutes (do not overbake). Cool on wire rack.
3. For frosting, cream shortening and butter until light and fluffy. Beat in confectioners' sugar a half-cup at a time, adding finely chopped pineapple and pineapple juice after beating in 2 cups of sugar. Add additional confectioners' sugar and pineapple juice to reach desired consistency.
4. Spoon frosting onto cupcakes. Top with toasted coconut and, if desired, chopped macadamia nuts.
NOTE: To toast coconut, bake in a shallow pan in a 350° oven for 5-10 minutes or cook in a skillet over low heat until golden brown, stirring occasionally.
1 FROSTED CUPCAKE: 533 cal., 29g fat (11g sat. fat), 51mg chol., 287mg sod., 67g carb. (55g sugars, 1g fiber), 3g pro.

TEST KITCHEN TIP

No fresh pineapple? Use canned pineapple tidbits and juice instead.

(5) INGREDIENTS

PINA COLADAS

Velvety-smooth texture and a taste of the tropics are what this tropical drink delivers. The easy drink can be mixed and chilled ahead of time. When ready to serve, just blend for a creamy and delicious beverage. —Linda Schend, Kenosha, WI

PREP: 20 MIN. + CHILLING
MAKES: 6 SERVINGS

- **2¼ cups unsweetened pineapple juice**
- **1 can (15 oz.) cream of coconut**
- **1½ cups light rum**
- **6 cups crushed ice**
- **Pineapple wedges**

In a 2-qt. pitcher, combine pineapple juice, cream of coconut and rum. Refrigerate, covered, until chilled. For each serving, add a generous cup of rum mixture and 1 cup ice to a blender. Process, covered, until smooth. Pour into a chilled hurricane or highball glass. Cut a 1-in. slit into tip of a pineapple wedge; slide wedge over the rim of the glass.

1¼ CUPS: 457 cal., 13g fat (10g sat. fat), 0 chol., 42mg sod., 55g carb. (52g sugars, 0 fiber), 0 pro.

PINA COLADAS

COCONUT CHICKEN & SHRIMP

SUSAN SEYMOUR
Valatie, NY

COCONUT CHICKEN & SHRIMP

I was looking for a fun, easy weeknight dinner based on our favorite shrimp dish from a restaurant. This simple meal has become a favorite! —Susan Seymour, Valatie, NY

PREP: 30 MIN. • **COOK:** 5 MIN./BATCH
MAKES: 6 SERVINGS

- **1 cup all-purpose flour**
- **1 cup lime-flavored seltzer water**
- **1 tsp. ground ginger**
- **1 tsp. salt**
- **1 tsp. pepper**
- **2½ cups sweetened shredded coconut**
- **1¼ cups panko (Japanese) bread crumbs**
- **1 lb. uncooked shrimp (31-40 per lb.), peeled and deveined**
- **2 boneless skinless chicken breasts (6 oz. each), cut into ¾-in. cubes**
- **Oil for deep-fat frying**
- **Salt and pepper to taste, optional**

MAUI MUSTARD

- **1 can (8 oz.) crushed pineapple, well drained**
- **½ cup red pepper jelly**
- **3 Tbsp. stone-ground mustard**

1. In a shallow bowl, whisk together first five ingredients. In another shallow bowl, combine coconut and panko. Dip shrimp in batter to coat. Dip in coconut mixture, patting to help coating adhere. Repeat with the chicken.

2. In an electric skillet or deep fryer, heat oil to 350°. Fry shrimp, a few at a time, until golden brown, 3-4 minutes. Drain on paper towels. Repeat with chicken. If desired, sprinkle lightly with salt and pepper.

3. For mustard, mix together pineapple, pepper jelly and stone-ground mustard. Combine shrimp and chicken; serve with Maui mustard.

1 SERVING: 659 cal., 31g fat (14g sat. fat), 123mg chol., 735mg sod., 69g carb. (39g sugars, 4g fiber), 29g pro.

SICILIAN POTATO SALAD

HONEY MUSTARD RED POTATO SALAD

PASS THE POTATO SALAD

Perk up the potluck standby with fresh recipes that take you from Cajun heat to oh-so sweet.

EAT SMART

HONEY MUSTARD RED POTATO SALAD

This summer cookout star is crunchy-delicious with a brilliant zesty dressing.
—Brittany Allyn, Mesa, AZ

PREP: 20 MIN. • **COOK:** 20 MIN.
MAKES: 16 SERVINGS

- **3 lbs. baby red potatoes, unpeeled**
- **½ tsp. sea salt**
- **2 green onions**
- **1 cup finely diced celery**
- **½ cup diced red onion**
- **1 medium carrot, grated**

DRESSING

- **¼ cup red wine vinegar**
- **2 Tbsp. honey**
- **2 Tbsp. Dijon mustard**
- **2 tsp. minced fresh thyme**
- **1 tsp. sea salt**
- **½ tsp. coarsely ground pepper**
- **½ cup extra virgin olive oil**

1. Place potatoes and ½ tsp. salt in a Dutch oven; add water to cover. Bring to a boil. Reduce heat; cook, uncovered, until tender, 10-12 minutes. Drain and cool.
2. Mince white portions of green onions; slice green portions and reserve. Combine minced onions with celery, red onion and carrot. For dressing, whisk together vinegar, honey, mustard, thyme, sea salt and coarsely ground pepper. Gradually whisk in oil until blended.
3. Cut cooled potatoes into 1-in. pieces, preserving as much peel as possible. Combine potatoes with onion mixture. Drizzle dressing over salad; toss to coat. Top with reserved green onion slices.

¾ CUP: 138 cal., 7g fat (1g sat. fat), 0 chol., 233mg sod., 19g carb. (3g sugars, 2g fiber), 2g pro. **Diabetic exchanges:** 1½ starch, 1½ fat.

EAT SMART

SICILIAN POTATO SALAD

Fresh basil is the star of this mayo-free, Italian-inspired take on potato salad.
—Sue Falk, Warren, MI

PREP: 20 MIN. • **COOK:** 20 MIN.
MAKES: 26 SERVINGS

- **10 small russet potatoes, unpeeled**
- **1½ tsp. salt, divided**
- **½ lb. fresh green beans, cut into 1½-in. pieces**
- **¼ tsp. pepper**
- **2 medium cucumbers, halved lengthwise and cut into ¼-in. slices**
- **½ lb. cherry tomatoes, halved**
- **1 large red onion, halved and thinly sliced**
- **1 cup thinly sliced fresh basil leaves, divided**
- **½ cup olive oil**
- **4 Tbsp. cider vinegar**
- **3 garlic cloves, minced**

1. Place potatoes and ½ tsp. salt in a Dutch oven; add water to cover. Bring to a boil. Reduce heat; cook, uncovered, until tender, 12-15 minutes. Drain; rinse with cold water. Pat dry.
2. Meanwhile, in a small saucepan, bring 1 cup water to a boil. Add green beans; cook, uncovered, just until crisp-tender, 3-4 minutes. Drain; immediately drop into ice water. Drain and pat dry.

3. Peel and cube potatoes; sprinkle with remaining salt and the pepper. Transfer to a serving bowl. Add beans, cucumbers, tomatoes, onion and ¾ cup basil leaves. Whisk together oil, vinegar and garlic. Drizzle over vegetables; toss to coat. Sprinkle with remaining basil.
¾ CUP: 96 cal., 4g fat (1g sat. fat), 0 chol., 143mg sod., 13g carb. (2g sugars, 2g fiber), 2g pro. **Diabetic exchanges:** 1 starch, 1 fat.

EAT SMART

SPICY CAJUN POTATO SALAD

We have a lot of get-togethers in the South, and if you want your dish to be chosen over all of the rest, it has to have a kick! This spicy salad does the trick.
—Amanda West, Shelbyville, TN

PREP: 20 MIN. • **COOK:** 10 MIN. + CHILLING
MAKES: 20 SERVINGS

- **5 lbs. medium Yukon Gold potatoes, peeled and cut into ¾-in. cubes**
- **1 large yellow onion**
- **½ medium lemon**
- **½ tsp. salt**
- **8 hard-boiled large eggs, chopped**
- **1½ cups mayonnaise with olive oil and coarsely ground pepper**
- **1 cup dill pickle relish**
- **¼ cup yellow mustard**
- **1 to 2 Tbsp. Cajun seasoning**
- **¼ cup minced fresh parsley**
- **Paprika**

1. Place potatoes in a Dutch oven; add water to cover. Cut onion in half crosswise; add one half to saucepan. Bring to a boil. Add lemon and salt to cooking water. Reduce heat; cook, uncovered, until potatoes are tender, 5-6 minutes.
2. Meanwhile, chop remaining onion. Combine with eggs, mayonnaise, pickle relish, mustard and Cajun seasoning.
3. Drain potatoes; rinse under cold water. Discard onion and lemon. Add potatoes to egg mixture; gently toss until well mixed (do not overmix, or potatoes will break down). Refrigerate 1-2 hours. Just before serving, sprinkle with parsley and paprika.
¾ CUP: 229 cal., 10g fat (2g sat. fat), 81mg chol., 400mg sod., 31g carb. (3g sugars, 2g fiber), 5g pro.

EAT SMART

TROPICAL SWEET POTATO SALAD

I had an abundance of sweet potatoes, so I put them to work and came up with this sweet and spicy salad.
—Crystal Jo Bruns, Iliff, CO

PREP: 20 MIN. • **BAKE:** 35 MIN. + CHILLING
MAKES: 8 SERVINGS

- **3 lbs. sweet potatoes, peeled and cut into ½-in. cubes**
- **1 medium mango, peeled and cut into ½-in. cubes**
- **1 medium red onion, thinly sliced**
- **Cooking spray**
- **1½ Tbsp. chili powder**
- **¼ tsp. salt**
- **¼ tsp. pepper**
- **½ cup Miracle Whip**
- **¼ cup plain Greek yogurt**
- **2 Tbsp. thawed pineapple juice concentrate**
- **2 serrano peppers, seeded and finely chopped, veins removed**
- **Thinly sliced serrano pepper, optional**

1. Preheat oven to 350°. Place sweet potatoes, mango and onion in a single layer in two foil-lined 15x10x1-in. baking pans. Spritz with cooking spray; sprinkle with chili powder, salt and pepper. Bake, turning vegetables at least twice, until tender, 35-40 minutes. Cool.
2. Combine Miracle Whip, yogurt, pineapple juice concentrate and serrano peppers. Fold into potato mixture. Refrigerate, covered, at least 1 hour. Serve cold. If desired, sprinkle with sliced serrano.
¾ CUP: 240 cal., 5g fat (1g sat. fat), 3mg chol., 317mg sod., 46g carb. (17g sugars, 7g fiber), 4g pro.

CRYSTAL JO BRUNS
Iliff, CO

SPICY CAJUN POTATO SALAD

TROPICAL SWEET POTATO SALAD

BURGER SEASON

Everybody loves a burger, and our Field Editors make some of the best. Their clever mix-ins and fun toppers make the cookout classic even more crave-able.

EAT SMART FAST FIX

CHICKPEA & RED ONION BURGERS

When the grill fills up with other goodies, I bake a batch of chickpea veggie burgers. Even die-hard meat eaters can't resist them.
—Lily Julow, Lawrenceville, GA

TAKES: 30 MIN. • **MAKES:** 6 SERVINGS

- **1 large red onion, thinly sliced**
- **¼ cup fat-free red wine vinaigrette**
- **2 cans (15 oz. each) chickpeas or garbanzo beans, rinsed and drained**
- **⅓ cup chopped walnuts**
- **¼ cup toasted wheat germ or dry bread crumbs**
- **¼ cup packed fresh parsley sprigs**
- **2 large eggs**
- **1 tsp. curry powder**
- **½ tsp. pepper**
- **⅓ cup fat-free mayonnaise**
- **2 tsp. Dijon mustard**
- **6 sesame seed hamburger buns, split and toasted**
- **6 lettuce leaves**
- **3 Tbsp. thinly sliced fresh basil leaves**

1. Preheat oven to 375°. In a small bowl, mix onion and vinaigrette. Place chickpeas, walnuts, wheat germ and parsley in a food processor; pulse until blended. Add eggs, curry and pepper; process until smooth.

2. Shape into six patties. Place on a baking sheet coated with cooking spray. Bake until a thermometer reads 160°, 10-15 minutes.

3. In a small bowl, mix mayonnaise and mustard; spread over cut sides of buns. Serve patties on buns with lettuce, basil and onion mixture.

1 BURGER: 386 cal., 12g fat (2g sat. fat), 72mg chol., 732mg sod., 54g carb. (10g sugars, 9g fiber), 16g pro.

FAST FIX

MOM'S FAVORITE OLIVE BURGERS

When she was in her 80s, my mom would reminisce about olive burgers at Coney Island. I used her instructions to make one and ended up pleasing both of us.
—Lorraine Hickman, Lansing, MI

TAKES: 25 MIN. • **MAKES:** 4 SERVINGS

- **1 lb. ground beef**
- **2 tsp. reduced-sodium soy sauce**
- **2 tsp. Worcestershire sauce**
- **¼ tsp. garlic powder**
- **¼ tsp. onion powder**
- **1 Tbsp. butter**
- **½ cup sliced green olives with pimientos, drained**
- **¼ cup Miracle Whip**
- **1 Tbsp. stone-ground mustard**
- **4 hamburger buns, toasted**
- **¼ cup crumbled feta cheese, optional**
- **Bibb lettuce leaves, optional**

LILY JULOW
Lawrenceville, GA

CHICKPEA & RED ONION BURGERS

1. In a large bowl, combine beef, soy sauce, Worcestershire, garlic powder and onion powder, mixing lightly but thoroughly. Shape into four ½-in.-thick patties, indenting the center slightly.
2. Melt butter in a large nonstick skillet; cook burgers over medium heat until a thermometer reads 160°, 4-6 minutes on each side.
3. Meanwhile, in a small bowl combine olives, Miracle Whip and mustard. Serve burgers on buns with olive mixture. If desired, top with feta cheese and lettuce.

1 BURGER WITH 2 TBSP. OLIVE MIXTURE: 425 cal., 24g fat (8g sat. fat), 79mg chol., 837mg sod., 25g carb. (5g sugars, 1g fiber), 25g pro.

GRILLED GREEN ONION BURGERS

Change up this super tasty burger with your favorite toppings. Whip some mayo with hoisin sauce to add extra tang!
—Darla Andrews, Schertz, TX

PREP: 35 MIN. • **GRILL:** 10 MIN.
MAKES: 8 SERVINGS

- 8 **bacon strips, cut in half**
- ½ **cup reduced-sodium teriyaki sauce**
- ¼ **cup hoisin sauce**
- 6 **green onions, chopped**
- 1 **Tbsp. garlic powder**
- 1 **Tbsp. ground cumin**
- ½ **tsp. pepper**
- 2 **lbs. ground sirloin**
- 8 **oz. sliced mushrooms**
- 2 **baby bok choy, quartered and core removed**
- 8 **large eggs**
- 8 **potato hamburger buns, toasted**

1. In a large skillet, cook bacon over medium-low heat until crisp. Remove to paper towels to drain; reserve drippings.
2. Meanwhile in a large bowl, combine teriyaki, hoisin, onions, garlic, cumin and pepper. Add beef, mixing lightly but thoroughly. Shape into eight ½-in.-thick patties. Grill burgers, covered, over medium heat until a thermometer reads 160°, 5-7 minutes on each side. Keep warm.
3. In the same skillet, cook mushrooms in 2 Tbsp. bacon drippings over medium-high heat until golden, 5-7 minutes. Add bok choy to skillet; cook until tender. Remove and keep warm.
4. In the same skillet, fry eggs in remaining bacon drippings over medium heat until desired doneness. Serve burgers on buns with bacon, bok choy, mushrooms and fried eggs.

1 BURGER: 481 cal., 22g fat (7g sat. fat), 247mg chol., 1230mg sod., 37g carb. (12g sugars, 4g fiber), 35g pro.

MOM'S FAVORITE OLIVE BURGERS

GRILLED GREEN ONION BURGERS

FIELD EDITOR FAVORITES

ON A ROLL

Classic cinnamon buns are pure yum, but why stop there? Field Editors bake up spirals with spice and all that's nice.

RED VELVET CINNAMON ROLLS

RED VELVET CINNAMON ROLLS

Turn a box of red velvet cake mix into this easy dessert—or breakfast! The icing tastes like Cinnabon's.
—Erin Wright, Wallace, KS

PREP: 20 MIN. + RISING • **BAKE:** 15 MIN.
MAKES: 12 SERVINGS

- 1 **pkg. red velvet cake mix (regular size)**
- 2½ **to 3 cups all-purpose flour**
- 1 **pkg. (¼ oz.) active dry yeast**
- 1¼ **cups warm water (120° to 130°)**
- ½ **cup packed brown sugar**
- 1 **tsp. ground cinnamon**
- ¼ **cup butter, melted**

ICING

- 2 **cups confectioners' sugar**
- 2 **Tbsp. butter, softened**
- 1 **tsp. vanilla extract**
- 3 **to 5 Tbsp. 2% milk**

1. Combine cake mix, 1 cup flour and yeast. Add water to the mixture; beat on medium speed 2 minutes. Stir in enough remaining flour to form a soft dough (dough will be sticky). Turn onto a lightly floured surface; knead gently 6-8 times. Place in a greased bowl, turning once to grease the top. Cover and let rise in a warm place until doubled, about 2 hours. Meanwhile, in another bowl, mix the brown sugar and cinnamon.

2. Punch down dough. Turn onto a floured surface; roll dough into an 18x10-in. rectangle. Brush with melted butter to within ¼ in. of edges; sprinkle with the brown sugar mixture.

3. Roll up jelly-roll style, starting with a long side; pinch seam to seal. Cut crosswise into 12 slices. Place in a greased 13x9-in. baking pan. Cover with a kitchen towel; let rise in a warm place until almost doubled, about 1 hour.

4. Preheat oven to 350°. Bake rolls until puffed and light brown, 15-20 minutes. Cool slightly.

5. Beat confectioners' sugar, butter, vanilla and enough milk to reach a drizzling consistency. Drizzle icing over warm rolls.

1 CINNAMON ROLL: 429 cal., 10g fat (5g sat. fat), 16mg chol., 311mg sod., 81g carb. (48g sugars, 1g fiber), 5g pro.

TEST KITCHEN TIP

Make these morning beauties your own by swapping in your favorite flavor of cake mix. We particularly love spice cake, devil's food and orange.

HONEY CINNAMON ROLLUPS

SUE FALK
Warren, MI

HONEY CINNAMON ROLLUPS

This cinnamony treat reminds me of baklava. But with only a few easy ingredients, it's a fraction of the work. My Aunt Adele shared the recipe with me, and I think of her whenever I make it.
—Sue Falk, Warren, MI

PREP: 35 MIN. • **BAKE:** 15 MIN.
MAKES: 24 SERVINGS

- **2 cups ground walnuts, toasted**
- **¼ cup sugar**
- **2 tsp. ground cinnamon**
- **12 sheets frozen phyllo dough, thawed**
- **½ cup butter, melted**

SYRUP

- **½ cup honey**
- **½ cup sugar**
- **½ cup water**
- **1 Tbsp. lemon juice**

1. Preheat oven to 350°. Combine walnuts, sugar and cinnamon.
2. Place one sheet of phyllo dough on a 15x12-in. piece of waxed paper; brush with butter. Place a second phyllo sheet on top, brushing it with butter. (Keep remaining phyllo covered with plastic wrap and a damp towel to prevent it from drying out.) Sprinkle with ¼ cup walnut mixture. Using waxed paper, roll up tightly jelly-roll style, starting with a long side, removing paper as you roll. Slice roll into four smaller rolls; transfer to a greased 13x9-in. baking dish. Repeat with remaining phyllo dough and ¼ cupfuls of walnut mixture. Bake until light brown, 14-16 minutes. Cool on a wire rack.
3. Meanwhile, in a small saucepan, bring syrup ingredients to a boil. Reduce heat; simmer 5 minutes. Cool 10 minutes. Drizzle over rollups; sprinkle with the remaining walnut mixture.

1 CINNAMON ROLLUP: 132 cal., 8g fat (3g sat. fat), 10mg chol., 43mg sod., 15g carb. (12g sugars, 1g fiber), 1g pro.

CINNAMON TWIRL ROLY-POLY

My whole house smells incredible when this cake is in the oven. Change it up with other extracts—maple is heavenly.
—Holly Balzer-Harz, Malone, NY

PREP: 40 MIN. + CHILLING
BAKE: 10 MIN. + COOLING
MAKES: 12 SERVINGS

- **3 large eggs**
- **¾ cup granulated sugar**
- **⅓ cup water**
- **1 tsp. vanilla extract**
- **1 cup all-purpose flour**
- **1½ tsp. baking powder**
- **Dash salt**
- **6 Tbsp. butter, softened**
- **½ cup packed brown sugar**
- **2 tsp. ground cinnamon**

FILLING

- **4 oz. cream cheese, softened**
- **¼ cup butter, softened**
- **1 cup confectioners' sugar**
- **½ tsp. ground cinnamon**
- **1 to 2 tsp. half-and-half cream or whole milk**
- **¼ cup finely chopped walnuts, optional**

GLAZE

- **¼ cup butter**
- **1½ cups confectioners' sugar**
- **1 tsp. vanilla extract**
- **2 to 3 Tbsp. half-and-half cream or whole milk**
- **¼ cup chopped walnuts, optional**

1. Preheat oven to 375°. Line bottom and sides of a greased 15x10x1-in. baking pan with parchment paper; grease paper.
2. Beat eggs on high speed until thick and pale, about 5 minutes. Gradually beat in sugar until well mixed. Reduce speed to low; beat in water and vanilla. Whisk the flour, baking powder and salt; add to egg mixture, mixing just until combined.
3. Transfer batter to prepared pan. Bake until cake springs back when lightly touched, 10-12 minutes. Cool 5 minutes. Invert onto a kitchen towel dusted with confectioners' sugar. Gently peel off parchment paper. Roll up cake in the towel jelly-roll style, starting with a short side. Cool completely on a wire rack.
4. Meanwhile, beat butter, brown sugar and cinnamon until creamy. Unroll cake; spread brown sugar mixture over cake to within ½ in. of edges.
5. For filling, beat cream cheese and butter until creamy. Beat in confectioners' sugar and cinnamon; gradually add cream until mixture reaches a spreadable consistency. Spread filling over brown sugar mixture. If desired, sprinkle with walnuts. Roll up again, without towel; trim ends if needed. Place on a platter, seam side down.
6. For glaze, heat butter in a small saucepan over medium-low heat until foamy and golden, 6-8 minutes. Remove from heat. Stir in confectioners' sugar and vanilla, then add cream 1 Tbsp. at a time, stirring well, until mixture reaches a pourable consistency. Slowly pour glaze over top of the cake, allowing some to flow over sides. If desired, top with chopped walnuts. Refrigerate, covered, at least 2 hours before serving.

1 SLICE: 396 cal., 18g fat (11g sat. fat), 93mg chol., 341mg sod., 56g carb. (47g sugars, 1g fiber), 4g pro.

CINNAMON TWIRL ROLY-POLY

O CHRISTMAS TRIFLE

A luscious holiday dessert that you can make ahead is a gift all by itself.

CANADIAN CRANBERRY TRIFLE

RAYMONDE BOURGEOIS
Swastika, ON

CANADIAN CRANBERRY TRIFLE

Cake, hand-whipped custard and cranberries give you a lot to celebrate. In summer, I make this showstopping dessert with fresh-picked blueberries and homemade blueberry wine.
—Raymonde Bourgeois, Swastika, ON

PREP: 30 MIN. + COOLING
COOK: 25 MIN. + CHILLING
MAKES: 16 SERVINGS

- **2 cups fresh cranberries**
- **1 can (14 oz.) whole-berry cranberry sauce**
- **1 cup sugar**
- **1 cup water**
- **½ cup sweet white wine**
- **¼ tsp. coconut extract**

CUSTARD

- **1 cup sugar**
- **2 Tbsp. cornstarch**
- **¼ tsp. salt**
- **3 cups 2% milk**
- **6 large egg yolks, beaten**
- **¼ tsp. coconut extract**

CAKE

- **1 frozen pound cake (16 oz.), thawed**
- **3 Tbsp. sweet white wine, optional**
- **½ cup slivered almonds, toasted**
- **Whipped cream**
- **Additional fresh cranberries and toasted slivered almonds**

1. In a large saucepan, combine cranberries, cranberry sauce, sugar and water. Bring to a boil, stirring to dissolve sugar. Reduce heat to medium; cook, uncovered, until thickened, 10-15 minutes. Add wine and coconut extract. Remove from the heat; cool completely.

2. For custard, mix sugar, cornstarch and salt in another large saucepan; gradually whisk in milk until smooth. Cook and stir over medium heat until thickened and bubbly. Reduce heat to low; cook and stir 2-3 minutes longer. Remove from heat.

3. In a small bowl, whisk a small amount of hot mixture into egg yolks. Return all to pan, whisking constantly. Bring to a gentle boil; cook and stir 2 minutes. Stir in coconut extract. Cool 30 minutes. Refrigerate, covered, for 1 hour.

4. To assemble, cut cake into 1-in. cubes. In a 1-qt. trifle bowl or other glass serving dish, place half of the cake cubes; sprinkle with wine if desired. Layer with half of the almonds, cranberry mixture and custard. Repeat the layers. Refrigerate, covered, until serving. Top with whipped cream and additional fresh cranberries and toasted slivered almonds.

1 CUP: 323 cal., 10g fat (5g sat. fat), 114mg chol., 157mg sod., 53g carb. (42g sugars, 1g fiber), 5g pro.

TEST KITCHEN TIP

To make a blueberry-cranberry trifle, swap 2 cups fresh blueberries for the fresh cranberries and proceed as directed.

5 INGREDIENTS

WINTER WISHES TRIFLE

I created this light and fluffy trifle for a dear friend who was looking for a stunning dessert. This recipe hit the mark.
—Susan Stetzel, Gainesville, NY

PREP: 20 MIN. + CHILLING
MAKES: 12 SERVINGS

- 1 **prepared angel food cake (8 to 10 oz.)**
- 4 **oz. white baking chocolate**
- 4 **cups heavy whipping cream, divided**
- ½ **tsp. peppermint extract**
- 12 **peppermint candies, crushed**

1. Place mixer beaters in a large metal bowl; refrigerate 30 minutes. Cut or tear cake into bite-sized pieces; set aside.
2. Break white chocolate into smaller pieces; microwave at 70% power, stirring after 45 seconds. Microwave until melted, about 30 seconds more. Stir until smooth. Let stand 5 minutes; stir ¼ cup heavy cream into white chocolate until smooth.
3. In the chilled bowl, beat remaining heavy cream until soft peaks form. Gently fold two-thirds of whipped cream into white chocolate. Stir peppermint extract into remaining whipped cream.
4. In a trifle bowl, layer cake and white chocolate mixture, repeating layers. Top with peppermint-flavored whipped cream. Refrigerate, covered, until serving. Sprinkle with crushed candies.
1 SERVING: 392 cal., 32g fat (20g sat. fat), 90mg chol., 173mg sod., 25g carb. (12g sugars, 0 fiber), 4g pro.

WINTER WISHES TRIFLE

HONEY GINGERBREAD TRIFLE

HONEY GINGERBREAD TRIFLE

My husband's grandma made the most amazing honey gingerbread. It's wonderful all on its own, but when you add it to a trifle, your guests are sure to ask for the recipe.
—Tami Kuehl, Loup City, NE

PREP: 25 MIN. + CHILLING
BAKE: 25 MIN. + COOLING
MAKES: 12 SERVINGS

- 1 **cup sour cream**
- 1 **cup honey**
- 1 **large egg**
- ¼ **cup canola oil**
- 2½ **cups all-purpose flour**
- ½ **tsp. salt**
- 1 **tsp. baking soda**
- 1 **tsp. baking powder**
- 2 **tsp. ground ginger**
- ½ **tsp. ground cinnamon**

PUDDING LAYER

- 2 **cups 2% milk**
- 1 **pkg. (3.3 oz.) instant white chocolate pudding mix**

PUMPKIN MOUSSE LAYER

- 1 **cup 2% milk**
- 1 **pkg. (3.4 oz.) instant pumpkin spice pudding mix**
- 1 **carton (8 oz.) frozen whipped topping, thawed**

1. Preheat oven to 350°. Beat sour cream, honey, egg and oil until well blended. In another bowl, whisk together the next six ingredients; gradually beat into sour cream mixture. Transfer to a greased 9-in. square baking pan. Bake until a toothpick inserted in center comes out clean, 25-30 minutes. Cool in pan 5 minutes. Remove to a wire rack to cool completely.
2. Meanwhile, for the pudding layer, whisk milk and white chocolate pudding mix 2 minutes. Let stand until soft-set, about 5 minutes. Refrigerate. For the mousse layer, whisk milk and pumpkin spice pudding mix in another bowl for 2 minutes. Fold in whipped topping. Refrigerate.
3. To assemble, cut cake into 1-in. cubes. In a 3-qt. trifle bowl or other glass serving dish, layer a third of the cake cubes, white chocolate pudding and pumpkin mousse. Repeat layers twice. Refrigerate, covered, 4 hours or overnight.
1 CUP: 413 cal., 14g fat (7g sat. fat), 25mg chol., 514mg sod., 64g carb. (44g sugars, 1g fiber), 6g pro.

Substitutions & Equivalents

EQUIVALENT MEASURES

3 teaspoons	= 1 tablespoon	**16 tablespoons**	= 1 cup
4 tablespoons	= ¼ cup	**2 cups**	= 1 pint
5⅓ tablespoons	= ⅓ cup	**4 cups**	= 1 quart
8 tablespoons	= ½ cup	**4 quarts**	= 1 gallon

FOOD EQUIVALENTS

Macaroni	1 cup (3½ ounces) uncooked	= 2½ cups cooked
Noodles, Medium	3 cups (4 ounces) uncooked	= 4 cups cooked
Popcorn	⅓-½ cup unpopped	= 8 cups popped
Rice, Long Grain	1 cup uncooked	= 3 cups cooked
Rice, Quick-Cooking	1 cup uncooked	= 2 cups cooked
Spaghetti	8 ounces uncooked	= 4 cups cooked

Bread	1 slice	= ¾ cup soft crumbs, ¼ cup fine dry crumbs
Graham Crackers	7 squares	= ½ cup finely crushed
Buttery Round Crackers	12 crackers	= ½ cup finely crushed
Saltine Crackers	14 crackers	= ½ cup finely crushed

Bananas	1 medium	= ⅓ cup mashed
Lemons	1 medium	= 3 tablespoons juice, 2 teaspoons grated zest
Limes	1 medium	= 2 tablespoons juice, 1½ teaspoons grated zest
Oranges	1 medium	= ¼-⅓ cup juice, 4 teaspoons grated zest

Cabbage	1 head = 5 cups shredded	**Green Pepper**	1 large = 1 cup chopped
Carrots	1 pound = 3 cups shredded	**Mushrooms**	½ pound = 3 cups sliced
Celery	1 rib = ½ cup chopped	**Onions**	1 medium = ½ cup chopped
Corn	1 ear fresh = ⅔ cup kernels	**Potatoes**	3 medium = 2 cups cubed

Almonds	1 pound = 3 cups chopped	**Pecan Halves**	1 pound = 4½ cups chopped
Ground Nuts	3¾ ounces = 1 cup	**Walnuts**	1 pound = 3¾ cups chopped

EASY SUBSTITUTIONS

WHEN YOU NEED...		**USE...**
Baking Powder	1 teaspoon	½ teaspoon cream of tartar + ¼ teaspoon baking soda
Buttermilk	1 cup	1 tablespoon lemon juice or vinegar + enough milk to measure 1 cup (let stand 5 minutes before using)
Cornstarch	1 tablespoon	2 tablespoons all-purpose flour
Honey	1 cup	1¼ cups sugar + ¼ cup water
Half-and-Half Cream	1 cup	1 tablespoon melted butter + enough whole milk to measure 1 cup
Onion	1 small, chopped (⅓ cup)	1 teaspoon onion powder or 1 tablespoon dried minced onion
Tomato Juice	1 cup	½ cup tomato sauce + ½ cup water
Tomato Sauce	2 cups	¾ cup tomato paste + 1 cup water
Unsweetened Chocolate	1 square (1 ounce)	3 tablespoons baking cocoa + 1 tablespoon shortening or oil
Whole Milk	1 cup	½ cup evaporated milk + ½ cup water

Cooking Terms

AL DENTE An Italian term meaning "to the tooth." Used to describe pasta that is cooked but still firm.

BASTE To moisten food with melted butter, pan drippings, marinade or other liquid to add flavor and juiciness.

BEAT To mix rapidly with a spoon, fork, wire whisk or electric mixer.

BLEND To combine ingredients until just mixed.

BOIL To heat liquids until bubbles that cannot be stirred down are formed. In the case of water, the temperature will reach 212 degrees at sea level.

BONE To remove all bones from meat, poultry or fish.

BROIL To cook food 4 to 6 inches from a direct, radiant heat source.

CREAM To blend ingredients to a smooth consistency by beating; frequently done with butter and sugar for baking.

CUT IN To break down and distribute cold butter, margarine or shortening into a flour mixture with a pastry blender or two knives.

DASH A measurement less than ⅛ teaspoon that is used for herbs, spices and hot pepper sauce. This is not a precise measurement.

DREDGE To coat foods with flour or other dry ingredients. Most often done with pot roasts and stew meat before browning.

FLUTE To make a "V" shape or scalloped edge on pie crust with your thumb and fingers.

FOLD To blend dissimilar ingredients by careful and gentle turning with a spatula. Used most commonly to incorporate whipped cream, beaten egg whites, fruit, candy or nuts into a thick, heavy batter.

JULIENNE To cut foods into long thin strips much like matchsticks. Used often for salads and stir-fries.

KNEAD To work dough by using a pressing and folding action to make it smooth and elastic.

MARINATE To tenderize and/or flavor foods, usually vegetables or uncooked meat, by placing them in a mixture that may contain oil, vinegar, wine, lime or lemon juice, and herbs and spices.

MINCE To cut into very fine pieces. Often used for garlic, hot peppers and fresh herbs.

PARBOIL To boil foods, usually vegetables, until partially cooked. Most often used when vegetables are to be finished using another cooking method or chilled for marinated salads or dips.

PINCH A measurement less than ⅛ teaspoon that is easily held between the thumb and index finger. This is not a precise measurement.

PULSE To process foods in a food processor or blender with short bursts of power.

PUREE To mash solid foods into a smooth mixture with a food processor, mill, blender or sieve.

SAUTE To fry quickly in a small amount of fat, stirring almost constantly. Most often done with onions, mushrooms and other chopped vegetables.

SCORE To cut slits partway through the outer surface of foods. Often required for ham or flank steak.

SIMMER To cook liquids, or a combination of ingredients with liquid, at just under the boiling point (180-200°). The surface of the liquid will have some movement and there may be small bubbles around the sides of the pan.

STEAM To cook foods covered on a rack or in a steamer basket over a small amount of boiling water. Most often used for vegetables.

STIR-FRY To cook meats, grains and/or vegetables with a constant stirring motion, in a small amount of oil, in a wok or skillet over high heat.

General Index

This handy index lists every recipe by food category, major ingredient and/or cooking method, so you can easily locate recipes that suit your needs.

✓Indicates an EAT SMART *recipe*

CHOCOLATE

COCONUT & COCONUT MILK

CONDIMENTS

COOKIES

CORN

CORNBREAD & CORNMEAL

CORNED BEEF

CRANBERRIES

CREAM CHEESE

POTATOES

PRESSURE-COOKER RECIPES

PRETZELS

PUMPKIN

QUINOA

RAISINS

RASPBERRIES

RHUBARB

RICE

SALADS & DRESSINGS

Dressings

Green Salads

Main-Dish Salads

Other Salads

SALADS & DRESSINGS (continued)

SALSA

SANDWICHES

(*also see Burgers*)

SAUERKRAUT

SAUSAGE

SEAFOOD

SIDE DISHES

Alphabetical Index

This convenient index lists every recipe in alphabetical order, so you can easily find your favorite dishes.

✓Indicates an **EAT SMART** *recipe*

D

E

F

G

H

I

J

S

T

U

V

W

Y

Z